THE FOUNDATIONS OF ADULT EDUCATION
IN CANADA

Dedications

To Mary
(Gordon Selman)

To my companion learners—Paige, Kimberly and Lesley
(Paul Dampier)

The Foundations of Adult Education in Canada

GORDON SELMAN
University of British Columbia

PAUL DAMPIER
The Justice Institute of British Columbia

THOMPSON EDUCATIONAL PUBLISHING, INC.
Toronto

Additional copies of this publication may be obtained from:
  Thompson Educational Publishing, Inc.
  11 Briarcroft Road, Toronto
  Ontario, Canada M6S 1H3
  Telephone (416) 766-2763 Fax (416) 766-0398
Please write for a full catalogue of publications.

Canadian Cataloguing in Publication Data

Selman, Gordon R., 1927-
    The foundations of adult education in Canada

Includes bibliographical references and index.
ISBN 1-55077-029-2

1. Adult education - Canada - History.
I. Dampier, Paul, 1948-   . II. Title.

LC5254.S44 1990   374'.971   C91-093071-6

ISBN 1–55077–029–2

Printed and bound in Canada by John Deyell Company
    3 4 5 6   95 94 93 92

Table of Contents

Preface

The authors of this book are self-confessed Canadians. We have been increasingly uncomfortable in recent years over the fact that although we have a lively adult education scene in Canada, and a deeply interesting history in this field which goes back for at least 150 years, there is no book which attempts to do justice to this subject. We hasten to add, however, that the present volume is not essentially a history book. It is rather a discussion of the nature of adult education in Canada, with emphasis on the most recent decades, and on the relationship between adult education and the society of which it is a part. We believe that Canadians are not an inward looking people and that in adult education, as in other areas of activity, we have been open to and influenced by what has happened in other parts of the world.

The readership which the authors had in mind for this book are those persons who have an interest in the nature of adult education in this country. Many of these, we assume, are practitioners who may welcome an attempt to describe the unique character of the enterprise of which they are a part. Both authors of this book have been practitioners of adult education and also teachers of those seeking professional education in this field. In this latter role we have been all too aware of the lack of Canadian materials with which to work. And we have witnessed the frustration of many of our students who looked, frequently in vain, for Canadian perspectives on the field. We pay tribute to the work which has been done in the past by other Canadians on aspects of the field, and we rely to a considerable extent on that work in parts of the book which follows. We hope that the present volume adds significantly to the Canadian resources we can all call upon.

The table of contents indicates the approaches we have taken to our task. The first chapter deals with some basic questions of definition. Chapter 2 presents a discussion of the functions which adult learning performs in the life of individuals and society, and describes some philosophical perspectives concerning the nature of the enterprise. From there we turn in Chapter 3 to the relationship between Canada's experience as a nation and the nature of the adult education programs and services which we have developed. If, in some broad way, adult education has been responsive to individual and social needs, then what have been—and are—some of the features of our experience as a people to which the field has responded? Although this volume in the main focuses on the most recent decades, an attempt has been made in this third chapter to provide some historical perspective on the field as well.

The fourth and fifth chapters contain an examination of adult education in operation. In Chapter 4 there is a close look at who participates in such activity—and who does not. The nature and variety of the providers of adult education are analyzed. And in the fifth chapter, we examine some of the ways in which programs of adult education are conceived and developed. The latter is done not in an effort to provide anything approaching a thorough coverage of the methodologies of program planning, but rather as a further description of the adult education enterprise at work.

Commentators on the Canadian scene frequently stress the degree to which we have used government and other public agencies to accomplish national goals. Chapters 6 and 7 look at the matter of public policy and adult education, paying considerable attention to the complexities of the Canadian scene, in which three levels of government, local, provincial (and territorial) and federal, all have played a role in this field.

Chapter 8 examines the discipline and the "workforce" of adult education. The transition is reviewed which saw the field change from what was at one time largely a social movement, based in the voluntary sector, to one which has become more professionalized and institutionalized. Certain aspects of the emerging profession—the roles performed by adult educators, the development of professional associations, the growth of professional education programs, and the expansion of research and publication activity—are also examined.

The ninth chapter takes a closer look at the two most recent decades—since approximately 1970. In some respects this constitutes a drawing together of the contemporary developments in many of the areas covered in the earlier chapters. There is an attempt as well to identify some of the trends and prominent features of the current scene, and to use these insights as a basis for some speculation about the future.

In Chapter 10, the authors have commented upon the nature of the literature (mostly Canadian) relevant to the main subject matter areas dealt with in the book. We have done so in a way which hopefully will be helpful to other students of the field who may wish to pursue particular topics.

The authors wish to express their gratitude to Dr. Mark Selman of Continuing Studies, Simon Fraser University, for contributing to this volume the section of Chapter 2 on "Philosophical Considerations." This aspect of the foundations of adult education has for too long been neglected by the broader field of educational philosophy in Canada and Dr. Selman's contribution represents a significant and helpful corrective step in that regard.

We wish to say a few words about our decision to make this a book about adult education as it has developed primarily in English-speaking Canada only. We look upon this with regret, but as a necessity. Neither of the authors is fluent in French (indeed we sometimes wonder about our English!) and we did not feel we could do justice to the nuances of the field as it has developed in Quebec and other predominantly French-speaking regions. Our regret over this matter is real, but tempered by the fact that in many respects, adult education in English and French-speaking Canada have functioned in two different worlds. The "two solitudes" are very much a fact of life in adult education, as in other areas of activity. In his book, *Culture and Adult Education*, Hayden Roberts has shown us some of the differences and has helped to explain why they exist. There have been some regular contacts between the two solitudes of adult education. Since the early sixties the two national associations, the Canadian Association for Adult Education and the Institut canadien d'education des adultes, have maintained effective contact and have joined together in several projects. They have co-operated in securing and maintaining ties with and financial support from the federal government. They have frequently worked co-operatively in their relationship with the international body, the International Council for Adult Education. As individuals, some leading figures from both communities have worked together in the Canadian Commission for UNESCO, which at times has been active in the field of adult education. There has been active participation from both language communities during the eighties in the Canadian Association for the Study of Adult Education. We will be richer someday for an account of our field which does present the picture of both language communities in Canada. This, regretfully, was beyond our reach in the present case.

From time to time, some of us who are involved in this field ask ourselves: "What is Canadian about Canadian adult education?" The writing of this book was an attempt by the authors to identify some of these characteristics. We discovered, with no great feeling of surprise, that Canadian adult education owes its distinctiveness to the attributes of the country itself: size, diversity, abundance, youthfulness, eclecticism and determination, among others. Historically, Canadians—nationally and regionally—have utilized adult education as a means of both making their history and responding to it. It seems to us that both traditions are of great importance and that adult education itself and the society of which it is a part will be the poorer if the values which have traditionally inspired the adult education movement are lost by those who work in this field.

1

Definitions and Boundaries

It is important to any field of practice, and certainly to any field of study, to be able to identify the essential characteristics of the enterprise. These matters are far from settled in the field of adult education. Or perhaps it is more accurate to say that they have been settled repeatedly to the satisfaction of particular scholars or practitioners, but have not remained settled. It is small comfort that many other fields are in the same situation at the present time.

The matter is complicated by the fact that as Knowles has pointed out,[1] the single phrase, "adult education," is used to refer to at least three different phenomena. It refers, first of all, to a set of activities. The sum total of all acts of participation by individuals, and programs offered by a vast range of institutions, provides us with an overall picture of adult education as an activity in our society. Secondly, the term is used to refer to the intellectual process by means of which adults seek, or are assisted to learn things. This comes close to what might be termed the discipline of adult education. And thirdly, the phrase is used to refer to the social system which is made up of individuals and organizations which are concerned with the education of adults. This field, or "movement," as it has frequently been termed, has worked towards the increased recognition by our society of the importance of adult education and has tried to gain greater resources and policy support for the work. Adult education is dealt with in all three of these dimensions in this volume. Fascinatingly complex, it is; tidy, it isn't. An insistence on orderliness, precision and tight typologies may just be a distinct liability in coming to a full appreciation of the nature of adult education.

In this chapter, the term adult education will be examined and defined, with some attention to its historical evolution. This is followed by the description of two other sets of terms, the first group of which are frequently used synonymously with adult education and a second group which are related, but quite distinctly different from adult education. Finally, some general methodological terms will be described and distinguished.

Naming the Enterprise

It is a standing joke in adult education circles that there is such lack of agreement about some basic terminology in the field. The problem—to the ex-

---

[1] M.S. Knowles, *A History of the Adult Education Movement in the United States* (Huntington N.Y., Krieger, 1977) p. viii.

tent that it is one—is not just that practitioners are not clear what the terms mean as they use them; it is that, there being no agreed upon set of terms in the field, people use different terms for the same thing. Adult educators, depending on their institutional setting, may refer to their work as community education, continuing education, further education, adult training, continuing studies, extension—or even adult education. There is no standardized lexicon of terms in the field, though Verner[2] and others, from time to time, have suggested terminological schemes. Perhaps the field is too diverse, too subject to regional and occupational idiosyncrasies and developing too rapidly to make the prospect of standardized terminology a realistic one.

There has come to be a significant difference in meaning between the two terms, the education of adults and adult education. "The education of adults" is used as a more inclusive term, and refers to all purposeful efforts by which adults seek to learn, or are assisted to learn. The term "adult education," though somewhat fluid in meaning, tends to refer to a narrower spectrum of such activities, ones which are designed especially for adults, and usually are part-time or, if full-time, of relatively short duration. For instance, adults who decide to return to college or university on a full-time basis are certainly adults engaged in education, but would not normally be included in the statistics of adult education activities.

In this and related cases, "adult education" can be seen to be an administrative category. Under one set of circumstances, the adults may be considered "regular" students; under another, "adult education" students. If the persons referred to above studied the very same subject, but did so on a part-time, evening course basis, they might well be counted as adult education students. If they attended full time, they would not.

In many of its settings, be it school board night classes or company training programs, for instance, adult education has developed historically as an "added on," and often secondary or marginal activity for the sponsoring organization. And for the vast majority of adult learners, participation in educational activities is a part-time, or if full-time, a short duration activity. As a result many definitions of the term adult education which were developed in the early years of the movement included the idea of its part-time nature. One such, for instance, is that provided by Bryson in what is generally considered the earliest text book for the field. He defined adult education as "all activities with an educational purpose that are carried on by people engaged in the ordinary business of life."[3] Other definitions of this type referred in some way to the part-time or short-term nature of adult education activities.

---

2   C. Verner, *A Conceptual Scheme for the Identification and Classification of Processes* (Chicago, Adult Education Association of the USA, 1962); C. Verner, "Definition of Terms" in G.Jensen, A.A. Liveright & W. Hallenbeck, *Adult Education: Outlines of an Emerging Field of University Study* (Washington, Adult Education Association of the USA, 1964).

3   L. Bryson, *Adult Education* (New York, American Book Co., 1936) p. 3.

Although it is clearly the case that most adult learners pursue their further education on a part-time basis, most definitions of adult education no longer include such a reference. In what is considered the starting point of many modern developments in adult education, *The 1919 Report* to the British Ministry of Reconstruction by its Committee on Adult Education defined adult education as follows:

> ... all the deliberate efforts by which men and women attempt to satisfy their thirst for knowledge, to equip themselves for their responsibilities as citizens and members of society or to find opportunities for self expression.[4]

The perspective represented in this definition was that of the adult learner and emphasized the purposes for which the adult engaged in this activity. In his well-known work, *The Design of Education*, Houle reflected this, and added to it. Adult education is the process by which men and women

> ... seek to improve themselves or their society by increasing their skill, knowledge or sensitivities; or it is any process by which individuals, groups or institutions try to help men and women improve in these ways.[5]

Houle concluded by placing emphasis on the process by means of which the providers of adult education relate to the adult. It was this element on which Verner chose to concentrate:

> Adult education is the action of an external agent in purposefully ordering behavior into planned systematic experiences that can result in learning for those for whom such activity is supplemental to their primary role in society, and which involves some continuity in an exchange relationship between the agent and the learner so that the educational process is under constant supervision and direction.[6]

These two elements are combined in what is currently perhaps the most frequently cited definition of adult education, one contained in the Recommendation on the Development of Adult Education, which was prepared by UNESCO at the request of member states and formally approved in 1976. It defined adult education as:

> ... the entire body of organized educational processes, whatever the content, level and method, whether formal or otherwise, whether they prolong or replace initial education in schools, colleges and universities as well as in apprenticeship, whereby persons regarded as adult by the society to which they belong develop their abilities, enrich their knowledge, improve their technical or professional qualifications or turn them in a new direction and bring about changes in their attitudes or behavior in the twofold perspective of full per-

---

[4]   *The 1919 Report* (Report of the Adult Education Committee to the United Kingdom Ministry of Reconstruction) (Nottingham, University of Nottingham, 1980 (1919)) p. 34.

[5]   C.O. Houle, *The Design of Education* (San Francisco, Jossey-Bass, 1972) p. 32.

[6]   C. Verner, *A Conceptual Scheme*, p. 2–3.

sonal development and participation in balanced and independent social, economic and cultural development ...[7]

This somewhat cumbersome, but inclusive definition acknowledges the awkward issue of how to define adult. Even within any one society, it is not a simple matter to deal with this question. Age is certainly the key factor, but status of adulthood is variously defined in various social roles, such as in the courts, the right to drive a motor vehicle, to get married, or to vote. The framers of the UNESCO Recommendation, faced with the problem of relating to all countries in the world, acknowledged the necessity of defining adulthood but termed it, "persons regarded as adult by the societies to which they belong."

It is important to make the distinction between adult education and adult learning. Learning is the intended end-product of education. Much, if not most of adult learning in our society takes place outside of our educational institutions and the programs which they offer. As Thomas has put it, "education floats in a sea of learning."[8]

The creation of educational programs comes about when the learning of certain things in our society is seen by constituted authorities as desirable or necessary, or when opportunities to learn are so consistently in demand by individual adults that there is clearly merit—or profit—in providing the services. If the society decides that certain kinds of vocational or technical training for adults is necessary in order to make possible the economic advancement of the country as a whole, then educational programs are created, or purchased, to meet that need. Similarly, if it is realized that a lack of basic education or that a lack of working knowledge of the language of the country on the part of adult immigrants is limiting to both the individuals and the community, services are put in place to correct the situation. From the adults' point of view, if they cannot speak the language used around them, or if, in view of technological change, they now need to become computer literate, for instance, then they will in many cases go seeking the opportunity to learn these things and there will be a response in the form of educational programs—from the public or the private sectors.

Parallel or Overlapping Terms

There are several terms related to adult education, some used synonymously with it, which are commonly encountered in the field.

---

[7] UNESCO, *Recommendation on the Development of Adult Education*, published in Canada (Ottawa, Canadian Commission for UNESCO, 1980 (1976)) p. 3.

[8] A.M. Thomas, "Government and Adult Learning," in F. Cassidy & R. Faris (Eds.), *Choosing Our Future* (Toronto, Ontario Institute for Studies in Education, 1987) p. 109.

Continuing Education. This term is used by many as synonymous with adult education. In a number of institutional settings, however, there is the connotation of furthering one's education beyond a significant level which has already been achieved. Universities, for instance, tend to be comfortable with the term on the assumption that it implies the subsequent education of their graduates, or at least educational activities at a reasonably advanced level. There is a relatively recent movement in the field to broaden the meaning of the term by extending it to cover any situation where the person is "moving on," particularly within the more formal, credential-related aspects of education.[9] The term further education is sometimes used with a similar meaning (though in Britain it tends to be vocational in emphasis).

Extension. The term extension has had two main uses in North America. The first is often referred to as "agricultural extension" and relates to educational services provided particularly to those who live in rural and small town settings, and is often vocational in emphasis. There is a long tradition of such work in North America, where governments, universities and other agencies have provided a wide variety of vocational, social and cultural programs for rural people.[10] There has also been a strong tradition in North America of universities referring to most or all their adult education activities as university extension. The term was borrowed initially from Great Britain, and in the early decades involved universities mainly in providing in another place or at another hour of the day a version of many of the same kinds of teaching (usually without written assignments) which they delivered to their "regular" students on campus. In the early years of this century, a new, more varied and broadly-based type of university extension service was developed in North America and it generally retained the use of the term extension. In recent decades, however, the term extension has been seen by some in the universities as reflecting a concept of the institution's role which is too broad in character and a number of universities have changed the name of their "extension" units to such terms as continuing education, continuing studies, or some variation on the theme.

Community Education. This term is used by some synonymously with adult education. This is true particularly of those working at a local or community level. The adult education unit of a local school board, for instance, is frequently called by such a name. But in many instances there is also a significant philosophical or value-related dimension to the use of this term which sets it apart from the field of adult education as a whole. For many practitioners of "community education" there is a wish and intention that what they are doing should

---

[9] A.M. Thomas, "Government and Adult Learning," p. 106.

[10] D.J. Blackburn (Ed.), *Extension Handbook* (Guelph, University of Guelph, 1984).

have a vital connection with the character of community life in the region they are serving. Rather than simply respond to the expressed needs of individuals for educational services, they wish to relate their programs to forces working for change and improvement in community life. They wish to make a difference to the quality of life in their communities.[11] Such a point of view goes back in Canada at least as far as the "lighted schoolhouse" movement of the 1920s,[12] the folk school movement of the 1930s and later,[13] and the community school movement of more recent decades.[14]

Related Terms

There are a number of terms which are a step further removed from adult education than the ones dealt with in the previous section but which are closely related or overlapping in some respects.

Lifelong Education and Lifelong Learning. Perhaps because adult educators have been among those who have promoted the concept of lifelong education in recent decades, and of course because lifelong education does include the adult years, there has been a tendency in some quarters to confuse—or use inter-changeably—the terms adult education and lifelong education. In fact they are quite different; lifelong education refers to educational influences on the person over the entire life span—during childhood and youth, as well as the adult years—and adult education refers only to the latter. The confusion of the two terms was reinforced by the classic report of the Adult Education Committee of the U.K. Ministry of Reconstruction in 1919, which stated that adult education should be a "permanent national necessity, an inseparable aspect of citizenship, and therefore should be both universal and lifelong."[15] In more recent decades,

---

[11] S. Brookfield, *Adult Learners, Adult Education and the Community* (New York, Teachers College Press, 1984).

[12] R. England, *Living, Learning, Remembering* (Vancouver, University of British Columbia, Center for Continuing Education, 1980).

[13] J.R. Kidd (Ed.), *Adult Education in Canada* (Toronto, Canadian Association for Adult Education, 1950).

[14] P.F. Prout, *Community Schools in Canada* (Toronto, Canadian Education Association, 1977).

[15] *The 1919 Report*, p. 5.

the concept of lifelong education is one which has been developed in the work of the United Nations Educational, Scientific and Cultural Organization (UNESCO), since approximately 1960. The idea was given great impetus by the report of UNESCO's International Commission on the Development of Education (the Faure Commission) and its report, *Learning to Be*,[16] which appeared in 1972. In this report and several publications which have subsequently been produced by the UNESCO Institute on Education (Hamburg), the idea of lifelong education and of "the learning society" have been further developed.[17] Within such a framework, the society's formal educational institutions (schools, colleges, universities, etc.) are seen to be only part of the resources in society for the education of the individual; the home, the workplace, one's social and recreational activities, and other aspects of life are all seen to be the settings for educational activities in "the learning society." Canadians played a significant part in developing the concept of lifelong education. Dr. J. Roby Kidd explored the territory in two books[18] before the term gained wide currency and Dr. Alan Thomas published several papers during the sixties which analyzed the implications of the concept.[19]

From one point of view, lifelong learning can simply be recognized as a fact. It is clear that individuals, some perhaps more actively than others, do go on learning throughout their whole life span—from the cradle to the grave. The desirability of lifelong learning has been expressed in the literature of societies since ancient times, but has received more focused attention, in tandem with lifelong education, in the last few decades. Although lifelong learning may be associated with learning for any purpose, there has been a strong, perhaps dominant philosophical thrust which associates it with liberal-democratic values, "education for liberation" and "self-fulfilment."[20] The writings of Paul Lengrand[21] in the late sixties and the UNESCO report, *Learning to Be,* of 1972, helped to establish this philosophical direction, and this has been developed further in the work of UNESCO's Institute of Education at Hamburg. The terms lifelong edu-

---

[16] UNESCO, *Learning To Be* (Paris, UNESCO, 1972).

[17] R.H. Dave (Ed.), *Foundations of Lifelong Education* (Oxford, Pergamon, 1976); A.J. Cropley (Ed.), *Towards a System of Lifelong Education* (Oxford, Pergamon, 1980); C.K. Knapper & A.J. Cropley, *Lifelong Learning and Higher Education* (London, Croom Helm, 1985).

[18] J.R. Kidd, *How Adults Learn* (New York, Association Press, 1959); and J.R. Kidd, *The Implications of Continuous Learning* (Toronto, W.J. Gage, 1966).

[19] A.M. Thomas, "The Learning Society" in CAAE/ICEA, *National Conference on Adult Education* (Toronto/Montreal, CAAE/ICEA, 1961); and CAAE, *A White Paper on the Education of Adults in Canada* (Toronto, CAAE, n.d. (1966)).

[20] C.K Knapper & A.J. Cropley, *Lifelong Learning and Higher Education*, p. 19.

[21] P. Lengrand, *An Introduction to Lifelong Education* (Paris, UNESCO, 1970).

cation and lifelong learning have now become coin of the realm in educational discussion, embracing but going far beyond the field of adult education.

Open Learning. The term open learning has emerged in the last few decades. It is related to the idea of "the learning society," which is in turn associated with lifelong learning. The terminology was borrowed in part from the British institution, the Open University, which began operation in 1971.[22] Open learning, like many educational terms, is rather variously defined, but the connotation is that of open accessibility to and utilization of resources for the assistance of learning. Rather than be limited to particular curricula, places or times for study, the learner has access to a wide range of resources which may be utilized when and as the learner sees fit. The emphasis is on giving learners the optimum degree of control over their own learning, and in such a situation the teacher, if there is one present (often the expert is present in the form of books, programmed or modularized instructional units, etc.) is seen as a facilitator or advisor, rather than as a content expert who directs the educational process. The term open learning is used in various ways. One emphasizes that all learners have access to instructional resources, not only those who have certain levels of formal education or certification. Another use of the term refers to a local learning centre—in an industry, for instance—where the employee has access to a range of educational resources and may utilize these as they are relevant to his or her needs, and at a time and pace which are convenient.

Recurrent Education. Although the term recurrent education is used rather loosely in the field, it is appropriately restricted to forms of organization of the world of work and the world of education in such a way that the individual may move back and forth between the two during the adult working years.[23] The concept was developed in Sweden in the sixties and introduced by that country to the Organization for Economic Co-operation and Development (OECD), where it relatively rapidly gained acceptance among some of the more industrialized countries. The key to a system of recurrent education is paid educational leave, which makes it possible for employees to take time off from their working careers in order to return to full-time or part-time education and not suffer undue disadvantage in either setting—work or education. Legislation in support of various forms of recurrent education has existed in Europe since the late sixties.[24] Recurrent education should not be understood only as a way for workers to keep up to date with their vocations. The originators of the concept saw various social benefits as well. Youth who were restless in school could go into the world of work at the end of grade 10, with opportunities provided for them to

[22] N. MacKenzie, N. Postgate & J. Scupham (Eds.), *Open Learning* (Paris, UNESCO, 1975); W. Perry, *The Open University* (San Francisco, Jossey-Bass, 1977); E. Stabler, *Founders* (Edmonton, University of Alberta, 1986).

[23] OECD, *Recurrent Education: Trends and Issues* (Paris, OECD/Center for Educational Research and Innovation, 1975).

[24] C. Titmus, *Strategies for Adult Education* (Chicago, Follett, 1981).

return to education when they had a clearer sense of what they wanted to do with themselves. In conditions of high rates of unemployment, many persons could be productively employed in furthering their education. And older workers, who may have received relatively limited formal education in their youth, could return to education. Recurrent education as a formal or comprehensive policy has received some study in North America and has found its way into some settings (often through union or other agreements) but has yet to be widely adopted on this continent.

Community Development. Community development is an educational and social process which has been closely associated with adult education—and vice versa. There have been adult education specialists who have claimed that community development is a sub-division of their field,[25] but that is not the general view. Community development is usually seen as a process by which members of a community, however defined, determine to take stock of their community, set goals for desirable change, and work towards those goals. It is clear that in the process of community development there is need for a great deal of learning on the part of those involved—about the state of their community, the goals which can be agreed upon, the resources available to assist the community in its actions, the range of options available, and the management of the group processes involved in all these efforts. As set forth so effectively by Lovett[26] and Brookfield,[27] the community development process, far from being contained within the field of adult education, properly requires the leadership of a range of professionals—in such fields as social work, community planning and public administration—as well as a range of content experts, selected in accordance with the goals identified by the community. Canada has a rich experience in many aspects of community development, as revealed in Draper's volume, *Citizen Participation: Canada*, and other sources.[28]

Some General Methodological Distinctions

It may also be helpful at the outset to describe some broad categories related to the methodology or organization of content in the field. They help us to think in a more systematic way about the multiplicity of methods and approaches which are employed.

---

[25] C. Verner & A. Booth, *Adult Education* (New York, Center for Applied Research in Education, 1964).

[26] T. Lovett, *Adult Education, Community Development and the Working Class* (London, Ward Lock Educational, 1975).

[27] S. Brookfield, *Adult Learners, Adult Education and the Community.*

[28] J. Draper (Ed.), *Citizen Participation: Canada* (Toronto, New Press, 1971); Department of Adult Education, Ontario Institute for Studies in Education, *Second National Workshop on Community Development* (Toronto, Dept. of Adult Education, O.I.S.E., 1969); J. Lotz, *Understanding Canada* (Toronto, NC Press, 1977).

Social Organization of the Learner. The popular image of adult education activity is that of the class, being taught by an expert or teacher who knows more about the subject than do the students and who sets about teaching it to them. Indeed a vast amount of adult education follows that pattern. The instructional techniques utilized by the teacher may vary, according to what is being taught— be it Greek history, how to manage your investments, how to repair your outboard motor, how to perform certain technical tasks on the job, how to bake bread, or how to draw the human figure—but the basic relationship of student to teacher may be essentially the same. There are other kinds of group activities, however, where there is no acknowledged expert present. These may be discussion groups where those present are sharing their experience and knowledge. They may be groups in which the members take turns studying up on topics and presenting information about them to their colleagues. It may be a case of a group of citizens discussing a subject for the purpose of making a decision about future action. Another variation of such "peer" groups consists of the members all having shared some experience—reading a book, seeing a play, hearing a record or listening to or watching a broadcast and then engaging in a discussion of the topic or the experience. Some such peer groups have designated discussion leaders and some do not.

The other setting in which the learner may be situated is to be alone. Considerable research has been carried out in recent years, by Tough[29] and many others into what Tough has termed the self-directed learner. This refers to individuals who set about to learn something but who do not go to a class or in any other way put themselves under the tutelage of some teacher or agency, and who remain in control of the educational process themselves. The research into this phenomenon indicates that almost everyone engages in such self-directed education. In many cases, however, the learner is studying or learning alone, but under the direction of some other agency. Study in such a setting is a rapidly growing phenomenon in our society, a development which is spurred on by technological change, most notably in the use of the computer. The traditional form of such education was the correspondence or guided reading course. The student was directed to read certain texts or carry out certain work and then submit an assignment for marking to a tutor or sponsoring agency. The course often concluded with an examination. This method relied on the printed or written word and usually involved mailing assignments back and forth. What was at one time called correspondence education has in recent years become distance education (that is the teacher or agency is at a distance removed from the student) and whereas instruction and response traditionally involved only the mails, now there is considerable reliance on the telephone, audio and video tapes, broadcasts to augment other materials, and in some cases, local study and tutoring centres where students can seek needed assistance or contact with other students. An-

---

[29] A. Tough, *The Adult's Learning Projects* (Toronto, Ontario Institute for Studies in Education, 1971).

other major form of study by oneself is modularized instruction, sometimes computer-based. The student is "led through" a course of instruction, asked to respond frequently in order to demonstrate whether the material has been learned, and then given further instruction, depending on the success of the feedback. A third type of setting for the individual learner consists of the local resource or open learning centre. In this case the student is provided with a range of learning aids—books, tapes, programmed instruction, manuals, etc.—and is able to utilize these resources at the time and to the extent he or she wishes.

In addition to the group settings and individualized settings illustrated above, it may be appropriate to refer as well to community settings. These are group situations as well but may be distinguishable on the basis of their focus of interest. Gatherings which are part of the community development process, for instance, may be organized in order to take stock of community opinion or to come to a conclusion about choices to be made. There may be a substantial element of education or learning as part of the occasion, but the ultimate focus may not be on the learning so much as on securing satisfactory community representation and making decisions.

Organization of Content. Current thinking about the way in which education, including adult education, is organized in terms of the content and the relationship between the learner and the sponsor of the activity sees the field divided into three main approaches, formal, non-formal and informal education. Such terminology is in use among educational planners at the national and international levels,[30] and has readily been adopted by adult education in that it fits well with the large variety of approaches utilized in that field. Formal education is the type of program format associated with full-time study in the traditional educational institutions. It usually involves comprehensive curricula, is staged or graded into multi-year levels, and is linked to a graduated system of certification or accreditation. It has been described by Coombs as "institution bound" or "time bound," in that normally students are required to move at a certain pace through the system.

Non-formal education is comprised of all other organized, systematic educational activity which is carried out in society, whether offered by educational institutions or any other agency. It is aimed at facilitating selected types of learning on the part of particular sub-groups in the population. It may, for instance, take the form of a one-week short course, a one-day conference, a series of evening classes, a correspondence course, or some other form of instruction, the essential characteristic being that the event has been consciously planned as an educational experience. Non-formal education may include such activities as a literacy class, a short course for up-dating a professional person, an agricultural extension course for farmers or rural women, a short course for the training of volunteers, community programs in the field of health, nutrition, family planning

---

[30] P.H. Coombs, *The World Crisis in Education: The View from the Eighties* (New York, Oxford, 1985); J. Lowe, *The Education of Adults: A World Perspective* (Toronto, Ontario Institute for Studies in Education, 1982).

or co-operatives, or a class in music appreciation. This approach is well suited to many learning needs, and to societies in various stages of development. Similar activities have in some circles traditionally been called non-credit courses, but that term does involve another set of issues.

The third type of educational approach, informal education, is frequently unorganized, unsystematic, and at times perhaps even unintentional. Coombs states that this third type "accounts for the bulk of any person's total lifetime learning" and he defines it as "the lifelong process by which every person acquires and accumulates knowledge, skills, attitudes and insights from daily experiences and exposure to the environment—at home, at work, at play."[31] International planners in the field of education such as Coombs and Lowe suggest that in considering the educational system and resources of any society, it is appropriate to consider not only the formal educational systems in operation but also the network of non-formal and informal educational capabilities as well.[32]

The Relationship of the Learner to Educational Resources

While this topic overlaps in some respects with ones covered elsewhere in this section, it is of such major relevance to adult education practice, it deserves separate mention. It has to do with the accessibility of instructional resources in the variety of educational settings among which the adult moves, and may make choices. At one end of the spectrum, perhaps, is the case of an institution or set of institutions which has the exclusive right to grant certain credentials and which prescribes the means by which these credentials may be earned. An example might be a medical or other professional faculty at a university, which limits its intake, prescribes the program and means of study and constitutes the only means of gaining entry to professional practice. A further step along the continuum may be represented by a college which controls certain certification (a degree, diploma, certificate) but where entry into the program is reasonably open and the courses are available by full or part-time study, and perhaps by distance education delivery as well as face to face. Another type of situation may be represented by a proprietary secretarial school. Entry may be open to anyone who is reasonably competent in the basics, intake may be on a continuous basis, and instruction may be individualized and self-paced, utilizing instructional materials which are available to students and non-students alike. Further, the skills being learned may be achievable by other means and the opportunity for gaining employment based on those skills may not be limited on the basis of how they were achieved. (Employers may be quite accustomed to doing their own testing of prospective employees for their competence in office or technical skills, but they are frequently prepared to take some other institution's word for the knowledge or skills acquired in a university, an accountancy program, or in some other

---

[31] P.H. Coombs, *The World Crisis in Education*, p. 24.

[32] P.H. Coombs, *The World Crisis in Education*; J. Lowe, *The Education of Adults*.

educational program.) A next step along the continuum may be represented by the distance education student, for instance someone taking a correspondence course. Having enrolled, the student typically acquires instructional resources in the form of a manual of instruction and text books. The student is then free to proceed at whatever pace he or she chooses (usually within certain limits), calling on the resources provided and any others available. But if the course is for some form of credit, there will be restrictions in terms of what assignments should be written, and there will likely be examinations to be completed. The student is working "on his own" but subject to some conditions imposed by the accrediting institution. A further stage in the direction of self, as distinct from institutional control of the conditions of learning, is represented by the individual's use of a local learning centre, for example a learning centre in a factory or a storefront drop-in learning centre for adult basic education. Here the flexibility in terms of the time, duration and form of study undertaken may be very great, limited by the materials and experts available on which the student may call. Perhaps the "learner autonomy" end of the spectrum is appropriately represented by the "self-directed" learner. In this case the person may decide what to learn, may start (and stop) at any point, adjust the learning goals at any time, choose the style or educational process or resources which will be called upon, consult any persons or other resources available, and have control over the costs to be incurred. There are many hazards in the path of self-directed learners, as there are for full-time study in a professional university program, but they are very different ones. The former maximizes independence and flexibility, but also the hazards which accompany lack of structure and imposed discipline. The full-time institutional student faces—willingly in most instances—quite the reverse.

2

Functions and Philosophical Considerations

What is adult education for? Such a question can be answered at several levels, and from different perspectives. At the most profound level, the answer leads us to an examination of the ideas of philosophers who have had something to say about education and human development. At a more applied or policy related level, the matter is often approached by examining the "functions" of adult education, seeing them from the point of view of both the individual and the society as a whole.

The Functions of Adult Education

Perhaps the most common typology of functions, as seen from the individual's point of view, is comprised of four categories:

1. Vocational—this has to do particularly with the knowledge and skills required to perform a job.

2. Social—This relates to the individual's social roles in life as family member (parent, child, etc.), as a member or leader of social groups and organizations (at work, in community life, etc.) and as a citizen (a voter, volunteer, community worker, etc.).

3. Recreational—this relates to the individual's recreational activities, be it playing a game, appreciating or performing in the arts, or keeping up to date on a field of interest.

4. Self-development—this is a rather amorphous category, and to varying degrees may overlap with the other three. It may be seen to relate to the sorts of goals we associate with liberal education— learning how to think critically, express oneself, broaden one's horizons. Feelings about oneself, others and the ultimate values in life may be said to fall into this category as well.

The foregoing kind of formulation was fairly common in the literature of the field some decades ago and is based on the roles or "fields of action" of the individual.[1] Other formulations put forward in the 1960s, when adult education

---

[1] See for instance A.A. Liveright, *A Study of Adult Education in the United States* (Boston, Centre for the Study of Liberal Education for Adults, 1968).

as a field of study was under active development, put more focus on the functions as they related to intellectual functioning. In his chapter in the American *Handbook*, which appeared in 1960, Hallenbeck made reference to such terms as remedial, assimilative and compensatory.[2] In the textbook by Verner and Booth, which appeared four years later, the terms used were expansional (the acquiring of new knowledge and skills), participational (citizenship), integrational (combining knowledge with experience), and personal (the development and maturing of the individual).[3]

Sir Josiah Stamp, 19th century British economist and industrialist, described the functions of adult education as to assist the adult "to earn a living, to live a life and to mould a world."[4] In a somewhat similar vein, Thomas Kelly, in presenting an historical overview of adult education in Great Britain in recent centuries, has used the terms: education for salvation, for vocation, for civilization, for participation, and for recreation.[5] In a rather sweeping and colourful attempt to present all this more simply, Dwyer, in his *Ivory Towers in the Marketplace*, suggested that for the individual, the essential functions of adult education were two, to increase the "life chance" and the "life space" of the person.[6] The first term refers to basic education, vocational training and personal development which permitted the person to get ahead in terms of the kind of career or life situation that the person wanted. "Life space" referred to broadening the horizons of the person's life, in terms of interests and the capacity for enjoyment and appreciation.

Three examples will be presented of the functions as seen from the social or community view. The first is from Hallenbeck again, in which he uses the more personally related headings which were common at the time, but describes these consistently in terms of how the individual will use these powers (communications skills, improved human relations, expediting personal growth and facilitating participation) in the community setting.[7] In his international review of the field, Lowe approached the description of functions largely from the point of view of nations and governments. He saw occupational training as the most

[2]   W. Hallenbeck, "The Function and Place of Adult Education in American Society," in M.S. Knowles (Ed.), *Handbook of Adult Education in the United States* (Chicago, Adult Education Association of the U.S.A., 1960) pp. 29–38.

[3]   C. Verner & A. Booth, *Adult Education* (New York, Centre for Applied Research in Education, 1964).

[4]   Cited in G. Selman, *The Invisible Giant* (Vancouver, University of British Columbia/Centre for Continuing Education, 1988).

[5]   T. Kelly, "The Historical Evolution of Adult Education in Great Britain," in M. Tight (Ed.), *Education for Adults* (London, Croom Helm, 1983) vol. II, pp. 3–19.

[6]   J. Dwyer, *Ivory Towers in the Market Place* (New York, Bobbs-Merrill, 1956).

[7]   W. Hallenbeck, "The Function and Place of Adult Education in American Society."

widely accepted function. He felt there was support for two other functions in the less developed countries: inculcating a sense of national identity and helping to overcome poverty (economic development). Other functions seen for adult education included "helping societies adjust to the interaction of social and technological change," fostering social justice (by enabling more people to gain the benefits of economic development), and "reducing conflict in the political and employment spheres."[8]

The most recent of these social views of adult education comes from Peter Jarvis. He lists the functions as follows:

- Maintenance of the social system and reproduction of existing social relations.
- Transmission of knowledge and the reproduction of culture.
- Individual advancement and selection.
- Leisure time pursuit and institutional expansion.
- Development and liberation.[9]

In their textbook for the field, which appeared in 1982, Darkenwald and Merriam attempted to combine the personal and social functions. They stated the functions of the field as follows:

- Cultivation of the intellect.
- Individual self-actualization.
- Personal and social improvement.
- Social transformation.
- Organizational effectiveness.[10]

Such formulations of the functions of the field are cast in general enough terms to have application to Canada, and perhaps most if not all other societies. They would not all be embraced with equal enthusiasm by a totalitarian regime, or for that matter, as Lowe has pointed out, by all governments.[11] From a Canadian point of view, all of the functions described are familiar. It is not surprising that in a country which has been so pre-occupied at times with the socialization of immigrants and with developing a sense of national identity, many of the most noteworthy achievements in the field have been related to citizenship and social development functions of the field. The other point which should be made is that the community, through government, although it may realize the value of all the functions of adult education, may not regard all functions as equally deserving of public financial support. There may be a willingness to spend public funds for vocational or academic training, for instance (in the belief that these are crucial

---

[8] J. Lowe, *The Education of Adults: A World Perspective* (Toronto, Ontario Institute for Studies in Education, 1982) pp. 33–35.

[9] P. Jarvis, *The Sociology of Adult and Continuing Education* (London, Croom Helm, 1985) pp. 133–50.

[10] G. Darkenwald & S. Merriam, *Adult Education: Foundations of Practice* (New York, Harper & Row, 1982) pp. 43–64.

[11] J. Lowe, *The Education of Adults: A World Perspective*.

to the economic development of the nation) but an insistence that recreational types of learning should be fully paid for by the "consumer." A fuller elaboration of this matter is to be found in the chapters on public policy further on in this book.

Philosophical Considerations
by Mark Selman

This section is intended to provide an introduction to some of the philosophical approaches and issues which are relevant to the practice of adult education. It describes some important distinctions between kinds of claims, distinctions based on the different sorts of evidence or support needed to establish their acceptability. Next, some of the major ways in which adult educators and theorists have held differing assumptions are examined. These include fundamentally different views about the nature of society, the role of adult education within society, and the basis of our knowledge of the world. In each case, some connection is made between these general positions and the views of adult educators. In particular, some of these ideas are applied to an examination of the concept of the adult learner's "autonomy," and other matters involved in the andragogical perspective.

Adult educators do not usually think of their day to day decision-making as proceeding from philosophical premises. Commonly, like people working in most other fields, they act in ways which seem appropriate or natural, and in many cases, according to standards of accepted practice within their place of employment. But if we stop to think about it, we see that educators do make decisions about how to proceed, and these decisions are based on their values and their fundamental beliefs about the way things are. As Robert Blakely succinctly puts it, "We can—and usually do—refrain from asking philosophical questions, but we cannot avoid acting according to philosophical assumptions."[12]

Given that our assumptions may be a result of all sorts of accidents of upbringing and experience, and that they may well be based on little evidence or ill-founded inference, or may even be in contradiction with one another, some questioning of them is in order. In fact it might be argued that some relatively self-conscious reflection on one's fundamental beliefs and values is part of what makes an individual more than a simple product of environmental pressures, part of what accounts for a person's ability to be autonomous or self-determining.

In addition to this general reason for examining one's assumptions, educators have particular reasons to be consciously reflective about their views. Insofar as learning implies change, educators are in the business of changing people, or at least of helping people change themselves. Participation in such activities carries with it certain responsibilities—among them a responsibility to have examined the beliefs and values which may be conveyed through an educator's words and actions.

---

[12] R. Blakely, "The Path and the Goal," *Adult Education*, 7, 2 (1957) pp. 93–98, p. 93.

Further, educators are constantly faced with the task of trying to understand how other people make sense of whatever is being studied. This task is obstructed if there is a failure on the part of educators to recognize their own basic assumptions, which make certain conclusions seem obvious to them, but which may not be shared by others.

Without suggesting that such reflection should in any way be restricted to the early, formative stages of a person's professional career, it is also worth noting that reflection on fundamental assumptions may inform or help shape one's outlook and one's aspirations. It could influence, for example, one's choice of education or employment. Also, it may well become more difficult to find the time, or sufficient detachment from day to day pressures, to think through some important issues as one becomes involved in a career. So, there are important reasons for trying to reflect on philosophical issues at a relatively early stage of professional practice, as well as during one's subsequent career as a practitioner.

Some Philosophical Distinctions

In examining some of our more fundamental beliefs and values, and those of theorists and practitioners in the field of adult education, it is useful to have some conceptual tools. A few distinctions will therefore be introduced and explained. In order to establish the relevance of these distinctions, they will be discussed in the context of an adult educator who is trying to make practical decisions about how best to conduct her class.

Imagine, for this purpose, that an educator is teaching a class for nurses who are interested in learning how to orient and instruct new and inexperienced nurses who are being hired in a particular jurisdiction. One of the issues raised by one of the members of her class is that the experienced nurses feel that something should be done to help the new nurses think more critically about situations, rather than having to follow instructions rigidly and being at a loss when even relatively minor obstacles interfere with standard procedures. The instructor, let's call her Sharon, has looked at a couple of articles about critical thinking but feels ill equipped to address adequately some of the issues raised by her class. They want to learn how to teach critical thinking but, through class discussion, Sharon realizes that none of them, herself included, has a very clear idea about what critical thinking really is, or how they could promote critical thinking in this context. Some of the issues raised in the discussion include:

- What does critical thinking mean, or what does it mean to be a critical thinker?
- Do you have to be an expert to teach critical thinking or can any teacher learn to do it?
- Are general courses of instruction in critical thinking worthwhile or should they develop a specialized program of their own?

Each of these questions raises different kinds of issues, calling for different sorts of answers which require different types of support. Distinctions have been developed by philosophers to categorize different kinds of issues or claims according to the sort of grounds which serve to support or undermine them. Conceptual claims, for instance, are claims which are true or false depending on the meaning of words exclusively. That is, the truth of a conceptual claim is evident to anyone who has a relatively complete understanding of what the words in it mean. While this might seem to indicate that conceptual claims are not contentious or uninteresting, it will be recalled that many of the central concepts in adult education (see Chapter 1) are sometimes used in confusing and contradictory ways. Given that the language that we use both in thinking about the world and in communicating with others affects what we can see and what we can say, conceptual issues have fundamental importance to the enterprise of education. In fact, many of the enduring issues in philosophy and education turn out to be conceptual ones.

The issue raised by Sharon and her class about what critical thinking means is a conceptual question. Sometimes people speak and write as if it is quite clear what even complex terms mean, as if the meaning should be clear to any competent language user with a dictionary. This is certainly not the case for terms such as "critical thinking," which are used by different people for different purposes. Often such words are used as theoretic terms, in which case they may take on a special meaning. "Learning" is another example of such a term. If it is used by a behaviourist psychologist to mean "a change in behaviour," we as readers of this literature must be careful not to extend any conclusions drawn using this definition of learning, to the more general and varied uses of the term. It may be very relevant to learning to duck when passing under a low doorway but have little application to learning in the sense that one learns to care about one's workmates. Sometimes different senses, uses, or ways of understanding a concept are called "conceptions."

Philosophers have developed various strategies for clarifying the meaning of terms. Space precludes any serious examination of these strategies but one thing that is crucial to note is that conceptual questions cannot be settled by more research, at least not research in the traditional sense of conducting experiments and observing the results. If Sharon and her class want to find out what critical thinking means, there will be no point in looking to see what research has "proven" or in conducting their own experiments. Rather, they would have to look closely at what people who are teaching or writing about critical thinking are trying to achieve, or to examine the philosophical debate over the nature of critical thinking.

A second type of issue is called empirical. Empirical issues are those which are determined on the basis of evidence supplied by our senses, either directly or indirectly. Claims about observable states of affairs in the world are the most obvious examples of empirical claims but other claims for which only supporting evidence is available are also included. Examples of this latter category include claims about past events, claims about unobservable events such as sub-atomic collisions, or conditional claims, that is, claims about what would happen if such and such were the case.

If Sharon's class wanted to know whether special expertise was required or whether they would be able to teach their own students to think more critically on the job, they would be considering an empirical issue of this latter sort. This is the sort of issue for which they might be able to find an answer in the research, although it would require some care in evaluating whether or not the cases of published research that they were able to find provided examples which were close enough to their own situation to be relevant. They would also want to be sure that the indicators of success or failure in the relevant research studies were a reasonable match for the conception of critical thinking which was relevant to their interests—in this case defined as more independent thought on the part of their students while on the job.

Generally speaking, it may be noted that we do not employ reflection or philosophical methods of inquiry in order to establish the soundness of an empirical claim. If inquiry is required, we are more likely to rely on the standards and practices developed in the sciences, or in the study of history. In certain areas of human endeavour, however, empirical issues are inextricably connected to other sorts of issues. In education, for instance, it has often proven extremely difficult to sort out whether one method works better than another for accomplishing a given objective. This does not seem solely a matter of complexity, but also arises from the fact that education involves human intentions and feelings.

Value issues form a third category. Statements made with regard to these issues are called value claims or value judgments. While many value claims are not generally referred to as being either true or false, reasons can be offered for or against accepting them, and some judgments are more justifiable than others. If, for instance, a particular taxation policy can be shown to be producing undesirable social consequences, such as drastically increasing unemployment, or if it could be shown to be in conflict with some fundamental principle of human justice, we would have reasons for accepting the value judgment that it is a bad taxation policy.

Thus, while value related issues are often thought of as contentious and irresolvable, it is not the case, as some have thought, that value judgments are simply expressions of opinion which lack any rational or cognitive basis. On the contrary, trying to establish a relatively stable, consistent and coherent set of values is no less a rational enterprise than is the project of establishing a stable, consistent and coherent system of beliefs. Indeed, it seems to be the case that the two are closely related and are jointly involved in our coming to be a mature person. As the issue of what constitutes maturity is of central importance to defining the field of adult education, it is one to which we will return.

When Sharon and her class were considering whether general instruction in critical thinking is *worthwhile* or whether they *should* consider developing a more specialized program for their own purposes, they were considering value issues. Value judgments are often identifiable because they employ value terms such as "worthwhile" or "good," or because they express judgments about what "should" or "ought" to be done. It is of particular importance in a practical field such as education to realize that practical judgments, such as those employing "should" and "ought," are value judgments. As such, their acceptability is not determined by empirical research alone. Whether they are acceptable is also a matter of meeting other sets of standards. Which standards are relevant will depend on the sort of judgments being expressed.

Two broad categories which are particularly relevant for present purposes are those judgments which express epistemological and ethical claims. The first of these express judgments according to standards of adequacy for claims to knowledge. Such standards are of obvious significance to the educational enterprise. Whether one is preparing a lecture, evaluating a textbook, reacting to a comment made in discussion, or judging an assignment, an important issue will be to judge the adequacy of statements as assertions of knowledge. This will involve assessing whether they are true, whether there is evidence offered in support of claims that are made, and whether the claims are significant or relevant to the points under discussion. If Sharon's class wanted to know whether improved results on a certain kind of standard test were good evidence for the quality of a critical thinking program, they would be raising an epistemological issue.

Ethical judgments are those made about the adequacy of a person's (or a group's) conduct, especially as it relates to the interests of others. Two types of ethical issues which commonly arise in educational settings are those involving the treatment of individual students with (or without) respect and issues involving the distribution of educational resources. If, for instance, one of Sharon's students pointed out that they ought to equip their students to think independently, rather than teaching them in a way which encouraged blind obedience to instructions because that was the only approach which was consistent with treating their students as mature persons, she would be making an ethical argument.

One fact worth noting about ethical disputes in particular, is that there is often agreement at an abstract level about the values to be realized in a given situation (e.g. respect for persons, fairness, solidarity) but disagreement at the level of practice about what counts in a particular context as acting according to these values, or about how to balance conflicting values. This can be seen from the example of Sharon's student who wanted to encourage independent thought. It is comparatively easy to get people to agree that adult students ought to be treated as mature persons, but rather more difficult to get agreement about what that means in terms of teaching methods.

Some Fundamental Assumptions in Adult Education

Having now some shared understanding of these distinctions, we will turn our attention to some of the ways in which adult educators differ over fundamental assumptions. One thing that is important to recognize is that no simple set of categories can do justice to the range of differences which exist between educators on such matters. As we will see, thinkers who share many assumptions can disagree sharply over others.

Functionalism and Conflict Theory

One particularly important area in which educators disagree about fundamental issues is in their views of society and its relation to individuals. Only some aspects of this disagreement are, strictly speaking, philosophical, but it bears examination here because the different viewpoints have significant consequences for how the role of the educator is conceptualized.

The disagreement can perhaps be captured most succinctly by means of two contrasting metaphors, one seeing society as an organism, the other viewing it as a scene of conflict or struggle. The former is derived from a theory called functionalism, and is commonly associated with liberal thought. The latter is more common among Marxist and other more radical critics of existing Western social structures. It should be stressed, before exploring what is at stake in the acceptance of these metaphors, that theorists may vary greatly in how they make use of these metaphors—that while the metaphors may be used to point out general areas of disagreement, some liberals may have more in common with some more radical thinkers than they do with some other liberals, and vice versa.

According to those who see society as an organism, the various different parts of society contribute to its overall efficient functioning in the way the organs of a body each fulfill a necessary role. Schools, labour unions, the courts, businesses and other segments of society, each function as required for the operation of society as a whole. Under changing circumstances, the system adapts by making (usually incremental) adjustments in the relations between the various segments of society or in the roles of its institutions.

Usually associated with this view is the belief that society rewards most highly those roles which are most important. Thus, the most able individuals are attracted to those positions which are most critical to the welfare of the society as a whole. For educators who hold these sorts of beliefs about the way society works, the role of adult education is most likely to be seen as facilitating the adjustment or improvement of society, particularly by increasing the number of qualified people for positions which are in social demand. Individual students will, it is thought, be able to improve their position by equipping themselves to take on more important functions, ones which are more highly valued and rewarded. In addition, society as a whole will benefit by having more capable people in important positions.

Conflict theorists have a very different view of the way society works. They see it as being composed of groups with fundamentally different and often incompatible interests. Relations between different groups are not based on mutual adaption for the overall smooth functioning of society, but rather on constant struggle, with some groups trying to maintain positions of entrenched wealth and power over those without. For those who take this view, the belief that individuals succeed by equipping themselves better to fulfill roles important to society is seen as a myth, moreover as a myth which is useful for those in power as it tends to promote satisfaction with the status quo.

Educators who subscribe to this second view tend to see the role of educators in three possible ways. The first suggests that most educational efforts are merely window dressing, that real change in societal relations can proceed only on the basis of a different economic structure. Educational reform, in this view, is likely to be seen as a distraction from the real problems which are economic and political, or at best as treating the symptoms rather than the root causes of social inequality.

Others, however, have seen a more positive role for educators, believing that education can at least help to create the conditions necessary for the amelioration of political and economic inequities. In the field of adult education, Paulo Freire has been a particularly important writer who has taken this position. Based primarily on the experience of literacy work in Brazilian villages, Freire and his colleagues developed what he called a "pedagogy of the oppressed." In his book by that title, Freire argues that education is by its nature a political activity in that it either promotes the assumptions of the existing political and economic structures or it brings people to question them. In either case, it serves a political function.[13] In the context of the very poor villages in which Freire worked, the very fact of increased literacy among the villagers had significant political consequences. By becoming literate, they gained access to information about a range of possibilities unknown in the circumscribed world of their villages. They were no longer as completely dependent on their employers, the landowners, as they found out about other alternative social arrangements. They could begin to question the apparent inevitability of existing states of affairs and social relations. Freire describes this as a first step in the process of "conscientization," the process of becoming aware of contradictions in one's situation and becoming capable of acting to resolve them. Notice that for Freire meaningful or authentic education could not simply involve the passing on of facts, or even a deeper initiation into the cultural traditions of a society, but necessarily involves the fostering of critical thought regarding the socio-political context in which the learners are situated. Quite naturally, Freire's ideas have had the most influence in situations which resemble those in which his ideas were developed. In Canada, this has tended to be in working with groups facing the most severe obstacles to economic well-being and political autonomy, such groups as Native Indians, immigrant labourers, illiterate adults, and prisoners.

A third conception of the role of educators is offered by the Italian Marxist, Antonio Gramsci. In contrast to Freire, Gramsci offers a rather traditional, even conservative account of school age education. His primary concern was that children of lower class families were prevented from obtaining the best education available, not that the education they obtained was ideologically biased.[14] It is only in adulthood, when people have started to work, that education should be focused on specifically political objectives, primarily under the auspices of

---

[13] P. Freire, *Pedagogy of the Oppressed* (New York, Herder & Herder, 1970).

[14] H. Entwistle, *Antonio Gramsci* (London, Routledge & Kegan Paul, 1979).

worker controlled organizations such as labour unions and community based groups.

Subject-Centred and Learner-Centred Approaches

It may be noted here that the general distinction between the views of Freire and Gramsci are roughly paralleled by differences among liberal educators. On the one hand, educators who adopt a progressivist approach, usually derived in some way from the thought of John Dewey, tend to emphasize the active role of the learner, in a social context, in creating and defining the value of what is learned. Often this results in what is referred to as a "learner-centred" curriculum. On the other hand are those who, often drawing on the work of R.S. Peters, emphasize the importance of initiation into our cultural traditions and the intrinsic value of what is commonly called a liberal education. This approach tends to result in what is called a "subject-centred" curriculum.

Peters has associated this view with the idea that education is to be valued for its own sake, not primarily or essentially because of its utility or its value as a means towards achieving other goals. This is in contrast, of course, to those who see education's value as residing in its contribution towards individual advancement or social reform.

Many of these positions have entered into debates in adult education. The notion that educational planning should be driven by the interests of the participants is evident in a common saying from 30 years ago which was that "adult education has no curriculum." In 1966, the Canadian Association for Adult Education issued a "White Paper," in which it was stated, "Whatever a citizen chooses to learn is important simply because he chooses to learn it."[15] On the other hand, Colin Griffin has argued that "the primary conceptual framework for adult education ... has been constructed in terms of needs, access and provision rather than in terms of knowledge, culture and power." We need, he says, "a curriculum theory of adult education; one which is primarily concerned with the social and political definition, distribution and evaluation of knowledge."[16]

The view that education is to be valued for its own sake is evident in the 1936 statement of H.F. Munro, the President of the Canadian Association for Adult Education, who wrote of "the enterprise of turning an individual into a genuinely competent and wise adult" and of "the love of learning for its own sake, with the consequent enlargement of our philosophical frontiers and the wisdom which knowledge, rightly pursued, brings in its train."[17] George Grant, the well-known

---

[15] Canadian Association for Adult Education, *A White Paper on the Education of Adults in Canada* (Toronto, CAAE, n.d., 1966) p. 1.

[16] C. Griffin, *Curriculum Theory in Adult and Lifelong Education* (London, Croom Helm, 1983) pp. 38, 68.

[17] H.F. Munro, "Editorial," *Adult Learning*, *1*, 2 (1936) pp. 2–3.

Canadian political philosopher, who once worked for the same association, wrote in the Association's journal in 1953 that adult education stands for "no limited social ends, but for the highest end, the self-liberation of the human soul by the systematic examination of its own activities."[18] Northrop Frye, the eminent literary critic and educator, goes so far as to say, in his book, *On Education*, that attempts to be "relevant" are inimical to the realization of the most important values of education.[19]

On the other hand, Canada in particular has a long tradition of adult education projects undertaken with specific political, economic and social ends in mind. One of the most famous of these is the Antigonish Movement in the Maritimes, using adult education as a focus for the organization of co-operative ventures among exploited fishermen and their families. The leading figure in the Antigonish Movement, Rev. Moses Coady, believed, according to his biographer, that "the adult educator worth his salt was an aggressive agent of change and adult education a mass movement of reform."[20] In 1941, E.A. Corbett, in his Director's Report to the Canadian Association for Adult Education, said, "That's our job, to show people what a living, shining thing democracy can be."[21]

Three Philosophical Orientations

Positivism

In order to gain some appreciation of the issues which lie behind these different positions, one must understand something of the place of epistemological concerns in the development of Western philosophical thought. Perhaps the most central project of Western philosophy has been to identify the grounds on which our knowledge is based, that is, on what basis can we identify the difference between those of our beliefs which are true and justified and those which are false or merely speculative. Philosophers such as Descartes have believed that it is possible to derive a foundation for our knowledge of reality from reason alone. This is referred to as rationalism. English philosophers John Locke, Bishop Berkeley and David Hume, believed that our knowledge of reality is based entirely on impressions of the world received through our sensory organs. Because, as mentioned above, claims which are based on information which can be verified through our senses are called empirical, this position is referred to as empiricist.

---

[18] G. Grant, "Philosophy and Adult Education," *Food For Thought, 14,* 1 (1953) pp. 3–8, p. 5.

[19] N. Frye, *On Education* (Markham, Ontario, Fitzhenry & Whiteside, 1988).

[20] A.F. Laidlaw, (Ed.), *The Man from Margaree* (Toronto, McClelland & Stewart, 1971), p. 83.

[21] E.A. Corbett, Director's Report to Annual Meeting of Canadian Association for Adult Education 1941, quoted in G. Selman, *The Canadian Association for Adult Education in the Corbett Years: A Re-evaluation* (Vancouver, University of British Columbia/Centre for Continuing Education, 1981), p. 7.

Since the end of the 18th century, this argument has been modified somewhat, largely because of internal contradictions in each of the major positions. Rather than searching for a foundation on which all knowledge could be grounded, philosophers have turned more to the problem of identifying those areas of knowledge or kinds of claims which can be said to be held on the basis of good reasons. One of the most celebrated moves in this direction was Kant's argument that human knowledge and understanding is restricted to the world as it appears to us, that we have no access to any ultimate or unconditioned reality. One of the implications of this argument is that many of the positions taken by earlier philosophers, arguments which attempted to determine the true nature of reality, quite apart from how the world appears to human beings, are meaningless as they are based on a confusion about how language can properly be used.

In this century, there have been several major streams of philosophy which have emerged as responses to these historical positions. In the English speaking world, three have been particularly influential and each of these has had significant influence on educational theorizing. These three strains are positivism, pragmatism and analytic philosophy.

The project of positivists generally has been to develop a scientific language which is more precise than our ordinary way of speaking, one which includes only claims which are logically true (analytic) and those which can be verified unambiguously by reference to observable states of affairs (empirical). While this has been an extremely influential philosophical doctrine, attempts to apply these notions in understanding human behaviour and social interactions have been quite contentious. One of the most dramatic of these attempts has been the psychological theory of behaviourism. Behaviourism is worth considering in some detail both because of its historical influence on educational practice, and as an example of a practical theory based on this philosophical doctrine.

Behavourists have argued that a scientific understanding of human action is desirable and is possible only by operationalizing the concepts by means of which we understand human states and traits in terms of their observable behaviours. In practical terms, this has been interpreted to mean that educators ought to state their aims in terms of the behaviours that they wish their students to exhibit. Thus, educators can develop clear, unambiguous criteria for the achievement of an educational objective, and can eventually establish what means of education are effective in bringing about different objectives.

Simple as this program sounds when described in a few sentences, it is fraught with conceptual difficulties. Chief among these has been that many of the concepts by means of which we can ordinarily make sense of educational activities do not entail any determinate set of behaviours. The fact that someone has learned something, understands something, or has developed an interest in something, implies normally that he or she has developed some new capacity or inclination, but not necessarily that these changes will be manifest in any observable change in behaviour. A deeper understanding of classical music may not produce any observable changes even while the person in question is listening to classical music. Many of the words which are most central to understanding what other people are doing depend for their meaning as much on inferences about people's purposes and intentions as they do on people's observable behaviour. Because purposes and intentions are, however, not observable states, they are excluded from behaviouristic analysis. Behaviourists are faced with an unattractive choice: either they accept that much of what we want to understand under the description of educational activity and achievement cannot be captured within their theoretical structure (because the concepts cannot be operationalized adequately) or they conclude that their strictures on what counts as scientific are too rigid. Either many of the questions we most want to understand cannot be addressed or some of the basic premises of behaviourism must be given up.

As a result of these and other problems, behaviourism has fallen from being one of the most dominant psychological theories, especially in the field of education, to having a rather restricted role in explaining learning in which understanding or cognition is thought to play a limited role. Examples would include learning which is limited to rote memorization, repetitive drill aimed at the development of physical skills, or the training of those with very limited mental capacity. Nonetheless, behaviourist language and assumptions are common enough still in educational writing that sensitivity to these issues is required if one is not to adopt them unwittingly.

The history of behaviourism is typical of many of the more positivistic theories, especially in the human or social sciences. Most current philosophers and theorists hold that there is no clear way of separating logical and empirical claims from questions of intention and value. Thus, there is no way to establish a completely neutral, value free method for establishing the truth. This kind of realization, however, can give rise to concerns that there is no such thing as knowledge, in general. It suggests that all claims to knowledge or truth are relative to the purposes, interests, and intentions of whoever is making the claim. But this suggestion seems to raise possibilities that run strongly against some basic intuitions, intuitions that most people do not want to give up. For instance, some have taken it to mean that there is no reality, only versions of it as viewed by different individuals or different social groups. Further, it has been taken to imply that agreement or shared understanding between people with different backgrounds and purposes is unlikely, or even impossible, as they live in essentially different realities. Claims to truth by one individual or group would then have no more force than statements of preferences or opinions.

Pragmatism and Analytic Philosophy

Philosophers and others have differed greatly over how seriously to take this problem and its apparent consequences for communication between individuals and social groups. One very important tradition in philosophy, especially American philosophy, is called pragmatism. Pragmatists, as the name implies, treat this and other philosophical issues as practical problems to be worked out in experience. Thus, a pragmatist would be inclined to ignore the problem about the nature of reality, and discuss the issue of relativism in terms of its practical consequences in human communication. If, in fact, it turns out that we can successfully communicate with others with very different interests and experiences, if we can translate from language to language and obtain reasonably coherent reactions on the basis of our translations, then the worst fears raised by the issue of relativism can be put to rest.

John Dewey, one of the most important of the pragmatists, especially for those in the field of education, was little troubled by this issue. He had a strong faith in human nature, in democracy, and in science. He believed that if human beings were given the freedom to pursue their own interests within a supportive environment, human knowledge and understanding would flourish. A dominant metaphor in Dewey's work is the notion of education as growth. A common objection to this idea is that people's mental lives, unlike plants and other things which grow, have no natural or predetermined shape. Allowing the uneducated person's own interests to guide the educational process is, according to this objection, an abrogation of the educator's responsibility.

One of the sources of this objection is the analytic school of philosophy of education. These philosophers believe that many educational theories and programs are based on misunderstandings of the concepts with which we make sense of educational activities and achievements. But, rather than arguing for the development of a new, more scientific language in which to formulate educational theories, as the positivists did, analytic philosophers have argued that we should pay very close attention to the structure of ordinary language and the way we ordinarily use certain important concepts. They point out, for example, that the notion of a person's interests, which is so central to Dewey's arguments, is ambiguous in an important way. Persons' "interests" may refer either to that which they are interested in or to what is in their best interests. It is obvious that people should be educated in a way which advances their best interests, but this is quite different, they claim, from using what they are interested in as the determining factor in what they will study.

R.S. Peters and Paul Hirst, two of the most influential analytic philosophers of education, go on to argue that, on the basis of an analysis of the way that the concept of education is employed, only some of the achievements and some of the activities of educational institutions are truly educational. By being careful with the way we use the term, they argue, we could avoid confusing activities which are indoctrinatory, for instance, with those which are genuinely educational. They also argue that "being educated" implies a certain breadth and depth of knowledge, typically taken to mean that an educated person has some acquaintance with each of the traditional disciplines of knowledge. Thus, according to these philosophers, it is the traditions of the academic disciplines, rather than the interests of students, which provide the most significant guide to planning educational activities.

This point returns us to the issue of whether program planning or curriculum development ought to proceed primarily on the basis of the structure of the academic disciplines and other fields of study, or whether it ought to be determined primarily by the interests of those studying. It may be that individual educators will need to determine the most satisfactory way of dealing with this issue on a situation by situation basis. Nonetheless, it seems important that educators do consider some of these issues because whether or not philosophers come to agreement about which of the possible positions is most reasonable, educators will end up making judgments and decisions which presuppose some position, at least for a given context.

Autonomy as an Example of an Educational Ideal

Presumably people do not want to have their professional practice based on ideas which are in fundamental conflict with other of their deeply held beliefs about reality, human nature, etc. To provide an example of how an educator's basic beliefs and values might be connected with, or be in conflict with some of these positions, we might consider the related concepts of maturity and autonomy. Most of us are committed to the idea that autonomy is an important character trait, one which we ought to foster in ourselves and enhance in others. Maturity is a particularly important notion for adult educators in that it is one of the characteristics which is typically thought to distinguish adults from children. It is on the basis of a presumption of greater autonomy (in the sense of independence of judgment) that adults are entitled and expected to take an active role in legal and democratic processes, for example.

The issue of autonomy is relevant to an evaluation of each of the major positions discussed. It can be argued that behaviourism, for example, obscures our sensitivity to the issue of students' autonomy, focusing as it does simply on observable inputs and responses. In fact, it tends to treat human beings simply as objects of study which react in this way or that, without regard for their purposes and intentions, which are inextricably related to the issue of autonomy. Notice, for instance, that the fostering of autonomy is not a legitimate educational objective according to the principles of behaviourism, as it cannot be operationalized in terms of any specific set of behaviours. Thus, unless there is reason to doubt one or more of these descriptions of behaviourism, an approach based on behaviourist theory is inappropriate if we agree that issues involving autonomy are critical to the responsible practice of education.

The dispute between philosophers inspired by Dewey and the analytic philosophers can also be understood as crucially involved with the issue of autonomy. Dewey inclines us to think that it is through the practice of autonomy in choosing their educational pursuits that students both express and develop their autonomy. Peters and other analytic philosophers argue that autonomy in its richest sense is closely connected with the ideal of an educated person and that without a relatively broad and deep understanding of our culture/academic traditions, the freedom to pursue one's interests is of limited value. It is perhaps like the freedom to vote without any real understanding of the issues at stake in the election.

The fact that there can be such fundamental differences between sincere and intelligent people concerned with issues in education, people who are equally concerned about virtues of character such as autonomy, is an indication that this is an area in which human judgment plays a significant role. This issue is not likely to be settled by some scientific discovery or by some startling new argument that no one has ever thought of before. More likely, through reflection and study of others' work, we can develop a deeper appreciation of the connection between our ideals, such as maturity and autonomy, and our various practices. By considering the importance of autonomy, we become more sensitive to the ways in which common educational practices may pre-empt students' autonomy and encourage them to be dependent on the reasoning or intellectual/political authority of others.

Many kinds of study can enhance our understanding of these issues. Historical and literary texts can often provide insight into the ways that other individuals and groups have made sense of these issues. Another source which is not often included in the study of issues in adult education is the writing of philosophers themselves. Consider these comments by Immanuel Kant, one of the greatest of Western philosophers, about the nature of enlightenment. Kant understands enlightenment as both an individual and a socio/political ideal.

> Enlightenment is man's release from his self-imposed immaturity. This immaturity is man's inability to make use of his understanding without direction from another. It is self-imposed in that its cause lies not in lack of reason but in lack of resolution and courage to use it without direction from another ... Laziness and cowardice are the reasons why so great a portion of mankind, long after nature has discharged them from external direction, nevertheless remains in a state of immaturity, and why it is so easy for others to set themselves up as their guardians ... and kindly assume superintendence over them ... It is not easy to be of age. If I have a book which understands for me, a pastor who has a conscience for me, a physician who decides my diet, and so forth, I need not trouble myself.[22]

Even this short passage raises some critical issues for adult educators. Kant links enlightenment and maturity with ideas we have considered under the notion of autonomy. Notice that he thinks that the most crucial factors which interfere with autonomy are "lack of resolution and courage," not the development of reason or discipline based knowledge, as suggested by the analytic philosophers. If Kant is right, it may be that educators should devote far more of their attention to fostering these virtues on the part of their students. It may be that these virtues are best fostered in a situation which emphasizes the shared nature of intellectual inquiry and de-emphasizes the traditional disciplines as established bodies of knowledge. (Given the changing content of knowledge in the disciplines, many philosophers have come to regard them more as traditions of practice which are

---

[22] Version adapted from I. Kant, *Foundations of the Metaphysics of Morals* (New York, The Liberal Arts Press, 1959 (1784)), p. 85.

modified over time, in part through the use of critical practices which form part of a discipline's structure.)

Another crucial point in this excerpt from Kant is the notion that people are apt to slide into a position of either dependence or superintendence. This is a constant danger in the practice of adult education. Many students and educators find it easier to think according to the book or to act on the basis of some theory they are taught, rather than to use their own judgment and take responsibility for their own decisions. Many others may, quite without malicious intent, assume superintendence of them by taking the place of the book, the pastor or the physician in Kant's examples. This draws attention to the danger of adult educators trying to emphasize the place of their professional expertise, to the extent of interfering with the autonomy of adult students.

Obviously, this is not an argument against the development of knowledge in the field of adult education, any more than Kant's is an argument against books, pastors or doctors. What it does point out is that there is a dangerous link between the development of knowledge, especially in fields which involve knowledge of people, and conditions in which people's autonomy is limited or discouraged. As adult educators, involved with the education of those who are at least presumed to be in a state of relative maturity, we might be expected to be particularly cautious about acting in ways which might discourage maturity and autonomy in Kant's rather rich sense.

Philosophy and the Language of Adult Education

The above was an example of a way in which philosophical writing, like literary and historical writing, may be a useful aid to reflection on the practice of adult education. Another way in which philosophical inquiry may contribute to an understanding of this field is in providing what might be called "perspicuous accounts" of central ideas and terms. What is meant by this is that philosophical inquiry may be useful in clarifying conceptual confusions, in showing how certain word uses are related to each other, or by providing a more overarching perspective than that obtained by a more specific or narrowly focused theory. Of particular significance is the recognition of value implications, or the normative force, included in this broader perspective.

In order to see what this might mean in a particular case, it will be useful to consider one of the most influential concepts in the field, the notion of andragogy. This is a particularly useful example, both because of its impact on the field and because of its relation to the concepts of autonomy and maturity, which were discussed in the previous section. By seeing how this concept is applied and by seeing its relation to the more general concepts of adulthood, maturity, and autonomy, we will get some sense of the relation between theoretic, and more broadly philosophic, understanding.

Malcolm Knowles has suggested that the practice of "the science and art of helping adults learn," which he calls andragogy, is significantly different from at least the traditional approach to teaching children, or pedagogy.[23] It is different because adults are more mature than children, and so their experience is more extensive and plays a more significant role in defining their self-concept. They are also more likely to be self-directed rather than dependent on others for direction. Unlike children, they expect whatever they learn to have quite direct and immediate application to their daily lives.

This characterization is based broadly on theories of humanistic psychology, and the criteria which are used to differentiate adult learning from children's learning are psychological characteristics of the learners.[24] But the psychological characteristics of learners are only one of the many types of criteria by means of which we differentiate the activities of adults from those of children in ways that are relevant to understanding education. Thus, it is to be expected that the phrase "adult learning" when employed by Knowles and others who have adopted his criteria may be applied more specifically than the same phrase would be by other competent language users, but also that the "knowlsian" use would fail to recognize some of the other, non-psychological criteria implied in the ordinary non-theoretic use. In particular, it is to be expected that a theoretical concept designed to be used in an empirically testable hypothesis will fail to incorporate the normative character of our language of rights and entitlements. But this normative feature of concepts such as adulthood is also relevant to the practice of education, even if it is not part of the "operationalized" concepts of a psychological theory.

In particular, it is important to note that adults are considered to be autonomous agents for legal, political, and contractual purposes. Philosophers have pointed out that what it means to act autonomously is that the act is committed freely, in the sense that it is not the result of coercion or compulsion; that it is informed, in the sense that the individual has some idea what is at stake in possible alternative courses of action; and that the individual has a relatively stable set of values or purposes. In our society, barring special circumstances, it is presumed that adults' actions, including those aimed at educational goals, are made under these conditions. In the case of children, it is presumed that these decisions are made under conditions of reduced autonomy.[25] But to make this

---

[23] M.S. Knowles, *The Modern Practice of Adult Education* (Revised and Updated) (Chicago, Association Press, 1980) p. 43.

[24] As Sharan Merriam has pointed out, this is one of three types of criteria used in the field to make this differentiation. The other two are "the adult's learning situation," and "changes in consciousness." None of these approaches, as characterized by Merriam, identify adult learning as distinctive according to socio/political and legal criteria although the "change in consciousness" approach is a part of explicitly political approaches to education, such as Freire's. S.B. Merriam, "Adult Learning: A Review with Suggestions for the Direction of Future Research" in R.A. Fellenz & G.J. Conti (Eds.), *Building Tomorrow's Research Agenda for Lifelong Learning* (Kellogg Centre for Adult Learning Research: Montana State University, 1989) p. 9.

[25] For a more detailed argument of this point, see Mark Selman, "Learning and Philosophy of Mind," *The Canadian Journal for the Study of Adult Education*, 2, 2 (1988) p. 39.

claim is not only, or even primarily, to point out a set of empirical differences between children and adults, or even about differences in the way they are treated. Adults are entitled to be treated as self-determining agents and only in unusual cases is it acceptable to interfere with this right. It is on the basis of this right that adults are treated differently from children in law, and in many other contexts. Surely educational contexts are one of these.

These considerations are not raised in order to criticize or cast doubt on the utility of Knowles' concept of andragogy. Rather they are used to point out that a concept which is defined in relation to a theoretical framework such as humanistic psychology necessarily is applied according to a narrower and more specific set of criteria than our ordinary language concepts are. This is part of what makes a theoretic concept useful in making claims which can be tested through empirical research. But the price to be paid for this increased precision is the loss of some of the richness of our ordinary, non-theoretic language. Philosophical inquiry may be useful both in retaining normative dimensions of ordinary language and in clarifying the relationship between theoretic concepts and that ordinary language.

3

The Canadian Movement in Context

The enterprise of adult education, like any field of social practice, responds to the nature of the society within which it is functioning. One would expect, therefore, to find that the field of adult education in Canada reflects many features of our history as a people and our present social context. That this is the case can be amply demonstrated. Indeed some features of the history of the field would be difficult to understand without some knowledge of the history and nature of the society that produced them. It is the purpose of this chapter to examine some of these features and relate them to developments in the field of adult education.

It may justifiably be said that in large measure adult education here in Canada, as elsewhere, does not have an agenda of its own, but rather relates itself to the interests of others. Exceptions will be noted in the account which follows, but adult education tends to be the servant of the purposes of other elements in the society. This fact is caused, or at least reinforced, by the fact that in the vast majority of cases, adult education is a marginal enterprise sponsored by organizations whose chief aims and objectives lie elsewhere. In most of its settings, the education of adults is seen to be a means to an end rather than as an end in itself. The goal is most frequently not more fully functioning people, as such, but more productive workers, more expert practitioners, more informed citizens—and perhaps more institutional clients.

Because adult education, in most of its settings, is a servant of interests other than its own, it is not surprising that it reflects in its nature the characteristics of the society within which it operates. Canada being a nation which has continuously throughout its history received large numbers of immigrants, it is to be expected that citizenship education in its various dimensions, and carried out by various means, should be a prominent feature of the adult education scene. In fact a case can be made for citizenship education being the area in which Canadian adult education has made many of its most significant contributions to the field. To take another example, education having been assigned under the constitution of Canada as a provincial responsibility and economic development patterns having been very unequal from region to region, one would expect very great differences in the nature and extent of adult education development from one region to another. Indeed this is a prominent feature of the field in Canada. To move to a more negative example, the relative difficulty (some would say failure) in Canadian society to build effective understanding between English and French-speaking regions of the country is all too evident in adult education, just as it is in society as a whole. It appears to be justified to state that adult education in Canada reveals, illustrates or reflects many of the characteristics of the society of which it is a part.

External Influences

Although it is clear that many of the most outstanding projects in Canadian adult education were distinctively Canadian in origin and character, we have as well borrowed many institutional forms from elsewhere. The two most obvious sources have been Great Britain and the United States, but other countries have contributed as well. In the most recent decades particularly, Canadian adult education has drawn heavily on ideas about the field which have come from the international community.

British Influences

It was only natural—and to be expected—that as the large number of immigrants came to Canada from Great Britain, they would bring with them a knowledge of certain educational programs and institutions with which they had been familiar in their former homes. In addition, there was a great deal of travel back and forth between the two countries and many British newspapers and other publications were read by Canadians. In view of this, it is not surprising that Canadians adopted a number of British institutional forms in the field of adult education, as they did in other areas of life as well. Five examples, spread over some 150 years, will be described: the mechanics' institutes, the Y.M.C.A., university extension, the Workers' Educational Association, and the Open University.

Mechanics' institutes were created in Great Britain as a means of providing scientific and technical information for workers, especially skilled workers, or "mechanics." These tradesmen knew how to carry out the procedures of their trades, but frequently had not had an opportunity to learn the scientific background or the "why" of those procedures. Started with a mixture of self-help and philanthropic motivation, mechanics' institutes were experimented with as early as 1800 in Edinburgh, but the movement did not begin in earnest until the foundation of the London Mechanics' Institution early in the 1820s.[1] Within

---

[1]   T. Kelly, *A History of Adult Education in Great Britain* (Liverpool, Liverpool University, 1962); J.F.C. Harrison, *Learning and Living 1790–1960* (London, Routledge and Kegan Paul, 1961).

twenty years there were more than 300 institutes in Britain. (In subsequent years most institutes in Britain strayed from their original purpose and became general cultural organizations for their communities.) In the meantime, the movement had come to Canada—or more accurately, to the Canadian colonies. In late 1830, an institute was established in Toronto. The following year the first was established in Halifax, and at about the same time, in Montreal.[2] Institutes were established in British Columbia as well, but not until the early 1860s.[3] Ontario was where the institutes were most fully developed, there being 311 of them by 1895. The Department of Education in Ontario for a period even saw the institutes as the chief agency through which "the upgrading of workers in the technical arts could be achieved."[4] In Canada, as in Britain, the mechanics' institute movement was almost entirely gone by the end of the century, many of the organizations turning their libraries over to the municipality, to be used as the nucleus of, or as an addition to the municipal library services.

A somewhat similar process can be seen in the case of the Young Men's Christian Association (Y.M.C.A.), except in this case, the institution took root in Canadian soil and continues to be active. The Y.M.C.A. was established in London in 1844 and was originally intended as a place where young men who had come to the city from the rural and small town areas could go to find healthy, constructive social activities. Within 50 years there were 651 Y.M.C.A.'s in Britain alone and the movement had spread around the world. In 1853, nine years after the first branch had been founded in Britain, a Y.M.C.A. was established in Toronto, and soon began to offer evening classes and other educational activities.[5] The organization soon spread across Canada, first to the larger centres and then to many smaller towns as well, frequently providing evening classes of various kinds before the public educational authorities took up the task.

University extension activity (although there were precursors of various kinds) is generally seen to have begun at Cambridge University in 1873, at the instigation of James Stuart.[6] Oxford University soon took part as well. The early work consisted of the production of syllabuses and the delivery of series of lectures in the cities of Britain, delivered in the main by university faculty. It tended to consist of the same kind of lecturing which was performed at the university, followed by oral or written questions. (Written work came later.) By 1890, extension centres had been established in 250 communities. Between 1885

---

[2] C.B. Fergusson, *Mechanics' Institutes in Nova Scotia* (Halifax, Public Archives of Nova Scotia, 1960); F. Vernon, *The Development of Adult Education in Ontario 1790–1900* (Unpublished Ed.D. Thesis, University of Toronto, 1969).

[3] G. Selman, "Mechanics' Institutes in British Columbia," *Continuous Learning, 10*, 3 (1971).

[4] F. Vernon, *The Development of Adult Education in Ontario*, p. 481.

[5] M. Ross, *The Y.M.C.A. in Canada* (Toronto, Ryerson, 1951).

[6] T. Kelly, *A History of Adult Education in Great Britain.*

and 1905, Oxford alone had arranged for 32,146 extension lectures in 577 centres, for 424,000 students.[7] University extension came to both the United States and Canada during the 1890s. This lecture type of extension work was apparently not well suited to North American society, however. A number of American institutions, in at least 28 states, got into the field during the Nineties, but by the end of the century, such work had declined almost to the vanishing point. A new, North American model of university extension was to emerge soon. In the meantime, Canadian universities entered the field. Although in both cases some earlier experiments can be identified, Queen's University and the University of Toronto were the first universities to enter the field on a regular basis, Queen's in 1888 and Toronto three years later.[8] A Canadian Association for the Extension of University Teaching, based on this early British model of extension work, was formed at a founding conference in Toronto in 1891, but it appears to have died within a year.[9]

A fourth institutional form of adult education which was "imported" from Great Britain is the Workers' Educational Association (WEA). Founded in Britain in 1903, the WEA represented a partnership among the working class, the co-operative movement and the universities, the latter delivering the instruction and the former two, the students.[10] The working class in Britain was generally denied access to higher education at the time and the WEA provided a means to deliver instruction of a university level to working-class leaders. Albert Mansbridge, the founder and Director of the Association, made a tour of Canada and other "Dominions" in 1917 and out of his visit to Canada came a WEA organization, founded in Toronto the following year.[11] This organization has had a continuous history in Ontario since that time, but its existence elsewhere in Canada was short-lived.[12]

The final example which will be mentioned is that of the Open University. This institution was formally established in 1969 and began instruction two years later.[13] The Open University had the effect of modernizing and revitalizing the

[7]   J. Creese, *The Extension of University Teaching* (New York, American Association for Adult Education, 1941).

[8]   G. Selman, *A History of The Extension and Adult Education Services of the University of British Columbia 1915 to 1955* (Unpublished M.A. Thesis, University of British Columbia, 1963); J.A. Blyth, *A Foundling at Varsity* (Toronto, University of Toronto/School of Continuing Studies, 1976).

[9]   E.A. Corbett in J.R. Kidd, *Adult Education in Canada* (Toronto, Canadian Association for Adult Education, 1950).

[10] T. Kelly, *A History of Adult Education in Great Britain.*

[11] Workers' Educational Association of Canada, *Workers' Educational Association 1903–1953* (Toronto, W.E.A., 1953).

[12] See for instance, G. Selman, *A History of ... Adult Education Services.*

[13] N. MacKenzie, R. Postgate & J. Scupham (Eds.), *Open Learning* (Paris, UNESCO, 1975); W. Perry, *The Open University* (San Francisco, Jossey-Bass, 1977); E. Stabler, *Founders* (Edmonton, University of Alberta, 1987).

approach to distance education, with its combination of correspondence instruction, supplementary broadcasting and publishing, residential short courses, and support services at the local and regional levels. This example has inspired significant new developments in the field of distance education in Canada, most notably, perhaps, Athabaska University in Alberta and the Open Learning Agency of British Columbia.

American Influences

While it is true that many immigrants have come to Canada from the United States, as was the case with Britain, perhaps a stronger reason in the American case for the influence of American educational ideas was the fact that the societies in the two North American countries were faced with similar kinds of nation-building tasks. In both cases, these were "immigrant societies." Newly-arrived residents needed to learn about their new homelands and its ways, and in many cases learn a new vocation. Both nations were faced with the challenges and opportunities of establishing their cultural identities, and of developing their far-flung national territories. And both developed federal government structures and had to work out systems for dividing responsibilities and delivering government services through a network of national, provincial/state and local authorities. There have been profound differences in the approach of the two nations to these tasks but many of the challenges have been essentially the same and it is not surprising that many similar approaches have been adopted. In the selective list of examples which follows, brief reference will be made to five institutions or program models: agricultural extension, Chautauqua and correspondence education, the North American model of university extension, school board and college approaches to adult education, and human relations training.

The field of agricultural extension is perhaps a classic case to cite of a challenge which faced the peoples of both countries, and which they set about addressing in similar ways. Clearly in both Canada and the United States, the opportunities for agricultural development in their huge territories were enormous and important. Ways had to be found to provide information, education and other forms of assistance to those who moved into the field of agriculture, for many an entirely new occupation. Faced with a similar task, the two countries followed distinctive courses of action. From small beginnings, often on a very localized basis, agricultural activities began in both countries. Agricultural extension was carried out by three main types of organizations: voluntary associations of producers such as farm organizations and commodity groups, government and other public agencies, and the private sector—fertilizer companies, financial institutions or other proprietary firms.[14] In the case of agricultural extension, Canadians developed many ideas of their own. The scale of the American agricultural economy and of their government initiatives in the field, however, were

---

[14] D.J. Blackburn (Ed.), *Extension Handbook* (Guelph, Ontario, University of Guelph, 1984).

bound to have an influence on Canada. As well, many leaders and public officials in Canadian agriculture had received their advanced training in the United
States and became aware of American methods. Voluntary organizations of farm
people—the Grange, the Farmers' Union, and the American Farm Bureau Federation—had branches or stimulated similar organizations in Canada, such as the
Farmers' Institutes. In the area of public policy, the American Morrill Act of
1862 was of basic importance in setting the goals for agricultural extension and
creating the Land-Grant colleges in each state, which were to serve as the base of
operations for much extension work. The institutional framework was further
developed with the passage of the Smith-Lever Act in 1914, which created the
Co-operative Extension Service, a co-operative venture of the state and federal
governments.[15] In Canada, agriculture was designated as a shared federal and
provincial responsibility and each jurisdiction has developed its own approach.
The federal government has exercised a strong influence on this work, however,
through cost-sharing provision for particular activities, research activity and "information and the direct provision of service through demonstration and research
facilities and personnel in the regions."[16] "Extension agents" or "agricultural
representatives" have been widely used in Canada, as in the United States, but
here they have been employed on the whole by provincial departments of agriculture rather than by the Extension Service, as in the United States. It is fair to
say that both countries have learned from the experience of the other in this field,
but it is clear that the American example has had a strong influence on Canadian
practice in various ways.

A second area in which American experience had an influence on developments in Canada combines two related features of the American scene, the Chautauqua Institution and a methodology which it pioneered, correspondence
instruction. What started out as a residential summer training program for Sunday school teachers in 1874 at Chautauqua in up-state New York developed over
the years into a flourishing institution with widespread influence and many imi-
tators.[17] Chautauqua was a pioneer in many areas of education—methods of
foreign language teaching, the Literary and Scientific Study Circle movement,
and correspondence education being among the best known. Its work in correspondence education had important influence on the development of that methodology in subsequent years in university and other circles, and throughout
North America.[18] Quite separate from the original Chautauqua Institution, companies of travelling "Chautauquas" sprang up in the United States, taking educa-

[15] M.S. Knowles, *A History of the Adult Education Movement in the United States* (Huntington, New York, Robert Krieger, 1977).

[16] D.J. Blackburn (Ed.), *Extension Handbook*, p. 7.

[17] T. Morrison, *Chautauqua* (Chicago, University of Chicago, 1974).

[18] M.S. Knowles, *A History of the Adult Education Movement*; J.R. Kidd, *Adult Education in Canada.*

tion and entertainment to towns throughout the country, typically in the familiar Chautauqua tents. Sheila Jameson has told the story of the operation of some of these Chautauqua circuits in Canada in the period from shortly after the First World War until the Thirties.[19]

We have seen that university extension on the British model had influence in Canada late in the Nineteenth century, but that an effort to build a national movement and organization on that basis had foundered—in Canada, as it did in the United States. In 1907, the University of Wisconsin began the development of a new type of university work, one which took as its starting point not the kind of teaching and subject matter which had been traditional university fare, but rather the educational needs of the people to be served.[20] Instead of relying on the traditional lecture method and restricting itself to the usual academic content, the university devised other ways of serving the educational needs of adult citizens—correspondence instruction, audio-visual devices of various kinds, short courses and workshops, information pamphlets, travelling "field men" who were expert in the practical application of their fields of knowledge, and scientific and consulting support services. The "Wisconsin idea" hit a responsive chord elsewhere in North America and was perhaps the dominant thrust of such work at the time of the creation of the National University Extension Association in 1915.[21] In the meantime, the University of Saskatchewan had begun agricultural extension work (1910) and the University of Alberta had created an Extension Department (1912), very much on the Wisconsin model.[22] Other Canadian universities were to do the same.[23]

---

[19] S. Jameson, *Chautauqua in Canada* (Calgary, Glenbow-Alberta Institute, 1979).

[20] F.M. Rosentreter, *The Boundaries of the Campus* (Madison, University of Wisconsin, 1957); M.S. Knowles, *A History of the Adult Education Movement*; T.J. Shannon & C.A. Schoenfeld, *University Extension* (New York, The Centre for Applied Research in Education, 1965).

[21] M.S. Knowles, *A History of the Adult Education Movement.*

[22] P.J. Blenkinsop, *A History of Adult Education on the Prairies: Learning to Live in Agrarian Saskatchewan 1870–1944* (Unpublished Ph.D. Thesis, University of Toronto, 1979); R.J. Clark, *A History of the Department of Extension at the University of Alberta 1912–1956* (Unpublished Ph.D. Thesis, University of Toronto, 1985).

[23] F. Peers in J.R. Kidd, *Adult Education in Canada*; J.R. Kidd, *Adult Education in the Canadian University* (Toronto, Canadian Association for Adult Education, 1956).

Two other institutional forms were to have a strong influence on Canadian practice in adult education as well—the school board-sponsored "night class" program and the community college. In both Canada and the United States, ways had to be developed in those vast territories to create educational authorities at the local or municipal level which would share responsibility with provincial/state governments in the delivery of appropriate education for children. In the case of both countries, this was accomplished through the creation of a system of elected school boards at the local level.[24] Beginning in the 1830s and expanding rapidly in the subsequent decades, adult education services were provided as well by school boards in many of the American states.[25] Although the story is not known in detail as yet, school board night classes appear to have begun in Canada in the 1850s, although their development—and even their existence—was somewhat sporadic for some time after that.[26] While clear evidence of the American model having influenced Canada in this case is difficult to document, it seems obvious given the sequence of events. It is certainly the case that when Canadian governments were examining the alternatives before them in the 1960s with respect to the development of college systems, the varied American models were carefully studied, and in some instances, emulated.[27]

Finally, reference will be made to human relations training. In its contemporary forms, the human relations and leadership training movement arose in large measure from the research of Kurt Lewin and the pioneering work of the National Training Laboratory in Group Development which began operation in 1947 in Bethel, Maine.[28] This work had a direct influence on Canada as Canadians took part in programs in the United States and brought the techniques back for application in their home areas. This aspect of adult education has not been well documented in Canada, but it is clear that subsequent work in this field in Vancouver, Fort Qu'Appelle and other centres was directly influenced by the American experience.

---

[24] L.A. Cremin, *American Education: The Colonial Experience 1607–1783* (New York, Harper and Row, 1970); J.D. Wilson, R.M. Stamp & L-P Audet (Eds.), *Canadian Education: A History* (Scarborough, Ontario, Prentice-Hall Canada, 1970).

[25] M.S. Knowles, *A History of the Adult Education Movement.*

[26] J.R. Kidd, *Adult Education in Canada*; J.R. Kidd, *18 to 80: Continuing Education in Metropolitan Toronto* (Toronto, Board of Education, 1961).

[27] J. Dennison & P. Gallagher, *Canada's Community Colleges* (Vancouver, University of British Columbia, 1986).

[28] L.P. Bradford in M.S. Knowles (Ed.), *Handbook of Adult Education in the United States* (Chicago, Adult Education Association of the U.S.A., 1960).

Other Countries

It is possible to trace the influence in Canada of adult education experience in a number of other countries, especially in the current period. One example will be provided from the earlier years, that of the influence of the folk school. Established first in Denmark in the 1840s and stimulated by the ideas of N.S.F. Grundtvig, the Danish Folk High School movement soon became famous and for at least a hundred years provided an inspiration for adult educators and others in many countries.[29] A number of well-known leaders in Canadian adult education, among them key figures in the formation of the Canadian Association for Adult Education in the 1930s, made pilgrimages to Denmark. There was as well a lively folk school movement in Canada, especially in Ontario and the West. Its history in Canada is not well documented, and the boundary line between what may appropriately be called folk schools and other types of residential education is vague, but it may be stated that the period from the late 1930s to the late 1950s was the high point of the folk school movement in Canada.[30]

The influence from other countries in the most recent period has been more in the form of ideas than institutional structures. The first example to be cited is that of recurrent education. This concept was described in the first chapter. It was created in Sweden in the late 1960s and soon gained widespread acceptance in Western Europe and the Organization for Economic Co-operation and Development (OECD).[31] Canada, which is a member of OECD, has taken an interest in the idea and the federal government has conducted two substantial studies of its application to Canada.[32] The second example is that of lifelong education and lifelong learning. Some early developmental work on the idea was carried out in Canada, but the chief impetus to the idea as far as the international community was concerned has come from reports produced by UNESCO and by its Institute on Education in Hamburg. The terminology surrounding the concepts has become coin of the realm in the field of adult education in Canada and featured

[29] E. Stabler, *Founders*.

[30] J.K. Friesen in J.R. Kidd, *Adult Education in Canada*; J.K. Friesen & J.M. Parsey, *Manitoba Folk Schools* (Winnipeg, Manitoba Co-operative Services Branch, 1951); E. Loosley, *Residential Adult Education: A Canadian View* (Toronto, Canadian Association for Adult Education, 1960).

[31] C. Titmus, *Strategies for Adult Education* (Chicago, Follett, 1981).

[32] Commission on Educational Leave and Productivity, *Education and Working Canadians* (Ottawa, Labour Canada, 1979); National Advisory Panel on Skill Development Leave, *Learning For Life* (Ottawa, Department of Employment and Immigration, 1984).

prominently in two well-known provincial royal commissions on education which reported in 1972, the Worth Commission in Alberta and the Wright Commission in Ontario. A third example of such influences has been the impact on thinking in Canada of the concept of development as it has been conceived in the international community, and more particularly the prominence given to the significance of non-formal and informal adult education in this context.[33] Finally, reference should be made to the work of several "radical" writers in the last two decades whose ideas have encouraged Canadian adult educators to consider the social and political implications of their work. Three examples which might be mentioned, among many, are Tom Lovett, Ivan Illich and Paulo Freire.[34] The work—and personal visits—of these and other adult educators have had major impact on the thinking of many Canadian adult educators, encouraging them to re-examine their liberal and "service ethic" approach to the field and to consider the relevance of the field as a factor in social change.

Canadian Responses to the Canadian Context

Canadian adult education has a high reputation in the international community of adult educators. Studies of the field which take a world view of its history and characteristics consistently cite Canada's contributions, frequently mentioning such projects as the Antigonish Movement, National Farm Radio Forum, the Women's Institutes, Frontier College, the National Film Board, and the work of outstanding Canadian individuals, most notably J.R. Kidd and Allen Tough.[35] Canadians are widely considered to have responded to their situations and challenges as a people by devising educational responses which not only successfully meet their own needs, but in many instances have useful application elsewhere.

There are a number of features of the Canadian experience in the northern portion of the North American continent which may be seen to have had an impact on aspects of Canadian adult education. As well, they may be seen as forces which elicited from Canadians who were involved in the provision of adult education the particular institutional forms, selection of goals and content, and educational procedures which have been developed here.

---

[33] P. Coombs, *The World Crisis in Education: The View from the Eighties* (New York, Oxford University, 1985); B. Hall & J.R. Kidd (Eds.), *Adult Learning: A Design for Action* (Oxford, Pergamon, 1978).

[34] P. Freire, *Pedagogy of the Oppressed* (New York, Herder & Herder, 1970); P. Freire, *The Politics of Education* (Massachusetts, Bergin & Garvey, 1985); I. Illich, *Deschooling Society* (New York, Harper and Row, 1970); T. Lovett, *Adult Education, Community Development and the Working Class* (London, Ward Lock Educational, 1975); T. Lovett, C. Clarke & A. Kilmurray, *Adult Education and Community Action* (London, Cromm Helm, 1983).

[35] A.S.M. Hely, *New Trends in Adult Education* (Paris, UNESCO, 1962); J. Lowe, *The Education of Adults: A World Perspective* (Paris, UNESCO, 1982); T. Lovett et al., *Adult Education and Community Action.*

Citizenship in an Immigrant Nation

First, and perhaps most obvious, Canada is a nation of immigrants. Except for the Native people (who may themselves have been immigrants to this land in the distant reaches of unrecorded history) Canadians—the present generation or their ancestors—have come as immigrants from other lands. The two "founding races" of Canada are seen to be the immigrants who came in such large numbers in the colonial period from Great Britain and from France. Since that time, immigrants have come from many lands. This unique ethnic or racial mix has led to the present Canadian social and cultural policy of "bilingualism and multi-culturalism." Canadians are fond of comparing their own social policy of "the Canadian mosaic" with the policy adopted in the United States, which is often referred to as "the melting pot."

The essential point is that Canada having throughout its history received relatively large numbers of immigrants, one of its most essential tasks has been to provide educational opportunities needed by many of these newcomers. Beyond the immediate requirements of the immigrants, however, there has been an on-going pre-occupation in Canada with "the Canadian identity." What should be the essential characteristics and goals of this collection of people who make up the Canadian nation? It is significant that the landmark Royal Commission on National Development in the Arts, Letters and Sciences, which reported to the Canadian people in 1951, and which has been the most profound study of Canadian cultural policy ever carried out, introduced their report with the following quotation from St. Augustine:

> A nation is an association of reasonable beings united in a peaceful sharing of the things they cherish; therefore to determine the quality of a nation, you must consider what those things are.[36]

Canadians have been struggling with that question throughout their history as a people, in the light of both the changing ethnic and cultural mix resulting from continuous immigration, and also the concern on the part of many Canadians over the influence on Canadian development of its large and dynamic neighbour to the south, the United States of America.

The education of immigrants has been a constant pre-occupation of Canadian society, including adult education. This has taken the form of both language and citizenship education. The federal government has for many decades assumed the cost of language instruction (English or French) for recent immigrants and has shared the cost of such work beyond the initial period. This language instruction was carried out by a variety of agencies, mostly local educational institutions or voluntary agencies. The senior level of government established a Citizenship Branch in the federal administration in the late 1940s which fostered in a variety of ways the assimilation of newcomers to Canada and effective communication between the ethnic communities and the Canadian mainstream.

---

[36] Royal Commission on National Development in the Arts, Letters and Sciences, *Report* (Ottawa, King's Printer, 1951) p. xxiii.

The federal government undertook much of this work on its own, but also co-op-erated closely with other bodies, most notably the Canadian Citizenship Council, and for a time beginning in the 1950s, a series of local citizenship councils across the country which were formed as a result of Citizenship Branch initia-tives and supported in their activities by both the Branch and local leadership.

With respect to the broader field of citizenship education, it may justifiably be claimed that this is the main thrust of many of the best known Canadian contri-butions to the field of adult education. Defining the term citizenship education presents a problem. A narrower or "civics" approach might include only a knowledge of the structure and processes of government and a knowledge of particular issues on which decisions must be made by the community. A more comprehensive definition—the one that is being used in the present case—ranges much more widely and has as well to do with the various ways in which citizens play a role in determining the nature of the society of which they are a part, and also their attitudes and disposition towards such participation.

The importance of citizenship education in this broad sense in the Canadian adult education tradition has been noted by various observers. The opinion which is perhaps most valuable in this regard is that of Gordon Hawkins, who was Associate Director of the Canadian Association for Adult Education for several years during the 1950s and who was well informed about adult education in both Canada and Britain. In an article written in 1954 and intended for publication first in Britain, Hawkins pointed out that whereas adult education in Britain had a tradition of academic study and tutorial work, the situation in Canada was very different. In Canada:

> the concern is more with what one might call the "community" aspects of adult education. Partly this is a consequence of geography and time. With newly formed and changing communities, with immigrant groups, with the awful challenge of distance, methods and aims are bound to be different. But there is also a newer, consciously evolved philosophy of adult education. It stems from a deep concern with the processes of democracy—with *how* the individual and the group and the community work, as much as with *what* they set out to achieve. Hence the emphasis in their scheme of things on group work, commu-nity organization, discussion methods and techniques, leadership courses and so on, and, as a background to all that, on the use of mass media to spread a common basis of information for their discussion and their social actions.[37]

---

[37] G. Hawkins, "As Others See Us," *Food For Thought, 14*, 8 (1954) p. 2.

A number of Canadian adult education projects which have made a contribution to the field of citizenship education, broadly conceived, will be briefly described.

Perhaps the most famous adult education project in Canada and the best known outside our borders is the "Antigonish Movement"—the extension work in co-operative education of St. Francis Xavier University in Antigonish, Nova Scotia. It is also the best documented of adult education projects in Canada.[38] St. Francis Xavier University, a Roman Catholic institution, under the leadership of the Rev. James Tompkins and Rev. Moses Coady, decided to devote effort to the economic improvement of the fishermen, farmers and industrial workers of its economically depressed region. The work began officially in 1928 and the major strategies adopted were that of community development and the creation of co-operative and credit union organizations. Remarkable results were achieved and the Antigonish Movement soon became well known internationally. The methods used for social and economic development were soon seen to have application in the emerging societies of the Third World, and over the years hundreds of persons from other nations came to Antigonish to study the extension methods being employed. The university constructed special facilities to house such visitors, and as well has sent teams of instructors abroad to train leaders in other regions.

The co-operative movement is based on the idea that the membership of the organization should participate actively in management decisions. Because this participation needs to be conducted on the basis of appropriate information and understanding, most co-operatives are actively involved in educational activity. As Ian MacPherson, the historian of the co-operative movement in Canada has put it, "co-operators most caught up in their movement have been essentially adult educators."[39] Educational activities sponsored by the co-operative movement in Canada have been traced back to the early years of this century. An educational institute for the co-operative movement in the West was formed in 1951, and a Western Co-operative College established in 1959 (a building of its

---

[38] G. Boyle, *Father Tompkins of Nova Scotia* (New York, Kenedy & Sons, 1953); M.M. Coady, *Masters of Their Own Destiny* (New York, Harper & Bros., 1939); I. Delaney, *By Their Own Hands* (Hantsport, Nova Scotia, Lancelot Press, 1985); A.F. Laidlaw, *The Campus and the Community* (Montreal, Harvest House, 1961); A.F. Laidlaw (Ed.), *The Man from Margaree* (Toronto, McLelland & Stewart, 1971); M. MacLelland, *Coady Remembered* (Antigonish, Nova Scotia, St. Francis Xavier Press, 1985); P. Milner (Ed.), *Human Development Through Social Change* (Antigonish, Nova Scotia, Formac Publishing, 1979); E. Stabler, *Founders.*

[39] I. MacPherson, in F. Cassidy & R. Faris (Ed.), *Choosing Our Future* (Toronto, Ontario Institute for Studies in Education, 1987).

own becoming available three years later).[40] A somewhat parallel movement took place in French-speaking Canada, a training institution eventually being established at Levis, Quebec.

A second major sector of citizenship education in Canada is represented by the two crown corporations, the Canadian Broadcasting Corporation and the National Film Board of Canada. Both were created in the 1930s and both were given the mandate, among others, to educate Canadians about their country, their fellow citizens, and the issues facing Canadian society.[41] Canadians have from the very beginning of their national experience looked upon government as a constructive instrument for social development. Various writers have contrasted the attitudes in this respect in Canada and in the United States. The Canadian attitude towards the role of government has been described as "constructive socialism."[42] Richard Gwyn has stated that it is taken for granted in Canada that "the state, for all its periodic inefficiencies, will cause the society to progress for the benefit of all the individuals in it."[43] Canadians, in the words of E.H. Carr, have accepted the idea of "the strong state exercising remedial and constructive functions."[44] Part of the reason may be that Canada has had a relatively small population, considering the size of its territory, and in many instances if socially important functions were to be performed, only government had the resources to make it happen. Canadians have been willing to see enormous quantities of public resources go into the construction of the first transcontinental railway and to see the subsequent national railway and our first national airlines created by crown corporations. These are just a few examples of the great reliance Canadians have placed on the public sector.

The Canadian Broadcasting Corporation was created in 1936, a successor to the Canadian Radio Broadcasting Commission, which had existed since 1932.[45] It was to provide education as well as entertainment for the people of Canada. Especially in the early decades of its existence, the Corporation was anxious to establish co-operative working relationships with other educational organizations. Its involvement with the Canadian Association for Adult Education and the Canadian Federation of Agriculture in National Farm Radio Forum, with the

---

[40] I. MacPherson, in M.R. Welton (Ed.), *Knowledge for the People* (Toronto, Ontario Institute for Studies in Education, 1987).

[41] G. Evans, *John Grierson and the National Film Board* (Toronto, University of Toronto, 1984); F.W. Peers, *The Politics of Canadian Broadcasting 1920–1951* (Toronto, University of Toronto, 1969).

[42] C. Berger, *The Writing of Canadian History* (Toronto, Oxford, 1976).

[43] R. Gwyn, *The 49th Paradox* (Toronto, Totem, 1985) p. 160.

[44] E.H. Carr, *The New Society* (Boston, Beacon Press, 1951) p. 78.

[45] F. Peers, *The Politics of Canadian Broadcasting*.

former in Citizens' Forum, and with the Canadian Institute on Public Affairs on the Couchiching conferences are outstanding examples.

The National Film Board of Canada (NFB) was created in 1939, the successor organization to the Government Motion Picture Bureau, which had functioned since 1923.[46] Its mandate was in large measure to inform Canadians about their country. It, like the Canadian Broadcasting Corporation, was part of a nation-building strategy. The first Director of the NFB was a charismatic and controversial figure, John Grierson, who was a genius in the genre of the documentary film.[47] The NFB, from its earliest existence displayed a capacity to create world-class documentary films. That level of excellence has been maintained over the years. No sooner was the NFB created (in 1939) than Canada was plunged into World War II. Canada did not enter that conflict wholeheartedly united about the issues involved and so for the first few years of the NFB's existence, the Board was serving at least two causes—the original one in its mandate, to strengthen the Canadian identity and sense of common cause, and as well the task of rallying the Canadian people behind the war effort. Propaganda thus became a major function of the Film Board from the beginning, a role with which Grierson was perfectly comfortable. As he frequently put it, "Art is not a mirror, but a hammer."[48] Grierson stayed with the NFB for only six years, but he left his stamp on the organization.

It is one thing to make marvellous documentary films; it is another to get people to watch them. During World War II and immediately thereafter, the Film Board tackled that challenge, and with brilliant success.[49] Through the activities of its field staff across the country and with the co-operation of agencies in each province (frequently the extension department of the provincial university) the NFB took the leadership in establishing "film councils" in hundreds of cities and towns across Canada and established support services for these organizations. Film depositories were established in each province or region and "film circuits" were created which involved providing a variety of films for each community for a period of time, at the end of which those films would be sent on to the next town on the circuit, and the first community would receive a fresh collection. The local film council had the responsibility of finding audiences to see the films in their care. This was done by various means, largely by arranging for other community organizations which were interested in the content of particular films to show them at their meetings, but also through regular "film nights" organized by the film council itself. By these and other means, the Film Board was success-

---

[46] G. Evans, *John Grierson and the NFB*.

[47] G. Evans, *John Grierson and the NFB*.

[48] D.B. Jones, *Movies and Memoranda* (Ottawa, Canadian Film Institute, 1981) p. 6.

[49] G. Evans, *John Grierson and the NFB*; C.W. Gray, *Movies for the People* (Montreal, National Film Board, 1976).

ful in having its films seen by a remarkably large audience across the country. Evans states that at the end of the war, there was an average monthly attendance of 465,000 at Board films. Rural circuits alone were reaching a quarter of a million viewers a month.[50] The Board also made high quality "instructional" films, which were widely used by educators in various settings across the country. The film circuit system was maintained until the 1950s, when the advent of television and other factors brought it to an end, at least in its original form.

Another aspect of the NFB's work which is of interest, and has been highly regarded internationally, is its role in placing film-making (and later videotape) facilities in the hands of those involved in the community development process. The activity was one element of what was termed "Challenge for Change," a project which was launched in 1966. The first experiment with this technique was conducted on Fogo Island, Newfoundland, in a project conducted in co-operation with the Extension Department of Memorial University and the local people. Part of the community development process involves the community in assessing itself. Film-making equipment was placed in the hands of the local people, to be used as a tool in creating a film or films which reflected, to the satisfaction of those involved in the process, the thinking of the community about its present state, and aspirations. The films also became a powerful instrument for conveying the community's wishes to agencies such as departments of government which had resources or powers at their disposal on which the local community wished to call. The Fogo and other early experiments with this technique were eagerly seized upon by planners in other countries, especially in the developing countries, and the key actors—in the Film Board and Memorial University—were soon in great demand in other countries to advise on similar projects. A second element of the Challenge for Change project was a series of short films which were designed as discussion starters for courses or community meetings about matters related to citizenship and dealing with the bureaucracy, etc. Not officially part of Challenge for Change, but similarly closely related to action for social change are such special units as the Women's unit of NFB, which have produced important films about issues in Canadian society.

The Canadian Association for Adult Education (CAAE), under the leadership of its first Director, E.A. Corbett, took the initiative in the creation of two important educational projects involving print, broadcasting and local study groups, National Farm Radio Forum and Citizens' Forum. The former, being the original venture, gained a world-wide reputation and has been adapted for use in many other countries.

It has already been pointed out that one of the major tasks facing Canadian society was to extend education to the rural parts of the population. This had to do with the vocational and technical aspects of agricultural pursuits, but also with building a society in Canada which included rural people in a meaningful way. E.A. Corbett had formerly been for many years involved in university

---

[50] G. Evans, *John Grierson and the NFB.*

extension work in Alberta and had a keen sense of what was most needed in rural Canada. The CAAE, in co-operation with the Canadian Federation of Agriculture, and building on earlier experiments in Ontario, approached the CBC about a proposed national educational program, which was to become National Farm Radio Forum.[51] Farm Forum was a program which involved four principal elements: the local listening and discussion group; a printed pamphlet on each week's topic; a weekly radio broadcast, also on the topic for the week; and feedback to the program organizers concerning the group's opinions on the topics discussed (and also feedback to all listening groups on what opinions had been throughout their region on the previous week's topic). The CAAE, through its provincial allies (often the university extension departments) organized the groups and produced and mailed the pamphlets. (The Federation of Agriculture assisted in these tasks.) The CBC produced the broadcasts. The listening groups, having read the pamphlet and having met to listen to the broadcast, then turned off the radio and went on to discuss the subject, afterwards conveying their opinions or consensus to a "provincial secretary," who went on the air at the end of each broadcast in order to report back to all groups on reactions to the previous week's topic. By these means, rural listeners in all parts of Canada were engaged over a 26-week season in the consideration of a range of topics generally related to the interests of rural people—topics on agricultural policy, international trade, community and family life, or other public affairs topics. The program went on from 1941 until 1965 and over that period involved persons from all parts of Canada in the consideration of significant questions affecting their lives and the welfare of their communities. There were seen to be benefits for the individuals involved, but there was also an intent to contribute to the sense of common interest among Canadians. It was part of a strategy on the part of Corbett and other leaders of the enterprise to play a part in building the Canadian national community.[52] Development planners from other countries saw potential in the Farm Forum approach for their own development plans. UNESCO requested the CAAE to prepare a study of the project through which its methods could be made known to the international community. This was carried out by Alex Sim, one of the pioneers of Farm Forum, and was published in 1954

---

[51] R. Faris, *The Passionate Educators* (Toronto, Peter Martin,1975); R.A. Sim, *Canada's Farm Radio Forum* (Paris, UNESCO, 1954).

[52] E.A. Corbett, *We Have With Us Tonight* (Toronto, Ryerson, 1957); R. MacKenzie in J.R. Kidd, *Adult Education in Canada*; R. Faris, *The Passionate Educators*.

by UNESCO.[53] It has been stated that over 40 countries subsequently made use of some form of the project.[54]

In the period of reconstruction thinking during and immediately after World War II, it was decided to develop a program which utilized the methods of Farm Forum but which would be aimed at a more general, perhaps mainly urban listening audience and would focus on general citizenship and public affairs topics. Thus was created Citizens' Forum, a joint project of the CAAE and the CBC, which began on the national network in 1943 and continued for 20 years.[55] It is clear that this program arose from a conscious feeling on the part of many adult educators that the movement should contribute to the "reconstruction" of Canadian and international society, following a decade of depression and world war.[56] This project represents a further major contribution of the instigator, E.A. Corbett, to the development of the Canadian nation. Corbett has been seen by observers outside the field of adult education as "a leader of the intellectual mafia" who were "promoters of a Canadian national consciousness."[57]

Another important and distinctive Canadian contribution to education in the field of citizenship, social and cultural development was the Joint Planning Commission (JPC). Created in 1947 at the instigation of E.A. Corbett, this "organization" brought together, usually three times a year, the representatives of many national agencies—departments of government, voluntary agencies, churches, labour and business groups—a wide range of groups actively involved in the educational, social and cultural development of Canada.[58] The word "organization" is put in quotation marks because there was no such thing as membership, in the usual sense. The CAAE provided the secretariat and called the parties together for the regular meetings, but the participating organizations sent representatives only because the meetings continued to be useful to them, not because of a membership commitment. Indeed it likely would not have been possible to maintain the useful mix of organizational representation—the private and public sectors together—if a formal membership had been required. Emphasis was

---

[53] R. Sim, *Canada's Farm Radio Forum.*

[54] J.R. Kidd, *Learning and Society* (Toronto, Canadian Association for Adult Education, 1963).

[55] R. Faris, *The Passionate Educators*; I. Wilson in J.R. Kidd, *Adult Education in Canada*; I. Wilson, *Citizens' Forum: Canada's National Platform* (Toronto, Ontario Institute for Studies in Education, 1980).

[56] I. Wilson in J.R. Kidd, *Adult Education in Canada*; I. Wilson, *Citizens' Forum.*

[57] W.R. Young, *Making The Truth Graphic: The Canadian Government's Home Front Information Structure and Programs during World War II* (Unpublished Ph.D. Thesis, University of British Columbia, 1978) p. 22–23.

[58] C. Clark, *The Joint Planning Commission* (Toronto, Canadian Association for Adult Education, 1954).

placed on exchange of information about the activities, plans and concerns of the various bodies. Laidlaw indicates that during the program year 1954–55, for instance, participants in the JPC included 114 organizations: 49 voluntary organizations, 18 government departments and agencies, 17 university extension departments, 15 business and professional groups, 6 provincial departments of education, 5 church organizations and 4 labour organizations.[59] There were valuable exchanges of information and views about matters of mutual interest, and programs which informed the participants about important national issues such as broadcasting policy, national royal commissions and other significant government actions, the educational potential of television and similar topics. The JPC continued in operation until 1968, one high point having been reached in 1964, when the Prime Minister, L.B. Pearson, addressed the group (on International Co-operation Year).[60] The organization had been the object of study by many visitors from other countries over the years. The maintenance of such clearing house or coordinating bodies in adult education had proven to be a very difficult achievement and many came to study this success story in Canada.

The final example of citizenship education—the Women's Institutes organization—is of a distinctly different type. It may be said that the Women's Institutes, now a world-wide movement, were a Canadian "invention." The first local institute was founded in Ontario in 1897 at the instigation of Adelaide Hoodless, an active leader in women's organizations. The aims of the W.I.s as they have subsequently developed have generally to do with citizenship and with the quality of life for rural and small town women. They contribute to community betterment, are advocates to government and others concerning the welfare of children, women and the family, and sponsor a wide range of educational activities on household arts and related matters for their own membership and other interested persons.[61]

The Challenge of Distance and Regionalism

The Canadian story has to a very large extent been one of coping with the hugeness of scale of the country, especially in view of the relatively small population. One of the major schools of interpretation of Canadian history has seen the St. Lawrence waterway and the extension of its influence westwards by means of modern transport and communications as the key to Canadian survival and development.[62] In the early decades of Canadian nationhood, there was an awareness of the fragility of the country and a realization that the nation must be

---

[59] A.F. Laidlaw, *The Campus and the Community*.

[60] G. Selman, *Alan Thomas and the Canadian Association for Adult Education 1961–1970* (Vancouver, University of British Columbia/Centre for Continuing Education, 1985).

[61] E. Chapman in J.R. Kidd, *Adult Education in Canada*; R. Collins in J.R. Kidd, *Learning and Society* (Toronto, Canadian Association for Adult Education, 1963); E. Rand, *Federated Women's Institutes of Canada: A History 1919–1960* (Ottawa, F.W.I.C., 1961).

[62] C. Berger, *The Writing of Canadian History*.

bound together East to West (to some extent in defiance of the North-South geographical regions which linked parts of Canada more naturally with American territory than with the rest of Canada) by such means as the railways and the telegraph, and when it became available, by broadcasting. In more recent decades there has also been an awareness on the part of many of a threat of cultural rather than physical domination from the United States, and conscious efforts have been made to strengthen the quality of communications and cultural development within Canada.

The educational activities of the Canadian Broadcasting Corporation and the National Film Board, some of which have already been referred to, are clearly a part of the Canadian nation's deliberate efforts to combat the distances that are a fact of life in Canada. Similarly, National Farm Radio Forum and Citizens' Forum may be seen as projects which attempted to offset the problems of distance—by means of the mails and radio broadcasting—in order to engage Canadians in all parts of the country in an informed consideration of issues in which Canadians have a common interest.

There have been other significant adult education projects in Canada which may be seen in the same context. One is the co-operation of the CBC and a voluntary agency, the Canadian Institute on Public Affairs in the organization and broadcasting of major conferences on public affairs topics—summer meetings at the Lake Couchiching conference centre of the Y.M.C.A. and winter conferences held in Toronto.[63] Several national organizations in Canada which focus on national and international affairs have developed strong programs over the decades by means of establishing local branches or chapters in the main population centres and servicing these by means of print—newsletters and other publications—and by sending speakers on tours or circuits so they could speak to many of the branches. Canadian organizations which flourished by these means have included the Men's and Women's Canadian Clubs, the Canadian Institute on International Affairs, and the League of Nations Society and its successor, the United Nations Association.

It has been pointed out that in a variety of ways, some successful adult education projects have involved means of coping with the geographical separation of the far-flung regions of the country. The other side of the coin is the tendency in Canada towards regionalism or sectionalism. Our outstanding cultural critic, Northrop Frye, has termed it a "garrison mentality" and has characterized the regions of the country as "solitudes touching other solitudes."[64] The most obvious feature of this phenomenon in Canadian life is the gulf which exists between the French-speaking Canadians in the Province of Quebec and the rest of English-speaking Canada. Here the facts of geography are reinforced by differences in language, culture and provincial rights. Significant contributions to

---

[63] F. Peers in I. Wilson et al., *Education in Public Affairs by Radio* (Toronto, Canadian Association for Adult Education, 1954).

[64] N. Frye, *Divisions on a Ground* (Toronto, Anansi, 1982) p. 59.

adult education within Quebec are hardly known to the rest of the country. And because education is a provincial responsibility under the Constitution, the pace and character of adult education services also varies greatly from one province to the next.

There have been important regional developments in adult education in Canada. Three examples will be cited. The Antigonish Movement has already been described briefly. What might be noted in addition at this time is the fact that not only did St. Francis Xavier University serve its own immediate region with its co-operative education program, but it also inspired similar (though less lasting) programs of much the same kind in the neighboring provinces of New Brunswick and Prince Edward Island as well.

There was a provincial and regional concept behind the Banff School of Fine Arts (as it was originally called) from the very beginning. Founded in the depths of the Great Depression, the School was from the outset seen as a resource for people throughout Alberta and beyond who were interested in the arts but did not have available at the local level the expertise of instruction and other resources which would enable them to advance their skills to the higher level which they sought.[65] Under the leadership of Donald Cameron, the Banff institution grew from its small beginnings to a large residential and educational facility which operates on a year-round basis and in a wide range of subject matter. It operates many programs under its own auspices and acts as a hotel or residential educational facility for many other groups as well.

There has always been a "sense of partnership" between librarians and adult educators. Indeed in the years before the emergence of a self-conscious adult education movement in Canada, librarians were among the most forceful advocates of the need for adult education services. The importance of library services as a resource for adult education activity is obvious. In the early decades of the development of library services in Canada, they tended to be highly local in character. The Public Library Commission in British Columbia launched an experiment in the late 1920s which helped to set a new course for library development in that province, and elsewhere in Canada and the world.[66] It involved creating a library organization which would serve a whole region (the Lower Fraser Valley in British Columbia), some 24 municipalities, and moving the holdings around the region, as required, to meet local needs and requests. This experiment was financed initially by the Carnegie Corporation of New York and it was a manifestation of its success that when that grant ran out, in the depth of the Depression (1932), 22 of the 24 municipalities involved voted to continue the

---

[65] D. Cameron, *Campus in the Clouds* (Toronto, McClelland & Stewart, 1956); and *The Impossible Dream* (Privately printed, 1977).

[66] M.C. Holmes, *Library Service in British Columbia* (Victoria, Public Library Commission of B.C., 1959); M. Gilroy & S. Rothstein (Eds.), *As We Remember It* (Vancouver, University of British Columbia/School of Librarianship, 1970).

service as a charge against local taxation. Helen Stewart, who had headed up the project, subsequently received many invitations from other countries to consult about the establishment of similar systems elsewhere.[67]

Another dimension of the effects of the size of Canada on the development of adult education has been that of the "frontier." The consciousness of a frontier has been a continuing phenomenon in the life of Canada from its earliest days. In the early years, this was thought of mainly in terms of "the West." More recently the focus has been on the northern parts of Canadian territory. Our most famous historian, H.A. Innis, has pointed out that by contrast with the United States, Canada has had a "hard" frontier. Many of Canada's resources are hard to get at; the climate in much of the country is inhospitable, many of the resources are hidden in the earth's crust and difficult to extract and move to market. As S.D. Clark has put it: What was called for in the opening up of this northern half of the continent were massive accumulations of capital, large scale forms of economic organization, long lines of communication and transportation, and extensive state support.[68]

It was against this background that another unique Canadian adult education institution, Frontier College, did its work.[69] Founded in 1899 as the Canadian Reading Camps Association, the work of the College has for most of its history concentrated on English language instruction (most of the students were recent immigrants) and what today we would term adult basic education. Frontier College arranged with the employer in the camp to provide a regular job for a worker to be supplied by the College. The latter then recruited persons, usually from the universities, who agreed to perform such jobs, and also in the evenings and on weekends, to organize educational activities for any of the workmen who could be interested in such activity. The "worker-teacher" earned his wage from the employer, for his regular daytime duties, and received little or no pay for his role as educator. This project went about its work quietly for many decades, largely unnoticed even in the world of adult education. But when in the 1960s, Canada began to take note of the extent of illiteracy and under-education in the country and began to mount substantial programs in those areas, it was "discovered" that Frontier College had extensive experience in adult basic education and was a valuable resource in helping Canadians prepare themselves for this work.[70] Frontier College subsequently became involved in community development programs as well, and has in the most recent decade concentrated on inner-city projects. It has been a model for serving frontier camps or communities which has been studied by persons from various other countries and it has received international awards for its contributions to literacy education. Frontier College

---

[67] M. Gilroy & S. Rothstein, *As We Remember It.*

[68] S.D. Clark, *Canadian Society in Historical Perspective* (Toronto, McGraw-Hill, 1976) p. 55.

[69] A. Fitzpatrick, *The University in Overalls* (Toronto, Hunter-Rose, 1920); G.L.Cook in M. Welton, *Knowledge for the People.*

[70] I. Morrison in M. Brooke (Ed.), *Adult Basic Education* (Toronto, New Press, 1972).

is a clear example of how an institutional form and a methodology were developed in response to the social and economic circumstances pertaining in the areas to be served.

The Federal-Provincial Context

Under the Canadian Constitution, education is assigned as a provincial responsibility. Each of the ten provinces has in many respects gone its own way in this field, and institutional arrangements vary markedly from one province to another, especially (though not only) at the post-secondary level. The federal government has certain tasks in the field of education assigned to it—education in the Northern Territories, of Native people, those in the armed forces (and their dependents), and those in federal penal institutions. In addition, by agreement with the provinces, the national government has played a role in several other areas of education, such as: language and citizenship training for immigrants; bilingualism education for civil servants and others; citizenship education and the promotion of inter-ethnic communication and understanding; grants to the provinces to share in financing post-secondary education; support of museums; rehabilitation of disabled persons; and in recent decades, direct assistance to various local groups (older persons, for instance). The federal government has also provided direct assistance to educational activity within the labour movement by providing supporting grants for such work to national labour bodies.

The outstanding further example of how the federal government has "co-operated" with the provinces in the field of adult education is that of adult occupational training.[71] A detailed account of federal-provincial relations in this field is provided in a subsequent chapter. It is simply noted here that up until the late sixties, the federal authorities sought to encourage the provinces to be more active in this area by indirect means—by providing funds which could be drawn upon by the provinces on a matching basis. With new legislation in 1967, the federal government assumed a more direct role in the provision of such training.

An important "side effect" of the legislation of the 1960s and beyond may be seen in the field of Adult Basic Education (ABE)—literacy to high school completion and English (or French) as a second language (ESL) training. When, as a result of the funds made available by legislation of 1960, greatly expanded facilities and programs for vocational training began to become available, it was revealed just how many people in Canada were not able to cope with the programs offered because of lack of basic education and/or lack of knowledge of the language. The federal authorities were therefore drawn into having to finance ABE and ESL activity on a very large scale. The Canadian government's "War on Poverty" measures which were launched in the mid-sixties added emphasis to such work. The new legislation in 1967, the OTA, made more direct and ade-

---

[71] J.D. Wilson et al., *Canadian Education: A History*; J.S. Dupre et al., *Federalism and Policy Development: The Case of Adult Occupational Training in Ontario* (Toronto, University of Toronto, 1973); J.W.G. Ivany & M.E. Manley-Casimir (Eds.), *Federal-Provincial Relations: Education Canada* (Toronto, Ontario Institute for Studies in Education, 1981).

quate provision for such work, six out of the ten provinces taking up the federal offer to wholly fund provincial "NewStart" corporations, which were designed to provide leadership in ABE activities in the regions.

Such federal initiatives had the effect of revealing the extent of the need for ABE and ESL in Canada and of beginning to meet the need. However, when austerity budgets in the early seventies forced the federal authorities to cut back on its work in ABE and ESL, the task fell into the hands of the provinces. Nothing was more obviously a provincial responsibility, after all, than basic education. The provinces responded very unevenly to this challenge—as they have to all aspects of adult education—but for better or for worse, the ball was largely back in their court. The 1960s had been a period of strong federal government leadership in adult education. But as in the case of Canadian federation as a whole, the late sixties and the subsequent decades brought strong decentralizing tendencies.[72] In this latter case, one can see a further demonstration of how trends and developments in the broader context of national life were reflected in the field of adult education.

Community and Communitarianism

During the great debate over the Free Trade Agreement with the United States which took place during the federal election campaign of 1988, there was a great deal of attention focused by those opposed to the Agreement on distinctive features of Canadian culture and society which might be endangered by the creation of a "level playing field" between the two countries.[73] Perhaps the most prominent aspects of Canadian life which were identified in that connection were Canadians' greater confidence in government as an instrument of public benefaction, and the greater tendency in Canada to care for each other's welfare, or as Robin Matthews and others have termed it, "the communitarian tradition in Canada."[74]

Reference has already been made to the tendency in Canada (usually seen in contrast to American views) to rely on government as an instrument to facilitate

---

[72] R. Bothwell, I. Drummond & J. English, *Canada Since 1945* (Toronto, University of Toronto, 1981); J.M.S. Careless, *Canada: A Story of Challenge* (Toronto, MacMillan, 1970); M.S. Cross & G.S. Keeley (Eds.), *Modern Canada: 1930–1980s* (Toronto, McClelland & Stewart, 1984); D.V. Smiley, *Canada in Question: Federalism in the Seventies* (Toronto, McGraw Hill, 1972).

[73] E. Finn (Ed.), *Canada: Don't Trade It Away* (Ottawa, Canadian Union of Public Employees, 1978).

[74] R. Matthews, *Canadian Identity* (Ottawa, Steel Rail, 1988).

social well-being and progress. Our leading historiographer has termed it "constructive socialism"[75] and another historian, "the social service state."[76] In a landmark sociological study of Canadian society published in 1961, Kaspar Naegele pointed out that Canadians were more ready to trust government than were Americans.[77] We have seen earlier how the crown corporation, be it in the form of a national railway or airlines, broadcasting network or film production organization, has been used repeatedly in Canada as a means of serving the economic, social and cultural strengthening of the nation. One of our leading historians, A.R.M. Lower, has put it this way: "At every critical juncture of our national life, when we have been faced with a choice between individualism and socialization, we have chosen socialization."[78] This may help to explain also why in Canada there has been such a heavy emphasis on public educational institutions—schools, colleges, universities—as the means of delivering adult education services.

It has been stated by Leslie Armour, a contemporary Canadian philosopher, that "communitarianism and its outcomes" is one of the sets of ideas which has most strongly shaped Canadian life.[79] He has placed a great deal of stress on the community as the source of Canadians' identity. Our most prominent cultural historian and critic, Northrop Frye, has frequently stressed the tendency of Canadians to draw strength—and in the case of our artists, vision—from the local community.[80] Perhaps in the ideas of such writers it is possible to see the reason why community education and community development have found such fertile ground in Canada.

Community development has been at the heart of a number of significant and well-known adult education projects in Canada. National Farm Radio Forum led to many community improvement projects at the local level. The Joint Planning Commission, which has already been described, may be seen as having made an important contribution to the social and cultural development of the Canadian community and sense of identity for two decades in the post World War II period. The Antigonish Movement in Nova Scotia proceeded largely by means of community development methods. Mention has also been made of the important

---

[75] C. Berger, *The Writing of Canadian History*, p. 200.

[76] R. Bothwell et al., *Canada Since 1945*, p. 311.

[77] K.D. Naegele in B.R. Blishen et al. (Eds.), *Canadian Society: Social Perspectives* (Toronto, MacMillan, 1961) p. 27.

[78] Cited in B. Ostry, *The Cultural Connection* (Toronto, McClelland & Stewart, 1978) p. 55.

[79] L. Armour, *The Idea of Canada* (Ottawa, Steel Rail, 1981) p. 109.

[80] See for instance, N. Frye, *Divisions on a Ground*.

contribution of the National Film Board to community development methodology through its Challenge for Change project.

Canadian communities were the site of many other community development projects. Examples of community development activity abound in the Canadian story. Robert England has described how he and his wife developed the prairie "lighted schoolhouse" into an instrument of community development in the early 1920s. His work and that of his staff in the ethnic communities along the Canadian National Railways route across the prairies (under the sponsorship of the railway) deserves to be better known than it is.[81] Mr. and Mrs. Harry Avison conducted a community development project at The Pas, Manitoba, under the auspices of the Canadian Association for Adult Education in the late thirties.[82] Florence O'Neill's memorable articles on the work she carried out in the small towns of Newfoundland during the early 1940s represent and important stage in this work as well.[83] The Royal Commission on Agriculture and Rural Life, which carried out its work in Saskatchewan from 1952 to 1956, was an important pioneer in the use of a public inquiry and its related research activity as an instrument of community development. Shortly thereafter the Government of Manitoba decided to launch "one of the first official community development programs in Canada,"[84] a program among Metis people of that province.[85] It is clear that the Quiet Revolution in Quebec during the sixties and thereafter involved several forms of community development work, as did aspects of the federal government's War on Poverty measures of the latter half of the decade. The latter included, for instance, community development activities under the Agricultural Reconstruction and Development Act, and community development projects carried out under the Company of Young Canadians, Opportunities for Youth, and the Local Improvement Projects. Mention should be made as well of a series of projects carried out in the early 1970s in Eastern Ontario under the sponsorship of Algonquin College in Ottawa.[86] In the very early seventies the federal government entered into a series of agreements with groups of Native people in Canada to provide community development services.[87] At about this same time, the National Film Board was getting into its Challenge for Change project, which has already been described. As well, Frontier College, which had mainly concentrated on its worker-teacher activities, began in the early seventies

---

[81] R. England, *Living, Learning, Remembering.*

[82] M.R. Welton, "'A Most Insistent Demand': The Pas Experiment in Community Education," *Canadian Journal for the Study of Adult Education, 1,* 2 (1987) pp. 1–22.

[83] F. O'Neill in J. Draper (Ed.), *Citizen Participation: Canada* (Toronto, New Press, 1971).

[84] J. Draper, *Citizen Participation: Canada,* p. 246.

[85] J. Legasse in J. Draper, *Citizen Participation: Canada.*

[86] A. Stinson in J. Draper, *Citizen Participation: Canada.*

[87] J. Lotz in J. Draper, *Citizen Participation: Canada.*

to enter into contracts with provincial governments under which the College provided personnel to conduct community development projects in designated towns.[88]

The early and mid-seventies brought a wave of fiscal austerity in Canada and in some quarters a turning to more conservative government philosophies. The years of flourishing community development activities were over. Once again, the linkage between events in the broader Canadian society and those in adult education were obvious.

The Impact of General History on the Development of Adult Education

While many more detailed examples could be given to illustrate further the clear connection between the general history of Canada and that of adult education—and the necessity of having knowledge of the broader history in order to fully understand developments in adult education—two examples will be provided in greater detail.

The first is that of "The 1943 Manifesto," which was approved and published in that year by the Canadian Association for Adult Education (CAAE). The Manifesto was a declaration of principles endorsed (unanimously) by a national conference of the organization. It was a brief statement containing a general introduction and a statement of seven principles. It refers to the need for "a new Canadian and world society" and invites interested individuals and groups to join in the "urgent educational task" of working towards that end.[89] It declares that "academic aloofness and neutrality are not enough" and declares itself in support of certain principles. Among these, for instance, is the assertion that "social controls and planning are necessary" and that it is "probable that the area of public ownership and control should be extended ... " This declaration, it is fair to say, had little practical effect on the program of the Association[90] and was replaced three years later by another declaration, but it earned the CAAE a reputation for being anti-free enterprise, gained it some enemies, and colours some public attitudes towards the organization to this day. When one comes to examine this incident closely, in terms of what was going on in the rest of society at that time, the action, while perhaps politically unwise in some ways, was hardly surprising. The depression had left a legacy of doubt about the future of Canadian society and some elements of socialist thinking had become quite broadly accepted.[91] There was great concern—in the armed forces and at home—that the end of the war would bring a return to economic problems and

---

[88] See for instance F. & N. McLeod in J. Draper, *Citizen Participation: Canada.*

[89] Full text in J.R. Kidd, *Learning and Society,* pp. 108–109.

[90] G. Selman, *The Canadian Association for Adult Education in the Corbett Years: A Re-evaluation* (Vancouver, University of British Columbia/Centre for Continuing Education, 1981).

[91] D. Creighton, *The Forked Road: Canada 1939–1957* (Toronto, McClelland & Stewart, 1976).

unemployment. At this time in the war, much attention was being given to the problems of reconstruction, and ideas for reform were in the air. Indeed the following year the Liberal government brought in several significant welfare measures. Faris has shown that there were ideological and social forces which converged at this time in the CAAE and which help to explain the concurrence on such a manifesto.[92] There may be many questions still to be considered in providing a full and satisfactory explanation as to why such a manifesto was passed, but it is clear that any attempt to explain it only in terms of the views of a few key leaders or relationships internal to the CAAE would fall far short of the mark. There were forces at work in the broader Canadian society which were clearly powerful in explaining the action that was taken in this adult education organization.

A second such example has to do with the emergence, mainly during the 1960s and early 1970s, of provincial organizations of adult educators, and of their relationship with the national organization, the Canadian Association for Adult Education. The CAAE was formed in 1935, and except for a few short-lived regional bodies which came and went from time to time, by 1950 was still the only organization of adult educators, at least in English-speaking Canada.[93] During the fifties, provincial organizations emerged in two provinces, Saskatchewan and British Columbia. In 1961, after a review of its operations, the B.C. body decided to alter its nature and asked the national organization, the CAAE, to change its constitution in order to create "divisions," provincially-based bodies which would be integral parts of the CAAE, not just affiliates. This change was made and during the course of the sixties, adult educators in six provinces created divisions of the CAAE. But as the sixties progressed, regionalism and the decentralization of initiative within Canadian confederation as a whole greatly increased,[94] and populist ideas were strengthening in various aspects of Canadian life. When in 1967, educators in Alberta came to form a provincial body, they decided that it would remain an autonomous organization rather than be a division of the national one. Pressures began to increase within the CAAE of a populist and provincially-based nature to abandon the tightly integrated form of national organization and to enable the provincial bodies to become autonomous (but affiliated) organizations. This was brought about in the early seventies. The point which needs to be stressed is that an awareness of what was going on in the broader society—the turbulent populist movements and the basic shifts in power and initiative within confederation—places the developments within the adult education movement in an entirely different light. There were forces within the

---

[92] R. Faris, *The Passionate Educators*.

[93] G. Selman, "Specialization or Balkanization: Organizations of Adult Educators," *Canadian Journal of University Continuing Education*, xiv, 1 (1988).

[94] R. Bothwell et al., *Canada Since 1945*; J.M.S. Careless, *Canada: A Story of Challenge*; D.V. Smiley, *Canada in Question*.

field of adult education which provide some explanation for these developments,[95] but an awareness of the broader picture can make clear some of the
connections between a particular field—adult education—and the society of
which it is a part.

Aside from the two specific examples just described, there have been many
instances of how developments in the field of adult education have reflected
other events. The two world wars are particularly obvious examples. These traumatic crises in the life of the nation catapulted enormous numbers of persons into
unaccustomed roles—men and women in the armed forces, many into new or
expanded wartime industries, many women into the work force for the first time,
etc.—which required them to learn many things, and quickly. The Great Depression of the 1930s placed many persons into altered circumstances, requiring
major adjustments on their part, and also elicited from governments a wide range
of new policies and provisions in adult education.[96] A combination of forces in
the late fifties—economic recession, high rates of unemployment, and the
"shock" which came with recognition of Soviet leadership in space technology—
combined to produce a large scale attempt to upgrade the competence of the
Canadian work force (The Technical and Vocational Training Assistance Act of
1960). The "War on Poverty" policy of the federal government, announced in
1965, resulted in various pieces of legislation which profoundly altered government policies towards adult education. Many of the social movements which
emerged in the sixties and seventies, such as the women's movement, the environmental movements, disarmament groups and the like, have added important
new dimensions to the adult education enterprise in Canada. The neo-conservative policies of federal and many provincial governments in the late eighties
brought a shift in adult education to a greater concentration on vocational or
occupational training, and a shift of a major portion of such work from the public
to the private sectors.

It is clear that adult education is predominantly a "reactive" enterprise in our
society. It responds to the circumstances and the "agenda" of the community
within which it functions. Whereas back in the 1930s and 1940s, the field could
be said to have been a social movement, with goals of its own and with a vision
of what kind of society it wished to help to create, the field has changed profoundly since that time. While there are still sectors of the field which are
inspired by those kinds of goals, adult education today is overwhelmingly dominated by what has been termed the "service ethic."[97] With increased professionalization and institutionalization of the field, adult education is seen increasingly
as a service to individuals rather than as a force to shape the nature of the

---

[95] G. Selman, *Alan Thomas and the CAAE 1961–1970.*

[96] G. Selman, *Adult Education in British Columbia During the Depression* (Vancouver, University of British Columbia/Centre for Continuing Education, 1976).

[97] See K. Rockhill in R. Taylor, K. Rockhill & R. Fieldhouse, *University Adult Education in
England and the USA* (London, Croom Helm, 1985).

community. Such changes are lamented by some adult educators, including many involved in the Canadian Association for Adult Education, which continues to represent the social movement elements of the field, but its membership is small. Most adult educators appear to welcome the professionalization of the field and see no necessary philosophical implications in their calling. They are content to leave decisions about how knowledge will be used to the individual learner. Many social movements in Canada, however, such as the labour movement, the women's and environmental movements, co-operative and many church-related groups, have a different view, and may be the basis of an emerging "popular education" movement in this country.

Stages in the Development of Adult Education in Canada

In the brief account which follows, the history of adult education in this country is divided into five periods.[98] Such time frames are artificial creations, but they are sometimes helpful in identifying significant trends and notable milestones.

Before 1867

This was largely a period of scattered, informal beginnings, under private and voluntary auspices. It was a time of book clubs, literary and scientific societies, music, handicraft and art associations. It was also a time of heavy reliance on institutional forms which were imported from elsewhere—a kind of adult education colonialism. This included mechanics' institutes, the Y.M.C.A. and voluntary organizations of agricultural producers, for instance. Certain cultural organizations which were to have a long history, the Institut canadien of Montreal (1844) and the Royal Canadian Institute of Toronto (1849), were established in this period. There appears to have been little in the way of publicly financed adult education, though public libraries began to appear in some areas, the government of Upper Canada began to subsidize the mechanics' institutes, and the Toronto School Board offered night school classes for a few years beginning in 1855.

1867–1914

Adult education was still largely under private auspices in this period, but important steps were taken which laid the groundwork for the expansion of the public sector.

As the population increased and settlement pushed West and North, there was a continuation of the phenomenon of study groups, institutes and associations devoted to educational and cultural matters. Mechanics' institutes, Y.M.C.A.s and after 1868, Y.W.C.A.s were formed in increasing numbers. Representative of the wide range of other voluntary organizations which became active in the field

---

[98] For a more detailed account, see G. Selman, "Stages in the Development of Canadian Adult Education," *Canadian Journal of University Continuing Education*, 10, 1 (1984) pp. 7–16.

are the National Council of Women (founded in 1893) and the forerunner of the home and school movement founded in Beddeck, Nova Scotia, two years later.

Agricultural extension, under both private and public auspices, came into its own in this period. The Grange (the first in 1872), Farmers' Institutes (the first in 1894) and other agricultural societies flourished. The C.P.R. and the federal government operated experimental farms beginning in the mid-eighties. After the turn of the century, the federal and some provincial departments of agriculture became engaged on a large scale in educational activities. Co-operative education in relation to agriculture was under way early in the new century. In 1913 the federal parliament passed the Agricultural Instruction Act, which made federal funds available for use by the provinces for agricultural extension work, an important step in itself, but also significant in that it pioneered the means subsequently to be used by Ottawa to fund other types of vocational education as well. Other departments of government, for instance Marine and Fisheries and the Geological Survey, began to offer educational services in this period.

Public educational institutions began in greater numbers to get into the field. The Toronto School Board reinstituted its night classes in 1880 on a permanent basis. Night classes in technical subjects were greatly expanded at the turn of the century. Queen's University became the first university in Canada to begin extension work on a permanent basis in 1889, and Toronto and McGill soon followed suit. After the turn of the century, with the creation of provincial universities in Saskatchewan and Alberta, these two adopted the more broadly based approach to university extension which had been pioneered at the University of Wisconsin.

Three other important organizations had their origins in this period. The first Women's Institute was founded in Stoney Creek, Ontario in 1897. An organization devoted to the education of rural women and to improving the quality of rural life, the women's institute movement subsequently spread quickly and became worldwide. The Canadian Reading Camp Association began its activity in 1899 and has continued its work in frontier camps and communities until very recent times, changing its name in 1919 to Frontier College. The origins of co-operative education in Canada are obscure, but the founding of the Caisse Populaire in 1900 should be noted in that connection.

1915–1939

A traumatic period in the life of the country, these twenty-five years also witnessed the beginning of a conscious adult education movement in Canada and the creation of a number of noteworthy projects. The best known program during World War I was Khaki College, which provided educational services to servicemen in Britain and Europe. The counterpart in the Second World War was the Canadian Legion Educational Service, which served both overseas and Canadian-based troops.

A number of important adult education institutions were created in Canada during these years. University extension was begun at many universities, the best known project being the co-operative education project of St. Francis Xavier University in Nova Scotia, often referred to as the Antigonish Movement. The Workers' Educational Association was established in several centres in Canada in 1918, but was short-lived everywhere but in Ontario. Sir George Williams University, long an evening college and an important source of part-time degree study, was founded in Montreal in 1926. The Banff Centre, originally the Banff School of Fine Arts, was founded under University of Alberta auspices in 1933. And in the late thirties, two of our most important national institutions were created, the Canadian Broadcasting Corporation and the National Film Board of Canada.

A sign of the growing maturity of the field of adult education was the creation in 1935 of the Canadian Association for Adult Education. Organizational meetings the previous year had laid the groundwork for this step and had commissioned the first national survey of adult education activities.[99] Founded largely by university and government people, the CAAE was originally intended to be a clearing house and information centre for adult education in Canada, but under the dynamic leadership of E.A. Corbett, and influenced by the crisis presented by the World War, the organization was transformed into a direct programming agency, largely in the field of citizenship education.

Certain government services developed extensively during this period. In 1919, with the passage of the Technical Education Act, the federal government provided funds for use by the provinces in vocational training, the same device, essentially, which continued to be used until the mid-sixties. Important measures were enacted both federally and provincially as a response to the Great Depression of the 1930s, aimed at providing training and work, but also at improving the morale of the people.

The crisis of the depression and the deep concern about the future of Canadian (and the world) society produced many efforts during the thirties to study and rethink the basic elements of the citizen's relationship to fellow citizens, and the nature and role of government. A great deal of this effort was directly related to politics and produced several political movements. But much of such study activity was carried out under other sponsorship, for instance groups under United Church auspices which prepared and issued a major proposal, "Christianity and the Social Order," and other policy statements. The Social Gospel movement was very lively in those desperate days, as were many forms of radical political advocacy.

1940–1959

This was a vibrant time in the life of Canada, in war and peace, and also in the field of adult education. Many of the best known accomplishments in Canadian adult education were created or gained prominence during these years and there was considerable expansion of provision in this area by public authorities.

---

[99] P. Sandiford, *Adult Education in Canada: A Survey* (Toronto, University of Toronto, 1935).

The wartime period mobilized Canadians to unaccustomed tasks on an unprecedented scale. Whether in the armed forces, wartime industries or the vast network of civilian and voluntary support services, Canadian men and women responded—and learned—as never before. Canada emerged from the war with an expanded economy and a new sense of identity as a nation. The educational efforts of the Wartime Information Board and of many other organizations during the war years contributed to these changes.[100]

The CAAE, under the leadership of Corbett and Kidd, made remarkable contributions in these two decades. Foremost among these were the three projects in the field of citizenship education, Farm and Citizens' Forum and the Joint Planning Commission, which have been described earlier in this chapter. The postwar period was one of continuing large scale immigration to Canada and both government, through the newly-formed Citizenship Branch, and the voluntary sector, with the effective leadership of the Canadian Citizenship Council, provided many services to "New Canadians."

Cold War tensions and Canada's active role as a leading middle power on the world scene at this time encouraged the activities of several important organizations concerned with education about international affairs, including the United Nations Association, the Canadian Institute on Public Affairs and the Canadian Institute on International Affairs. Canadian adult educators, most notably J. Roby Kidd, also began to play an important role at UNESCO and elsewhere in the international adult education movement.

Local and provincial governments in many parts of Canada became involved more actively in the field. The community centre movement swept the country, creating new means of making educational and recreational services accessible at the neighbourhood level. School board adult education programs began to expand rapidly in some areas, most notably in British Columbia. Whereas in 1945, only one province in Canada had a formally constituted adult education section within its department of education, by 1957 seven provinces had taken that step, and by 1961 they all had done so. In Manitoba, the provincial government launched an important community development project among the Metis people. The federal government also began to expand its educational work with the Native people.

The National Film Board gained world recognition in this period for the excellence of its productions. In order to carry out its mandate of interpreting Canada to Canadians, it devised an outstandingly successful domestic distribution system, which has already been described and which resulted in the Board's productions being seen by a remarkable percentage of the Canadian population.

This was a period, especially in the 1950s, in which a sense of professionalism was emerging in adult education (see Chapter 8). Organizations of adult educators began to appear in some provinces and the CAAE inaugurated series of regional conferences in both the Maritimes and the West. Several universities

---

[100] W.R. Young, *Making The Truth Graphic.*

offered credit courses on the subject of adult education for the first time in the fifties, and in 1957, the University of British Columbia introduced the first full degree (Masters) program in Canada in this field.

1960–The Present

The most recent period has seen enormous strides made in the field of adult education and this account can at best mention only some highlights. Developments such as the vast expansion of national investment in vocational and technical training, the "War on Poverty" begun in the mid-sixties, the political strains within Canadian confederation, the emergence of a series of important new social movements, the development of a whole new system of educational institutions (the community colleges), and the gradual acceptance of the fact that education must be seen not as "preparation for life," but as an ongoing part of life—these and other significant changes have led to the vast expansion and increased acceptance of adult education and lifelong learning.

In very broad terms, the 1960s may be seen as a period of important federal initiatives and the subsequent years as ones of more active (but in some cases, transitory) provincial measures. Canada's international stature in the field of adult education was demonstrated in 1960, when UNESCO's Second World Conference on Adult Education was held in Montreal and J. Roby Kidd was elected as its President. The conference is generally seen to have articulated for the field the conviction that adult education had passed the stage of being seen largely as a remedial activity, something one engaged in to make up for what was missed earlier, and instead should be seen as part of a normal pattern of adult life.

The federal government has made enormous contributions to adult education in these years. The character of technical and vocational education has been transformed by a great infusion of federal funds, as well as by the decision taken in the mid-sixties by the federal authorities to move into the direct provision of vocational and technical training, rather than leaving it to the initiative of the provinces. Related to the expansion of vocational education has been the federal role in the development of adult basic education and English (and French) as a second language instruction. In both areas, federal efforts have accelerated educational provision and have resulted in pressure being placed on the provinces to increase their efforts as well. Another important area of federal contributions flowed from the "War on Poverty" approach begun in the sixties, which spawned a great range of community development, local initiative and social development activities. The bilingualism and multiculturalism policies endorsed by the federal government have spurred much educational activity. Finally, in this selective list of federal initiatives, mention should be made of the large federal grants to the labour movement in recent years to help strengthen its educational activities.

Developments at the provincial level are perhaps even more diverse, and reference to them will be left in the main to Chapter 9, which deals with contemporary activities. The increasingly obvious fact that adult education was a growing enterprise in Canadian society was confirmed by statistical reports. Government reports, as detailed in the following chapter, indicated that whereas in 1960, the beginning of this final period, approximately one in 25 Canadians took part in some form of adult education course during the year, a similar report for the year 1983 showed that by that time, one in every five Canadians had registered for courses during the year.

This chapter has been concerned with describing the connection between Canada's historical experience as a nation and the form and content of the adult education enterprise which has been developed. In addition to borrowing various institutional forms from other countries, Canadian adult educators have responded in outstandingly creative and innovative ways to conditions in our own society. Many of these Canadian programs and projects, developed to meet Canadian circumstances, have been judged by authorities in other lands to be of value to them, and have been studied and adapted for use elsewhere. It is likely true to say that no other aspect of education in Canada has had as much impact outside our borders than the field of adult education.

4

Participation, Participants and Providers

The Interest in Adult Learning

Every day and each evening in Canada a significant number of adults are involved in learning activities of one kind or another. They pursue their learning in a variety of settings and with the assistance of numerous kinds of organizations. Evidence of this pursuit of learning include cars parked around school buildings in the evenings, displays of course brochures in public settings, and impressive industrial training centres.

Two observations are at the root of the interest which adult educators hold in studying adults' participation in learning. The first is that the greatest amount of adult learning is done completely on a voluntary basis. Even when freed from the compulsion to attend grade school, adults in substantial numbers choose to continue learning. In most cases the choice is entirely of the individual's own volition, while in some cases there are compelling reasons to participate such as keeping up in one's employment. For the most part, however, participation in adult education is based on adults exercising their free will. The second observation is that adults need to continue learning in order to maintain and advance themselves in their society. Whereas in earlier times continuing one's education was seen as a way of getting ahead, and particularly in the context of the workplace, nowadays continued learning is necessary just to keep current with the ever quickening pace of change. Taking both observations, a common question arises which adult educators are interested in having answered: why do some adults continue with learning while others do not? While much is known about the factors which both promote and discourage participation, our understanding is by no means complete, and this chapter will address the question rather than answer it.

The term which has been favoured to describe adults who are active learners is "participants," and the observable behaviour of adults who are active in their learning quest is described as "participation." This seems reasonable enough, and hence to define the term "participation" as it relates to adult education would appear to be straightforward. After all, by definition to participate is to join; thus participation in adult education is the act of joining some form of adult learning activity. As with much in adult education, however, it cannot be quite that simple, and one of the purposes of this chapter is to help clarify what is meant by participation. As an example of the difficulty, the initial question might be asked,

"Is it necessary that an adult, in order to participate in adult education, must join in with others to learn, or can an adult also learn in a solitary manner?" As we shall see, there is debate on this question, and has been for some time.

Before starting to examine adult participation it will be helpful to first identify why the concept of participation in adult education is seen as being important. This can be done by adopting the viewpoint of the several "stakeholders" in adult education, i.e., those with a particular interest in it. To begin there is the viewpoint of Canadian society. Numerous writers on adult education point to the need of adults to participate actively in the affairs of the society in order to preserve and strengthen the democratic ideal.[1] As citizens we are aware that, given Canada's ethnic mosaic beginning with the Native peoples, then the dual cultures of the French and the English, and its current evolution to a multicultural society, there is an ever increasing reliance on a tolerance of differences in order for the weave of Canadian society to remain strong. We know tolerance is derived from understanding that is based on knowledge, as opposed to intolerance which is based on ignorance and fear. In addition, Canada is faced with perplexing and often conflicting issues such as environmental protection and economic development, individual rights and community welfare, and national priorities and regional recognition. In our democratic society it is ultimately the citizen who must make informed choices, and participation in adult education is seen as an important way to become informed.

The next viewpoint is that of the providers of adult education, whether they be large institutions such as a community college or small associations such as an Alzheimer Disease support group. These providers all offer what they believe to be interesting and useful programs, some of which are intended to have a general appeal while others are directed at specific groups. In desiring to fill the available space in the class—that is the number of seats for attenders—these providers need to know how to promote attendance. Further, once a person is motivated to attend it is the instructor (or facilitator) who needs to be aware of participation factors in order to design the appropriate instructional strategy to meet the learning need.

Another viewpoint is that of adult learners. Generally speaking, the more that is known about adult learning needs and desires, and the factors which influence the decision to participate, the more that will be able to be done to meet these same needs and desires. This should in turn increase the availability of opportunities to participate. Not only will there be more opportunities, but these opportunities will be more accessible to adults as the sponsoring organizations become more adept at overcoming the difficulties adults experience which stand in the way of their participation. For example, in an effort to enable homebound parents to enroll in a course on child development, the course which is normally

---

[1] For example, G. Hawkins (Ed.), *A Design for Democracy* (New York, Association Press, 1956); J. Draper (Ed.), *Citizen Participation: Canada* (Toronto, New Press, 1971); G. Selman, "Adult Education and Citizenship," in Cassidy and Faris (Eds.), *Choosing Our Future: Adult Education and Public Policy in Canada* (Toronto, O.I.S.E. Press, 1987).

offered in the evening at a far off community college might now also be offered during the daytime at a neighbourhood church hall with child minding provided.

Another viewpoint is that of adult educators who believe fervently that through continued learning an adult enjoys a more productive and satisfying life. By increasing the number of adults who successfully participate in learning activities, the adult educator is fulfilling a role, indeed a mission, that contributes to the well-being of individuals and society alike. This is a moral viewpoint, and differs completely from a self-serving one which instead simply seeks participation for participation's sake, thereby providing employment for adult educators. At the same time it is important for adult educators to be able to point to high enrollment figures as an indication of adult learning. Such figures help to advance the day when decision makers accept lifelong learning as the basis for all educational policy.

In summary, Canadian society places a very high value on learning by youth and adults alike, and large amounts of public resources are made available to enable learning to take place. Because in adult learning the basis for participation differs in a number of significant ways from that of youth, and adult learning has no prescribed format, the concept of participation in adult education takes on its own fascination. Participation is viewed as being admirable—even virtuous— and non-participation, rather than being viewed disdainfully, is instead understood in terms of the presence of some impediment to participation which must be overcome. The admirable traits of participation include the following:

- it is a manifestation of the concept of lifelong learning;
- it is an indication of a learning society, with the likelihood of greater understanding and tolerance existing among citizens;
- it reflects a constructive use of leisure time and a productive use of work time;
- it is an available mechanism for people in the conducting of their lives, i.e. staying abreast with change, coping with problems, taking advantage of opportunities, bringing understanding to perplexing situations;
- it represents activity versus passivity, striving versus stagnation, enterprise versus indolence, positiveness versus negativeness;
- it is reminiscent of an earlier time in Canada when small communities depended on participation to sustain a quality of community life.

Three Central Ideas to Participation

There are three ideas which are central to the topic of participation: (1) determining what is meant by participation in adult learning; (2) examining who participates and for what reasons; and (3) identifying the providers of adult learning activity. As a backdrop to examining these ideas the methodology and findings of a major survey conducted on adult education in Canada will be presented. The survey is introduced here and will be referred to throughout this chapter.

In 1984 Statistics Canada and the Education Support Branch of the Secretary of State jointly published a report alluringly titled, *One in Every Five: A Survey of Adult Education in Canada.*[2] The title borrowed from the findings of a survey conducted in January, 1984 to determine, among other things, the extent of participation in adult education in Canada. This Adult Education Survey found that nineteen per cent—approximately one fifth—of adult Canadians participated in at least one adult education course in the calendar year 1983.

While this was not the first survey on adult learning to be conducted in Canada—the CAAE and the ICEA had done a considerably smaller version two years earlier and in 1960 the Dominion Bureau of Statistics conducted a survey similar to that of 1984—it does provide the most recent and statistically reliable picture of participation in adult education in Canada.[3] (Other countries have collected participation data on a regular basis but in Canada, because there is no national body with such a mandate, this has not been the case.)[4] In order to interpret the survey's findings, it is necessary to now address the three central ideas outlined above.

The Idea of Participation

As noted above the term "participation" has become accepted as a way of describing the act of engaging in adult learning. There are two reasons which can be advanced for this acceptance, both of which indicate the importance of nuance when describing aspects of adult education. The first is that by using the term the operative notion of voluntarily engaging in adult learning is thereby emphasized. One participates by choosing to join, and one can also choose to discontinue participating. This contrasts with the synonym "enrollment" which, even though the enrollment may be voluntary, still suggests the giving of oneself over to the organization which accepts the enrollment. The second reason is that in adult education the common term used to identify an adult learner is "participant" rather than, for example, student. This use is by no means universal but just as participation is suggestive of voluntary involvement, so participant is

---

[2] Statistics Canada, *One in Every Five: A Survey of Adult Education in Canada* (Ottawa, Ministry of Supply and Services Canada, 1985).

[3] For the 1982 survey see CAAE/ICEA, *From the Adult's Point of View* (Toronto, CAAE, 1982). For the 1960 survey see Dominion Bureau of Statistics, *Participants in Further Education in Canada* (Ottawa, Queen's Printer, 1963). The DBS had been keeping some data on adult education participation since 1929. See Chapter 6, "The Participants in Adult Education," in R. Kidd, *18 to 80: Continuing Education in Metropolitan Toronto* (Toronto, Board of Education, 1961). For the report of a provincial study see Ignacy Waniewicz, *Demand for Part Time Learning in Ontario* (Toronto, O.I.S.E. Press, 1976).

[4] For example the National Centre for Education Statistics of the U.S. Department of Education publishes participation statistics triennially and the Swedish National Bureau of Education maintains annual statistics. Also there are two landmark USA studies on participation, one by Johnstone and Rivera, *Volunteers for Learning: A Study of the Educational Pursuits of Adults* (New York, Aldine, 1965) and the other by Clark and Sloan, *Classrooms in the Factories: An Account of Educational Activities Conducted by American Industry* (New York, New York University Press, 1958).

suggestive of one who joins to share in the learning experience with the "facilitator" (as opposed to "teacher"). The voluntary nature of joining gives the participant a greater sense of equality with the facilitator in the learning activity. Thus the subject of this examination is the act of participation on the part of the participant.

There are two approaches to understanding participation as it relates to adult education. The first approach can be thought of metaphorically as a turnstile. With this approach it is the act of entering, of being counted as one attends at a certain time and place, that denotes participation. While the turnstile description of this approach seems somewhat crass, the approach is based on the administrative necessity found in any formal system of keeping count. Such systems have a constant need to justify their existence, and the easiest way of doing so is to employ quantitative measures to denote activity. Thus departments of continuing education within institutions are able to report on the number of persons who participated, that is enrolled, in their various programs during a given period of time. The label "enrollment" would well apply to this approach. By labelling this as the enrollment approach to participation it is not intended as a condemnation. The very fact an organization continues to have statistics to report indicates its adult education operation is viable. The point, though, is how with this approach the emphasis is placed on the statistical fact of initial participation, i.e. enrollment, rather than on the purpose of the participation, namely learning.

The second approach looks at the ways in which adults engage themselves in learning beyond their formal education. This meaning emphasizes the occurrence of adult learning wherever and however it occurs. It acknowledges that beyond one's formal education an adult may exercise freedom of choice in deciding to continue to be engaged in learning and is free to engage in learning in whatever way desired. It may involve enrolling in a course at a night school or it may involve learning at home with the assistance of a self study manual purchased at a book store. With this meaning the importance is placed on the act of learning rather than the fact of enrolling. The label "engagement" would well apply to this second approach as the emphasis of this approach is on the variety of ways in which adults continue to engage themselves in learning.

Of the two approaches, enrollment and engagement, the former is the more readily understood. There is a numeric simplicity to it, a mere matter of counting individuals who sign up and attend. As noted this is an important measure of participation in adult education. From the viewpoint of the providers of adult education courses, this approach is basic to their ability to continue offering courses, dependent as they are on people enrolling. The latter approach of engagement, however, is more attuned to the activity of learning as construed by adult learners. To pursue an understanding of this approach it is helpful to first liberate one's traditional understanding of learning.

Learning is a natural activity of the human species. All of us take on extraordinarily complex learning tasks at the outset of our lives, such as learning to talk, to walk, and to discriminate shapes and sizes. By necessity we are innate learners. We also discover that our innate ability to learn is enhanced by having another person (and even through a stimulus such as a television) assisting us in our learning efforts. Indeed these efforts can be made much more effective and efficient by having another person directing them in a manner which they prescribe for the learner. This all important role is filled by a person acknowledged by the designation, "teacher."

The role of teacher is introduced very early in a child's life. In the example above of learning to talk, walk and discriminate, it is usually a child's parents who perform as teachers. Before long the child is introduced to school, and it is here that the roles of teacher and learner become formalized. An indication of the powerful influence of the role of the teacher is to observe how for many children teachers quickly become role models, and in games of, "Let's play school," it is the role of teacher, not student, which is coveted. This role of teacher is important to consider because all societies have built their educational systems around it. When parents enroll their child in school it is the teaching resource it contains which they desire for the child.

It is precisely because a system must be organized in order to place students with teachers that learning becomes the subject of an administrative orientation. Students are arranged into classes, provided with text books and accounted for each school day morning. The taxpaying public demands such efficacy in the school system. What occurs, however, is that learning becomes highly administrated, and this dominates our view of the human learning process. It is no wonder then that this administrative view carries forward into adulthood once a student's formal education is concluded. Most significant for adult education, however, is the understanding that this view no longer needs to dominate the conception of how individuals engage in learning activities.

The view in adult education is to return the learner to the pre-eminent role. This return is heralded by the fact that the adult enjoys the freedom to choose whether to continue learning or not, and also to choose the circumstances in which any learning will take place. It is precisely this freedom of choice that gives "engagement" participation its meaning. That adults do continue to engage themselves with learning in the ways they do constitutes the true phenomenon of participation. Equally though, the phenomenon includes reasons for adults who are not continuing to be engaged with their learning. These reasons for non-engagement suggest impediments which, if overcome, might well lead to participation. This latter point will be examined further in this chapter under the heading of "Barriers to Participation." For the present the emphasis will be on those who are considered participants.

From this discussion it is seen that the idea of participation in adult education is associated with learning. This association requires, however, that there also be an understanding of what is meant by learning, and it is here that there exists a divergence of thought as it relates to adult learning. One direction leads along the path of learning theory as developed by educational psychologists and which emphasizes the importance of planned learning, i.e., instruction, to learning. In this direction every effort is made to understand the internal mental processes connected with learning so as to determine the instructional strategies most likely to influence learning. It is apparent that this direction is of particular interest to the professional educator, whose task it is to direct the strategies which will likely have the greatest potential for bringing about learning in the individual. Indeed the presence of an educator is seen as being necessary in order for planned learning to take place.

The second direction leads along a path where there is much less emphasis on the role of an educator in bringing about planned learning and instead sees the adult learner as now being capable of also assuming some or even all of this task. Adherents of this direction regard the adult learner as having reached a state of both self-awareness and self-determination sufficient to make his or her own learning decisions. Thus it is the adult learner who intentionally and voluntarily places himself or herself in a learning situation and measures it to determine the extent to which learning will occur so as to meet personal learning objectives. This direction is not to be seen as being counter to that of the educational psychologists, indeed the definition of learning is common to both, incorporating as it does the elements of a change which is brought about in physical or mental ability and which is sustained over time.[5] Instead an adult is viewed as being in a position to exercise considerable autonomy and discretion over his or her learning, and this includes the option of taking on some or all of the responsibility for planning the instruction, including the evaluation criteria. As Brookfield notes, "At the heart of self-directedness is the adult's assumption of control over setting educational goals and generating personally meaningful evaluative criteria."[6] Indeed the ultimate situation for any teacher must be when the teaching which has been provided enables a person to become an independent learner. Thus participation in adult education, when understood in terms of the presence of learning, can include much more learning activity than occurs when only a teacher or facilitator is instructing.

In light of the suggestion that the presence of learning indicates participation, it would be wrong to suggest that whenever learning takes place there is necessarily participation. The respected adult education theorist, Gale Jensen, referred to learning which takes place as a result of the everyday experiences of life as

---

[5] For example the educational psychologist, Robert Gagne, describes learning as "a change in human disposition or capability, which can be retained, and which is not simply ascribable to the process of growth." R. Gagne, *The Conditions of Learning* (2nd ed.) (New York, Holt, Rinehart & Winston, 1970) p. 3. The adult educator, Alan Thomas, similarly describes learning as being "a voluntary act, which occurs each time a member of society comes to know something, to be able to do something, or to be able to feel something he or she could not previously." A. Thomas, "Learning in Society—A Discussion Paper," in *Learning in Society—Toward a New Paradigm* (Ottawa, UNESCO, 1985) p. 21.

[6] S. Brookfield, *Understanding and Facilitating Adult Learning* (San Francisco, Jossey-Bass, 1986) p. 19.

being learning in the "natural societal setting." This learning he characterized as being both casual and serendipitous and in terms of this discussion would not be associated with participation. Jensen contrasted the natural societal setting with the "formal instructional setting," which includes the presence of an educational "agent" (teacher) to guide and direct learning.[7]

For many adult education theorists it is the formal instructional setting that constitutes adult education's field. (The term formal instructional setting is intended to emphasize the necessity of the educational agent, and not to imply an actual classroom.) By this is meant that purposefulness is necessary to distinguish intended learning from that which occurs serendipitously. The responsibility of the educational agent, then, is to ensure the purposefulness of the learning activity. The educational agent accomplishes this by designing "a sequence of tasks using specific learning procedures to help an adult achieve a mutually agreeable learning objective."[8] Thus another respected adult education theorist, Coolie Verner, defined adult education as being, "a relationship between an educational agent and a learner in which the agent selects, arranges and continuously directs a sequence of progressive tasks that provide systematic experiences to achieve learning."[9]

The delineation of the field of adult education in terms of the formal instructional setting, with its inclusion of organized educational activities and an ongoing relationship between learner and educational agent in order to ensure purposefulness in the learning activity, has more recently been challenged by researchers of adult learning. They have concluded that adults can and do learn in a purposeful manner without necessarily needing to be in an organized educational activity complete with an educational agent. Further, their findings indicate that adults are capable of conducting their own learning activities and that the role of the educational agent (teacher) is one that the learner can assign to another as he or she sees fit. In some cases the learner will assign this role to a class instructor; in other cases the learner might assume a large portion of it, thereby enabling the learner to self-direct much of the learning activity, consulting with a subject expert only if assistance is required. In fact this is a distinguishing aspect of the engagement approach to adult education, namely the belief that the learner can assume some or even all of the responsibilities of the "agent." In this approach the learner is participating, but this act of learning, this engagement, may never be evidenced on any class list.

It is apparent that the view of adult learning which gives credence to the idea of self-directed learning embraces both directions to learning noted above, that is

---

[7]   G. Jensen, "The Nature of Education as a Discipline," in G. Jensen (Ed.), *Readings for Educational Researchers* (Ann Arbor, Ann Arbor Publishers, 1960).

[8]   C. Verner and A. Booth, *Adult Education* (Washington, The Center for Applied Research in Education, 1964) p. 1.

[9]   C. Verner, "Basic Concepts and Limitations," in J.R. Kidd (Ed.), *Learning and Society* (Toronto, CAAE, 1963) p. 235.

the need for a professional educator to direct learning and the ability of the learner to assume responsibility for planning his or her own learning. In self-directed learning the role of the educational agent can be divided between the learner and the educational agent, as determined by the learner. There is even the option of the learner assuming all of this role. In this latter option, however, the educational agent will still be present in an impersonal form, e.g. as the author of a book, the organizer of a lecture series, or the script writer of a television documentary. (Note, however, that in such cases the term "educational agent" would be inappropriate as the author, the lecture organizer and the script writer are not acting in the capacity of a professional educator, as is intended by the term.) This self-directed view should not be associated with serendipitous learning in the natural societal setting, as the essential element of purposefulness is still present.

The person most identified with self-directed learning is Allen Tough of the Ontario Institute for Studies in Education. According to Tough, adults commonly undertake "learning projects," which he defines as being "a series of related episodes, adding up to at least seven hours. In each episode more than half a person's total motivation is to gain and retain certain fairly clear knowledge and skill, or to produce some other lasting change in himself."[10] Tough's research work confirmed the idea that adults were competent in directing their own learning and, when necessary, even teaching themselves. The term "adult's learning projects" was introduced by Tough to emphasize the intentionality with which adults commit themselves to their learning.

The findings by Tough and others as to the extent of adult participation in learning projects are most revealing:[11]

1. almost everyone undertakes at least one or two major learning projects a year, and the median number of projects conducted annually is eight;

2. it is common for an adult to spend 700 hours a year engaged in learning projects;

3. almost seventy per cent of learning projects are self-planned.

By adopting the understanding of participation as purposeful learning which utilizes both enrollment and engagement approaches, it is possible to appreciate the shortcoming of using enrollment figures alone to measure the extent of participation. Enrollment figures indicate some, but not all, of the adult learning phenomenon. To illustrate this point the Statistics Canada Adult Education Survey determined that approximately twenty per cent of Canadian adults took at least one course, class or instructional activity in the calendar year 1983 (up from

[10] A. Tough, *The Adult's Learning Projects: A Fresh Approach to Theory and Practice in Adult Learning* (2nd edition) (Toronto, Ontario Institute for Studies in Education, 1979) p. 6.

[11] A. Tough, *The Adult's Learning Projects*, p. 1.

four per cent in 1960). Another finding, this time from research conducted earlier by Tough, determined that virtually all adults engage in several "learning projects" each year, and were thereby participating in adult education. Tough's research concluded that 90 per cent of the adult population is engaged in carrying out their own "learning projects."[12]

The discrepancy between the two findings is easily enough explained by the approach to identifying participation. In the case of Statistics Canada's survey it was enrollment while in the case of the research on learning projects it was engagement in learning. Further, the Adult Education Survey (and many similar surveys) defined adult education in terms of a course, class or instruction, i.e. the formal instructional setting, whereas for Tough's purposes learning was defined in terms of an adult learning project, which is "a major, highly deliberate effort to gain certain knowledge and skill (or to change in some other way.)"[13]

From reviewing the findings of both Statistics Canada's and Tough's efforts at quantifying participation in adult education, one is left with two distinctly different impressions. According to the engagement approach to participation (as posited by Tough and embodied in self-directed learning) most adults are satisfying their learning needs and wants, while the enrollment approach to participation used by Statistics Canada suggests cause for great distress, considering the high level of non-participation (80%). What is to be concluded from such an apparent discrepancy?

Firstly the reasons for the gap can be readily determined, i.e. the definition of the term participation and the basis for measuring participation (enrollment versus self-directed learning project). Secondly, adult education researchers continue to grapple with the phenomenon of adult learning and with efforts to describe it accurately. This means rethinking many of the conventional ideas about education, even adult education, such as the requirements for learning: a classroom, a collection of students, a curriculum and a teacher. Adult education is still an emerging field of research and practice. Thirdly, when one uses the term participation, the approach to its meaning—enrollment versus engagement—must be made clear.

In summary it is recognized that while participation in adult education is an empirical fact, there are different points of view regarding the idea of participation. Depending on how one believes that the learning process takes place, the rate of participation in adult education in Canada varies from a discouraging low level (20%) to an encouragingly high level (90%). Whatever one's point of view, however, behind these statistics are the participants, and it is helpful to appreciate their individual circumstances.

---

[12] A. Tough, "Major Learning Efforts: Recent Research and Future Directions" *Adult Education* (U.S.A.), 1978, *28*, pp. 250–263.

[13] A. Tough, *The Adult's Learning Projects*, p. 1.

The Idea of Participants

Who exactly is a participant in adult education? It is interesting when walking down a busy street or riding on the public transit to speculate on whether individual adults one encounters are participants, and what might be the subject of their learning interest. Initially by way of intuition, and more recently by way of surveys and research, a fair amount of knowledge has been gained about participants and their motivations for learning. Using the enrollment approach, these are the twenty per cent recorded in the Statistics Canada Adult Education Survey and from whom information has been gathered as to their reasons for participating. Of equal if not greater interest to the adult educator are the other eighty per cent, but our knowledge of this group is scant by comparison. It is easier to ask an adult who is participating why he or she chose to participate than to identify a non-participant and ask why he or she is not participating. Further, in the case of the non-participant it is difficult to determine whether he or she would in fact participate if the declared impediment to participation were to be removed.

One of the first questions which arises when determining who is a participant is what constitutes adult education. Is a thirty-year-old university graduate student a participant? Is an eighteen-year-old school dropout who is now enrolled in a high school completion program a participant? There is no categorical answer to these questions, rather it depends on the context of the question. In the two instances raised here both persons may be identified as adult learners by virtue of their age. Also both are accumulating a growing amount of life experiences, and these experiences influence their ways of thinking and provide them with an adult self concept. But because the university student is registered in the formal educational system, which is considered outside of adult education's purview, while the high school dropout is registered in a program sponsored by a school board's adult education department, administratively one will not be counted as an adult participant while the other will. In adult education, then, it is helpful to take a broad view of who is a participant. The motive for identifying a participant is not to draw a line of demarcation so as to arbitrarily separate participants as being either included or excluded. Instead the emphasis is on identifying the individual's circumstances, and using these to suggest that he or she is a participant. Three factors are used in determining an individual's circumstances so as to distinguish them as being a participant in adult education: age, psychological maturity, and social role.[14] Each will be examined in turn.

One apparently straightforward approach to identifying who can be considered as an adult participant would be to use the age separating youth from adult and suggest anyone who has achieved chronological adulthood is thereby automatically an adult participant. What, then, might be the age? Not too long ago in Canada and elsewhere the so called "age of majority" signifying adult status for

---

[14] C. Verner, "Definition of Terms," in *Adult Education: Outlines of an Emerging Field of University Study*, Jensen et al. (Eds.) (Washington, Adult Education Association of the USA, 1964).

such purposes as voting in national elections and purchasing liquor was twenty-one years. This arbitrary age has subsequently been lowered to eighteen years. At eighteen, however, an individual may already have taken on considerable responsibilities normally ascribed to adulthood, such as marriage, parenting and soldiering, and because of this it is usual to bestow adult status and privilege on the individual. Another approach, that of using the official school leaving age (usually 16 years), poses similar difficulties. Can we consider the significant numbers of students who remain in school beyond this age in order to complete their high school matriculation as suddenly being different, i.e. adult, and thus deserving of adjusted teaching methods? Such a suggestion would be totally impractical, just as the basis for it is fallacious. Age alone, therefore, is not a means of distinguishing an adult participant.

Psychological maturity refers to the point in time when the individual is prepared to assume responsibility for him or herself and at the same time assume a productive role in the community. Seen in these terms it is the individual's state of mind as evidenced by social maturity which indicates when the individual is prepared to enter adulthood. While every society has developed certain bench marks leading up to a complete acknowledgement of adulthood, e.g. ascribing legal adult status, granting privileges such as driving a car, and bestowing the right to vote, the total elapsed period for all this to come to pass may be several years. Thus an individual who considers him or herself to be an adult, and is accepting of adult responsibilities, should be so acknowledged and supported by the society, even though all the "rights of passage" might not yet have been attained.

The third factor is that of social roles. As this factor will be elaborated on shortly, for now the essence of the idea will suffice. Throughout life there are social roles appropriate to certain ages which individuals assume as they grow and develop. For example a child must learn to relate with other children of the same age. Somewhat later in life a young adult must learn to live with a marriage partner. There is a difference, however, in how the learning is acquired. Whereas a child for the most part learns about these social roles from teachers in the school and from parents in the home, for the adult the onus is on the individual to seek out other opportunities for learning about the social roles which they as adults are now assuming. Thus an adult participant is one who is assuming a social role appropriate to adulthood, and sets out to learn about it.

There have been two recent efforts in Canada at developing a working definition of an adult so as to enable the collection of participation data. In 1982, the Canadian Association for Adult Education (CAAE) and its francophone counterpart, the Institut canadien d'education des adultes (ICEA) commissioned a Gallup survey to examine the state of adult education and training in Canada, and they defined adult to include "all persons beyond the compulsory school attendance age in each Canadian jurisdiction who have interrupted their continuous attendance at an educational institution for a significant period of labour force participation or other activities."[15] Subsequently the Statistics Canada Adult Education Survey of 1984 defined adult participant as an individual 17 years and over who did not attend an educational institution full time, unless as a full-time student that person took a course, class or instruction on a part-time basis in addition to his or her full-time course load.[16] In terms of the three factors noted above, both definitions incorporate the age factor while only the CAAE/ICEA definition additionally implies the presence of the psychological maturity factor with its reference to labour force participation "or other activities." The Statistics Canada definition obscurely hints at the social role factor by its suggestion of a full-time student taking a course in addition to his or her course load. Neither definition is seen to be totally satisfactory as both of necessity employ arbitrary distinctions. For instance in the case of the CAAE/ICEA definition, all full-time students beyond compulsory school attendance age seem not to be adults for the purpose of adult participation statistics, even though they may participate outside of their full-time studies. In the case of the Statistics Canada Survey definition it suggests that a woman who returns to college after raising a family in order to complete a diploma program is not an adult participant. Both examples of exclusion are quite unsatisfactory and point to the limitations—and difficulties—in developing working definitions in adult education.

There is an approach to identifying an adult participant other than by using the factors of age, psychological maturity, and social role already noted, and that is to use the content and sponsorship of the education as the distinguishing criteria. Using the approach of formal, non-formal and informal education as presented in Chapter 1, the suggestion is that persons involved in—more precisely registered informal education are not considered as participating in adult education, even though they may unquestionably be considered as adult, as in the example of the middle aged woman returning to college to complete a diploma. The reasoning is that the formal education system has conditions which it imposes on students in order to award credentials, and that the various requirements which are a necessary part of academic conformity are incompatible with the tenets of adult education. For instance one of these conditions is that the student learn at a certain rate or else suffer consequences such as failing the course, being denied the certification, or being forced to withdraw. Adult education practice, by comparison, acknowledges that adult learners learn at varying rates and good practice makes provision for this without the consequence of failure, denial, or withdrawal. Adult education's purview, then, is seen as being with non-formal and informal education.

In some respects this distinction seems clear enough but it is certainly one which does not see the matter from the adult participant's point of view. By way of example, is an adult who registers full time in a community college's diploma

---

[15] CAAE/ICEA, *From the Adult's Point of View*, p. 4.

[16] Statistics Canada, *One in Every Five: A Survey of Adult Education in Canada*, p. 1.

program a different learner from another adult who registers for a course offered part time by the same community college through its continuing education department? From an administrative and even conceptual point of view the answer is "yes" while from the adult's point of view it is "no."

It is necessary to further understand this administrative arrangement because it is telling of adult education's status within the formal educational system, and thus the status of adult learners. It is the educational planners (be they policy makers, administrators or whoever is part of making the educational opportunity available to adults), who must plan and manage the formal educational system established for that society. Because resources for this purpose are finite and because the system needs to be coherent in order to best serve the society, it must be structured on an organized basis. For this system to function distinctions must be made so as to determine for whom it does and does not have legislated responsibility for providing education. Beyond this mandate the system can then determine who it does or does not desire to serve. Because for the most part the legislation governing the formal educational systems in the provinces does not provide for non-formal adult education, adult education has existed by and large on sufferance within these systems. Using the example above, the adult who is registered full-time is considered a bona fide student at the college while the adult who is registered in the continuing education course is distinguished as being a "participant."

In keeping with the formal educational system's need to define as a way of distinguishing, it will be helpful to now provide a definition of an adult participant. The definition is simple enough, and it is contained in a broader UNESCO definition of adult education adopted at its 19th Session held in Kenya in 1976.[17] This definition acknowledges that adulthood is a stage of social development, and the age at which this stage is attained by the individual varies from society to society. For this reason the definition remains open, and adult participants are defined as "persons regarded as adult by the societies to which they belong." By way of the content of their learning, these adults participate in the "entire body of organized educational processes, whatever the content, level and method, whether formal or otherwise, whether they prolong or replace initial education in schools, colleges and universities as well as in apprenticeship … " This definition would suggest that for the purpose of identifying an adult learner in Canada, the federal voting age of eighteen would be accepted as when society regards an individual as being an adult by way of enjoying full citizenship.

Before leaving the discussion on who is a participant, it is fair to suggest that adult participants have caused some difficulty for formal educational systems. Most often educational systems have sought to distinguish adult participants for reasons of exclusion or for separate treatment, e.g. the setting of academic admission requirements or the charging of cost recovery fees. The paucity of legis-

---

[17] UNESCO, "Recommendation on the Development of Adult Education" (Ottawa, Canadian Commission for UNESCO, nd).

lation recognizing adult learning needs is one indication of the difficulty which adult education poses for the formal educational system. As a consequence adult education's frequently described marginal status as viewed by the formal educational system is often visited upon the adult participant, or would-be participant.

Having answered the question of who is an adult participant from various perspectives the next question to raise is, "Why do adults participate?" (See also Chapter 2 for a discussion on the functions of adult education.) The common conception about education is that it is something one does during the early part of life in order to then get on with the business of living. "First learn, then earn" has been viewed as the logical life sequence upon which educational systems are built. Indeed while attending school, college or university the goal of attending is typically described as being to "complete" one's education or to be "finished with school." With these limiting notions in mind, the fact that adults choose to continue their education understandably raises the curiosity of those who observe the phenomenon. Because this phenomenon is neither recent nor incidental, however, and because the curiosity of researchers and theorists have been piqued and their findings publicized, it is possible to interpret the motivations of participating adults. This interpretation is contained in the adult education literature on motivation, and it is by studying motivation that a clearer picture emerges of learning's pervasive influence on the lives of adults.[18]

Motivation to Participate

As human beings, adults are motivated by needs, wants and desires. There is a considerable degree of conformity among adults in the objects of these three motivators, as well as some individuality. For many the strength of the motivation is not sufficient to bring about action on the part of the individual, while for others their motivation leads to, in the case of adult education, participation. By simply being attuned to the normal circumstances of adulthood and the influences of socioeconomic conditions, it is possible for an adult educator to determine what are compelling needs, wants and desires which are likely to solicit a participatory response by at least some adults.

A particular set of assumptions about the learning needs of individuals has been gathered together under the heading of andragogy, meaning the art and science of helping adults learn. The term andragogy has been championed by Malcolm Knowles to juxtapose it with the term pedagogy, meaning the art and science of teaching children. In his acclaimed book, *The Modern Practice of Adult Education*, Knowles identifies four assumptions of andragogy, one of which describes adults' readiness to learn.[19]

---

[18] See for example R. Wlodkowski, *Enhancing Adult Motivation To Learn* (San Francisco, Jossey-Bass, 1985) and P. Cross, *Adults As Learners: Increasing Participation and Facilitating Learning* (San Francisco, Jossey-Bass, 1981).

[19] Malcolm Knowles, *The Modern Practice of Adult Education* (2nd ed.) (Chicago, Follett Publishing Co., 1980) p. 43.

Adults are aware of specific learning needs generated by real life tasks or problems. Adult education programs, therefore should be organized around "life application" categories and sequenced according to learners' readiness to learn.

This readiness to learn refers to the learning needs of adults as they develop through their adult life. Adult education as a field of practice has been greatly influenced by developmental psychology, and an understanding of it can provide insights into why adults learn.

One of the earliest proponents of the relationship between developmental psychology and adult learning was Robert Havighurst.[20] Havighurst identified and sequenced what he called the "developmental tasks" of childhood and adulthood, and suggested that these tasks are faced in turn by the individual as he or she grows in age and maturity. Havighurst believed that in order to meet the demands of each developmental task, learning was required, and that this need for learning gave rise to a "teachable moment," i.e. when a person is most receptive to learning information and skills pertaining to the particular task. Havighurst further indicated the importance of successfully achieving each developmental task in order for the individual to contend with life in a satisfying manner.

There are three periods of adult life identified by Havighurst which contain developmental tasks appropriate to that life period. These are:

Early Adulthood, ages 18–30
- selecting a mate
- learning to live with a marriage partner
- starting a family
- rearing children
- managing a home
- getting started in an occupation
- taking on civic responsibility
- finding a congenial social group

Middle Age, ages 30–55
- achieving adult civic and social responsibility
- establishing and maintaining an economic standard of living
- assisting teen-age children to become responsible and happy adults
- developing adult leisure time activities
- relating to one's spouse as a person
- accepting and adjusting to the physiological changes of middle age
- adjusting to aging parents

Later Maturity, age 55 and over
- adjusting to decreasing physical strength and health
- adjusting to retirement and reduced income
- adjusting to the death of a spouse

---

[20] R. Havighurst, *Developmental Tasks and Education* (3rd ed.) (New York, McKay, 1972).

- establishing an explicit affiliation with one's age group
- meeting social and civic obligations
- establishing satisfactory physical living arrangements

In addition, Havighurst identified ten social roles which adults might assume during adulthood, namely: worker, mate, parent, home maker, son or daughter of aging parents, citizen, friend, organization member, religious affiliate, and user of leisure time. As an individual moves through the three phases of adult life there is adjustment in the carrying out of these social roles, and this gives rise to additional developmental tasks.

Other writers have built on this notion of developmental tasks in an effort to increase their knowledge of what the learning needs of adults are at stages of their adulthood, and what are the implications of these learning needs for adult education practice. For example Alan Knox's book titled, *Adult Development and Learning* is subtitled, "A Handbook on Individual Growth and Competence in the Adult Years for Education and the Helping Professions."[21] Because of this enhanced understanding of adult learning needs, adult educators are in a better position to anticipate what adults are most likely to want and need to learn, and why. A simple example will illustrate this point. A young couple wishing to get married has the opportunity to attend a marriage preparation course covering such topics as finances, inter-personal communication, and family planning. The course has been developed to deal with the nuptial issues the couple is now facing. Later on, after several years of marriage, the couple might well attend a parenting course in order to strengthen their relationship with teenage children. Much later yet, one marriage partner might need to join a support group concerned with caring for a loved one who suffers from Alzheimer's disease.

Arguably the most lucid thinking on the question of why adults participate is that of Cyril Houle. In his book, *The Inquiring Mind*, Houle identified three major types of adult learners on the basis of their motivational orientation to learning: the goal oriented, the activity oriented, and the learning oriented.[22] According to Houle the goal oriented are those who use education in order to accomplish fairly clear cut objectives, for example a person wishing to advance within his or her work situation. The activity oriented are those who partake because they find in the circumstances of learning a meaning which has no necessary connection, and often no connection at all, with the content or announced purposes of the activity. This recognizes that many persons participate in continuing education courses, for example, because they provide a break from routine and an opportunity to meet new people. The learning oriented are those

---

[21] A. Knox, *Adult Development and Learning* (San Francisco, Jossey-Bass, 1981).

[22] C. Houle, *The Inquiring Mind* (Madison, University of Wisconsin Press, 1961).

who seek knowledge for its own sake. Such persons are often described as having a thirst for knowledge because of the satisfaction it brings to them.

Houle constructed his typology on the basis of extensive interviews with twenty-two acknowledged continuing learners. Since reporting his findings in 1961, there has been considerable further investigation by other researchers to corroborate and elaborate on Houle's conclusions.[23] While others have indeed elaborated on the categories none have surpassed the clarity of Houle's typology, with its readily identifiable categories.

Houle's conclusions as to motivational orientation to learning are compatible with the engagement approach to adult learning. Another effort at determining motivational orientation, in this case consistent with the enrollment approach, is the 1984 Statistics Canada Adult Education Survey. Its findings are based on data which have been subjected to statistical analysis. Whereas Houle deduced his typology from the interviews which he conducted, the Adult Education Survey's findings were simply reported, leaving any deduction up to the user of the data. It is interesting to note that while both efforts are subject to criticism for their respective methodological shortcomings, each provides additional insight into the complex and highly personal realm of individual motivation.

The Adult Education Survey questioned participants as to their motive for participating, using five motivational categories: (1) academic, (2) job related, (3) personal development/general interest, (4) hobby/craft/recreation and, (5) other. (It will be recalled that these participants were not attending an educational institution full-time, rather they were part-time learners.) Included in each category were the following topics: "academic" referred to courses taken at a high school, college, or university for credit toward a diploma, certificate or degree; "job related" referred to courses which provide skills applicable to either the job held by the participant or for a prospective job; "personal development/general interest" referred to courses which are taken for the benefit or interest they provide to the participant without that person wanting to accumulate credits leading to some form of certification; "hobby/craft/recreation" referred to courses taken as a leisure pursuit by the participant, e.g. photography, woodworking. (It was possible to include job related topics in this category if the participant's motivation was leisure oriented, not job related); "other" referred to courses which did not reasonably fit into one of the four specified categories, e.g. marriage preparation. Table 1 shows the percentages of total number of participants for type of course taken.

This data has been analyzed using variables such as age, gender, educational attainment, mother tongue, place of birth, the respondent's employment status, and the institutional provider of the instruction. (The data has also been prepared

---

[23] For corroboration see R. Boshier, "Motivational Orientations of Adult Education Participants: A Factor Analytic Exploration of Houle's Typology" *Adult Education* (U.S.A.) *21* 2 (1971) and for elaboration see Morstain and Smart, "Reasons for Participating in Adult Education Courses: A Multivariate Analysis of Group Differences" *Adult Education* (U.S.A.) *24* 2 (1974).

Table 1: Adult Education Survey: Percentages of total number of participants for type of course

Job related	41%
Personal development/general interest	23%
Hobby/craft/recreation	20%
Academic	12%
Other	2%
Don't know/not stated	1%

for each province.) When so analyzed the data becomes more revealing, for example in the case of gender 57% of the men who participated took job related courses compared with only 28% of the women who participated. This is contrasted with the finding that 27% of the women participants took personal development/general interest courses compared with only 18% of the men. Interestingly enough, in the case of job related courses 56% of the men compared with 44% of the women had their fee paid by the employer.

Another example indicates that while 21% of Canadian adults have 0 to 8 years of education, only 4.7% of them participated. This is contrasted with the 10% of adults with a university degree, of whom 40.8% participated.

The survey's findings provide illuminating statistics which suggest some of the reasons why adults participate; however their use must be prefaced with caution. The specific findings are like a photograph in that they capture only a point in time and space and, like the lens of the camera, the survey questionnaire can only focus on a certain area. Thus the findings describe but one "episode" of participation, using definitions and parameters chosen by the researchers. It is possible to compensate for this by conducting the survey in a like manner on more than one occasion, as in a longitudinal study, so as to develop something like a motion picture. This allows for useful comparisons to be drawn which in turn permits more reasonable inferences to be made. Unfortunately such has not been the case with the Adult Education Survey. Nonetheless there has been sufficient research into motivation to enable the drawing of some conclusions.

In reviewing the literature on motivation to participate in adult education Rubenson came up with the following summary:[24]

- The strongest motives for participating are "work" and personal satisfaction.
- Typically about one third give personal satisfaction as their main reason for participation.

---

[24] K. Rubenson, "Barriers to Participation in Adult Education," Background Paper 4 prepared for the Report of the National Advisory Panel on Skill Development Leave, *Learning for Life* (Ottawa, Supply and Services Canada, 1984) p. 9.

- One powerful reason for participating is the desire to make practical use of the knowledge acquired.
- Preparation for new jobs are mainly emphasized by persons under 30 and by women in the process of changing from child care to gainful employment.
- Interest in job related goals begin to decline at age 30 and drops off sharply after age 50.
- Professionals and college graduates are more likely to be seeking advancement in present jobs than blue collar workers.
- Pensioners look for courses where they can acquire knowledge which will help them to adjust to their new role in society.
- Women working at home tend more than others to state that they participate to "get out of the rut" and "see new faces."
- Personal satisfaction is a stronger motive among the upper classes than among the lower.
- There is a steadily growing number of people taking courses for recreational reasons.

Barriers to Participation

Knowing why adults participate enables adult educators to better meet learning needs. Participants, however, are those who have acted on their motivation. Much more difficult to determine are the reasons why adults do not participate. While non-participants may be equally motivated by their circumstances as participants, and in some respects more so, for some reason or reasons they do not act on this motivation. One of the concerns of adult educators has been to identify and if possible remove these so called barriers to participation.

Just as studies have been conducted to determine what it is that motivates an adult to participate in adult education, similarly studies have been conducted in an attempt to determine why such a large percentage of adults—approximately 80% in Canada according to the Adult Education Survey—do not participate. The question is asked, "Is there some impediment, some barrier, to their being able to participate—or feeling inclined to participate?" Presumably if providers could determine the barrier(s) which stands in the way of participation, removal of the barrier would result in a measurable increase in participation figures. Thus considerable effort has gone into identifying these barriers and assessing their metaphorical height.

Before looking at the barriers to participation in adult education it is wise to introduce a caution. While indeed numerous barriers can be identified it is important to understand that there is not a simple "cause and effect" relationship between any one barrier and participation. To suggest that by simply removing a particular barrier, for example a substantial tuition fee, there will automatically result an oversubscription of a class is to ignore the intensely individual make up of voluntary action (in this case participation) on the part of the adult learner. Thus our understanding of non-participation must not be based on the assumption that all adults are eager to participate but for the fact that barriers stand in their way. As discussed earlier this notion of participation is based on the enrollment approach. According to the engagement approach, where studies have found participation rates ranging from 70% to 100%, adults are able to conduct their learning without necessarily needing to enroll. Expressed another way, it might well be that many adults simply prefer not to enroll and instead to be completely self-directed.

Research into non-participation has found that it is possible to divide barriers into three categories: situational, dispositional, and institutional.[25] The situational barriers are the circumstances of the potential learner and include such describable items as disposable income, means of transportation, and availability of child minding services. The dispositional barriers likewise belong to the learner, but in this case are a function of the individual's personality. Psychological factors such as fear of returning to the evaluative attention of a teacher, the feeling of intellectual inadequacy after being away from schooling for a long time, or a general disinterest in learning once a good job has been secured are three examples of dispositional barriers. The last category of barrier, institutional barriers, are those put up by the institutional sponsor of the learning activity. These barriers are not seen as being intentionally erected by the institution to discourage participation, rather they reflect the operating practices of the particular institution which have adverse consequences. Thus the decisions taken by the institution in offering an adult education course such as scheduling, class location, pre-requisites, instructor selection, etc., will for some potential participants become reasons for their not participating. Of the three barriers to participation, then, it is evident that "ownership" of the situational and dispositional barriers resides with the individual while the institutional barriers resides with the provider. Thus any attempts to lower these barriers to the point where participation is enabled requires understanding and communication between the non-participant and the provider.

The number of specific barriers which can be identified is endless, and hence the need for a grouping. As an indication of the more prominent barriers, the findings of the participation study undertaken by the CAAE and the ICEA are presented. These barriers were derived from a series of consultations with "persons who come from social groups known to experience difficulties when they seek to access learning opportunities from public institutions."[26] Out of these consultations emerged fourteen consistent themes:

1. financial aid policies which have the effect of discouraging learning by imposing penalties on recipients who enroll in courses, or where the financial aid in support of learning is inadequate

---

[25] See P. Cross, *Adults As Learners* (San Francisco, Jossey-Bass, 1981).

[26] CAAE/ICEA, *From the Adult's Point of View*, p. 11.

2. lack of coordination between referral agencies and educational institutions

3. lack of support systems such as orientation, counselling, child care and tutoring

4. lack of information on available courses

5. geographic barriers which discriminate against those in rural areas due to the concentration of educational opportunities in the urban centres

6. institutional practices which are incompatible with learner needs

7. fatigue experienced by part-time learners who have other activities

8. lack of time to engage in learning due to employment, family and personal reasons

9. attitudinal barriers either directed by others at the learner or felt from within which cause the learner to be sensitive about learning

10. fees and other costs

11. scheduling which is either inappropriate or which changes

12. employers' recruiting policies whereby unnecessary credential requirements are used as a screening device to employ young graduates in preference to retraining existing employees

13. residency requirements of universities for degree programs

14. reluctance of institutions, in the absence of academic credentials, to accredit an individual's life experiences as part of entrance requirements

15. curriculum and learning are often organized not with anxious learners in mind, but experienced learners.

Ten of the fifteen barriers can be seen as being institutional while three are situational (#s 5, 7, 8) and two are dispositional (#s 9 & 15).

Much can be made of these barriers and their detrimental influence on participation; however, they should be viewed contextually. At the beginning of this chapter an account of the institutionalizing of learning was presented, and the confining legacy it imposes on the idea of learning in our society and on the lives of individuals. What is lacking is a supportive educational framework which is designed to: (1) remove institutional barriers by eliminating adult education's marginal status; (2) remove situational barriers by providing access; and (3) remove dispositional barriers by uplifting the educational experience. Some of the work necessary for this lies with policy makers and their responsibility for resource allocation, but equally there is the need to develop a shared attitude within the society which views continued learning as central to individual and societal well-being.

The Idea of Providers

It is understandable that most people immediately associate adult education with "night school." After all, the use of grade schools in the evening has historically been the most apparent evidence of adults continuing with their education, and it now serves as a convenient stereotype. Two things, however, indicate that this conception is now misleading: (1) the proliferation of organizational sponsors which provide adult education at all times of the day and evening; and (2) our contemporary understanding of how adults satisfy their needs and interests in learning without necessarily resorting to the traditional classroom setting.

Adult education is now recognized as being sponsored by a large number of agencies and conducted in many settings, be they public lecture halls, workplace training facilities or the privacy of one's home. Thus in considering the providers of adult education it is important to distinguish the provider, i.e. the sponsoring agency, from the particular building in which the activity is conducted. With formal education the sponsor and the building most often go hand in hand, whereas that is not necessarily the case in adult education. Instead the important factor when describing the provider of adult education is the sponsoring agency. As an example, many school boards have converted former grade schools buildings which no longer serve a school age population into adult learning centres. The reason for this is to congregate many of the school board's multiplicity of adult education programs into one facility and offer them during the daytime as well as in the evening. To look at the particular institution, i.e. the building, one would rightly say it was devoted to adult education. The sponsoring agency, however, is a school board which was established with the primary purpose of meeting the learning needs of youth, and its adult education work is secondary to this primary purpose. It is likely that the adult learning centre has been funded with grant monies which, because they are not guaranteed in legislation, can be withdrawn with little notice. This is a different funding arrangement to the grade school system. Another example is the situation of a voluntary association utilizing the facilities of a church hall for its particular weekly program. The provider of the adult education activity is the voluntary organization, not the church.

No one organization is perceived to have jurisdiction over adult education's offerings, nor are its activities required to be conducted in a particular type of institution, for example an educational facility. An agency can be any organization that is involved in sponsoring opportunities for adult education, be it an educational institution, a voluntary association, an industrial concern, a public agency, or whatever.

It is also now accepted that many adults are capable of conducting independent learning projects of their own instigation, seeking assistance from an appropriate agency only if needed. Thus adults need not receive their education only through the auspices of some sponsoring organization. Furthermore, because adults have different learning needs at various stages of life, they will turn to different sources for assistance, as suggested by the particular learning need. Thus a vocational institute will provide upgrading in technical areas while an accounting firm will put on a workshop in pre-retirement financial planning. What is needed, then, is a way of identifying agencies which have a place in adult learning, be it through direct sponsorship of courses or through being considered a supporting resource for the self-directed learner.

Various typologies have been developed in an attempt to capture and categorize the number of organizations which sponsor or support adult education. The one developed by Schroeder[27] is an amalgam of several of these and identifies four types of agencies. These agency types are:

- Type I: Agencies established to serve the educational needs of adults—adult education is a central function. Agencies of this type are not numerous when compared with the number concerned with the educational needs of youth; however the number is growing. Type 1 agencies typically have a specific adult "market" which they are serving. Schroeder identifies proprietary schools (e.g. business schools, correspondence schools and technical schools such as are listed in the Yellow Pages of the telephone directory under "schools") and independent residential and non-residential adult education centres (e.g. Banff Centre, Frontier College, and the Justice Institute of B.C.) as being of this type.

- Type II: Agencies established to serve the educational needs of youth which have assumed the added responsibility of at least partially serving the educational needs of adults—adult education is a secondary function. Agencies of this type are the ones most often identified with adult education, and for the most part are publicly funded (even though their adult education offerings are to a large degree dependent on user fees). Examples include public schools, community colleges and universities, each with their adult and continuing education divisions or departments.

- Type III: Agencies established to serve both educational and non-educational needs of the community—adult education is an allied function employed to fulfil only some of the needs which these agencies recognize as their responsibility. This type constitutes a significant number of agencies, e.g. libraries, museums and public health clinics, and many of these recognize the need to educate in a specific area in order to achieve their particular purpose, e.g. public health.

- Type IV: Agencies established to serve the special interests (economic, ideological) of special groups—adult education is a subordinate function employed primarily to further the special interests of the agency itself. There is a vast amount of adult education that is conducted by such agencies, e.g. churches, advocacy groups, voluntary associations, labour organizations, business and industry. Schroeder suggests that agencies of this type are generally concerned with adult education "to

---

[27] W. Schroeder, "Adult Education Defined and Described," in Smith et al. (Eds.), *Handbook of Adult Education* (New York: Macmillan, 1970).

the extent that such education contributes to the effectiveness of the agency in fulfilling its primary purpose ... "[28]

Schroeder's typology serves as a helpful means of differentiating among the numerous sponsoring agencies, and equally it demonstrates the diverse nature of adult education when analyzed according to sponsorship. This diverse nature also indicates the extent to which education is utilized by numerous agencies to promote individual, community and special interests. Adult education does not have a distinct institutional presence in the community, nor is there an institutional hierarchy as in the case of the formal educational system, with its elementary, secondary, college and university institutions. Nonetheless adult education does have a pervasive presence.

Schroeder's typology represents a classical approach to understanding providers of adult education, centring as it does on sponsoring agencies. This typology does not, however, account for self-directed learning, although it is understood that all agency types are available to the self-directed learner (subject of course to institutional policies which may limit accessibility). More recently another schema has been proposed in a new attempt to make coherent the diversity of providers of adult education, and this schema does take into account the self-directed learner.[29] Described by its originator, Jerold Apps, as a framework of providers of adult and continuing education, this classification system places the adult learner rather than agencies at the centre of its consideration. In graphically presenting the framework by way of circles containing the providers types, Apps places the adult learner in a circle at the centre of the diagram and stems the four provider types outwards from there. The four types are: tax supported agencies, non-profit agencies, for-profit agencies, and non-organized learning opportunities. Apps indicates that the framework "is based on the assumption that adult learners have choices for learning opportunities—a long-standing characteristic of the adult education field."[30] He also acknowledges the existence in some areas of mandatory continuing education, for example continuing education within some professional groups, but this does not detract from the framework as formulated. As for the self-directed learner, Apps suggests all four provider categories are available to the learner (also subject to institutional policies).

The provider types are described briefly as follows. Tax supported providers are those agencies and institutions which are fully or partially tax-supported and include educational agencies, correctional institutions, libraries, museums, etc. Non-profit providers are self-supporting agencies and institutions typically associated with the voluntary sector and including professional organizations. For-

---

[28] W. Schroeder, "Adult Education Defined and Described," p. 37.

[29] J. Apps, "Providers of Adult and Continuing Education: A Framework," in Merriam and Cunningham, (Eds.), *Handbook of Adult and Continuing Education* (San Francisco, Jossey-Bass, 1989).

[30] J. Apps, "Providers of Adult and Continuing Education: A Framework," p. 279.

profit providers encompass those companies whose adult education work is sustained by the profit motive and include the obvious proprietary and correspondence schools as well as conference centres, computer software publishers and workshop facilitators. Non-organized learning opportunities as a provider type is understood to be open ended, and this acknowledges that it is the self-directed learner who selects the provider. By way of illustration of this provider type, Apps includes television viewing and the other mass media, the work setting, and travel and leisure time activities.

Apps' effort to organize providers by way of a systematic framework rather than a classification schema which employs selection criteria (as evident in Schroeder's agency specific typology) is an attempt to reflect, as he suggests, "the situation of adult education in North America in the late 1980s."[31] Thus for Apps the providers of educational opportunities for adults are conceptualized as being all inclusive as opposed to being selective and include agencies, organizations, services, individuals, or simply the learning opportunity itself, however provided. Particularly noteworthy for Apps is the amount of adult learning opportunity made available by the for-profit providers, especially as its growth is an indication of successful entrepreneurial efforts to meet adult learning needs and wants. He concludes his conceptualizing by noting that, "We are entering a new era in adult education, and we must change our thinking about the way it is organized."[32]

It is interesting how the categorical aspect of both Schroeder's and Apps's typologies are being eroded by developments in formal education. Even though the categories as designated were intended more to be instructive than to be mutually exclusive, nevertheless a number of trends have appeared which are transforming perceptions and blurring delineations. The most significant trend is towards acceptance by the formal education system of the notion of lifelong learning. The belief that one can be educated for a lifetime within the first twenty years or so of one's life no longer prevails as a defensible idea in formal education. From the point of view of the individual, the rapidity, extent and omnipresence of change have virtually eliminated the grounds for being complacent about learning beyond one's formal education. For example, in the modern era a worker will likely experience more than one career change within the space of a working life, and each change will prompt a need for new learning. As part of this trend, a rather bewildering number of vocations now require educational certification, and this virtually compels an individual to enroll in upgrading programs of one sort or another with each career move. The outgrowth of this trend to lifelong learning by formal education institutions, and especially as driven by job related considerations, has been a re-orientation of emphasis by some agency types.

---

[31] J. Apps, "Providers of Adult and Continuing Education: A Framework," p. 280.

[32] J. Apps, "Providers of Adult and Continuing Education: A Framework," p. 285.

The Type II agencies of Schroeder's typology (agencies established to serve the educational needs of youth which have assumed the added responsibility of at least partially serving the educational needs of adults) have experienced the greatest developments in adult education. As an example community colleges, which initially were construed as an alternative to university at the post-secondary level for high school graduates, i.e. youth, have assumed a considerable adult education orientation and thus in certain aspects correspond more to a Type I agency (agencies established to serve the educational needs of adults). Indications of this shift by community colleges include the amending of registration criteria in credit programs to allow for a mature student category and the advertising in the media of their programs, promoting as they do for adults to return to college to enhance their career opportunities. Certainly the provision of distance education by agencies dedicated to this purpose such as Athabasca University in Alberta and the Open Learning Agency in British Columbia particularly accommodates the adult learner.

Another development in formal education concerns public funding. The Type II agencies are understood to be included in Apps's tax supported category. Apps notes, however, that the public funding of adult education is not secure by way of legislative enactment, as is the case with grade school education. In many cases adult education which is provided by a tax supported agency, e.g. a school board, is increasingly having to pay its own way, thereby diminishing the extent to which adult education is tax supported.

There are two other developments which blur the distinctions among provider types, institutional brokering and institutional collaboration. The brokering idea in education borrows from the free enterprise practice of an individual or company acting as an agent of exchange between two parties. In this case, however, it is not always necessary that there be the usual fee-for-service payed to the broker. In the Saskatchewan community college model, where the college was conceived of as an administrative entity and not as an educational facility, the college's function was to broker with other agencies, both educational and community based, for the delivery of courses, including adult education courses. These courses were intended to meet learning needs as identified from within the community. This represents brokering on a provincial scale. On a smaller scale brokering often takes place in instances where an educational institution arranges for another institution or organization to deliver instruction on behalf of a group of learners. This often occurs when, for example, an industry or community agency with a corporate learning need will turn to a local continuing education department of a school board or university and ask that it arrange for a particular program of another organization to be presented.

Among educational institutions there is also a trend to collaboration which goes beyond simple co-operation. In this case two or more institutions will formally agree to provide some service or program in combination with each other. An example is in British Columbia where the Open University of the Open Learning Agency is a consortium of three universities: the University of Victoria,

Simon Fraser University and the University of British Columbia. By way of this collaboration an adult learner is able to earn a baccalaureate degree from the Open University, having taking courses from all three universities. Another illustration is where a community agency will collaborate with an educational institution for the delivery of a course of studies at the facilities of the community agency. This often occurs where it is apparent the learners would not attend the course at the educational institution but are receptive to it being offered at the community agency. There are numerous examples of this in the area of literacy instruction and also with homogeneous groups of learners, e.g. Native peoples, who identify with their own surroundings rather than with those of the dominant culture as represented by the educational institution.

These trends which are taking place within many of the providers are symptomatic of the fact there is no assigned institutional form for adult education. As long as adult learning needs continue to be identified and met, whether prescriptively or instinctively, there will always be variations among providers. In Canada the lead role among providers has evolved initially from the voluntary sector to, second, the formal education sector and now increasingly to, third, the employer sector. At the same time, however, the importance to adult education is not that there be any dominant provider group but rather that there remain an assortment of providers, each addressing particular learning needs in a fashion helpful to the learners.

A categorizing of agencies which provides a comparison of "market share" among providers is presented in the Adult Education Survey where, rather than utilizing a conceptualization of providers as in Schroeder's typology, there is a simple grouping of agencies most associated with providing adult education. This basis is not very instructive as a number of agencies are grouped like strange bedfellows or else are grouped in an all encompassing category. The findings, however, are helpful, particularly in the case of the agencies which enjoy a category unto themselves. The nine categories are: (1) employers, (2) union and professional associations, (3) universities, (4) colleges, (5) school boards, (6) private schools, i.e. proprietary schools, (7) churches, (8) voluntary organizations, and (9) libraries.

In terms of comparisons between provinces and within Canada, the findings for the providers must be viewed in light of the provincial circumstance.[33] This differs from the participation findings which have national as well as provincial significance when used for comparative purposes. For example, at the time of the Adult Education Survey Nova Scotia did not have a community college system (although there were some colleges) and it was the school boards which were identified as being the most significant providers of adult education in that province. In Saskatchewan, by contrast, it was the community college system as created in the early 1970s which was identified as providing the greatest amount of adult education. In Alberta, where there is a system of Further Education

---

[33] See Chapter 7.

Councils which works to rationalize the program offerings of agencies within a given area so as to avoid duplication, no one provider dominated. The findings of the Adult Education Survey reflected these provincial differences. The school board provision in Nova Scotia was 25% of all courses taken by adults, in Saskatchewan 2% and in Alberta 11%. College provision was 6% in Nova Scotia, 27% in Saskatchewan and 17% in Alberta. The combined total of school board and community college provision was, however, comparable in all three provinces—Nova Scotia 31%, Saskatchewan 29% and Alberta 28%.[34]

We have already seen how participation in adult education is for the most part a voluntary act, and how for each individual the act of participating is determined by the interaction of several variables—some quite personal (situational, dispositional), others within the control of providing agencies (institutional). The providers of adult education, however, are seen as being very much instrumental to participation, appealing as they do to the learning needs and interests of adults. For this reason in adult education there has always been a widespread interest in providers, whose goals are to serve learning needs in helpful, often creative ways. In Canada, a country with a small population and a short history, there have been and continue to be a remarkable number of agencies providing noteworthy programs, and much of the record of adult education is related by way of accounts of these agencies.[35]

Up to this point the discussion of participation, participants and providers has dealt with these ideas in mainly inanimate terms. Of course nothing could be further from the fact of the matter: adult education is full of passion. Participants are understood as being human beings with learning needs unique to their individual situations. Providers are not inorganic edifices but rather vital organizations created with purposes sympathetic to adult learners. And participation is understood as being an adult behaviour driven by learning needs and desires which are very much part of the human condition. The dispassionate view develops, however, as it becomes necessary to bring some organization to our understanding of participation for purposes such as conceptualizing the phenomenon for study and advocating to government for financial support. The next chapter, Elements of Design in Programs, presents several illustrations of programs where it is the passion in adult education which is clearly evident as contrasted with the statistical and categorical presentation of participation.

---

[34] Statistics Canada, *One in Every Five: A Survey of Adult Education in Canada.*

[35] For descriptions of various providers and their programs in Canada there are three useful overviews: J.R. Kidd (Ed.), *Adult Education in Canada* (Toronto, Canadian Association for Adult Education, 1950); J.R. Kidd (Ed.), *Learning and Society* (Toronto, Canadian Association for Adult Education, 1963); and Kidd and Selman (Eds.), *Coming of Age: Canadian Adult Education in the 1960s* (Toronto, Canadian Association for Adult Education, 1978). In the U.S. the American Association of Adult and Continuing Education and its predecessor, the Adult Education Association of the USA, have published at intervals of approximately ten years (1934, 1936, 1948, 1960, 1970, 1990) handbooks on the study and practice of adult education, and each has a section devoted to describing agencies. Darkenwald and Merriam have a useful chapter on agencies and programs in *Adult Education: Foundations of Practice* (New York, Harper and Row, 1982).

Having now examined in turn the three central ideas of participation, participants and participants and providers, it becomes clear that in both the study and practice of adult education it is participation which is the underlying phenomenon. It is through participation that adults and agencies are linked for the satisfaction of personal learning needs and the carrying out of agency missions. Adult learners seek out agencies and agencies both receive and seek out adult learners. Whereas in youth education the link between the learner and the providing agency is fixed and is described as attendance, in adult education there are innumerable motivational influences at play in creating a participation link between learner and agency. Further, the nature of the participation link is specific to each situation, whether it be the borrowing of a book from the library or an interactive educational TV program via satellite technology.

The goal in adult education is generally understood to be participation by all adults so they may derive meaning in their lives and contribute to the well-being of their communities.[36] Both learner and agency are seen as being active in this effort to bring about participation, as is government through policy initiatives such as employment training. The continued interest by adult educators in the three central ideas of participation recognizes that there is still much to be learned and much to be done in order to reach the goal. Enabling non-participants is the single most important objective in attaining the goal, and for this reason it is necessary that adult educators maintain a perspective on the two approaches to participation outlined earlier. Taking the engagement approach and considering the research findings that the vast majority of adults are engaged in self-directed learning, the argument can be made that the existing provision for adult education must be adequate and that individual adults are apparently quite capable of meeting their own learning needs. This argument is obviously very attractive from a politician's point of view when it comes to allocating budget resources. And yet common sense indicates that with five million adult Canadians functionally illiterate, as determined by a survey in 1987,[37] there must be a very large number of adults who would find it difficult if not impossible to participate in adult education. For these adults alone, not to mention those with other compelling circumstances, government must be involved in making participation possible. When seen in this light, the concept of participation also becomes a matter of public policy.

For adult educators, then, participation is a key concept which must be seen from more than one viewpoint, as it is subject to interpretation. Participation is the dynamic facet of adult education which prompts research by academics and

---

[36] For example see UNESCO, *Recommendation on the Development of Adult Education* (Ottawa, Canadian Commission for UNESCO, nd) and John Lowe, *The Education of Adults: A World Perspective* (Toronto, O.I.S.E. Press, 1975), Chapter 1, "Changing Ideas and Functions."

[37] This was the finding of the Southam Literacy Survey and was reported in several Canadian newspapers. These articles have been collected in a booklet published by Southam News titled *Broken Words* (Toronto, Southam Inc, nd).

conjecture by practitioners as to what brings it about and what stands in its way. The fact of participation has inspired the creation of many distinctive providers of adult education, and it has resulted in untold numbers of adults being helped in the conduct of their lives. What is clear is that participation for participation's sake is not sufficient in adult education. There must be a purposefulness worthy of the involvement of the various stakeholders identified at the beginning of this chapter. The next chapter examines various elements of design in adult education programs which acknowledge this need for purposefulness.

S

Elements of Design in Programs

The most conspicuous aspect of adult education is its programs. Programs are regularly promoted in all the media as well as advertised in special catalogues, and they are conducted in any number of locations and at times throughout the day and well into the evening. Those who participate in programs talk about them with family, friends and co-workers. Not infrequently some form of action will result from a program which draws the attention of the wider community, for example neighbourhood watch programs for deterring crime. Some programs have even become so established as to have their own physical presence in the community—such as religious education centres attached to churches.

Most adults come to adult education by way of participating in some form of organized program. Providers such as school boards, recreation departments, private organizations, voluntary associations, businesses, churches, universities and libraries, to name but a few, offer innumerable programs in a myriad of formats. One can register for a class, attend a public lecture, enroll in a correspondence course, join in a study group, organize a reading program, and so on: the opportunities and options are many and varied.

This chapter is concerned with the idea of program in adult education, and is divided into two sections. The first section presents the main conceptual ideas associated with programs and briefly describes how they are planned. In the second section a number of elements of program design are highlighted by way of examples. The underlying belief expressed by this chapter's organization is that adult educators must draw from two sources when involved in program planning. There is what Knowles calls the "technology of adult education," that is the processes and procedures which have been devised to create programs which meet the needs and interests of adults.[1] There is also, however, the wealth of information and inspiration to be found in examining programs which in either the present or the past have proven successful.

The Concept of Program

Program is the basic unit of organized participation in adult education. It describes the bringing together of resources, no matter how modest or elaborate,

---

[1] M. Knowles, *The Modern Practice of Adult Education* (2nd edition) (Chicago, Follett, 1980) p. 130.

in order to facilitate learning. The participation is said to be organized by virtue of the fact someone besides the learner has been involved in planning the participation, and this involvement has resulted in a program being developed. There is a great spectrum of possibilities when considering what might be described as programs, from a reading program developed by a librarian in discussion with a borrower to a province-wide hunter awareness program conducted by a government department. There are no specifications for what constitutes a program other than the existence of a learning need or interest which has caused resources in support of the learning need to be purposefully brought together by an organizer. It is this learning purpose, then, which distinguishes an adult education program from a purely recreational or social program.

Despite the apparent generality surrounding programs in adult education a few basic elements begin to emerge. Learning is the focus of a program. There is a degree of organization to a program as provided by an organizer. Some resources are necessary for the learning to occur (e.g. facilities, instructor). And there needs to be participation in order to make the program viable. These four basic elements of program, then, are present in all adult education programs and they only grow by a matter of degree as programs take on greater complexity.[2] As well, programs with greater complexity in their design will undoubtedly have additional elements associated with them. Thus just as in Chapter 4 participation was seen as being the underlying phenomenon in adult education, in this chapter program is identified as being the basic learning arrangement.[3] As such, programs hold a particular fascination in adult education, and for a number of good reasons.

One reason is that there are no prescribed formats in adult learning, although there are a number of formats which have proven successful over the years. Thus the planner or planners of a program typically have several possibilities open for their consideration, and this allows for creative planning. Another reason is that adult education is viewed as being a positive force in society, and programs are adult education's main mechanism for contributing to a better society. A third reason is that programs are not the property of any one or a few organizations; rather, a multitude of organizations are involved in conducting programs. A fourth reason appreciates that organizing and conducting successful programs calls for a broad range of abilities and talents on the part of the planner or planners. Lastly there is the recognition that programs tell the observer some things about the organization offering the program, such as its purpose, its philosophy and its resourcefulness. After all, organizations are best understood as the means by which humans are able to collectively address themselves to some

---

[2] Brookfield identifies three features to program: purpose, order and finiteness. S. Brookfield, *Understanding and Facilitating Adult Learning* (San Francisco, Jossey-Bass, 1986) p. 204.

[3] For a detailed overview of the concept of program see Alan Thomas, "The Concept of Program" in Jensen, Liveright and Hallenbeck (Eds.), *Adult Education: Outlines of an Emerging Field of University Study* (Washington, Adult Education Association of the U.S.A., 1964).

mutually agreed purpose. The next aspect of program, then, is bringing some sense of coherence to the array of programs which have developed over the years.

There are two approaches that can be taken in attempting to bring understanding to the array of adult education programs. The first approach is to develop a system for classifying all programs and the second is to identify a number of bases which are helpful in distinguishing among programs while at the same time not attempting to be inclusive. The first approach is useful both from an instructive point of view and as a means of portraying the field of adult education through, for example, comparative surveys of participation in types of programs. The second approach is useful when one is expediently describing a program by distinguishing what it is from what it is not, e.g. a credit program from a non-credit program, or simply identifying it for what it is, e.g. a university extension program. This second approach acknowledges that most people have a general understanding of the common adult education program types.

As for the first approach, then, the classic conceptualization of the field is based on how participants are organized into programs.[4] This scheme recognizes how the natural pattern of human organization fits with the experience in adult learning, namely that adults can learn individually, they can learn in groups (small and large), and they can learn within the context of the whole community. Thus in adult education programs are developed which organize learners into: (1) individual programs, e.g. home study, computer assisted instruction; (2) group programs, e.g. classes, workshops, conferences; and (3) community programs, e.g. programs which take in the scope of an entire community as in the case of a community development project. These categories, then, of individual, group and community are the three formats for organizing programs.[5] This represents the organizational system for classifying programs. Another system is to use the content of the program.

The 1984 Statistics Canada Adult Education Survey provides a good example of an effort to classify programs on the basis of their content. For the purpose of this survey five categories were identified: (1) academic; (2) job-related; (3) personal development/general interest; (4) hobby/craft/recreation; and (5) other. The categories were defined as follows:

> Academic courses refer to those taken at a high school, college or university for credit toward a diploma, certificate or degree. Job-related courses are defined as those which provide skills applicable either to the job participants held or a job which they wished to qualify. Included in this category are courses in such areas as word processing, computer programming, auto mechanics, and TV repair. Hobby/craft/recreation courses cover leisure pursuits such as wood-

---

[4] Verner and Booth, *Adult Education* (New York, Centre for Applied Research in Education, 1964).

[5] The term originally given by Verner to this classification was "method." Knowles preferred the term "format." For a discussion on this see M. Knowles, *The Modern Practice of Adult Education* (1980), p. 131.

working, pottery, painting, photography, cooking, and sewing. Job-related subjects can also fall into this group if the participant's motivation was leisure-oriented. Personal development/general interest courses refer to classes in history, music appreciation, etc., and academic courses taken on an unstructured basis (as distinct from accumulating credits toward a diploma, certificate or degree). The final type of course—the catch-all "other" category—comprises training that does not fit neatly into one of the foregoing groups. Included here are marriage preparation, prenatal instruction, driver-training, first aid, etc.[6]

It can be seen that this content classification, while initially appearing quite reasonable, has inherent problems when faced with particular situations. For one, the fifth category of "other" is seen as an unsatisfactory way of accounting for a significant number of different programs. For another the categories are not mutually exclusive. It is instead the respondent's perception of the program which determines the category. Take, for example, a university course in art history. For the part-time student working toward a degree the course could be categorized as academic. For an art gallery worker the course could be job related. And for a retired person seeking more knowledge of art the course could be general interest.[7] It should also be noted that there are other program category descriptors besides the ones used in the Statistics Canada Survey that are commonly used to capture program groupings including liberal adult education, religious education, public affairs, and home and family life education. Attempting to group programs by content is thus seen as a difficult proposition, given the variety of programs in adult education and the perceptions of what they are as seen by the participants.

Another approach to this program categorization is to examine the content by way of the adult education function it is believed to serve. Using Bryson's five functions (as discussed in Chapter 2) the content categories in this case would be remedial, vocational/occupational, relational, liberal and political. In this approach, however, it is someone other than the participant who is designating a program as one or the other category. As pointed out, participants very often take the same course for different reasons.

Another possibility is to use the predominant learning domain to which the content is directed, be it the cognitive domain (i.e. learning information, intellectual skills and problem-solving strategies), the affective domain (i.e. interests, attitudes, values, beliefs), or the psychomotor domain (i.e. motor skills). This system is more difficult in that it is often the case that a program will deal equally with cognitive and affective learning—for example a public affairs program which attempts to help people form a reasoned attitude on an issue by presenting factual information.

---

[6] Statistics Canada, *One in Every Five: A Survey of Adult Education in Canada* (Ottawa, Ministry of Supply and Services Canada, 1985) p. 19.

[7] This example is taken from Dampier and Stalker-Costin, "Adult Education in British Columbia: A Discussion of the Statistics Canada Adult Education Survey" in Jindra Kulich (Ed.), *Advocacy for Adult Education in British Columbia* (Vancouver, Pacific Association for Continuing Education, 1988) p. 22.

From the above examples it can be seen that different approaches can be taken to the classifying of adult education programs. There is no one schema that can be used for all purposes and instead it is necessary to know the purpose for which the classification is intended. As well it is necessary to know from whose perspective the program categories will be selected—that of the adult education theorist/researcher or that of the participant.

The second approach to understanding program types does not attempt to be inclusive by way of a classification scheme but rather distinguishes or identifies a program on a commonly understood basis. The example above used the basis of a credential to distinguish credit programs from non-credit programs. This basis is quite clear cut as programs are either one or the other, i.e. credit or non-credit. Another basis which can be used is the method by which the program is delivered, for example distance education as contrasted with traditional classroom. Other bases have evolved through the generalizing and even stereotyping of programs. An example is the sponsorship of a program where one identifies the provider, for example a night school course (which implies an educational agency as the provider) as distinct from, say, a training course (which implies an employer as the provider) or a bible study course (which implies a religious organization as provider). Another example of this is to identify the environment in which the learning takes place, such as a home-study program, a residential program, or an educational travel program. Of course this approach to understanding programs is limited because it is neither systematic nor comprehensive; however it does recognize the general awareness that adults have as to different types of programs.

Having identified the two approaches to understanding programs in adult education—classification systems and distinguishing bases—the question is next raised as to what is the source of the need for these programs? Three general sources can be identified. The first is the potential learner, the adult who feels within him or herself the need for, or interest in, learning. Often an adult is already conscious of this need or interest, while in some cases this consciousness is brought about through such avenues as a conversation with a friend, a counselling session or, in the work setting, a performance appraisal. In an effort to ascertain the individual learning needs and interests of adults, frequently a provider will conduct a survey and use the results to plan programs.

The second source is that of subject area. Many areas are undergoing change based on new ideas, improved technologies or whatever, and in order for adults to keep up with these developments, programs are offered for this purpose. Examples can be drawn from virtually any subject area, be it history as reinterpreted though revisionist thought, social work identifying new options for dealing with disturbed youth, or computer applications through enhanced programs. Many adults become aware of their learning needs and interests as a result of seeing a program advertised, and the program may have been planned because of developments in that subject area. The third source is that of contemporary society. In order for society to continue to function, and particularly in a demo-

cratic society, it is necessary that there be an informed citizenry, able to participate fully in that society. Often it is government which identifies the learning
needs of society, or for at least a segment of society, as in the case of job
retraining for members of the labour force whose work skills are no longer of
productive value. Another example is the need in Canada, as a matter of government policy, for a federal civil service that is able to operate bilingually and
hence the need for language training. It is not only government, however, that
identifies the needs of contemporary society. Any organization is able to interpret
such needs and develop programs to address them. Thus libraries, for example,
are able to be part of a municipal effort at reducing the amount of landfill waste
by sponsoring a program on residential recycling.

Having examined the three general sources of the need for programs it is next
possible to suggest that programs satisfy the needs of individuals, of institutions,
and of society. In the case of individuals programs are the main avenue for
meeting learning needs through participation. It is important that there be a wide
range of programs available as it is only through the opportunity to participate in
programs that the multiplicity of individual learning needs can be met. This is
reflected in developments in distance education, for example, which seeks to
eliminate access barriers such as are imposed by geography and time constraints
in order to increase participation. Programs also satisfy the needs of the institutions which provide them. It is through participation that the institution is able to
carry out its adult education mandate, whether this be central or peripheral to the
institution's mission. For those institutions whose adult education is central to its
mission, offering programs which attract participation is necessary for the
institution's continued existence. As for society, programs of adult education are
a vitally important means for that society to maintain and advance. It is impossible to imagine how the society would function were individuals not enabled,
through participation in programs, to continue with their learning beyond the
formative years. Thus it is necessary that within the society there be institutions
providing programs which allow adults to act on their learning needs.

The foregoing discussion can be summarized by asserting that programs are
the most pervasive feature in adult education. The more one delves into the
concept of program, the more it is possible to recognize the richness in learning
opportunity made possible through programs. This assertion is substantiated by
the attention paid in the literature of adult education to the process of developing
programs, and this process is introduced in the next section.

Program Planning

In adult education the term used to describe the process of developing programs is program planning (also program development and program design).
This term is preferred to the one used in formal education, namely curriculum
development, because program planning is seen as being broader in its considerations. There are not nearly the constraints in adult education that there are in
formal education, such as prescribed curriculum, levels of academic progression,

regulations, and certification. Providers of adult education programs have the ability, generally speaking, to meet learning needs in ways which they believe to be most effective. The person who carries out the planning process is usually referred to as the program planner (also program developer and program designer), and often an important aspect of this person's task is to involve others in the planning, including prospective participants. In many instances the planning process itself becomes a learning experience for those involved, and this is seen as a desirable feature of program planning.

The term program planning has become central in the adult education nomenclature. It describes the process by which programs are researched and developed so as to meet the multitudinous learning needs and desires of adult learners. Its several phases have been variously described and are typically sequenced as follows: (1) diagnose needs, (2) set objectives, (3) plan methods and resources, (4) implement, (5) evaluate for re-planning.[8] In proceeding through these sequential phases the program planner makes numerous decisions such as matching the identified learning needs with suitable instructional resources, securing appropriate facilities, and setting fees. The aggregate of these decisions culminates in the final design of the program and it is by this design that the program is commonly recognized and described, be it a women's program, a general interest program, a personal development program, a vocational program, a certificate program, or whatever it is that the design suggests. Thus whereas the initial program planning is the process by which a program is developed, the subsequent program design is the overall statement of the program's purpose. Typically the design is perceived by such indicators as the program's title, its duration, the sponsoring organization, the intended participants, etc. While it is obvious that a program's design and the planning process applied to obtain that design are integrally related, for the observer it is only the design which is readily apparent. The decisions taken during the planning process by the planner can only be inferred from the final design.

Program planning is recognized as being a critically important aspect of adult education. As more and more adults act on their needs and desires for learning and turn to the providers for assistance, it is essential that the programs in which they participate satisfy their situations and foster an openness for further learning. This will only be the case if in the minds of the participants the programs are successful. For this reason program planning has always held a particular fascination for adult educators in their individual efforts to achieve program success and to avoid failure. Additionally in many program areas of adult education there is the effort to attract respectability by securing more predictable results, as in the cases of literacy education, skills development and corporate training.[9]

---

[8] R. Herman, "Planning for Learning: A Model For Creative Decision-Making," in Barer-Stein and Draper, *The Craft of Teaching Adults* (Toronto, Culture Concepts, 1988) p. 58.

[9] For a detailed treatment of the junction of adult learning and program planning see Brundage and MacKeracher, *Adult Learning Principles and Their Application to Program Planning* (Toronto, Ministry of Education, 1980).

There are two aspects to program planning. The first aspect is the various tasks associated with each of the planning phases outlined above. To take the initial phase of diagnosing needs, there are a host of tasks involved in completing this phase alone. Depending on the situation, a representative group must be identified, a method chosen for soliciting their learning needs (e.g. personal interviews, questionnaires, survey of employers), a diagnostic instrument developed, the research conducted, the results analyzed, and conclusions drawn. These conclusions may then have to be further verified. Thus there are numerous tasks to be carried out if the program is to be successful according to the criteria established for it. The second aspect is very much related to the first, namely the skills and abilities required of a program planner to carry out the various tasks. This, however, involves more than just carrying out the tasks. Using again the planning phase of diagnosing needs, a program planner might need to be competent in not only the tasks as indicated but also in such areas as committee work, statistical analysis, budget administration and report writing.

It is beyond the scope of this chapter to outline the planning tasks and the planning skills and abilities involved in program planning.[10] Instead a framework will be presented which integrates the concept of program with the dynamics of program planning.

Houle's Fundamental System

In his book, *The Design of Education*, Cyril Houle presents what he refers to as the fundamental system of educational design. It is so described because Houle indicates its applicability to any level or type of education, be it youth or adult, formal or informal. Houle directs his thinking, however, to adult educators in particular, and the fundamental system is briefly presented here by way of recommending it as a schema which is useful for both analytical and developmental purposes.

The fundamental system is guided by Houle's conception of adult education, which he describes as being, "the process by which men and women (alone, in groups, or in institutional settings) seek to improve themselves or their society by increasing their skill, knowledge or sensitiveness; or it is any process by which individuals, groups, or institutions try to help men and women improve in these ways."[11] For Houle the basic way that the process is carried out is through the design of an activity, and he defines activity as, "a specific educational action or

---

[10] There are a number of sources where these skills and abilities are enumerated. A comprehensive treatment is presented in a manual developed for the B.C. Ministry of Education by B. Lund and S. McGechaen, *CE Programmer's Manual* (Vancouver, UBC Centre for Continuing Education, 1981). See also M. Knowles, *The Modern Practice of Adult Education* (1980), p. 256.

[11] C. Houle, *The Design of Education* (San Francisco, Jossey-Bass, 1973) p. 32.

succession of actions … "[12] Thus Houle's activity equates with the concept of program as presented in this chapter.

The fundamental system takes the dual possibilities of people helping themselves to learn and people helping others to learn and develops two distinct but interrelated parts. The first part consists of an enumeration of the educational design situations out of which a learning activity, i.e. a program, occurs. Houle identifies eleven such situations, and categorizes them into four groupings: individual, group, institution, mass. These categories (noted as "C") are as follows:

Individual

C–1 An individual designs an activity for himself

C–2 An individual or a group designs an activity for another individual or group

Group

C–3 A group (with or without a continuing leader) designs an activity for itself

C–4 A teacher or a group of teachers designs an activity for, and often with, a group of students

C–5 A committee designs an activity for a larger group

C–6 Two or more groups design an activity which will enhance their combined programs of service

Institutional

C–7 A new institution is designed

C–8 An institution designs an activity in a new format

C–9 An institution designs a new activity in an established format

C–10 Two or more institutions design an activity which will enhance their combined programs of service

Mass

C–11 An individual, group, or institution designs an activity for a mass audience

This enumeration, then, covers the broad range of possibilities for programs in adult education. (The C–1 learning situation is seen as being outside the concept of program, i.e. organized participation, as developed at the beginning of the chapter as this represents self-learning. To the extent that the individual in this situation might also participate in one of the other learning situations, however, then this participation is seen as being organized and hence covered by one of the other categories. For example a person who sets out to learn navigation by reading books has designed a program for him or herself, and is self-learning. At such time as the person might take a night school course on the same subject so

---

[12] C. Houle, *The Design of Education*, p. 229.

as to confirm the knowledge gained through self-learning, then this participation is in a program designed as a result of one of the learning design situations in the institutional grouping, and thus is no longer self-learning.)

The second part of the system consists of the framework through which these activities, i.e. programs, operate. This framework is made up of the several considerations which together capture the planning and conducting of a program. These considerations are Houle's formulation of the phases of program planning, similar to the phases presented above. His phases are:

1. A possible educational activity is identified

2. A decision is made to proceed

3. Objectives are identified and refined

4. A suitable format is designed

5. The format is fitted into larger patterns of life

6. The plan is put into effect

7. Results are measured and appraised.

While there is a natural sequencing suggested by the phases of the framework as presented, Houle advises that these components are to be understood as a complex of interacting elements and not as a logical sequence of steps. Houle notes:

> In theory, the process of education usually goes through the stages of identification of objectives, selection of means of accomplishing them, conduct of the planned activity, and retrospective evaluation of it. If these various elements are to be identified and understood, they must be recorded in some fashion, and the temporal order is as good as any other for the purpose. But practice does not usually follow this logical pattern.[13]

Houle offers a number of possible reasons why there is a disinclination to follow a logical pattern. One is that often an educational activity is launched because some fortuitous resource or circumstance makes it possible for the activity to come to be. In such cases "the objective is chosen to fit the means, not the reverse."[14] Another reason advanced is that "the mind seldom works in a completely logical fashion."[15] Houle notes how the design of an educational activity typically undergoes numerous reformulations prior to its ultimate incarnation. The developmental process often implores spontaneity, and often considerations are dealt with out of their logical order, or are temporarily put aside, so as not to impede creativity.

The Fundamental System can be operated in two "modes." The first mode is to use it when contemplating the offering of a program (be it a course, workshop, public forum, etc.) so as to first think through the design options and the plan-

---

[13] C. Houle, *The Design of Education*, p. 39.

[14] C. Houle, *The Design of Education*, p. 39.

[15] C. Houle, *The Design of Education*, p. 39.

ning considerations. The applicable categories can be examined in turn to assess their appropriateness to meeting the learning need. From this review of the options the program can then be planned.

The second mode is to use the Fundamental System to study a particular program which is already planned. Used this way it is possible to place the program in the applicable category and examine its significant design elements. This mode permits both a comparative and an analytical perspective to studying programs. It is this feature which commends the Fundamental System as a helpful structure for appreciating adult education programs as it offers a complete view of the field of program and a realistic description of the operation of program planning. It is recommended that the reader study Houle's formulation in greater detail as the system outlined here represents only a summary.

Before leaving the discussion on program planning it must be noted there is a danger in program planning being approached too narrowly, as though the process is able to be carried out on a formulated basis so as to assure that identified learning needs can be met. This susceptibility arises because the steps involved in the process have been variously described in numerous adult education texts and guidebooks, and one might be led to conclude that planning adult education programs is simply a matter of working rationally through the steps. Knowles, for example, refers to andragogy as being "an emerging technology for adult learning."[16] A reasonable extension of this assertion is that those who work in the field are thus adult education technicians. While in some respects this is the case—after all good practice ensues from successful application of insight and knowledge of what has occurred previously—it does not convey the role of creativity, intuition and inspiration as essential ingredients of much that is present in adult education. To balance the view of an adult education technology Knowles also introduces the idea of adult education as an art form, whereby there is also merit to applying art principles to the design of programs.[17] Nonetheless there are a number of strong influences at work on program planners which constantly threaten to restrict the dimensions of their planning considerations.

The first such influence stems from the modern age of high technology. Without doubt North American society has an infatuation with technology, and we willingly allow our lives to be led by it. With the introduction of succeeding technological innovations, less and less time is required for each to become virtually a household item. Developments in this connection have had a direct influence on education generally as witnessed by the twin terms, "educational technology" and "instructional technology." Examples in adult education include the utilization of computers in adult basic education, the employment of interactive video discs in corporate training departments, and establishing dialogue

---

[16] M. Knowles, *The Modern Practice of Adult Education* (New York, Association Press, 1970) p. 37.

[17] M. Knowles, *The Modern Practice of Adult Education* (1980), p. 127.

through telecommunications in distance education. In the area of instructional design there are several "authoring" software programs available that simply prompt the adult educator through a curriculum development process. Technological developments such as these are truly dazzling in their capabilities, and their applications hold much promise. Certainly there will be yet further developments of this kind. By way of perspective, however, the place of technology in adult education is seen as being an assist to learning. Verner believed that the rightful purpose of the items of technology was to augment instruction in order to "make learning more certain."[18]

Another restricting influence on program planners results from the quite spectacular expansion in the number of public sector providers of adult learning and due largely to the development of community college systems in the provinces. With the profusion of these institutional providers the scope of the work of program planners has come to be delineated by the bounds which surround these institutions, and which are expressed by such delineators as mandate, geographical service area, subject matter, clientele, etc. These bounds impose practical limitations on program planning which have the effect of introverting the extent of thinking to within the institution. Further, it becomes necessary to harmonize institutional program planning with the instructional time cycle of the institution, such as its semester, term, program period, session, or whatever. Program planning in adult education, then, has come to suggest in a significant way the development of programs (courses, workshops, etc.) by adult education specialists working for institutional providers and which must fit into the parameters of the institution.

A third restricting influence on program planners is the suggestion of a overly structured approach to planning. Planning by its very nature connotes a set, deliberate and calculated process where everything is predetermined prior to the implementation. Indeed the rationality of planning lies in its promise that there will be no surprises once the program comes to be implemented. This conception of adult education, however, is in many cases much too presumptuous. One of the basic tenets of adult education is that the adult participants bring with them to the learning activity their own ideas and experiences with which to enrich and enlarge the activity. Over-planning has the potential for missing this opportunity as it implies that the planner has the ability beforehand to predict outcomes. Anyone familiar with the community development process, for example, knows that upon entering the process the animator (as the adult educator is referred to in this area) can offer no assurance as to the direction the process will take. Structuredness is not meant to intimate that program planning is counter productive to good adult education practice, in fact the opposite is the case in that when properly carried out, it is possible for program planning to account for such unknown factors. What is known, however, is that historically many exemplary

---

[18] C. Verner, *A Conceptual Scheme for the Identification and Classification of Processes for Adult Education* (Washington, Adult Education Association, 1962) p. 9.

adult education programs never underwent a systematic program planning process, rather it was considerable amounts of intuition, creative thinking, and spontaneous decision-making that represented the sum of the intellectual control of the specific program.

A fourth influence on program planners is decidedly philosophical in nature and stems from two differing views of the purpose of adult education, namely the liberal view and the social transformation view. In the liberal view the purpose of adult education is posited as being to provide opportunities for adults to improve their personal situations. By offering programs which hold promise for individual betterment, adult education is seen to be a means of overcoming societal inequities. Thus it is appropriate for the wide variety of adult education agencies to offer a potpourri of learning opportunities. This offering allows individual adults to choose from among the options in order to improve their social and economic lot in life. Opposed to this liberal view is that of social transformation. This view holds that through adult learning it is possible to bring changes to the social, political and economic structures in society as it is these structures which are responsible for the adverse conditions experienced by certain groups of people. Adopting this view, the purpose of adult education is not simply to serve the particular learning needs and interests of individuals which can bring about individual change but rather to serve the collective needs and interests of groups of people in such a way as to bring about specific social change. The philosophical point to be made is put forward by the social transformationists who argue that there is no neutral education, and that education is either a force for change or a way of reinforcing the status quo.[19]

The implication is that programs developed according to the liberal view only reinforce the status quo because while individuals might in fact improve their circumstances through participation, the oppressive structures remain. Increasingly, and in fact predominantly, the adult education programs offered in Canada are seen to promote this liberal view, especially as the large institutional providers are publicly funded, and program planning as carried out in these institutions has the effect of reinforcing the status quo. It is this connection of program planning with the liberal view which philosophically introduces a limiting suggestion to the process of program planning.

The above discussion of the restricting influences on program planners points out the need by adult educators to be conscious of the personal orientation which they bring to their planning activity. While there is nothing inherently mistaken about the program planning process, it is important to recognize that adult education, as expressed through programs, communicates the values and beliefs of its

---

[19] G. Selman, "Adult Education and Citizenship," in Cassidy and Faris (Eds.), *Choosing Our Future: Adult Education and Public Policy in Canada* (Toronto, Ontario Institute for Studies in Education, 1987) p. 44. Selman has further developed this idea of adult education being associated with change—change which is not always welcomed. See G. Selman, "The Enemies of Adult Education," *Canadian Journal of University Continuing Education 15*, 1 (1989) pp. 68–81.

planners and sponsors. Wittingly or otherwise these values and beliefs are thus visited upon participants.

Elements of Design in Programs

Having now examined the concept of program in adult education and the program planning process in the abstract, it is fitting next to regard some actual programs. As indicated at the beginning of the chapter, adult educators should be as interested in learning from developed programs as from the theoretical conception of program planning. How this can be pursued is a matter of individual appreciation. One way is to use a model such as Houle's Fundamental System in order to single out the different planning considerations which have resulted in a program design and then study the ones which offer the greatest interest. In this section, however, the orientation is away from technical considerations and instead is upon design elements. The intention is to present a more sensitive appreciation, and the term "design element" is used to identify a discernible part of the overall program which in some special way contributes to the program's overall impact on adult learning.

There is not a finite list of design elements in programs; rather the appreciation of the observer can identify any number of individual elements. Likewise a program is not made up of a set number of elements in order to achieve a design. When regarding a program, though, it is often the case that a single design element in a program can be noted which most apparently contributes to the program's impact. What follows is a selection of design elements, chosen on no particular basis although most would be recognizable in any adult education program. Each design element is elaborated upon by way of a thumbnail sketch taken from a Canadian experience. The intention is that these sketches convey some of the inventiveness, intuitiveness and inspiration which are also very much a part of planning adult education programs. The design elements include:

- the unsettled social circumstances
- the vision and the visionary
- the sponsorship
- the philosophical basis
- the learning tradition
- the collaboration
- the learner/s
- the instructor
- the learning environment
- the learning process employed
- the learning materials
- the educational technology utilized

The Unsettled Social Circumstances

Much of the history of adult education is rooted in the concern for overcoming the arduous social circumstances experienced by adults. Those with little or no education have always been especially susceptible to a life of subjugation at the hands of those with wealth, power and superior education. In addressing this oppressive situation it was recognized by early activists that education was a means of empowering individuals to gain a measure of control over their circumstances, and which could lead to a more satisfying existence. Furthermore, education which was undertaken on a community basis and combined with collective action was seen as a way to bring about basic change in a society. It was this conviction and the programs which emerged which provided adult education with its original impetus as a social movement.

Canadian society has not been stratified to nearly the extent as has Great Britain, with its formal system of class distinction. Nevertheless social circumstances in Canada have been adversely influenced by such factors as economic control by foreign interests of many resource based industries, rapid and unsettling social changes in light of Canada's development as an industrial nation, and even extremes in geography and climate. More so in earlier times than at present, for many adults and their families the impact of these factors has meant a life of eking out a minimal existence. Despite this, however, Canadians in the various parts of the nation have always had an idea of the way they believed they should reasonably be able to live, based on the country's rich natural abundance and their willingness to work hard for their living. The example of the unsettled social circumstances comes from Saskatchewan, where aspects of the social fabric were seen as needing to be protected in light of changes to the province's traditional rural way of life.

Saskatchewan in the 1950s was described as being a "province in ferment" where "almost every aspect of the earlier economic and social pattern is shifting."[20] These changes had been brought on by the steady trend to urbanization, resulting in the diminution of values associated with rural living. As an indication of how strongly these values were held, in 1956 a Royal Commission on Agriculture and Rural Life was conducted to examine ways in which the quality of life in rural areas could be stimulated. As well a Centre for Community Studies was established at the University of Saskatchewan to study the changes that were occurring. Nonetheless, throughout the 1960s the shifting continued and the negative consequences to the rural areas was such that the situation called for a positive response. In large measure the response was the development of the Saskatchewan Community College.

In 1973, the newly elected NDP government passed the Community Colleges Act, thereby putting in place a provincial community college system unique in all of Canada. The uniqueness stemmed from the expressed desire to sustain

---

[20] W.B. Baker, "A Centre for the Study of Community Dynamic," in J.R. Kidd (Ed.), *Learning and Society* (Toronto, CAAE, 1963) p. 224.

Saskatchewan's rural communities and the traditional values associated with them. These values were articulated by the Advisory Committee which had been formed earlier to investigate a suitable college system for the province. "The sense of community in rural Saskatchewan, built on traditions of community participation and co-operation blended with self-help, is among the province's most valuable attributes."[21] The community college system was intended to serve the particular needs of Saskatchewan as opposed to being simply a copy of any one of the systems being developed at the time in other provinces. Specifically, the system was designed to be an instrument of community development whereby each college would provide programs of community education and service as determined by the community. The Advisory Committee Report noted, "A Provincial education system develops within a specific social-historical context. New developments, to be relevant, should be in tune with not only the history, but also the spirit of the people."[22]

The Saskatchewan form of community college was portrayed as "the college is the community, the community is the college." At the outset it was not considered necessary to construct separate college facilities; instead colleges would make use of existing facilities within the community. The staff resource was likewise purposely kept to a minimum. The college was designed to operate with an administrator, an adult counsellor, and a small number of community educators whose jobs were to work with the community in identifying educational needs. Instructional staff were as much as possible contracted locally for specific programs. As for its academic programs, the college would not grant diplomas but rather would act as a broker of educational services in concert with the province's existing universities and technical institutes. In terms of governance, the provincial government appointed boards for each community college made up of members from within each of sixteen regions in the province. In summary, as one of the principal architects, Ron Faris, described the Saskatchewan community college system, it was made up of "colleges without walls but with foundations."[23]

The colleges were well received throughout the province. One assessment referred to the first ten years of their operation as "an era of remarkable achievement in the area of adult and continuing education" and noted participation rates as high as 20 per cent. Furthermore the original objective of improving the quality of Saskatchewan life, particularly in the rural communities, was judged to

---

[21] Province of Saskatchewan, *Report of the Minister's Advisory Committee on Community Colleges* (Regina, Department of Continuing Education, 1972) p. 6.

[22] Province of Saskatchewan, *Report of the Minister's Advisory Committee on Community Colleges*, p. 6.

[23] Ron Faris, "Colleges without Walls but with Foundations" as quoted in Dennison and Gallagher, *Canada's Community Colleges* (Vancouver, University of B.C. Press, 1986) p. 56.

be an unqualified success. "As community-based institutions, Saskatchewan's colleges had few equals."[24]

There have been a number of changes to the Saskatchewan college system such that today it has lost much of its original distinctiveness. Some of these changes were inevitable as differences developed between urban and rural colleges in their programming and administration. More significantly, a change in government in 1982 meant a different political philosophy along with a new set of educational priorities, which emphasized economic development as this period coincided with a serious recession. Nonetheless, as in the case of the earlier Antigonish Movement in Nova Scotia, for a time this "great experiment" in community education served to focus attention on unsettled social circumstances which required addressing, and adult education was seen as being the appropriate response.[25]

The Vision and the Champion: Adelaide Hoodless and the Women's Institute

Adult learning needs can arise from any number of circumstances. Whereas the fundamental concern of educators of youth is to provide education which anticipates future circumstances, in adult education the emphasis is much more on responding to the present circumstances of adults in an effort to bring about some change. With adults, however, learning needs often go unnoticed, at least until some progressive individual brings attention to particular needs. Even drawing attention to a learning need is not sufficient: there needs also to be a vision of what will be the new circumstances once the need is addressed. This vision then requires someone or some group to champion it in an effort to bring about the new circumstances.

There are several famous Canadian adult education programs which are examples of this combination of the vision and the champion, including the Antigonish Movement with Fathers Tompkins and Coady, the credit union movement (caisses populaires) with Alphonse Desjardins, and the Women's Institutes with Adelaide Hoodless. These programs were the products of fertile minds, and in each case a perceptive mixture of idealism and pragmatism created a vision of a more desirable circumstance which was possible to achieve using adult education as a means.[26] In every case, rather than simply relating the vision, its champion instead incited others with the vision such that it was acted upon in a large scale. Indeed the factors associated with a vision in the adult education context are that the learning need: (1) must be made recognizable and distinct from the prevailing circumstances; (2) it must be based on a straight forward premise of

---

[24] Dennison and Gallagher, *Canada's Community Colleges*, p. 113.

[25] Dennison and Gallagher, *Canada's Community Colleges*, p. 116.

[26] For biographical sketches of these and other early Canadian adult educators see H. Rouillard (Ed.), *Pioneers in Adult Education in Canada* (Toronto, CAAE, 1952).

an achievable change; (3) it must be able to be joined in on and then built upon by other leaders; and (4) it must be able to incite people to action. Further, the champion typically evidences the following attributes: a spiritual concern for the well-being of others, a pioneering determination which deliberates only on success, and an ability to communicate lucidly.

Adelaide Hoodless was an educational reformer devoted to women's causes. Even though her original vision was based on circumstances more prevalent in the nineteenth century, it has maintained its clarity even to the present. The first Women's Institute was founded in 1897 in Stoney Creek, Ontario, and within twenty years similar institutes had been formed in all provinces. In 1919 provincial representatives met in Winnipeg to establish the Federated Women's Institutes of Canada.

The Women's Institute, like several other early women's organizations including the Y.W.C.A., sororities and women's auxiliaries, came about as a counterpart to organizations established for men. In this case Farmers' Institutes had been in existence since the 1880s with the purpose of aiding farmers in adopting more effective farming practices. Hoodless recognized the need for a similar type of organization to assist women in improving their equally important domestic practices. The Institutes were particularly suited to the rural setting where opportunities for women coming together were more difficult and hence less frequent than in the urban setting. As well, the mutual dependence which is characteristic of a more rural way of life lent itself well to the sharing aspect of the Institute's activities. Most important, however, was the raised status which the Institutes accorded to the role of women and the merit of their views.

The initial concern of the Institute was with "domestic science," as home economics was referred to in those days. This base was soon broadened to include other areas such as the arts and citizenship, community improvement projects of various descriptions, and advocating on issues of importance to women. (Particularly in the period before women were given the vote, the Women's Institute was one of the few forums in which they could express their views on political matters.) Membership was open to all women and meetings were conducted in such a way that learning and action were shared efforts among the members, without reliance on outside resources. The meetings were usually held in members' homes and the social aspects of gathering together were emphasized. This format had a great appeal, and the Institutes both grew in numbers and flourished in their activities under the motto, "For Home and Country."

Hoodless died in 1910 at the early age of 52. In her day the vision she held of the role of women was resisted by many, and she was often referred to with disdain as one of those "new women." Today, eighty years later, the circumstances of women have changed from those seen by Hoodless yet the vision of women coming together for socializing, edification and action on issues remains unchanged. The Women's Institute continues to serve this vision in mostly rural communities throughout Canada and through its national organization. In other communities where there is no Institute, and especially in the cities, there are modern counterparts such as women's resource centres and women's clubs. At the national level there is the Canadian Congress for Learning Opportunities for Women which advocates on behalf of the special needs of women in accessing educational opportunity.

A particular feature of the Women's Institute vision is its international dimension. Not only did the idea of Women's Institutes spread to other countries (due in large measure to the championing efforts of one Margaret "Madge" Watt) but they also provided the basis for an international organization, the Associated Countrywomen of the World. This evolution of the original idea first realized in Stoney Creek in 1897 is a testament to the perceptiveness on the part of Hoodless of a vital human need, one which transcends national boundaries. Her vision and her championing of it serve as an outstanding example of that element of an adult education program which awakens and activates within individuals a deeply felt need for personal discovery and mutual understanding.[27]

The Sponsorship: The Carnegie Corporation of New York

Unlike the education of youth which is predominantly provided for by the state, the education of adults historically owes its presence to sponsorship by independent organizations. From this situation has emerged an array of private sponsors including voluntary associations, religious groups, and philanthropic foundations. This private sponsorship has not only been instrumental in shaping the field of adult education but it has also been responsible for enriching its history.

Sponsorship as used here is meant to indicate the financial commitment of an organization which enables a program to go forward. While any organization can sponsor an adult education program without necessarily making a direct or large financial investment, nonetheless the organization is undoubtedly making available other resources (staff time, facilities, supplies) and by virtue of this indirect financial contribution it is still acting as the sponsor. Every program has a sponsor, and frequently there is more than one as in the case of a co-sponsorship. An important distinction is made here between the agency which is offering a program and the agency which is affording it to be offered. While commonly it is the same agency doing both, this need not be the case. Instead it could well be that the providing agency is receiving funding from some other sponsoring agency source for this purpose. The essential question to ask when delineating sponsorship is, "Who is affording the program to the point where it is able to be offered?" In determining the essential nature of the sponsorship a further question is, "What would be the consequence to this program of the sponsor withdrawing financial support?"

For the adult participant the question of sponsorship can be either of no concern or of great concern. Some sponsors are seen as being neutral, such as a

---

[27] For a history of the Women's Institute see E. Rand, *Federated Women's Institutes of Canada: A History 1919–1960* (Ottawa, Federated Women's Institute of Canada, 1961).

school board continuing education department, while others are seen as having a specific purpose, such as a religious organization's educational unit. In other cases the sponsor acts as a "silent partner" in the offering of the program, and allows the providing agency complete freedom to offer the program as it sees fit.

Because there is no regulation of sponsorship in adult education, it is enlightening to regard a particular program's sponsor and determine the nature and extent of influence which it has on the program. This is not to imply covertness on the part of the sponsor but rather to suggest that the connection between the sponsor and the program is usually quite informative about both.

The story of the Carnegie Corporation's foundational work on behalf of adult education in the United States is well known and is to be found in other accounts.[28] Less well known, however, is how the Corporation also supported many adult education activities in Canada, as part of a provision in its charter which permitted a small portion of the foundation's income to be used within the British Commonwealth (exclusive of the British Isles, which was separately endowed). In the period between 1925, when the Corporation began specifically to support adult education, and 1959, when the Corporation made the decision to concentrated its "Commonwealth Program" funds on emerging countries, the foundation was involved in financing a considerable number of adult education projects in Canada. This support is seen as being instrumental to the initiation and sustaining of some of Canada's early work of note in the field.

The Carnegie Corporation is one of the philanthropic legacies of Andrew Carnegie, a self-made man who became very successful as an American industrialist in the latter part of the 1800s. Carnegie was born in Scotland in 1835, the son of a weaver. His father experienced difficulties finding work in Scottish factories, and this caused the family to emigrate to America in 1848. Andrew subsequently became involved in the manufacture of steel and, through the Carnegie Steel Corporation, amassed a personal fortune. Believing that the wealthy were "trustees" of their wealth for the good of the public, Carnegie established several endowments for this philanthropic purpose, one being the Carnegie Corporation of New York. This corporation was set up in 1911 to administer the remaining portion of Carnegie's fortune, and Carnegie himself directed the Corporation's activities until his death in 1919. The best known benefaction of the Corporation are the early public library buildings, most of which were built in North America (2,509 in total, 116 in Canada).[29] This recognizable gift of the foundation is but one aspect of its stated purpose, that being, "to promote the advancement and diffusion of knowledge and understanding."[30] It was this inter-

---

[28] For example see H. Stubblefield, *Towards a History of Adult Education in America* (New York, Croom Helm, 1988).

[29] F. Anderson, *Library Program, 1911–1961* (New York, Carnegie Corporation, 1963).

[30] Carnegie Corporation of New York, *1988 Annual Report* (New York, Carnegie Corporation, 1989).

est on the part of the foundation that caused it to become involved in adult education work in a most vital way.

The Corporation became interested in adult education generally as a result of determining that libraries alone could not carry out the foundation's purpose of diffusing knowledge for general use. Instead it would be necessary to experiment with new methods, and important to this experimentation was the principle that "knowledge should be adapted to make the information appropriate to the recipient and their needs."[31] This interest in adult education by the Corporation was held particularly by its then president, Frederick Keppel, and he initiated a comprehensive program of studies, research, demonstrations and experimentation. Grants from the foundation, rather than creating new, permanent adult education agencies, instead provided temporary support for existing agencies or else created new coordinating agencies.

To carry out its adult education program the Corporation provided the necessary impetus, which resulted in the formation of the American Association for Adult Education (AAAE). Subsequently grants for adult education were reviewed by the Executive Board of the AAAE on behalf of the foundation, and this is the reason for the close links between the American association and many of the Canadian projects so sponsored. (Note: Projects in Newfoundland, until 1949 a British colony, were also supported by the Corporation, on the same basis as Canada.) One of the earlier grants went to assist in the organization of adult education in Canada, and thus the creation of the Canadian Association for Adult Education in 1935.

Specific information regarding the Corporation's Canadian and Newfoundland sponsorship of adult education is too detailed to provide here except in general terms.[32] Besides the effectual support in establishing the CAAE, the Corporation also supported the coordinating efforts of the Newfoundland Adult Education Association and the Quebec Association for Adult Education. In the area of program support the Corporation made possible expansion of the extension work at the universities of British Columbia, Saskatchewan, Manitoba, McGill, and St. Francis Xavier (the Antigonish Movement). Funds supported programs at Acadia University, Banff School of Fine Arts, the Y.M.C.A.'s Lake Couchiching, Frontier College, and the Workers' Educational Association of Canada and in Ontario. Besides these specific adult education projects, there were numerous other grants made by the foundation which had tangential implications. For example in 1921, at the request of the colleges and the government of Nova Scotia, the Carnegie Corporation undertook a survey of higher education in the Maritime Provinces.

As indicated, since 1959 the Corporation has directed funds from its Commonwealth Program to educational projects in emerging countries, and since

---

[31] H. Stubblefield, *Towards a History of Adult Education in America*, p. 25.

[32] For details by way of brief description, dates and amounts see S. Stackpole, *Commonwealth Program, 1911–1961* (New York, Carnegie Corporation, 1963).

1979 this program has been referred to as the International Program. In keeping with the Corporation's charter, recipient nations are limited to those countries or territories outside the British Isles which were a member of the British Commonwealth of Nations or were a British colony as of April, 1948. Even though Canadian adult education projects are no longer given a priority to receive funds through Carnegie's foundation, the sponsorship which was provided in earlier years remains as a spiritual legacy in the same way as his libraries remain as a physical legacy.

The Philosophical Basis: Education for Co-operative Housing

The coming together by Canadians to form co-operatives for various forms of mutual aid traces its beginnings to the caisse populaire movement, i.e. credit unions, in Quebec starting in 1900. Historically, co-operatives have been rooted in the rural areas of the country where interdependence has always been an essential part of the way of life, given the general condition of economic and social deprivation. Since the Second World War co-operatives have also become conspicuous in urban areas, particularly by way of credit unions and, beginning in the 1960s, with the development of housing co-operatives. Like other types of co-operatives, housing co-ops present to Canadians an alternative form of economic and social participation to that provided by the free enterprise system, with its basis in capitalist theory. Thus instead of housing being available by such means as private ownership, rental from a landlord, or social housing, co-operative housing enables people to join together to provide their own housing through joint ownership. A housing co-operative operates as a non-profit business where the members, those people who occupy the housing owned by the co-operative corporation, control the organization.[33] It is this organizational factor which distinguishes co-operative housing from other forms of housing, and it requires that there be an educational resource available to assist members in the successful operation of the co-operative. In short, members have to know how to live co-operatively.

There are two aspects to the educational program for members of housing co-operatives. Not only must the members receive training in the necessary managerial skills to operate a business and the interpersonal skills to live in harmony with one another, but they must also be able to relate these skills to the principles of co-operation. This recognizes the fact that co-op housing as an alternative form of housing has a distinct philosophical foundation upon which all its operations are built. The Co-operative Principles were adopted in 1966 by the International Co-operative Alliance as a set of basic principles that apply to all co-operatives. (These principles are also known as the Rochdale Principles as they are the latest version of the principles adopted by the first co-operative in England.) They are:

---

[33] Co-operative Housing Foundation of Canada, *Communique* (Ottawa, Co-operative Housing Foundation of Canada, May, 1988).

1. Open and Voluntary Membership: Membership in the co-op should be voluntary and there should be no artificial restrictions that would prevent anyone from joining who could benefit from its services and is willing to accept the responsibilities of membership.

2. Democratic Control: Co-operatives are democratic organizations. Their affairs should be administered by people who are elected or appointed in a way that members have agreed to and who are accountable to the members. Members should have equal rights of voting and should partic-ipate in the decisions affecting them.

3. Limited Interest on Shares: Any share capital that a co-op may have should receive a strictly limited rate of interest, if any.

4. Return of Surplus to Members (Non-Profit Operation): Surplus, or sav-ings, if any, arising out of the operations of a co-op, belong to that co-op and should be distributed so that no member gains at the expense of any other.

5. Co-operative Education: Co-ops should make provision for the education of their members, officers and employees and of the general public in the principles and techniques of co-operation.

6. Co-operation Among Co-operatives: All co-op organizations, in order to best serve the interests of their members and their communities, should actively co-operate in every practical way with other co-ops.[34]

For many the motive to join an housing co-op has more to do with the shortage of affordable housing than it does with the Co-operative Principles or a sense of participation in what essentially is a reform movement. If, however, co-operative housing is to demonstrate to government and the public that it is indeed a viable housing alternative, then its members must become knowledg-able about its philosophy and means of operation, and conduct themselves ac-cordingly. Thus when educational programs are offered by co-op housing federations across Canada on topics such as Board Orientation, Property Man-agement, and Constructive Conflict Resolution, the Co-operative Principles pro-vide the philosophical basis for the content, and they must be evident to the participants. The more effective the educational programs are at instilling the philosophical basis, the greater will be the capacity of the co-operative housing movement to offer persons an alternative to the free market housing system.

Indeed this idea of providing alternatives is basic to the philosophy of adult education. A reiteration in 1986 of the CAAE's Declaration on Citizenship and Adult Learning asserts that "the adult education movement is based on the belief that people have, within themselves and their communities, the spiritual and

---

[34] Co-operative Housing Foundation of Canada, "Board of Directors' Course," (Ottawa, Co-operative Housing Foundation of Canada, 1986) p. 1.

intellectual resources adequate to the solution of their problems."[35] It is understandable, then, that organizations which have been established as an alternative to prevailing social and economic structures would rely on adult education in the effort to educate those who stand to benefit. Additionally, such organizations face the need to constantly work at imparting their philosophical ideals as a means of upholding them.

The Learning Tradition: The Couchiching Institute on Public Affairs

There are some adult education programs which conjure up images of a particular learning tradition. The most widely held learning tradition is associated with "night school." Try as adult educators might to change adult education's image of the night school stereotype with adults utilizing daytime schools in the evening, the term remains as being the most pervasive association of adults with learning. To many the name "Couchiching" similarly connotes an adult learning tradition, in this case the connection being with public affairs programming.

Couchiching takes its name from the lake north of Toronto where the National Council of the Y.M.C.A.s in Canada first conducted a staff and lay training program in 1907. Two years later the property, known as Geneva Park, was purchased by the "Y" and training events continued to be conducted each summer. In the depression year of 1932 the Y extended the philosophy of its training program so that, instead of training strictly young men for their work in the Y, the program emphasized a more worldly outlook. Issues of national and international concern were examined to assess their impact on Canadian society and the work of the Y.M.C.A.. This change was inspired by an energetic adult educator who worked with the Y.M.C.A., R.E.G. Davis, and in that year he organized the first conference of the Canadian Institute on Economics and Politics. The program was opened to outsiders as well as Y secretaries (the designation for professional Y staff), and in the second year the outsiders greatly outnumbered the Y trainees. In 1949 the CBC began national radio broadcasts of the conference's sessions, and its involvement made it possible to bring in payed speakers. Subsequently the sessions were even televised.

The learning tradition associated with the Couchiching conference has developed from the special combination of features that have been present from the outset. First there is the reflective setting of Geneva Park itself amidst Ontario's cottage country. Then there is the topic of each year's conference, developed with the awareness of Couchiching's tradition of tackling public affairs issues head on and often in advance of their being generally acknowledged. (For example the 1989 theme was "What On Earth Are We Doing: A Conference on the Environment, Examining the Compatibility of Nature and Civilization.") Thirdly there is the scheduling of the institute each year during the summer, a time when

---

[35] CAAE, *Building the Social Movement* (Vancouver, University of BC Centre for Continuing Education, 1986).

participants are in a relaxed and expansive mood. The fourth feature is the format, consisting of presentations by acknowledged experts followed by informed group discussion. Another feature is the alumni which the conference is able to point to as having been involved with Couchiching, thereby giving it an enhanced reputation by association. Pierre Trudeau, Henry Kissinger, Joe Clark, Lester Pearson and John Diefenbaker are among the notable political figures who have been present.

The conference continues to take place annually at the Y.M.C.A.'s Geneva Park Conference Centre, although the Y.M.C.A. no longer conducts the program and the CBC no longer broadcasts the sessions. Instead the Couchiching Institute on Public Affairs, as it is now called, is a registered charitable organization "dedicated to bringing together interested Canadians to discuss important public policy issues with experts and other members of the general public."[36] While the annual summer program is open to anyone on a first-come, first-served basis it has become somewhat of a parochial event in Ontario, although the learning tradition associated with it continues and is described as being "the intellectual Grey Cup of Canada."[37]

There are of course other continuing learning traditions in Canada, for example the Banff Centre (originally the Banff School of Fine Arts), the labourer-teachers of Frontier College, and the agricultural extension work of several universities. As well, night school remains as the most universal tradition in Canada, although with the advent of many post-secondary educational institutions it does not connote only the use of a grade school facility. These learning traditions provide reassurance that in an age of constant change and innovation, there continue to be adult education programs still meeting long established learning needs in proven formats. This helps to demonstrate the basic nature of many learning needs associated with adulthood. As well, the establishing of any tradition promotes stability, and in the context of adult learning this promotes acceptance and respect.

The Collaboration: The Open Learning Agency in B.C.

Most noteworthy programs in adult education are the result of collaboration between two or more agencies involved in the field. Such collaboration occurs on the basis of a synergetic relationship; that is, in order to produce a desired effect a collaborative action is required: a single agency acting on its own could not be successful, or at least not as successful, at conducting the program. An obvious example is the case of the National Farm Radio Forum, conducted through the collaborative efforts of the CAAE, the CBC, and the Canadian Federation of Agriculture. The absence of any one of these three sponsoring

---

[36] Couchiching Institute on Public Affairs, membership brochure.

[37] Gordon Donaldson, "Summer After Summer" *The Review*, Number 3, 1981.

agencies would have made it impossible to conduct the program as effectively as was the case.

Because adult education is for the most part free of prescribed curriculum—the exception being where adults are returning to complete academic credentials—it is quite open to opportunities for collaboration. Even in the case of academic credentials, especially at higher levels where program requirements are more flexible than the prescribed curriculum necessary for high school completion or vocational programs, collaboration is increasingly seen as both feasible and desirable. At the root of all collaboration is the intent to bring about the development of programs which are then able to be delivered to the greatest number of adult learners possible. In this way collaboration serves well the interests of both the agencies and the learners; however as the basis of participation in adult education is its voluntarism, the dominant interest to be served by collaboration is that of the learner. To the extent that learners are attracted to programs brought about by collaboration, then the interests of the agencies involved are also able to be well served.

Given the primacy of meeting the needs of learners, what then are the inducements for the agencies to come together in this synergistic relationship? Several can be identified. The first has to do with mandate and purpose. Mandate refers to the authorized mission given to an organization which is established by a superior organization. For example, the Federal Government established the National Film Board with the broad mission to interpret Canada to Canadians and to other nations, through the medium of film. In the 1960s the National Film Board embarked on a bold community development initiative known as "Challenge for Change," which attempted through the use of films to motivate Canadians to address issues of social disparity. However the National Film Board's mandate did not provide for it to assume the role of animator, working directly with community groups to bring about social change. In order to produce the films in the Challenge for Change series, the National Film Board determined to collaborate with various community groups whose purpose it was to animate change. These films then became available for use by other organizations such as university extension departments and the CBC for widespread viewing. In this way the National Film Board's mandate and the community groups' purpose came together in a successful collaborative effort.

Another factor in collaboration is that various agencies and organizations have defined constituencies and rather unique networks. Motivating these constituencies and "working" the networks can most often only be done by the particular agency and thus, when a project is identified that needs to involve the constituencies through accessing the networks, collaboration is called for. An example of this is when in the late 1970s the CBC collaborated with the CAAE to conduct the public affairs program, "People Talking Back." The CAAE's network of provincial adult education associations was used to provide for local organization of participants in the program.

Collaboration also works where there is a mutuality of philosophy between the agencies, as contrasted with a relationship developed along commercial lines. An example of this is a residential centre owned by a religious organization which collaborates with a church parish in conducting a course, rather than it being held in a hotel conference centre. This example also serves to note how collaboration is a combining of resources, in this case a physical resource with a constituency resource.

Very often collaboration is also driven by financial considerations. An organization may want to develop a program which combines the use of both printed materials and a video tape. While the organization may be well equipped to produce the printed materials, the cost of also producing the video tape portion of the program may be prohibitive. Instead a collaborative arrangement might be worked out with an educational institution equipped to produce video. Examples of this can be found in provinces which have established media production centres as part of their education ministries.

There are also pressures being placed on institutions to collaborate. Institutional mandates are contrived definitions of areas of activity and often the mandates of similar institutions overlap or are in contradiction. With the expansion of provincial educational systems over the last three decades this has been the case on numerous occasions as school boards, colleges, institutes and universities expand to meet educational and training needs and to open new educational "markets." The public as well as policy commentators are demanding that educational institutions increase their collaborative efforts in order to make the educational system more comprehensible and rational as well as cost efficient. The desired result is that the system will be accessible to a greater number of persons. One intriguing example of this prescribed collaboration is the Open Learning Agency of British Columbia.

The creation in 1987 of the Open Learning Agency (OLA) was in response to the need for an even greater access to learning opportunity than was available through the province's already well developed educational system. Difficulties of geography, the limitations of conventional educational institutions, and a demographic imbalance within the regions of British Columbia were just three of the factors which called for an innovative approach to meeting demands for increased access to higher and continuing education. Making it possible to meet the need were components such as improved distance education technology (e.g. the placing in space of the Anik C satellite), a demonstrated success in open learning (the British Open University), and an established educational system of schools, colleges, institutes and universities. What remained was the creation of an agency mandated to integrate the system so as to serve more openly the educational needs and interests of British Columbians.

Open learning as a defined term is still evolving, however it is used to describe the combining of educational technology with innovative teaching methods into a system of learning which maximizes access to educational opportunity. Because open learning as an approach is designed to be responsive to the diverse needs of adults who wish to continue with their education, it is of considerable interest to adult educators. This is particularly the case as open learning is seen as a significant advance in the providing of an institutional response to the call for lifelong learning. Interestingly, open learning, when organized into a learning system which involves a number of educational agencies as components, is well suited to collaboration. The reason for this is that the component parts are complementary rather than competitive. Educational institutions are typically very protective about their territory, whether it be seen in terms of geographical area, program content, or institute mandate. Anything which threatens to reduce institutional territory is viewed with alarm as any such reduction translates into a reduction of funding to the institution, an undermining of its influence in the territory, and a loss of institutional prestige.

Two features to the Open Learning Agency emphasize complementarity and hence enable collaboration. The primary feature is the underlying premise of OLA which places the situation of the prospective learner at the centre of decision-making. Programs are designed which recognize the individual's rightful part in choosing when, where and how he or she will learn. (It should be noted that the programs offered by OLA's Open College and Open University are those for which a credential is offered, e.g. a certificate, a diploma or a degree. It is also possible, however, for persons to take OLA courses out of general interest, and to casually watch programs on OLA's Knowledge Network educational television channel.) As a result of increasing access to programs, due to the lowering of participation barriers, the effect is calculated to enable more participation than previously was the case. The manner in which this feature is made operational (described below) has the desirable consequence of increasing the utilization of local educational resources and facilities.

The second feature is the innovative B.C. Educational Credit Bank. The purpose of the Credit Bank is to make it possible for open learning students who are working towards an educational credential to be given credits for their previous formal and non-formal learning. Credit Bank advisors assess course credentials awarded by other educational institutions and also skills and knowledge gained through non-formal learning experiences. The effect of this crediting system is to make the educational system considerably more open and responsive to individual learning situations. It does this by recognizing that learning is lifelong, that individuals today are highly mobile and therefore their educational endeavours should also be portable, and that non-formal education is often of very high quality and thus worthy of considered recognition.

The collaboration works between the Open Learning Agency's three program components—the Open College, the Open University and the Knowledge Network—and the other provincial educational institutions. In the case of the Open College this is with school districts, colleges, institutes and private sector organizations where students can combine credits earned through independent learning, i.e. Open College distance education courses, with those earned through traditional methods, i.e. classroom instruction, and through non-formal learning, e.g. company sponsored training courses, to earn credentials. Similarly in the case of the Open University, students are able to earn credentials through open learning offered not only by the Open University but also by the province's three other universities. As for the Knowledge Network, this facility acquires, produces and broadcasts educational programs which are both of general interest and which support the province's educational system, including courses of the Open College and the Open University.

As indicated, the Open Learning Agency is an example of prescribed collaboration, bringing a new approach to learning in an era where educational credentials at basic and advanced levels are emphasized. This kind of collaboration is seen to be more difficult to manage than that which occurs willingly. Nonetheless, prescribed or voluntary, the collaboration must work for the benefit of the learner.

The Learners: Elderhostels

Generally speaking participation in adult education programs is unrestricted by way of enrollment criteria. When attending a class offered by a school board, university extension department, or community centre, one is likely to notice among the participants a wide range in age, educational levels, occupational status and other variables. There are programs, however, which are developed for specific groups, and in these cases the criteria for membership become the noteworthy element of the particular program design.

There can be several reasons why a program is developed for a special group of learners. It may be that the learning to be accomplished is specialized, and only needs to be learned by the special group. Technical training is an example of this, where only those who instal and maintain the particular technology need learn about it. Another example is where the specific group has a unique learning circumstance, as in the case of education for those who are incarcerated. A third example is where a "target population" of people are defined in an attempt by the program's organizers to bring a particular homogeneity to the learning group. One such program developed with this in mind is Elderhostel.

Elderhostel is an educational program for older adults which combines travel with intellectual activity. While its start-up is quite recent, its initial inspiration drew on two well established foreign experiences in adult education. An American social activist and educator, Marty Knowlton, along with David Bianco, Director of Residential Life at the University of New Hampshire, conceived the idea of Elderhostel in 1974. It was their view that older adults were wanting to continue their informal learning, and would be encouraged to do so if novel opportunities could be made available. They looked to the youth hostelling movement in Europe and the folk high schools of Scandinavia for the combination which would become Elderhostel's successful formula. In particular Knowlton was impressed by the "way in which the availability of a network of modest accommodation encouraged and nurtured an adventuresome hostelling spirit in European youth. He also observed the very positive impact a residential setting had on adult education programs offered by the folk high schools."[38]

A number of factors suggested that a unique form of adult education could be developed with older adults in North America. Generally speaking older adults enjoy high health standards, have available time, are financially reasonably well off, are mobile, and are living in an age of truly fantastic developments. As well, the belief that older persons are incapable as learners, first refuted by Edward Thorndike in 1928, has been further exposed as a falsehood by many subsequent years of adult education programming involving older persons.

The older adult was singled out because of the concern that "one of the major problems of aging lies in the self-image of uselessness and futility that United States society foists on its older members."[39] Retirement is an aging life stage that frequently causes withdrawal from active life by the retiree. It was the belief of the Elderhostel innovators that through a program of physical and intellectual stimulation the withdrawal syndrome could be checked and even reversed. Experience was to bear this out.

The first Elderhostel program was offered in the State of New Hampshire in 1975 using a network of that State's universities and colleges. The experience confirmed the original thinking about the older adult learning audience, and the program expanded the next year to include all six New England states. In 1977 Elderhostel was incorporated as a Massachusetts non-profit corporation and in the following year a national office was opened. Subsequent programs included offerings in Canada (1980), Europe (1981) and Scandinavia (1981). In 1982 a Canadian office was established and in 1986 Elderhostel Canada was incorporated as a non-profit charity with a national office located in Toronto. By 1989 the number of elderhostlers participating in a given year had grown to 240,000 and of these 12,000 participated in the Canadian programs.[40]

The Elderhostel program follows, for the most part, a set format. A host organization (such as a university, community college, Y.M./Y.W.C.A., etc.) in a particular locality arranges for three courses to be conducted, the contents of which take advantage of the resources of that locality. The program runs from Sunday afternoon to the next Saturday morning and the classes are held during the Monday to Friday period. Each class runs from one to one-and-one-half hours each day, and it is possible for a participant to take all three courses or just one. Participants are responsible for their own travel to the locality of the program. The registration fee covers the cost of the program once there, and in-

---

[38] Elderhostel Canada, *Catalog*, Vol. 12, No. 3 (Spring 1990).

[39] M. Knowlton, "Liberal Arts: The Elderhostel Plan for Survival," in *Educational Gerontology*, 1977, 2, p. 88.

[40] Elderhostel Canada, *Fact Sheet for the Elderhostel Network* (Toronto, Elderhostel Canada, 1989).

cludes tuition, accommodation and meals. In 1990 the average cost per week was $275.

There are two important stipulations concerning the Elderhostel curriculum. The first is the requirement that the host organization offer courses which are intellectually challenging and of good educational quality. The second is that courses are not to be designed for the elderly. "Elderhostel is not interested in teaching the elderly how to be old, which is certainly the effect, and often the purpose, of courses designed for the elderly."[41] From these two stipulations has emerged a curriculum based largely in the liberal arts and also in the sciences. At the same time the courses are intended to attract older people regardless of their educational background, and there is no prescribed academic standard. The experience has been, however, that the Elderhostel program "tends to draw persons with higher educational levels, incomes, and community participation rates."[42]

The one proviso of the Elderhostel program is that participants be 60 years of age or over, and in the case of a spouse or a companion, that he or she be no younger than 50 years of age. This way the Elderhostel program can be developed in consideration of this age group's life experiences. Further, and most importantly, the host organization must maintain the special administrative dispensation which the program enjoys on behalf of the participants, namely that tuition, accommodation and meals be provided at cost.

Elderhostel is truly an international movement in adult education, a logical outgrowth of its eclectic genesis. Programs are now offered in 56 countries by more than 200 institutions. Its success clearly indicates how responsive adults can be to an educational program which is planned and organized in such a fashion as to acknowledge adult learning ability. For proponents of adult education, Elderhostel demonstrably confirms the conception of lifelong learning.

The Instructor: Frontier College

Basic to learning in a student-teacher relationship is the nature of that relationship. This can be understood both in terms of personality, i.e. compatibility and mutual respect, and in terms of role definition, i.e. formal expectations of the student and of the teacher. Thus, as individuals grow and mature as persons, similarly they grow and mature as students. This maturing develops in such a manner that the student-teacher relationship is modified and instead of being understood by way of an hierarchical distinction based on differences in age, life experience and knowledge, in adulthood there is much more of an equality based on a considerable lessening in the significance of the differences. Of course there is still recognition of the teacher's greater skill, knowledge or understanding in a specific content area, and hence the creation of the teaching situation, but this

---

[41] M. Knowlton, "Liberal Arts: The Elderhostel Plan for Survival," p. 92.

[42] D. Peterson, *Facilitating Education for Older Adults* (San Francisco, Jossey-Bass, 1983) p. 251.

superiority does not formally extend its influence to other aspects of the relationship.

The change in the student role and the need to accordingly alter the teacher role together form the basis of the original distinction made by Knowles between pedagogy—the art and science of teaching children—and andragogy—the art and science of helping adults learn.[43] While Knowles subsequently amended his thinking about pedagogy and andragogy so as to see them not as dichotomous but rather as two sets of assumptions to be made about learners, the andragogical assumptions nonetheless were descriptive of mature learning situations.[44] With this in mind, Knowles summarized the differentiation of pedagogy and andragogy as follows:

> ... andragogy is premised on at least these four crucial assumptions about the characteristics of learners that are different from the assumptions on which traditional pedagogy is premised. These assumptions are that as individuals mature: (1) their self-concept moves from one of being a dependent personality toward being a self-directed human being; (2) they accumulate a growing reservoir of experience that becomes an increasingly rich resource for learning; (3) their readiness to learn becomes oriented increasingly to the developmental tasks of their social roles; and (4) their time perspective changes from one of postponed application of knowledge to immediacy of application, and accordingly, their orientation toward learning shifts from one of subject-centredness to one of performance-centredness.[45]

In order to respond to these changes in the student role brought on by the student's maturation, it is the tenet of adult education that the teacher role must also change. One of the ways this is reflected is by use of the term, "instructor." The intent in adult education when using the term instructor is not to deny that teaching is occurring, rather the term more particularly recognizes the varied situations in which adult learning takes place. The use of the term teacher carries with it connotations of a formal learning environment where andragogical assumptions do not prevail. Indeed the role of instructor in adult education has not nearly the formality attached to it as does the role of teacher. This is a reflection of the largely informal nature of adult education, and the absence of an institutionalized tradition which defers to the all knowledgeable teacher.

There is no stereotype which characterizes an instructor of adults. In terms of work it may be a full-time career choice or part-time sideline. An instructor might be an employee of an institution, an independent contractor or a volunteer. The pecuniary rewards can be substantial (in excess of $1,000 per day for trainers in business and industry) to being very minimal when, for example, working for a non-profit agency. In many cases the motivation to be an instructor is intrinsic to the individual and it is often that a person gives of his or her time and

---

[43] M. Knowles, *The Modern Practice of Adult Education* (1970), p. 37.

[44] M. Knowles, *The Modern Practice of Adult Education* (1980), p. 43.

[45] Knowles, *The Modern Practice of Adult Education* (1980), p. 44.

talent voluntarily. The credentials required vary according to the course being instructed, and much instruction requires no credential other than an attested interest or ability in an area. Many instructors develop the course which they then teach, while others instruct using a prepared syllabus. There are even some seemingly paradoxical situations with instructors of adults; for example, it is easily possible that the instructor will be younger in age than any of the students. In another example the roles of instructor and student may be exchanged at times during the instructional session if the student has more knowledge, skill or insight in a particular area. These situations are understood by the fact that in adult education the student–teacher relationship is one of adult to adult. There is a basic equality in this fact, and one that exerts a pervading influence on the relationship.

In selecting an instructor for an adult education activity there is usually more to consider than the basic matching of the instructor's content expertise with the learning needs of the students. Very often the instructor's ability to instruct will also be dependent on a sincere motivation which is sympathetic to the students' circumstances, as well as an abundant enthusiasm. An outstanding example of this can be found in Frontier College, Canada's premier adult education institution.

Interestingly, the description applied to instructors of Frontier College's original educational work was "labourer-teacher." This description is now very much a part of Frontier College's proud history and tradition, but in light of the above discussion it does reflect an earlier conception of adult education which was based more on pedagogical assumptions.[46] What the account of the labourer-teacher illustrates so poignantly, however, is the prerequisite of an adult relationship between the learner and the instructor if learning is to be facilitated by the instructor.

The name, Frontier College, conjures a wonderful juxtaposition; the vast and desolate Canadian hinterland being tamed by, of all things, learning, the stuff of civilized centres. And yet that was precisely the conception of Frontier College. Initially (in 1899) it was called the Canadian Reading Camp Movement by its founder, the Presbyterian minister Alfred Fitzpatrick. From the modest early objective of bringing a civilizing presence to the rough railroad, lumbering and mining camps through the provision of suitable literature in rustic reading rooms, Frontier College soon evolved a more ambitious goal of bringing education to the labourers.

Initially many of the reading rooms had "instructors" assigned to them by the Reading Camp Movement who were supported by church congregations. Because the work day extended virtually from dawn to dusk there was little for the instructor to occupy himself with while awaiting the labourers return to the camp. One early instructor, Angus Gray, determined that he could enhance the rapport between himself and his students by working alongside the labourers by

---

[46] See J. Morrison, *Camps and Classrooms* (Toronto, Frontier College Press, 1989).

day and being their instructor in the evening. Thus began the celebrated labourer-teacher position with Frontier College.

The labourer-teacher is more than an inspirational happenstance, it is a natural realization of the role of the adult educator in such a circumstance. This role calls for the adult educator to know his or her students in such a way as to then be able to deliver instruction, aware of their learning needs and personal aspirations. Knowles, when examining processes of adult learning, correlates conditions of learning with what he regards as being superior principles of learning. Taking one example and applying it to the labourer-teacher position of Frontier College, it is abundantly evident why the position has enjoyed such success as a model for others to consider. As a condition of learning Knowles indicates, "The learning environment is characterized by physical comfort, mutual trust and respect, mutual helpfulness, freedom of expression, and acceptance of differences." Two of the principles of learning which he correlates to this are, "The teacher accepts the learners as persons of worth and respects their feelings and ideas" and, "The teacher exposes his or her own feelings and contributes resources as a co-learner in the spirit of mutual inquiry."[47]

In both principles it is the teacher who is understood to need to come closer to the students, and not to adopt a posture of aloofness. The labourer-teacher position exemplifies this understanding, and labourer-teacher has become a term which simply means "that teachers of adult learners not only go to where their students are to teach them, but also to work side by side with their students as well."[48]

The labourer-teachers of Frontier College continue to be placed in the various work camps across the country, but new learning frontiers have opened which call for an equally innovative response by committed instructors. While literacy remains the paramount learning need to address, the venue for Frontier College's programs has moved in from the geographical frontier. Now programs exist in urban workplaces, in penitentiaries, in Frontier College's own learning centres, and in locations of the students' own choosing. This opening of new frontiers is consistent with the College's fundamental conviction, "to take education to those who do not have it wherever they may be."[49]

A constant with Frontier College is its qualifications for those who wish to be teachers. A contemporary recruiting advertisement for the labourer-teacher program states the requirements to be: "A demonstrated commitment to voluntarism and community development. Experience in teaching and/or tutoring is helpful. Must be fit. Background in heavy labour preferred. Ability to live and work closely with others in an isolated environment." For its other programs Frontier College believes that, with training and support, a literate person can teach another person the literacy skills necessary to function as a proud individual and

---

[47] M. Knowles, *The Modern Practice of Adult Education* (1980), p. 57.

[48] J. Morrison, *Camps and Classrooms*, p. 3.

[49] J. Morrison, *Camps and Classrooms*, p. 22.

as a productive citizen. As an example, in the brochure outlining the College's Prison Literacy Initiative, the call for volunteer tutors maintains that, "volunteers, through their willingness to give of themselves and their time, demonstrate that the community cares and that it is prepared to give devalued people a second chance."

In these ways, then, Frontier College continues to attract instructors to carry out its educational mission. Perhaps most effectively, Frontier College is able to act as a connector between the learning needs of educationally disadvantaged adults and the humanitarian commitment of those intent on making enlightenment possible.

The Learning Environment: Residential Centres and the Native Education Centre

There are two illustrations to present regarding the element of the learning environment. The first, residential centres, is by way of general comment as there are numerous such centres across Canada, and all exhibit the same support for learning. The residential learning environment enables adults to leave behind the strictures of routine and instead establish a pattern which has learning as its focus. It is the function of the residential centre to assume for the learners many of the tasks of daily living which otherwise would distract or discourage them from concentrating on the learning at hand. As well, by typically being situated in outlying areas, or at least away from the mainstream of life, the centre offers a contemplative surrounding and a soothing ambience.

Another function of the residential centre is to bring together persons from different localities. This is particularly important in Canada where the country's vast geography mitigates against easy and prolonged contact among persons with similar learning interests. This coming together for an extended period of time has the intended effect of making possible communication which otherwise might have to be conducted by correspondence or telephone. As well there are many more communication opportunities which are present in a residential setting due to its informality and the occasions it provides for casual contact with resource persons and other learners.

Because attending a residential centre stands out in one's experience as being an uncommon event, the learning episode tends also to stand out and thus learning is reinforced by association. As well there is a heightened intensity to learning which takes place in an unencumbered environment as learners have more energy to devote to learning. This is typically supported by the freedom in a residential centre to manipulate the learning process as it is occurring through various means including: having the space to easily break into small groups; having groups work on learning tasks with the benefit of generous time allotments; determining a balance of time between learning sessions, social opportunity, recreation, and individual space.

Most residential centres in Canada are operated by organizations that utilize them for conducting their own programs and also make time available for other organizations. Despite all the attributes connected with learning at these centres, organizing for such learning experiences is often a difficult task. Adults find it difficult to make the time available, there is an accommodation cost above whatever might be the tuition fee, and it often takes longer to become accustomed to the different learning environment than is possible to schedule. Nonetheless residential centres do offer a supportive and interesting environment for adult learning which the program planner should be prepared to consider.

The second illustration of the significance of the learning environment draws on the experience of the Native Education Centre in Vancouver. In this case environment and architecture are dual elements as the learning centre is a magnificent structure, incorporating functional learning space and social area within a northwest coast Native longhouse design.

The Native Education Centre has conducted an adult education program in Vancouver since 1967, and since 1979 this has been operated by an all Native community non-profit society, the Urban Native Indian Education Society. At its inception the Centre served two broad purposes, namely to assist Native people with their basic education so as to promote the taking of further education or the securing of employment, and to assist Native people in the difficult transition between life on the reserve and life in the urban area by way of life-skills programs. More recently there has been a new sense of urgency to Native people acquiring education and skills training, namely the developments associated with Indian self-government. Up to the opening of the present building in 1985 the Centre offered its program using conventional space, and this period was spent proving the need for such a program.

Because Native people place great emphasis on their cultural beliefs and values it was seen as important to have a learning centre designed not only to support this emphasis but indeed to boldly reflect it. This need is expressed in the Society's constitution where one of its goals is stated as being, "To provide central and suitable facilities where educational meetings may be held." This has been successfully accomplished. The Centre is located in a light industrial section of the City of Vancouver and, when sighted, is immediately remarkable. A large totem stands at the street side of the building and serves as a ceremonial entrance way to the longhouse design. The exterior of the building is all wood, allowing the exposed massive beams and posts to make a solid statement about the structure's derivation from traditional Native architecture. Around the building a landscape has been created where students are able to walk among plants and trees that have been selected for their cultural significance. A waft of smoke from the chimney serves to further situate the student in a village setting, not in the midst of Canada's third largest metropolitan area. Upon entering through the main doorway one is greeted by a large social area with a fire pit as its focus. This area is the setting of many of the cultural activities which are part of the life of the Centre. A small kitchen serves up mainly Native foods, with lunch being the time for communal eating. The walls are hung with many reminders of Native peoples and events.

The distinctive aspect of the Native Education Centre's learning environment is how intentional it is, and it is readily apparent the Centre was created to appeal to Native people. The importance of this appeal to academic achievement is appreciated when one considers how for Native people there is no cultural equivalent to learning which takes place within a building designated for this purpose. For many Native people the association they have of institutionalized learning is in connection with the residential schools, and this experience is seen as having been culturally destructive. Furthermore the learning environments which dominate the educational systems in Canada are large in scale and are built to a design and with building materials which have been selected for practical rather than cultural reasons. Thus the Native Education Centre provides a culturally identifiable space where Native adults are able to learn together in a supportive environment. This illustration should cause adult educators to closely examine the learning environments which they utilize, and the extent to which these environments either support or interfere with learning activity.

The Learning Process Employed: The Lake Cowichan Food Bank

In adult education there is no one way in which learning is deemed to be most efficiently achieved. Partly this is because adult circumstances are complex, as contrasted to the circumstances of youth which are largely given over to the task of learning. Partly also it is because adult learning needs are varying, again as contrasted to those of youth which, because their needs are basic, are much more uniform. The result of this variation in adult education is that there are numerous ways in which learning can be organized so as to meet particular learning needs.

As noted in the first section of this chapter there are three general formats by which adult learning is organized, namely individual programs, group programs and community programs. The individual and group formats of learning are much more contained and predictable than is the case with the community format, which involves learning on a community-wide basis and is most often denoted by the term, "community development." This format is the one which adult educators have the least experience in organizing and yet, when observed and studied, stands out by way of its distinctive learning process.

There is also a touch of intrigue to community development (or CD as it is familiarity known) as the outcome of a particular CD effort is never predictable. By virtue of the involvement of a community of people in its learning process, CD arouses passion and motivates people to action, often embroiling them in contentious issues. With CD, however, the focus is on the learning process in which the participants are engaged: their success from an adult education point of view is not measured so much by whether the desired outcome is achieved but more by what the participants have learned as a result of the CD process in which they are engaged. This learning might be in terms of their personal capabilities, their knowledge of an issue, their ability to organize for collective action, or their understanding of the power structures which control community decision-making.

One of the reasons the community format of learning is not prevalent is that not many educational institutions believe they have a mandate to engage in CD, and in fact not many do, at least not officially. Adult educators working in this area typically do so under the auspices of some other organization. Community development is not usually considered as mainstream adult education by institutional providers, even though much profound learning by adults does occur through their involvement in such experiences.

There are several outstanding examples of community development in Canada, including the oft-mentioned Antigonish Movement, the NewStart Corporations of the 1960s and 1970s dealing with adult basic education, and the National Film Board's Challenge for Change film program dealing with poverty and social change.[50] It is not necessary, however, for the community learning method to be organized on a grand scale. An instructive example comes from the logging community of Lake Cowichan on Vancouver Island, British Columbia.

Lake Cowichan is a stable community of approximately 2,500 population, with another 4,000 or so persons living within the school district catchment area. The school district employs a Director of Adult Education, and this fact is instrumental to the community development events which transpired. Dorothy Clode, the school district's first full-time Director of Adult Education, was appointed to this position in 1968. She had moved to Lake Cowichan with her family fifteen years earlier and had immediately become an active and respected member of the community, including as a community organizer and as a teacher of adults. Once employed as Director she set about the task of meeting the community's adult learning needs which could be addressed in one way or another through the resources of the School District's adult education program. To enlarge her understanding of the field to which she was now giving leadership, Clode completed a Masters degree in adult education during the initial two years of her directorship.

As with any initiative there are circumstances which precipitate action. In the case of the Lake Cowichan, beginning in 1980 there was a serious, virtually unprecedented, downturn in the economy of the small town, long sustained by an abundant natural resource base. The economic downturn which began in 1980 soon made itself felt, and by 1982 the unemployment rate stood at 60%. The impact was immediate and devastating to the townspeople who, under normal circumstances, prided themselves on a self-reliant way of life. The only consolation, if it might be considered as such, was that Lake Cowichan was not suffering alone. The whole provincial economy was similarly caught in the grips of the recession. It is fair to say, however, that rural communities felt the blow much sooner and much harder than the metropolitan centres as rural communities were less insulated economically.

The community needed to come together to discuss the deteriorating situation, and Clode worked diligently at organizing a meeting. At this gathering a number

---

[50] See descriptions of these and other programs in Kidd and Selman (Eds.), *Coming of Age* (Toronto, CAAE, 1978).

of ideas were suggested, the most significant being to conduct a community survey so as to determine the recession's impact on the area and to identify the needs which required addressing. A committee was formed for this purpose and, going by the acronym, LESS—Lake Economic and Social Survey, completed the survey. One of the needs immediately identified was for a food bank, especially as other communities similarly affected by the economic downturn had responded in this manner. While the need to distribute food to the disadvantaged is not a response unique to the 1980s, the extent to which the whole community—individuals, organizations, businesses, agencies—became involved in this activity, and the organization that was brought to the effort, made food banks an expression of community caring in the face of the crisis at hand during that decade. In the case of Lake Cowichan, it also provided the opportunity for community development to take place.

Organizing and running a food bank requires community involvement and the utilization of many skills. Through the fall of 1982 the LESS Committee worked to open a food bank in the basement of an Anglican church. Donations of food, equipment and expertise were forthcoming and by November groceries were being made available to those in economic difficulty at wholesale cost plus one per cent, with the one per cent mark-up being placed in a special fund to afford groceries for those in greatest need. To run the food bank—which involves maintaining the dignity of the recipients and offering hope as well as distributing food—unemployed volunteers came forward and, where necessary, Clode organized for training in such skill areas as peer counselling, cashiering, book keeping, and general administration. Within a year of opening the food bank had 200 registered members, most with dependents. (There was a special concern for the needs of wage earners with dependents as it was recognized that in facing the decision about looking for work elsewhere, they could not so easily pick up and move on, plus the community wanted to keep its social fabric together as much as possible.)

Organizing learners by way of a community development effort is viewed by many as an unconventional approach to adult learning, despite its faithfulness to the tenets of adult education. Clode recalls with some delight an incident in connection with her food bank experience. A very senior official from the Ministry of Education paid an unscheduled visit to the school district and was surprised to find that Clode, rather than being in her office was instead at the food bank. As a result of this incident Clode was required to officially account for her food bank involvement.

Identifying the need for the food bank, and getting it established, were immediate responses to the need. Once this need was met, however, attention could be turned to understanding the root causes of economic dislocation and unemployment, and then taking some further action. In the case of the LESS Committee, the subsequent action was to develop a three year plan for social and economic recovery, including projects the citizens could take on themselves to improve the community's prospects. An Economic Development Committee was formed and set about to bolster the community's belief in itself. With the assistance of funding from the federal government, projects were initiated which enabled the residents to make their community more attractive so as to benefit from the tourism industry. Possibilities for new self-help ventures were explored and, for example, a number of people opened bed and breakfast type accommodations.

The recovery process continued, although the community did not return to its earlier situation. One of the lumber mills closed down completely and the other was modernized so as to produce greater output with fewer workers. The job market declined and some skilled tradespeople did move away. Nonetheless, new opportunities were opened up including tourism, the export of log buildings, and "twinning" of Lake Cowichan with a city in Japan (also dependent on the forest industry), which resulted in a number of exchanges between school groups. The outcome of these successful ventures is that the Economic Development Committee continues with its efforts and now reports through to the Village Council. Most hopefully, with a return to economic health the need for a food bank has been eliminated.

When asked to reflect on the food bank initiative, Clode stated that the learning to be had through community development is contained in the fact that people are provided with a learning process, "and it's ultimately the process that they remember."[51] This process brings people together who are in some similar need (in this case unemployment) and enables them to organize for action. Learning is seen as being a major part of the action plan as the people involved must take on the responsibility for doing things for themselves, and new skills and knowledge are required for this. The role of the adult educator is to initially animate the community in coming together and then to facilitate the learning process so that the action plan can be carried out. This learning process is understood to empower people at the very time when they are feeling most helpless by building their self esteem and providing them with their own source of hope. As Moses Coady, leader of the Antigonish Movement, described it in the title of his book, the participants in a community development project are "masters of their own destiny."

The Learning Materials: Citizens' Forum Study Guides

Learning materials are the various items used by an instructor to assist the learner in the learning task. In the case of independent learning these materials serve the additional purpose of providing direction to the learner through the instructions and suggestions incorporated into the materials. Learning materials can be anything which the instructor chooses, be they everyday objects, workbooks, films, audio/cassette tapes, etc. They can be eclectic in nature such as handouts or be a single source as in the case of a text book.

---

[51] R. Moss, *Dorothy Clode: Community Educator* (University of B.C., unpublished M.Ed. thesis, 1988) p. 25.

The most pervasive learning materials in adult education are those prepared in printed form. This is not a reflection of the instructional effectiveness of the printed word over, say, a video tape or a computer program. Rather it is an indication of the comparable cost effectiveness of print for preparation, production and distribution and its versatility for use in teaching. Additionally there is both a history and a tradition to the use of print in education and indeed one of the initial learning tasks of an individual seeking to be educated is learning to both read and write. Thus the printed word retains its preeminence as the means of communicating to learners when learning materials are utilized, which is almost always the case. For this reason what follows is exclusively a consideration of print materials, but this is not intended to discount the value of other types of learning materials, nor to suggest the superiority of print.

The printed word has a significance to society beyond its use in learning situations, indeed other than through verbal communication it remains as the most important method of common communication. This explains the emphasis placed on an individual having sufficient literacy skills to function as a member of society and as a citizen. Not surprisingly, much of the work in adult education has been directed at literacy instruction, and this is as true for the present as it is the record of the past. (Interestingly 1990 was International Literacy Year while the previous year, 1989, marked the 90th anniversary of the founding of Frontier College, Canada's outstanding institution dedicated to teaching adult literacy.) Historically speaking, an early move to promote adult learning was by the establishment of reading rooms, as was the case in Y.M.C.A. facilities, and the construction of public libraries, for example with funding provided by the Carnegie foundation.

Printed learning materials have several attributes which make them attractive to both instructor and learner. For one, they most often are a way in which the content of the course is "packaged" and, because these materials typically become the possession of the learner, they are retained and thus available for future reference. They also can be used and shared as determined by the learner. Part of the versatility of printed learning materials is their portability, and they can be accessed at the whim of the learner be it while riding public transportation, while relaxing on the beach, or wherever.

There is no prescribed format which governs the development of printed learning materials; rather, it is a combination of the nature of the learning and the learning situation which influence the format. Nature of the learning refers to the expected outcome of the learning, be it in terms of the learner acquiring knowledge, understanding, skills, attitudes, values or interests, or some combination of these.[52] Learning for each requires its own approach; for example, skills learning calls for demonstration of the skill, and in learning materials this suggests illustration work. The learning situation refers to whether the course is given on a credit or non-credit basis. Thus, in the case of an adult education course which

---

[52] M. Knowles, *The Modern Practice of Adult Education* (1980), p. 240.

leads to some form of certification, the learning materials typically reflect the course curriculum and are even used directly in the instruction as in the case of a workbook or text book. Included in this are those printed materials developed with a learning outcome very much in mind but which are intended for use in self-directed learning such as self-teaching publications, "how to" guides and manuals of all sorts. In the case of a non-credit general interest course the learning materials usually are much less structured from an instructional point of view—if at all—and the content is often derived from other sources, e.g. magazine articles, reports, and excerpts from books.

In adult education there is a relationship between the learning materials used in a course or program and the intended learning outcome. This relationship is that the greater the specificity in the learning outcome, as indicated by the stated goals and objectives, the more specific the learning materials will need to be. This suggests the necessity in many instances of developing unique learning materials, as adult education is so often called upon to address particular learning needs. As well, because in adult education there are innumerable sponsoring agencies, each with their own philosophies, the same content areas are often approached quite differently. Literacy is a good example of this, with differences noted between agencies engaged strictly in teaching literacy skills and those which teach literacy skills in relation to social justice issues.

The effectiveness of learning materials can be measured by several criteria, the foremost of which is how they were experienced by the learner. Contributing criteria include: adherence to principles of good typography, including page layout and use of graphics; clear organization of content; good composition; correct grammar and punctuation; appropriate use of vocabulary for the intended reading level; orientation of the content for adult learners; the extent to which the content is topical. There are numerous other criteria which could be identified, but the specific learning situation and the nature of the learning needs also to be considered.

An outstanding example of effective learning materials is found in the Citizens' Forum program which was jointly conducted by the CAAE and the CBC between 1943 and its formal discontinuance in 1966. This example is chosen for several reasons: the significant number of adults from across the country who were involved as learners; the topical nature of the content; the development in the participants of knowledge, understanding, skills, attitudes, values and interests; the long-standing life of the program; and the ability of the learning materials to be used in conjunction with two different media, radio and television.

Citizens' Forum was a national discussion group program which utilized printed study materials and a weekly broadcast to help Canadians form their opinions and conclusions on matters of general concern. As the name implies, the objective of Citizens' Forum was citizenship education, and the program was a joint venture of the CBC and the CAAE. The format called for discussion groups to be created under the auspices of a number of community organizations such as university extension departments. The groups would then receive study guide materials related to a weekly radio broadcast (and subsequently also television). The program was operated each year between October and April and the discussion groups would meet weekly to consider the topic which had been introduced earlier in the study guide materials and to then listen to the corresponding broadcast. At the end of each broadcast the groups were invited to forward their conclusions on the topic to the program's provincial offices, and summaries were aired as part of subsequent broadcasts.

In order for the program to be successful in attracting and maintaining a large enrollment of discussion groups, the topics presented needed to be challenging, debatable, and of current interest. Examples from the 1953/54 season include: "Is Professionalism Ruining Canadian Sports?", "Censorship: Safeguard or Menace?", "Canada: One Nation?". Equally though, the participants in the discussion groups, in order to derive the greatest benefit from each broadcast, needed to be versed in the points of view pertaining to the topic. This was the purpose of the Citizens' Forum Study Guides.

Each Study Guide was eight pages in length, and was printed in approximately an 8" x 5" size pamphlet. The covers contained information on the Citizens' Forum program, broadcast times, sources of additional information, and suggested discussion questions. The contents developed the topic by way of presenting background information and noting differences in points of view. There are several notable aspects about the Study Guides as learning materials. The first is in regards to their readability. It was necessary for the guides to be comprehensible by persons of varying educational levels while at the same time providing information and opinions on complex issues. This called for good organization of the material and clarity in the writing. Another aspect was the requirement for objectivity while presenting differing points of view on what were often contentious issues. In order to adequately prepare the participants for the broadcasts, where differing points of view would be represented, the materials had to clearly identify the bases of the differences. The materials also had to cover the topic with sufficient thoroughness that informed discussion could take place. While the nature of the program was such that the Study Guides were not intended as a treatise on each topic, nonetheless a digest was required. Skilled editing was necessary to meet this requirement in the limited amount of space available. In paying tribute to Isabel Wilson, the Study Guide editor for the life of the Citizens' Forum program, a former executive director of the CAAE, Alan Thomas, noted, "As journalist, Isabel possessed an unmatched skill in reducing numberless pages of public rhetoric, mazes of statistics, and bureaucratic argument to multiples of eight pages ... Her pages were full of clear, cogent, and thoughtful argument, designed so that ordinary people might understand these complex issues, and act with reference to them."[53] Yet another aspect was how the study guides helped to focus group discussion. This was the intention of the

---

[53] A. Thomas, "A Memory of Isabel," in *Learning* Vol. IV: 1, p. 17.

discussion questions printed in each pamphlet. Isabel Wilson maintained that formulating the discussion questions was one of the most difficult aspects of the program. For one, the questions as framed might not have the intended result of stimulating discussion. For another, a question might be ambiguous, causing the group to be distracted in attempting to clarify the meaning. Yet another difficulty was creating questions which were sufficiently open-ended while at the same time allowing for a conclusion to be reached.

What makes these learning materials particularly noteworthy is the sustained period over which they were produced. This effort is all the more remarkable in that the materials had to be written with a national audience very much in mind (excluding French speaking Canadians, who had a similar program, Les Idées en Marche, on the CBC French network). Interestingly, the quality and timeliness of the materials was recognized by individuals and groups such as university classes who were not registered in the Citizens' Forum program. The use of the Study Guides in this informal manner was not at all discouraged. "The pamphlets make a contribution in the general field of adult education quite apart from their special use in one project."[54] This is fair testimonial for any learning material but it doesn't stop there. In a reflection on Citizens' Forum, Selman comments on how with the passage of time the Study Guides become "an increasingly interesting reflection of concerns of Canadians throughout the life of the project."[55]

The Instructional Technology Employed: Image Projection

Today when one walks into virtually any educational facility an immediate impression is formed of how the stereotype classroom—desks arranged so as to face an instructor at the front of the room with a blackboard behind—has been done over. Instead there are numerous indications that what formerly was considered a classroom now represents a modern instructional setting. While a blackboard will likely still cover at least one of the walls, the presence of modular furniture will enable the room to be configured according to the nature of the instructional activity, and undoubtedly there will also be present audiovisual equipment such as an overhead projector, a television and video tape deck, and perhaps a cart with other pieces of media equipment on it. These are just the overt indications that the modern instructional setting employs a greater variety of instructional techniques than in earlier times.

The changes noted in the modern instructional setting involve all components of the learning process including the classroom environment, the roles of the students and the teacher, the instructional resources available, and the educational philosophy which guides the learning. These changes are summarized by the understanding that assisting individuals to learn has in the past thirty years or

---

[54] Wilson et al., *Education in Public Affairs by Radio* (Toronto, CAAE, 1954) p. 36.

[55] G. Selman, "Roby Kidd and the Canadian Association for Adult Education," in *Occasional Papers in Continuing Education* (Vancouver, U.B.C. Centre for Continuing Education, 1982) p. 25.

so become considerably more systematic than simply a teacher facing a classroom of students and delivering instruction. Three of the most obvious influences in creating a modern instructional setting are: (1) new understandings from research about the learning process, (2) technological innovations in communications equipment which are used for instructional purposes, and (3) less tradition bound approaches to education. Terminology has also changed in keeping with these developments, and whereas in the past the term "teaching methods" described the approach to instruction, today the term "instructional technology" describes all the considerations available to the teacher to facilitate learning. Gagne describes this instructional technology as including " ... practical techniques of instructional delivery that systematically aim for effective learning ..."[56] This description embraces the definition of technology as being scientific knowledge applied to practical uses, and this includes the application of research learning as much as the use of audiovisual equipment.

The developments which have had the most dramatic impact on instruction have for the most part originated outside of the field of education but have been readily applied to it, namely technical innovations in communications. Radio, motion pictures, television, and computers are striking examples of this. These developments, which will be referred to as media developments, have had such a profound influence on the providing of instruction that they merit closer consideration, particularly as the hardware associated with these media developments, e.g. projectors, televisions, computers, screens, are now commonplace in instructional settings. What follows is a brief sketch of this influence, along with an example of how one of these media developments, image projection, was quickly adopted by adult educators in Canada. It must be reiterated, however, that instructional technology refers to more than the use of media equipment alone, and that this use is but one way that technology, i.e. scientific knowledge, has affected the total process of learning and teaching.

The media developments that have occurred in the instructional setting (the successor to the classroom) impact adult education as much as they do the formal educational system. There are several reasons for this. For one, much adult education takes place in the same facilities and so there is an obvious exposure of adult education to these developments along with the opportunity to take advantage of them. For another, much adult education takes place in settings where media innovation is very much the culture, i.e. training for business and industry. Yet another reason is that many of the learning needs which adult education has been called upon to meet have required employing various technological and novel approaches, and adult educators have been forthcoming in this regard. The Farm Radio Forum program, with its national use of radio, is an example of this ingenuity.

---

[56] R. Gagne (Ed.), "Introduction," in *Instructional Technology: Foundations* (New Jersey, Lawrence Erlbaum Associates, 1987) p. 7.

There are, however, aspects of adult education that have impeded an awareness and utilization of these media developments within adult education. For example, a significant number of adult education instructors are only part-time: they have occupations other than instructing to which they devote their major attention. Further, many adult education instructors have had no training in instruction, or if they have, it likely represents more of an orientation than training. There are also budget and logistical reasons which often mitigate against the use of new instructional media, as in the case of the programs that take place in settings other than educational facilities and which therefore likely require either renting or transporting equipment, and this can pose difficulties. Nonetheless, because the purpose of instruction is to bring about learning, and developments in media are able to be readily utilized to enhance the learning situation, adult educators should be aware of these developments and be able to take advantage of them wherever possible. In this way they can be more discriminating in their instructional efforts.

There are various terms used to describe the use of media equipment in instructional settings such as instructional media, audiovisual equipment, and media technology. As noted, however, the term instructional technology is used today to note the systematic approach to providing instruction, and is not limited to describing the use of media equipment. At the same time, because developments in media have been so remarkable, it is helpful to trace these developments so as to gain an understanding of their contribution to the current state of instructional technology.

As education for children became organized in the 1800s, one of the first efforts made to improve instruction was to introduce objects which complimented the oral and written instruction. This was intended to assist in the teaching of more abstract ideas by enabling the teacher to use objects to provide meaning to things abstract. The term "object teaching" was used to describe this approach. In the latter part of the nineteenth century, and stimulated by the advent of photography, the first pieces of visual equipment were introduced, the most remembered of which was the "magic lantern." This was a device which, by way of a lamp and a lens, projected an image contained on a glass slide onto a screen so as to enlarge the image. These pieces of equipment began what was called the "visual instruction" movement, which included static visuals such as maps, wall charts and globes. This movement quickly advanced with the introduction of new projection equipment such as the motion film projector. Paralleling these developments were those in the audio field, including sound recordings and phonographs as well as radio. A quantum leap occurred when audio was synchronized with the visual such that the visual movement now became known as the audiovisual movement. Motions pictures, for example, were now referred to as the "talkies."

Use of audiovisual productions was spurred on by the outbreak of World War Two as extensive use was made of film for purposes of both military training and propaganda. In peacetime, film became very instrumental as a medium for communicating culture, and in the instructional setting, the increasing availability of films made them a popular aid to instruction. Not only were they capable of stimulating students by their portrayal of reality, as in the earlier case of object teaching, but their range of subject matter was much more extensive and animated. Another major development which impacted on education was the introduction of television in the 1950s. Television technology has continued to be advanced such that much of its earlier unrealized promise for educational purposes is now being achieved, particularly with the use of space satellites and cable networks for transmitting broadcast signals, and dedicated educational channels used by educational agencies. The next innovation of spectacular proportions to be introduced into the instructional setting was the computer, and especially because of its capability to be highly interactive, and even personal, with the learner. Other innovations have followed which are largely hybrids on earlier advances, including video and aspects of telecommunications such as teleconferencing.

By the 1970s the developments in communications were having such an effect on instruction that the various pieces of audiovisual equipment could no longer be considered as ancillary in the instructional situation. This fact, coupled with continued investigation into the learning process and an expanded theoretical understanding that resulted, led to the introduction of the term, instructional technology, to replace the concentration on audiovisual alone. Instructional technology was intended to describe the "systematic way of designing, carrying out, and evaluating the total process of learning and teaching."[57]

Image projection has an important place in the instructional technology of adult education. Today there are several types of image projection equipment commonly available to the adult educator, such as 35 mm slide projectors, 16 mm film projectors, and overhead projectors. More recently there has been introduced video technology for displaying not only prepared video materials but also footage created in the instructional setting by the participant and instructor. Another equipment item, liquid crystal display units, are coupled with overhead projectors in order to display information from computer screens. It is interesting to see how these and other media equipment have over time influenced the instructional format in adult education.

An early use of image projection equipment was the stereopticon, more familiarly known as the magic lantern. Particularly in the period when many university extension departments were delivering programs to rural areas, the magic lantern, as its name suggests, was a popular feature of the presentations because of it ability to illustrate the things being discussed. This occurrence has been delightfully recorded from personal experience by Ned Corbett in his book, *We Have With Us Tonight.*[58] The advent of motion pictures, especially when sound

---

[57] R. Reiser, "Instructional Technology: A History," in R. Gagne (Ed.), *Instructional Technology: Foundations*, p. 19.

[58] E.A. Corbett, *We Have With Us Tonight* (Toronto, Ryerson Press, 1957).

was added, resulted in widespread use of this medium in adult education. The establishment of the National Film Board in 1939 gave special impetus to the use of film. In the rural areas, where at that time over half of Canada's population lived, a projectionist with film, projector and screen would travel a "film circuit," showing various educational films. Subsequently, when projection equipment became more prevalent, film councils and film libraries were established throughout the country to distribute films.

Being able to project images enabled adult educators to present more stimulating sessions and to use new formats. The information communicated in this fashion was easier for the learner to retain as it appealed to the two dominant senses of sight and hearing. As well, the information and ideas which film was able to capture and communicate could be complex while still being comprehensible, as the learner was able to see real life situations with cause and effect relationships. Discussion groups could be formed around the content of the film presentation, particularly as the content had been developed with a specific purpose and hence discussion points could be prepared to suit the audience's interests. The adult educator, rather than having to be the subject expert, was able to facilitate the discussion.

In the period prior to television, film projection necessitated that learners (participants) come together for viewing. For this reason film was an excellent medium for promoting group discussion. The advent of the television changed this as it was now possible for adults to remain at home and privately view televised programs. This new option, while convenient, was no substitute for viewing and discussing in a group. Thus while television increased individual viewing opportunity, it also had the consequence of eliminating the educational process of substantiating individual learning through discussion. Of course film continued to be an important medium, however the introduction of the video format, including large screen viewing, has become an increasingly convenient substitute to film during the 1980s.

For the adult educator today there is now a greater range of choices involved when selecting the image projection most suited to the learning program, and choosing requires an understanding of the complete process of instructional technology.

Speculation on Future of Elements

One way of understanding the past is to view time periods as eras. Most often eras are distinguished on the basis of phenomena such as major events, charismatic leaders, and prevailing ideas. The examples of elements of program design provided above can each be seen to be products of their own eras, however the particular era may be distinguished. For example, the founding of Frontier College by the Reverend Alfred Fitzpatrick was part of the era of the social gospel while the creation of the Saskatchewan community college system was part of the era of expansion in provincial post-secondary education systems. What one can infer from this is that adult educators, when faced with novel situations within particular eras, have managed to create program designs which address these situations. In some cases the situations have been adverse, such as the Lake Cowichan Food Bank, in others the situation has been opportunistic, as in the case of collaboration among agencies. Whichever, adult educators have been able to be alive to the moment: they have made a contribution within the context of particular eras. The question arises as to the continued ability on the part of adult educators to respond to contemporary eras with imaginative program designs.

Certainly there continue to be easily identifiable eras which call for understanding through adult education. The decade of the 1980s, for instance, was an era of national crisis as evidenced in the constitutional struggles. The 1990s are likely to be viewed as an era where issues of quality of life are seen as fundamental to society being able to continue functioning, e.g. the environment, the redefined family, and cross-cultural understanding. If adult education is to be involved with these issues in a significant way then new program designs need to be found. Is this possible?

There is no question but that it is possible to create new program designs to address the modern era. Nothing stands in the way of this happening. There are, however, shifts occurring in how adult education is currently patterned in Canada, and these shifts will exert influences on the generation of new program designs different from previous eras. Six shifts are noted here, and there are undoubtedly others.

(1) The Decline of Nation-wide Adult Education Programming

Canada as a nation has grown more complex as it has grown, and one of the notable outcomes of this has been an increasingly regional and provincial focus on national matters by its citizens. Even national institutions such as the CBC reflect this fact in their organizational structure and their program delivery. For adult education it is difficult to believe that in the 1990s nation-wide programming such as the CAAE's forum programs could be so readily conducted. The national preoccupation, even at the constitutional level, has been to emphasize regional differences at the expense of national commonality. Within the regions there is increasing suspicion, even disdain, for national initiatives.

(2) The Spectacular Expansion of Provincial Post-secondary Educational Systems

Beginning in the 1960s and continuing even to the present, provincial governments have developed their post-secondary educational systems as a strategy for ensuring the skills and knowledge necessary for economic and social well-being. This development has reduced the influence of the voluntary sector by overshadowing—and even overtaking—many of that sector's adult education efforts. The development has also significantly widened the adult education network such that organizing for co-operative programming is made more complex. Whereas, for example, the extension departments of provincial universities were once the adult education contact points in each province (albeit informal), presently many provinces have more than one university and several colleges and institutes as well as a government department or ministry of continuing education.

(3) The Reorientation of Adult Education Values

Adult education has followed suit with society generally in being more comfortable in expressing its value orientation in secular rather than spiritual terms. This reorientation is reflected in the observation that adult education is no longer a movement born of the social gospel but instead is now an enterprise. While this observation is not by any means absolute, few would deny the influence of entrepreneurialism on adult education today. Unquestionably this influence has been forced onto many adult education operations, but adult educators have by and large adapted to the new business practices and concerned themselves more than ever before with the "bottom line."

(4) Episodic Approach to Participation

How adults perceive and use time, and how educational agencies organize activity for adults, has brought about an episodic approach to participation, i.e. participation in courses or sessions which are distinct and of short duration. For so many adults a telling consequence of living in an era which is affluent, highly mobile, and full of competing opportunities—to identify but three indicators—is the necessity of organizing their lives on the basis of a timetable. Such organization means there is only so much time which adults are prepared to make available for continuing education while also attending to other facets of their lives. Educational agencies are cognizant of needing to organize activities which can be fitted into the general patterns of adult living so as to facilitate participation. What has resulted, over time, is a way of arranging adult education into conventional time frames, e.g. courses and sessional terms, where the conclusion of the course brings about the completion of a predetermined amount of instruction. This approach is very much reflected in those adult education programs where fees are charged.

The episodic approach to participation is also a function of how adult education is packaged for marketing purposes. With numerous educational agencies involved in providing adult education, and indeed being in competition with one another, this packaging and marketing have developed this episodic approach to a high level, as evidenced by the seasonal catalogues of continuing education courses provided by school boards, colleges, universities, community centres, and other agencies.

Decision-making by adults on the use of their time is a matter of personal priorities and circumstances. In this regard it is interesting to note how the new learning options of open learning, distance education and independent study are further recognition of how difficult it is for adults to appropriate their time, even with the aid of timetables, and how adult education must come up with innovative scheduling accommodations. As a society, however, we may have reached the point where the episodic approach is proving to be inefficient, and where schemes such as paid educational leave and recurrent education are required to allow for sufficient time for substantive learning to take place.

(5) More Individualized Learning

Two developments have had a profound impact on determining the location where adults engage in learning. The first in a chronological perspective was the automobile. This ready means of transportation allowed adults to travel from their homes to attend a night school, a community centre, or wherever a course was conducted. The underlying notion was that people with a certain learning need or interest would join with others who had a similar need or interest and become a group for the purpose of learning. The second development, advances in electronic media, quite reversed this notion of personal mobility. Now it was possible for the learner to stay at home and have his or her learning need met through distance education, even though there was no greater distance involved than before. Thus the traditional arrangement of learning with reference to a group of learners has been undermined. Nowadays an individual's circumstances and inclination can determine when learning will be undertaken, not schedules and requirements. This option of learning on an individual basis is not likely to eliminate learning in a group, however the trend to individualizing learning is there and is further spurred on by the new administrative arrangements as part of the concept of open learning.

(6) Specialization in Adult Education as a Field of Practice

The breadth and depth of adult education has always meant there were particular areas of focus in practice, as noted in Bryson's five functional areas of adult education: remedial, occupational, relational, liberal, political. With these areas being increasingly taken up and even dominated by public educational institutions, and with even larger enrollments, there has been a definite segmenting of the practice of adult education. This trend is quite evident in the array of associations which have been created along these same lines, e.g. the Canadian Association for Distance Education, the Canadian Association for Community Education, and the Movement for Canadian Literacy, to name but three.[59] As the field continues to grow, and as adult learning needs are made more divisible and described in more finite terms, such segmentizing will correspondingly increase. There are several likely outcomes of this. Adult education, in order to be comprehensible to ministries of education and to administrators, will need to become more structured along both administrative and content lines. This in turn will have implications for staffing where adult educators' working arrangements will become the subject of negotiation by a staff association or a trade union. Of course, not all adult educators will be employed by large organizations which

---

[59] G. Selman, "Adult Educators and their Organizations, Specialization or Balkanization," *Canadian Journal of University Continuing Education, 14*, 1 (1988) pp. 24–44.

might be structured along these lines, but even this distinction will further segment the field.

Whatever might be the result of these and other shifts in adult education practice, there is no question but that programs will continue to be offered and that adults will continue to participate. And because adults will always have learning needs to meet and have discriminating interests to satisfy, programs will need to be developed which are perceptive of these needs and interests, and which reflect them in their elements of program design.

6

Public Policy Formation

The 1980s were active years in Canada for public policy regarding adult education: the federal government passed legislation which provided for it (National Training Act, 1982); one province summarily dismantled its Division of Continuing Education (British Columbia); another province reviewed its support for the continuing education of adults (Quebec); and a third province reiterated its commitment to the concept of further education (Alberta). In addition, the special learning needs of illiterate adults were formally recognized by the creation of a National Literacy Secretariat while at the same time the disparity of access to learning opportunities between those who are well educated and those who are not became more pronounced.[1]

All of these developments took place at a time when the need for continued learning in an age of ever accelerating change was an undisputed fact.[2] What sense, then, can be made of the place of adult education in Canadian society from a public policy perspective?

The diverse nature of adult education once again mitigates against the possibility of a clear depiction, in this case in terms of public policy. Adult education is not organized into a manageable system, nor is it directed by any central authority. Furthermore the matter of just what constitutes public policy itself requires elaboration and qualification as public policy is but one means by which government can take action in any given area. Added to both these qualifiers is the significant factor in Canada's federal structure of the sensitive interplay between the realities of constitutional jurisdiction and government initiative, and matters of adult education policy just happen to fall right in the middle of these two realities. The net result is that in Canada the attempt to understand adult education as indicated by public policy is not straightforward, but it is a matter of piecing together in each of Canada's legislative jurisdictions the situation as it relates to specific areas of adult education.

Because of this uneven nature to public policy development in Canada regarding adult education the subject will be presented across two chapters. This chapter will first present a theoretical understanding to public policy and its formation. Accordingly it begins with an examination of what is meant by the

---

[1]   CAAE/ICEA, *From the Adults' Point of View* (Toronto, CAAE, 1982).

[2]   Employment and Immigration Canada, *Learning A Living in Canada*, Vols. 1 & 2 (Toronto, Minister of Supplies and Services, 1983).

term public policy and then provides a framework for analyzing the process of public policy development. As a means of integrating this theoretical understanding within the Canadian political context, the example of public policy favouring adult literacy is then used as a case study. To conclude the chapter there is a review of international calls regarding public policy and adult education. Chapter 7 reviews the public policy actions which have been taken in Canada at both the federal and provincial levels. To help bring an international perspective to the Canadian situation brief descriptions are also provided of the policy situation in three countries: Sweden, Tanzania and China. To begin, then, we will look at what is meant by public policy.

The Meaning of Public Policy

Generally speaking the term "public policy" suggests a specific undertaking by government on behalf of the public. In its most forthright expression such an undertaking is made to the people through legislation, thereby ensuring that the undertaking can only be amended or withdrawn by way of a change to the legislation. In reality, however, this is only one form in which public policy can be made. Other forms are often much less explicit, and neither their development nor their pronouncement are necessarily done in a particularly public manner. Examples of this include the specific regulations developed so as to make operational the intent of the more general legislation and the in-camera deliberations and decisions of a cabinet, the executive council of government. It is quite often the case that government policy must be inferred from the perceived actions of government as opposed to looking only to its formal expression as communicated by legislation. Several reasons have been advanced for this:

1. the public utterances of politicians do not always reflect the intent of the government

2. statutes are normally cast in rather general language and typically include aspects of permissiveness or provide discretionary powers to various operating levels

3. the general language of a statute is made operational by rules and regulations or orders-in-council which do not require the assent of the legislature

4. the interpretation of statutes and regulations by civil servants may or may not be in accord with a government's intent.[3]

Another difficulty with the term public policy is its implicit suggestion that not only are policies developed publicly but that they are also developed necessarily in the public interest. This suggestion is challenged by Cassidy, who

---

[3] J. Ellis, "Government Policies," in Mugridge and Kaufman, *Distance Education in Canada* (London, Croom Helm, 1986) p. 27.

suggests, " ... many of the policies which are made for the public are made by private rather than public interests. In fact, it is frequently the case that public policy is neither developed in public nor by the public. Public policy is often public only in the sense that it is something which happens to the public."[4] According to Cassidy, when regarding public policy it is necessary to consider whose interests are being served by that policy, and why that might be the case.

A further difficulty with public policy is that we must in many instances look to the absence of an explicit public policy, in whatever form, in order to conclude what the government's policy is regarding a certain issue. This situation is common in the case of adult education where in many jurisdictions there is no specific public policy governing adult education. This does not indicate that publicly provided adult education is taking place outside of a legal framework but rather that the laws which govern and enable it are general rather than specific.[5] The government, while not wanting to forbid adult education, at the same time is not wanting to give it a statutory status equal to that of compulsory youth education which would thereby commit government to a significant level of public expenditure. Using the situation in British Columbia as an example, the legislation governing the grade school system, School Act (1989), allows for school boards to provide adult education by virtue of Section 94 subsection 8 which says, "A board may permit a person who is older than school age to attend an educational program in accordance with any terms and conditions specified by the board." Such permissive, but not obligatory, wording reinforces the oft made suggestion of adult education's marginal status.

To this point the consideration of public policy has focused on policy and regulations enacted by a legislative body, i.e. a provincial legislature, a territorial assembly, or the national government. There is also the policy developed by a lesser authority, e.g. a school board, and by individual providers, e.g. a university extension department, to provide guidelines for administrators as they confront situations, either in the present or in anticipation of the future. Policies made at these levels are also important to take into account when considering the policy provision for adult education. The above example of British Columbia demonstrates this, as the general provincial policy delegates the specific policy to the local school board level. Thus the term, public policy, is surrounded by a degree of ambiguity, and this situation was summed up in a review of educational policies in the Province of Saskatchewan:

> Broadly defined, policy includes all written documents, statements of philosophy, customary practices (of the Department of Education), and all statutes and regulations regarding administrative procedures (followed by Department offi-

---

[4] F. Cassidy, "Public Policy Development: A Learning Approach," *Journal of the Alberta Association for Continuing Education* Vol. 13 (1985) p. 13.

[5] Ellis makes this point in the case of distance education. J. Ellis, "Government Policies," p. 28.

cials). Those policies reflected in statutes and regulations have legal implications. Others are largely intended to guide education officials in carrying out duties derived from statutes and regulations ... Formal policy found in legislation and statutes is difficult to read. Less formal policy is not consolidated and is not widely understood or easily communicated.[6]

In this chapter the consideration of public policy will for the most part be kept to its expression in statutory form.

Education and the State

Having reviewed the difficulties in specifying what exactly is public policy it is necessary to step back further yet and take a philosophical point of view about public policy and adult education. In doing so it is necessary to consider all of education as provided by the state, not just adult education. The question is one of determining what is the nature of the relationship between education and society, and appreciating the crucial interdependence that exists between the two. It then becomes possible to see the need for government, through its allocation of resources, to provide direction to the education system. Once the need for this direction giving is apparent, it become further possible to distil the place of adult education within the total provision of state supported education.

Basic to any society is the need to ensure its survival. In most societies this basic need is advanced to a higher order of existence than merely surviving, and in the case of societies governed by democratic ideology, they additionally strive to uphold the principles of democracy. These principles promote the rights of the citizen within society, and this is seen as being the most just means by which people should be governed. In such societies the educational system, with its ability to inculcate beliefs, values and attitudes as well as knowledge, is a primary instrument of government for ensuring the society's continued vital and democratic existence. Much of this is evidenced in the curriculum prescribed for use in the grade school system where socializing students in the dominant values held by the society is as much an emphasis as is the developing of individual intellect. (It also explains why curriculum development is controlled centrally and why grade school attendance is compulsory.) By way of its resource allocation to the educational system, government assumes a controlling interest in the results produced by the system.

At the same time the educational system in a democratic society, while not an independent entity, exercises a degree of autonomy from government and is able in turn to exert influence on the state. This comes about by virtue of the fact that the educational system, and particularly at the higher levels, is the predominant creator and disseminator of the knowledge and skills essential to the continued survival of the society. It is the educational system which has the ultimate ability to respond to circumstances which threaten the continued well-being of the state.

---

[6] Minister's Advisory Committee, *Saskatchewan Education: Its Programs and Policies* (Regina, Saskatchewan Education, 1984) p. 7.

(The exception to this is a military threat which calls for a military response.) Because the state exists in an ever changing world, especially in post-industrial societies there is the need at a minimum to maintain the standard of living which its citizens have come to expect while at the same time making the significant adjustments brought about by changes in the technical, economic and social environments. It is the educational system that plays the crucial part, on behalf of the state, in mediating between the necessary changes and the ability of citizens to respond, thereby making the adjustments possible. An example of this is the Free Trade Agreement between Canada and the United States which has as one of its consequences the exposure of a number of Canadian industries to stiff competition now that protective tariff barriers have been removed. The education system has become involved in at least two ways, the first being the educating of industry managers to new manufacturing and marketing strategies and the second being the retraining of workers who find themselves displaced.

In identifying the mediating role of the educational system it is important to note that the system serves the learning needs not only of the state but also of individual citizens. Free thinking citizens in a democratic society pursue their learning motivated by personal needs and interests, and these may well be distinct from what are the specific needs of the state. This is not a discordant situation in a democratic society, although resource allocation by government may be perceived as skewing the balance between individual and state interests if individual interests are thought of as being compromised or even ignored. Thus, for example, government might make large sums available for vocational education, and even provide tuition subsidies, while not supporting at all programs for older workers on retirement preparation.

In Canada and indeed most post-industrialized countries the educational system has had to make adjustments consistent with changes brought about in the society in order that it better serve the needs of the state. The most pivotal of these adjustments by the educational system is responding to the fact that individuals need to continue their education beyond what was once considered sufficient, i.e. beyond youth and now into adulthood. Thomas identifies two principal sources for this adjustment, one intellectual and the second practical.[7]

The intellectual source is identified as being the report of the International Commission on the Development of Education (Faure Commission) titled, *Learning to Be*, and published in 1972.[8] The Commission had been established by UNESCO to review the results of the huge expenditures in education undertaken by most governments in the world since the 1950s. Thomas notes the

---

[7] A. Thomas, "Learning in Society—A Discussion Paper," in *Learning in Society: Toward a New Paradigm*, UNESCO Occasional Paper No. 51 (Ottawa, Canadian Commission for UNESCO, 1985) p. 17.

[8] International Commission for the Development of Education, *Learning To Be* (London, Harrap, 1972).

Report arrived at the conclusion that it had not been a mistake for countries to have invested heavily in education as a means of development but that it had been an error to concentrate the expenditures on the education of the young. According to Thomas the *Report* " ... laid to rest one of the most cherished illusions of the West, that you can bring about positive and controlled change in a society by concentrating on the education of the young."[9]

The practical source identified by Thomas stems from the discovery not only by governments but also by large organizations that "even for the maintenance of their societies and organizations, they are increasingly dependent upon learning, that is, upon learning undertaken by increasing numbers and types of individuals in their populations, over longer periods of their lifetimes—learning which cannot be accomplished by means of exposure to educational resources in the first twenty years of life."[10]

Distinction Between Learning and Education

From the above it is possible to recognize how the relationship between education and society is both essential and dynamic, and that the instrument of education is seen, by some at any rate, to extend to the education of adults as well as youth. There is one further implication to be drawn relating to education and society and that is the distinction between learning and education. Learning is understood as being an intellectual process within the capacity of the individual, an activity described by Thomas as being "voluntary and uncoercible."[11] Education, by contrast, is an organized way of providing for learning to take place, as in the case of a school system or an industrial training centre. This distinction is important when considering public policy in that the state can legislate and regulate education but it cannot do so with learning. This is evidenced in Canada by the fact that significant numbers of students drop out of high school upon, or shortly after, reaching the age where education is no longer compulsory. In terms of the formal curriculum, these persons have chosen to discontinue their education. There may be certain skills or knowledge, however, which these same individuals will subsequently need to learn (or relearn) in order to function effectively, and it is likely only through the opportunity to subsequently continue with their education that this learning will be made possible. Thus while the distinction between learning and education is easily made, managing the interaction between the two is considerably more difficult both for the state and for the individual citizen. The difficulty exists for the state in being able to provide educational opportunity for those times when a citizen has a learning need. For the individual citizen the difficulty lies in being able to access

---

9   A. Thomas, "Learning in Society—A Discussion Paper," p. 17.

10   A. Thomas, "Learning in Society—A Discussion Paper," p. 18.

11   A. Thomas, "Government and Adult Learning," in F. Cassidy and R. Faris (Eds.), *Choosing Our Future: Adult Education and Public Policy in Canada* (Toronto, O.I.S.E. Press, 1987) p. 109.

educational opportunity when a particular learning need arises. The appropriate balance is exceedingly difficult to maintain, and it is not easy to determine just what constitutes "appropriate." Of interest to adult educators is the fact that much of this managing needs to occur with persons who are beyond their years of formal education, as this is the purview of adult education.

In Canada the state's involvement in the management of education beyond the formal educational system, i.e. with continuing education, is not a new phenomenon, although particularly during and since the Second World War its involvement has intensified in response to military and economic threats. The response has been by way of identifiable public policy, and in order to understand why and how these responses were developed it is helpful to have available an analytic framework.

Analytical Framework for Public Policy Formation

It has already been noted that the rendering of public policy is often difficult to discern. This situation is made even more difficult by the fact that public policy formation is sometimes done for reasons that have as much to do with political expediency as with providing good government. Because of this situation, a framework for analyzing the formation of public policy must necessarily be general so as to accommodate the innumerable factors and interests which influence the developmental process. The following framework is put forward as a means of analyzing individual public policies and also of comparing one with another.

Four stages can be identified when analyzing the formation of public policy. These stages are:

1. the precursor circumstances which give rise to a call for a public policy response, and which lead to ...
2. the development process of a public policy, which leads to ...
3. the implementation of a public policy, which is followed by ...
4. the review of a public policy in light of subsequent circumstances.

As noted earlier public policy, however it is made public, is an indication of a deliberate action on the part of government. Similarly, the absence of a public policy can be construed as a deliberate action on the part of government, in this case one of deliberate inaction which in effect maintains the status quo or which allows developments to occur unimpeded by public policy. To account for this possibility the above framework must be amended in stages 2, 3 and 4 so as to indicate that public policy can be seen in terms of either deliberate action or deliberate inaction. Thus:

1. the precursor circumstances which give rise to a call for a public policy response, and which lead to ...
2. the development process of a public policy, which leads to ... *or the denial of a process.*

3. the implementation of a public policy which is followed by ... *or the refusal or failure to implement a public policy, which is perhaps followed by ...*

4. the review of a public policy in light of subsequent circumstances ... *or a review of the continued ignoring of the precursor circumstances, or the circumstances as they have since developed.*

Stage 1

By way of elaboration, at stage one there are always innumerable circumstances in a society which need addressing or which call for redressing. To the extent that these circumstances are able to garner sufficient attention and support, an issue may develop which is not only recognized by an advocacy group but is also acknowledged by the government. At stage one, however, the focus is on the garnering of sufficient attention and support for the circumstances. The cause of the modern women's movement, beginning in the 1960s, is an example of circumstances coalescing into an issue. It is important to also note that it is often the case where government itself is the body which identifies the precursor circumstances and initiates the call for a public policy response. The move by the Conservative government to implement free trade between Canada and the United States in light of global economic trends illustrates this point.

Stage 2

At stage two the response to a call for public policy lies squarely with the government. It is here that the government chooses either to acknowledge or ignore the circumstances. This is evidenced by the government either engaging in a public policy development process or denying such a process. The focus is on process in that government, in choosing to acknowledge the circumstances and engage in a public policy development process, may elect to make the process as public or private as it wishes. The appointment of Royal Commissions is an example of a public process which is intended to encourage broad public participation. Most often, however, public input into policy development is controlled or even non-existent. Democratically elected governments are in a position to decide whether public input is required or whether the input as supplied by the elected representatives of the people is sufficient. Political considerations frequently influence a government's decisions in this regard. Regardless of the extent of participation by the public in the policy development process, the next stage awaits.

Stage 3

Ideally, of course, at this third stage public policy flows out of the development process. The government selects what it believes to be the most prudent course of action as identified by the developmental process and begins on that course. However by virtue of engaging in a policy development process the government does not necessarily obligate itself to take action, whether by way of legislative enactment, order-in-council or other methods at its disposal. Indeed one of the strategies employed by government to defuse an issue is to appoint a study into it as part of the policy development process, and to then ignore or only selectively implement the findings of the study. Adult education has fallen victim to this strategy on more than one occasion.

Stage 4

The fourth stage indicates that a particular public policy need not last forever, and is reviewed and evaluated in terms of its effectiveness in addressing or redressing the original precursor circumstances. Similarly, in the event the government initially chooses to ignore the precursor circumstances or subsequent circumstances, it may want to review that decision if the issue still exists or has gathered strength. The situation of industry despoiling the environment illustrates an issue the government was able to ignore for a considerable period of time, but because of growing public concern it has now accepted environmental quality as being an issue which requires control through public policy.

For each stage there are a myriad of considerations which influence the progression or non-progression through the stages. For example in the first stage—the precursor circumstances which give rise to a call for a public policy response—the existence of precursor circumstances may be a debatable point. A particular advocacy group may be determined they do exist, while government may disagree or choose not to agree. An illustration of this is where an environmental lobby believes a certain adverse condition exists, such as the polluting of a watershed by an industry, but government studies come up with different findings. Even if the precursor circumstances do exist, their implications may be insufficient to arouse much interest among other advocacy groups, the general public, or with government. In adult education there is the example of the move to certify adult educators along lines similar to teacher certification in the grade school system. Nothing has come of this move despite there being proponents of it. Further yet, if sufficient interest is indeed generated the response by government can be something other than to develop public policy. Instead an insignificant enforcement action or the appointment of an inquiry commission might be other responses that have far less policy consequences for government.

Public Policy Consequences

Consequences are a major consideration for any government. In the case of Canada the form of government is the parliamentary system, in which political parties vie for the right to form the government, and this right is for a limited period (maximum five years) when it must again be conferred. This strongly suggests that the policy making process is prompted by political considerations in addition to the altruistic considerations attached to a particular issue. In reality both altruistic and political considerations must be present for public policy to be developed and the framework as outlined can be made operational by identifying for each stage the altruistic and political considerations which are present. Where the two considerations are compatible, the probability of public policy being developed is greatly increased. Where the two are incompatible, there is little likelihood, unless exigencies exist such as the example of the federal budgetary deficit and the government's introduction of the Goods and Services Tax.

Another consequence for government arises in the process of allocating resources or, more specifically, money. While economists will point out that government's ability to spend money is not restricted, as government has the ability to raise additional amounts through taxation, the situation today of a large public debt is causing government to be particularly conscious of its fiscal responsibility. The outcome of this is that funds available to government must be carefully distributed among different priority areas, and just because a public policy issue has harmonious political and altruistic considerations, it will not necessarily result in public policy if the required budget amounts are not available. An example of this is the long touted national daycare scheme, a proposal which has remained unimplemented for lack of funding.

There is a further financial consideration for government which bears directly on education and this is the issue of universality. In Canada the notion of universality applies to certain government programs whereby citizen access to the benefits of those programs is not influenced by socio-economic considerations. Health care and child allowances are two such programs of the federal government. Within the provincial jurisdiction, education through the elementary and secondary grades is a universal program for school age children. Operating this educational system involves hefty expenditures of public money, and this is without adding the equally substantial cost of operating the post-secondary system. Thus for government any extension of universal access to education beyond its current level, replete as it would be with financial implications, is not seen as being an attractive option to pursue when attempting to address the educational needs of adults. An interesting development, however, is that in some provinces access to free education to the high school completion level has now been extended to adults regardless of age.

Four Modes of Government Response to Demands for Learning

To complete this discussion of adult education and public policy there is a categorization of the responses which governments can make to demands for learning, including adult learning, which serves as another assist to analyzing government action. Developed by Thomas, the categorization is made up of four possible modes: Mode 1—to permit, Mode 2—to encourage, Mode 3—to direct, Mode 4—to forbid.[12] Depending on the learning objectives involved in the particular demand for learning, government can choose to respond in the mode which will most likely bring about the outcome most desired by government.

The first mode, to permit, suggests that unless otherwise prevented by law the citizen is free to pursue learning as a basic freedom. Because learning is so much

---

[12] A. Thomas, "Government and Adult Learning."

a part of the classic freedoms of speech, association and movement, it is absolutely necessary to ensure these freedoms remain untethered. These freedoms are part of the "social contract" between the state and its citizens. Providing there is no legal impediment to the learning objectives (Mode 4—to forbid), the response by government from Mode 1 is either to encourage (Mode 2) or to direct (Mode 3) the attainment of the learning objectives.

The second mode, to encourage, indicates that government believes learning *per se* should be encouraged, and it is thus appropriate that public provision be made for this to occur, even though the objectives of the learning might not be associated with a particular requirement of the government (which is the third mode, to direct). In this second mode the individual is free to choose from among a spectrum of agencies involved in providing learning, from museums, libraries and art galleries through to employers, labour organizations and voluntary agencies. While the form of encouragement made by government is most often financial, for example capital expenditure or tax credits for tuition costs, there are other means at its disposal to similarly encourage learning. Thomas cites the example of a municipal government's regulatory ability to influence the architecture of buildings so as to make them, in this case, congenial adult learning spaces.

The third mode, to direct, indicates that society, through government, has identified particular learning objectives which warrant a systematic provision at society's expense. Public institutions have been created for this purpose and are readily identified as schools, colleges, institutes and universities. Thomas notes the constant factor with regards to these providing agencies is that they all have the authority, through government, to certify the achievements of their students.

The fourth mode, to forbid, is the antithesis of the first, to permit, and refers to those aspects of teaching which government has identified as being seditious, racist, treasonous, hateful etc. and which are expressly forbidden by law. An example would be the laws against the promulgation of hatred. The maintaining of community standards through censorship is another example.

Thomas indicates there is a dynamic to this categorization, a movement amongst the modes, which directly relates to the management of learning by government. Government is able to determine in which mode it will respond to a demand for learning, and by using this categorization it is possible to ascertain whether a particular response is likely to bring about what government considers to be the desired outcome. This is the topic of the next chapter, in which the responses by governments in Canada to the requirements and demands for adult learning are reviewed.

The foregoing outline of public policy has been general so as to embrace the wide spectrum of possibility regarding adult education and public policy. It will be useful to now "ground" this outline by way of a contemporary example. Because adult literacy has been the subject of explicit public policy in Canada, and calls for policy have come both from within government and from the community, it is an instructive illustration of public policy related to adult education.

Adult Literacy: A Case Study in Public Policy

Beginning with Thomas's four modes, government has always responded to demands for adult literacy education from the standpoint of Mode 1—to permit. What is clearly discernible, though, is that whereas government for many years based its policies on Mode 2—to encourage, more recently, as the problem of adult illiteracy has become a political issue, government has had to shift more noticeably toward Mode 3—to direct. The policy analysis framework introduced earlier is useful in identifying the specific developments which have lead to public policy formation in the area of adult illiteracy.

1. The Precursor Circumstances Which Give Rise to a Call for a Public Policy Response

The fact of adult illiteracy in Canada has long been recognized. One of the country's most venerated adult education institutions, Frontier College (established in 1899), early on saw the need to provide adult basic education in an effort to address this very problem. More recently, in 1967 the Canada NewStart Program was launched under the auspices of the federal Department of Manpower and Immigration with the purpose of promoting experimentation in methods which would motivate and train adults who were "educationally disadvantaged." Most recently the federal government has created the National Literacy Secretariat (in 1987) to foster action and promote coordination in literacy related programming.

Historically speaking, illiteracy has been considered as a condition afflicting immigrants and the less well educated, i.e. those who never attended school or who dropped out along the way. The earliest attempts at attacking illiteracy included provision by the state for the compulsory education of youth and also the provision by voluntary organizations of language training for immigrants and basic literacy skills for others.

In the span of time from the turn of the century to the present the attitude towards those who are adult illiterates has evolved from them being considered as either foreigners or ill-fated persons by virtue of an incomplete education to now being considered persons who are required to assume their full role in modern Canadian society. The essential factor in this evolution has been the acceptance by government of the responsibility for overcoming adult illiteracy so that it is now shared between the individual and the society at large, and with this acceptance provision of public funds has been made for the necessary remedial education.

This acceptance of the responsibility occurred largely as a result of uncovering the extent of illiteracy and the effect it was having on the country's social and economic development. Prior to this uncovering, illiteracy as an issue had easily been able to remain out of public view; indeed one of the hallmarks of a developed country such as Canada is its educational system with the capacity to effectively deliver mass education. Acknowledging the existence of illiteracy can be seen as a condemnation of the educational system. In Canada the uncovering began as a result of the federal government's initiatives in the 1960s with manpower planning, starting with the Technical and Vocational Training Act (1960). As Thomas notes, "Very early in the decade, it was realized that an alarming proportion of those in need of vocational training did not have enough of the academic skills to enable them to participate in the vocational training programs."[13] As a consequence the federal government became actively involved in funding remedial education as part of its vocational training initiatives, beginning with the Adult Occupational Training Act (1967). Adult basic education programs such as Basic Training for Skill Development (BTSD) and innovative approaches such as the NewStart Corporations came into being to compensate for inadequate or incomplete formal education.

The extent of illiteracy has, however, never been a secret. Census figures have regularly reported educational attainment in the adult population and these figures, in the absence of more specific precise literacy statistics, have been used as a reasonable indicator of the number of Canadian adults who, by definition, are functionally illiterate.[14] UNESCO established the standard of less than nine years formal education to indicate functional illiteracy.[15] For the most part, however, the statistics remained cause for individual rather than societal distress, and it was not until much later in the 1980s when the statistics were placed in the compelling context of the cost to Canada's labour market that illiteracy drew concerted attention at both the national and the provincial levels.

Despite the federal provision for adult basic education, illiteracy persisted and even worsened. Aspects of the problem became politically charged when, for example, the findings of a Senate committee were published which stated that the federal funds were financing the costs of upgrading the adult drop-outs from the provincial school systems.[16] Another Senate committee, investigating poverty in Canada, underscored the connection between educational attainment and economic status and the inevitable link between poverty and illiteracy.[17]

---

[13] Audrey Thomas, *Adult Illiteracy in Canada: A Challenge*, UNESCO Occasional Paper No. 42 (Ottawa, Canadian Commission for UNESCO, 1983) p. 63.

[14] For example see E. Adamson, "The Need for Adult Basic Education," in Selman and Kidd (Eds.), *Coming of Age: Canadian Adult Education in the 1960's* (Toronto, Canadian Association for Adult Education, 1978) p. 124.

[15] For a full discussion on definitions and standards see J. Cairns, *Adult Illiteracy in Canada* (Toronto, Council of Ministers of Education (Canada), 1988) p. 4.

[16] Audrey Thomas, "Adult Illiteracy in Canada: A Challenge," p. 64.

[17] Government of Canada, *Poverty in Canada: Highlights of the Report of the Special Senate Committee* (Ottawa, Information Canada, 1971).

For an economically advanced and democratic country such as Canada, the fact of persistently high illiteracy rates was a source of national embarrassment, not to mention social dislocation. At a time of massive investment in post-secondary education, the adult illiteracy issue remained a perplexing problem, one which called for a direct public policy response.

There are many additional precursor circumstances which could be identified as being influential to the call for public policy. Certainly a number of advocacy groups had been active in the effort to influence governments' increased role in addressing the issue, including Frontier College, the labour movement, World Literacy of Canada, The Movement for Canadian Literacy, the Canadian Association for Adult Education, and Laubach Literacy of Canada. By the mid 1980s the issue was well documented and acknowledged by all concerned.[18] In some provinces special literacy programs had been developed, and in British Columbia during 1982 a policy statement on adult basic education was issued which stated, "It is the policy of the ministry to provide, to adult citizens and landed immigrants residing in the province, reasonable access to high quality adult basic education programs."[19] The major call for action, however, was directed at the federal government, and there was considerable pressure applied. Thus the precursor circumstances had by 1986 lead to ...

2. The Development Process of a Public Policy (or the Denial of a Process)

In the Speech from the Throne delivered October 1, 1986, the federal government pledged to "work with the provinces, the private sector and voluntary groups to develop resources to ensure that Canadians have access to the literacy skills that are the prerequisite for participation in our advanced economy."[20] This policy reference signalled the political acceptance of the literacy issue on the part of the Conservative government. By virtue of being included in the Throne Speech the reference also signalled the gravity of the issue, and by its wording indicated the concern was framed in terms of the human capital view of adult education. (This view holds that the predominant purpose of adult education is to develop the skills of members of the workforce, the "human capital" of the economy.) The government's acceptance of the illiteracy issue, however, was still non-committal in terms of specific actions. Throne speeches typically provide the government in power with the opportunity to acknowledge the existence of a particular issue without having to go further. They are simply an indication of likely future action, and do not outline specific commitments.

The Throne Speech announcement represented, of course, a significant breakthrough for adult literacy advocates. Even though the reference was fleeting, its

---

[18] J. Cairns, *Adult Illiteracy in Canada*, p. 13.

[19] As quoted in J. Cairns, *Adult Illiteracy in Canada*, p. 42.

[20] Hon. David Crombie, "Message," in *Learning* Vol. V: 1 (1988), p. 13.

significance lay in the willing acceptance of the moral responsibility for the issue on the part of the federal government. By taking on the commitment the federal government would not only make available public resources to address the issue but would also be publicly accountable for its actions or inactions. What remained was the development of the specific policy.

As noted earlier, the development process of a public policy has no specified format or procedure. In the case of adult literacy the process was limited to the federal government acting of its own accord, although not without input from other sources. In part this is explained by the delicate jurisdictional issue: education is a provincial, not federal, responsibility, and the federal government had only so much room in which to take initiative. The Department of the Secretary of State was assigned the task of developing a national strategy for substantially reducing illiteracy, and the Department undertook consultations with provincial governments, with groups from the voluntary, educational, labour, and private sectors and with other federal government departments.

The reference in the Throne Speech had the effect of galvanizing the voluntary sector into action. A coalition was formed of national organizations concerned with promoting adult literacy. Under the leadership of the Movement for Canadian Literacy, the coalition embarked on a campaign of public awareness by way of placing an open letter to the Prime Minister, the Provincial Premiers and the Territorial Government Leaders in two mass circulation publications, *Macleans* magazine and the *Globe and Mail* newspaper.[21] This letter summarized a statement on public policy, known as the Cedar Glen Declaration, which the coalition had produced shortly after coming together in December, 1986.

The Council of Ministers of Education was also part of the consultation process. This body of provincial ministers of education is, among other things, a focal point for consultation on education related matters between the provinces and the federal government. Always mindful of the provincial prerogative in the field of education, and not wishing to be usurped on the literacy issue, the Council embarked on its own survey of the issue and followed this publication with the provincial response outlining provincial measures already being taken to eradicate adult illiteracy.[22]

The single most influential contribution to the policy development process came unsolicited to the federal government. During September, 1987, newspapers of the Southam News chain published articles on adult illiteracy based on the findings of a literacy survey commissioned by Southam News. The survey determined that five million Canadians were functionally illiterate, according to criteria developed specifically for the survey.[23] The national impact of the find-

---

[21] *Macleans*, February 22, 1988, p. 27.

[22] J. Cairns, *Adult Illiteracy in Canada*.

[23] P. Calamai, *Broken Words* (Toronto, Southam Newspaper Group, 1987).

ings was enormous, all the more so due to such shocking revelations as illiteracy existing even among university graduates.

The results of the Southam Literacy Survey gave rise to another study being conducted, this time by the Canadian Business Task Force on Literacy, in February, 1988.[24] The purpose of the Business Task Force study was to estimate the cost of illiteracy to business in particular and society in general so as instigate a serious dialogue on the problem of illiteracy. The intended outcome of the dialogue was to have government and business "allocate resources adequate to the dimensions of the problem." The study, undertaken by an accounting firm, estimated that the direct cost to business of illiteracy was 4 billion dollars and to society as a whole was 10 billion dollars. The report's authors noted that, "These estimates are published not with absolute conviction of their accuracy, but from a need to contribute to the debate on the position that literacy should occupy on the national agenda." The findings, although not as widely reported as the findings of the Southam Literacy Survey, were nonetheless astounding.

The purpose of the Business Task Force study was well served. The Southam Literacy Survey had brought the issue into full public view and "established beyond a reasonable doubt the existence of a literacy problem in Canada."[25] It was the quantification of that problem, however, which confirmed the insidious economic effects of illiteracy, and this was a clearly understood consequence, free of the entrapping of "softer" social concerns. Writing in response to the Southam Literacy Survey but before the publication of the Business Task Force study, Darville had noted in regard to maintaining literacy on the national policy agenda, "The development, or lack of development, of a conception of costs may make or break the literacy issue as a focus for long-term government attention."[26]

Two years after the reference to literacy in the Throne Speech the policy development process within government, both planned and in response to unfolding developments, had received all the necessary input. (Darville refers to these inputs as being a discourse, "that kind of conversation in texts through which 'issues' in our society are defined, and terms are devised to describe 'problems' and what should be done about them. Many texts (speeches, policy statements, committee and commission reports, scholarly articles, media accounts) make up this conversation.")[27] More than ever the issue was ready for direct policy action.

---

[24] Canadian Business Task Force on Literacy, *Measuring the Costs of Illiteracy* (Toronto: Business Task Force, 1988).

[25] Canadian Business Task Force on Literacy, *Measuring the Costs of Illiteracy*, p. 3.

[26] Richard Darville, "Framing Il/literacy in the Media" in *Learning* Vol. V: 1 (1988) pp. 9–11, p. 11.

[27] Richard Darville, "Framing Il/literacy in the Media," p. 10.

3. The Implementation of a Public Policy (Or the Refusal to Implement a Public Policy)

There were two initial policy initiatives announced by the federal government prior to the revelation of the major policy initiative. The first, in March, 1987, was when the federal Solicitor-General announced a significant program to address the high illiteracy rate among the prison population, it being estimated that nearly one half of the inmates were functionally illiterate. The second, in September, 1987, was when the Secretary of State announced a $1 million allocation for the establishment of a National Literacy Secretariat and the granting of funds in support of literacy initiatives. The major policy initiative occurred on International Literacy Day, September 8, 1988, when the Prime Minister announced the federal government's National Literacy Strategy consisting of a $110 million fund to be made available over five years. This amount was earmarked to support literacy partnership initiatives with voluntary associations and joint program initiatives with provincial governments. "Funds are available for pilot or demonstration projects, but not for ongoing delivery. Other projects funded include research and needs assessment studies, conferences and public awareness initiatives, development of materials, resource networks and provincial coalitions."[28]

The question is able to be raised as to whether or not the National Literacy Strategy can properly be defined as a public policy. In an operational sense it is. Public commitments have been made by the Prime Minister (who announced the National Literacy Strategy), resources have been allocated (110 million dollars), and a bureaucracy established (the National Literacy Secretariat). In a strict policy sense, however, it is not. There is no legislation which outlines the government's policy towards literacy. There is no official definition of literacy against which to measure the outcomes of the National Literacy Strategy. The partnership arrangement of the strategy distributes decision-making among numerous partners and thereby reduces the policy's cohesiveness. It also makes the avenues for accountability unclear. Lastly, the funding commitment is for five years only. In this regard the public policy is seen as not having gone far enough to ensure the policy's objectives can be met, i.e. the substantial reduction of adult illiteracy. This is compared to, for example, the National Training Act (1982) in which the federal government's job retraining policy was spelled out by way of legislative enactment and unilateral action. Despite this definitional question, the federal government has clearly acknowledged its lead role in bringing resources to bear on the literacy issue. Attention turns, then, to Stage 4 of the policy development process.

---

[28] Provincial Literacy Advisory Committee, *Opening the Doors to Lifelong Learning: Empowering Undereducated Adults* (Vancouver, Ministry of Advanced Education, Technology and Job Technology, 1989) p. 9.

4. The Review of a Public Policy in Light of Subsequent Circumstances
(A Review of the Continued Ignoring of the Precursor
Circumstances, or the Circumstances as They Have Since
Developed)

In the case of the literacy policy it is too early yet for a policy review to take place, the funding policy being only in its third year of five and there having been no subsequent circumstances to cause a deviation from the announced policy. With 1990 being International Literacy Year it is likely the National Literacy Strategy will be showcased, and statistics developed to suggest some degree of success at reducing the incidence of illiteracy. By virtue of having taken policy action, the federal government now holds the strategic high ground on the issue, above the advocacy groups and even the provincial governments. Whether it intends to hold this position remains to be seen as the five-year period draws to an end. Certainly the circumstances surrounding the literacy issue, as they subsequently develop in light of the National Literacy Strategy, will largely determine further policy initiatives.

The manner in which Canada is responding to the literacy issue is also of international significance. Canada sees itself as a responsible member of the international community, a view that is reinforced by its "middle power" status. This status positions Canada between the super power nations and the developing third world countries, thereby enabling it to be influential in mediating differences and in exercising leadership in the promotion of peace and human well-being. As evidence of this Canada participates thoughtfully at international gatherings, and often guides the deliberations so as to produce constructive outcomes. This certainly describes Canada's actions in the area of international adult education, and this country has participated at all four of the United Nations Educational, Scientific and Cultural Organization (UNESCO) sponsored international conferences on adult education (Elsinore—1948, Montreal—1960, Tokyo—1972, and Paris—1985).[29] As a recent example of Canada's role in these deliberations, at the 1985 Paris conference Canada introduced the Declaration on the Right to Learn which was subsequently passed by the assembly.[30] It is useful, then, to briefly examine the international calls for public policy regarding adult education.

---

[29] For reports on these conferences see UNESCO, *Summary Report of the International Conference on Adult Education* (Paris, UNESCO, 1949); UNESCO, *World Conference on Adult Education: Final Report* (Paris, UNESCO, 1960); UNESCO, *Third International Conference: Final Report* (Paris, UNESCO, 1972); UNESCO, *Fourth International Conference on Adult Education* (Paris, UNESCO, 1985). An excellent synthesis of the Third Conference is contained in J. Lowe, *The Education of Adults: A World Perspective* (Toronto, O.I.S.E. Press, 1975).

[30] Desmond Berghofer, "The Right To Learn," in *Learning*, Vol. IV: 2 (1985) p. 11.

International Calls for Public Policy

The work of the United Nations agency, UNESCO, has been particularly instrumental in bringing adult education into the mainstream of educational policy planning. One manner in which this has occurred has been the convening of the above noted international conferences on adult education. Two other manners also stand out: the establishing of an International Commission on the Development of Education in 1971 and the adoption of a Recommendation on the Development of Adult Education in 1976.

The International Commission on the Development of Education was established by UNESCO to look at the development of education worldwide, to study its problems and to put forward new strategies for planning educational systems. Its conclusions were published in a landmark report titled, *Learning to Be*, and which is commonly referred to as the Faure Report after the Commission's chairman, Edgar Faure. In a broadly considered approach to the provision of education worldwide, the Commission reviewed the adequacy of existing educational systems and their abilities to be responsive to both the requirements of their societies and the needs of individuals. The whole concept of education was examined in terms of its pedagogy and its occurrence throughout life. The Report's conclusions were necessarily general, given the scope of the inquiry and the international community to which they were addressed. Twenty-one conclusions were advanced with the intention that they become "elements for contemporary strategies" within individual countries in the desire to engender "learning societies." As an example, the first conclusion asserted the principle that, "Every individual must be in a position to keep learning throughout his life. The idea of lifelong education is the keystone to the learning society." From this principle came the recommendation that lifelong education be considered as "the master concept for educational policies in the years to come for both developed and developing countries."[31]

A subsequent UNESCO General Conference, held in Nairobi, Kenya, in 1976, adopted a Recommendation on the Development of Adult Education.[32] The principles contained in the Recommendation were commended to the signatory nations for attention and implementation by "authorities, departments or bodies responsible for adult education and also of the various organizations carrying out educational work for the benefit of adults, and of trade union organizations, associations, enterprises, and other interested parties." This Recommendation is significant on many counts, one being its effort at integrating into a policy document the products of previous international gatherings which dealt with aspects of adult education. The Recommendation is also comprehensive in its consideration of the areas of adult education which call for policy development,

---

[31] International Commission on the Development of Education, *Learning To Be: The World of Education Today and Tomorrow* (Paris, UNESCO, 1972) p. 181.

[32] UNESCO, *Recommendation on the Development of Adult Education* Occasional Paper 34 (Ottawa, Canadian Commission for UNESCO, nd).

as seen in its organization under the following headings: (1) Definition, (2) Objectives and Strategy, (3) Content of Adult Education, (4) Methods, Means, Research and Evaluation, (5) The Structures of Adult Education, (6) Training and Status of Persons Engaged in Adult Education Work, (7) Relations Between Adult Education and Youth Education, (8) Relations Between Adult Education and Work, (9) Management, Administration, Co-ordination and Financing of Adult Education, and (10) International Co-operation. The Recommendation has no binding authority on those governments which supported it, including Canada. Instead the Recommendation points the direction for member states as they develop their provision of adult education, " ... to give effect to the principles set forth in this Recommendation."

Other UN agencies which have also been active in calling for adult education measures include the International Labour Organization and the Food and Agriculture Organization, although these calls have been limited to the context of the specific mandate set out for each. In other global initiatives, adult education has been identified as a means to achieving particular objectives set by the UN General Assembly in its attempt to create a more just world economic and social order. Examples of this include the sustained effort to reduce the gap between rich and poor nations during the First and Second Development Decades of the 1960s and 1970s, and the declaration of international years to focus attention on specific areas of concern such as International Literacy Year in 1990.

Another international organization, the Organization for Economic Co-operation and Development (OECD), through its Manpower, Social Affairs, and Educational Directorate and its Centre for Educational Research and Innovation, has also been active in advocating to national governments various adult educational policies for implementation. In particular the OECD, beginning in the early 1970s, embraced the concept of recurrent education.[33] As proposed by the OECD, a recurrent education policy would consist of three main elements:[34]

1. that individuals, at the end of compulsory schooling, should have the right to defer the continuation of their education up to higher levels, to times of their own choosing, together with the right to re-enter the educational cycle;

2. that individuals should have the right to such occupational training as may be required to enable them to upgrade their job, to change it or to find a new one should they become redundant;

---

[33] OECD, *Recurrent Education: A Strategy for Lifelong Learning* (Paris, OECD, 1973).

[34] As noted in Employment and Immigration Canada, *Learning a Living in Canada*, Vol. 1, p. 47.

3. that positive measures should be taken to ensure that the expansion of adult learning opportunities should not accentuate inequalities.

In 1976 the OECD conducted a review of Canada's educational provision and in its subsequent report urged Canada to adopt the idea of recurrent education as the master strategy for its educational system.[35]

The Council of Europe is an organization of European countries which has also researched the need for adult education among its member nations.[36] The Council champions the concept of permanent education, which it describes as being a coherent and integrated educational system for all stages and sectors of life. In studying the existing provision of education, the Council found a significant lacking in the ability of educational systems to respond to new social and economic realities. By member nations adopting a system of permanent education the arbitrariness of educational provision which is made only for youth would be supplanted with a system which acknowledges the need for providing ongoing educational opportunity. This need arises because both developed and developing countries must continue to expand their economic and social systems in a world that is ever changing. While the concept of permanent education is particularly applicable to economic development with respect to education and training for work, its proponents also include all social and cultural activities with an educational content so as to additionally promote social development.

There are also many international non-governmental organizations concerned with adult education which have been active within their own spheres of influence at calling upon governments to support the provision of adult education. The International Council for Adult Education (ICAE), founded soon after the Third UNESCO Conference in Tokyo in 1972, is but one example. In 1976 the ICAE adopted a position on adult education and national development known as the Declaration of Dar es Salaam.[37]

There are also a number of individuals whose ideas have had a marked impact on international thinking about education, including adult education. The two who are arguably the best known due to the radical nature of their views on the educational process are Paulo Freire (*Pedagogy of the Oppressed*) and Ivan Illich (*Deschooling Society*). There are others, however, who through publications and attendance at international gatherings have lent their thoughts to the call for public policy. Two Canadians who are notable in this regard are Alan Thomas of the Ontario Institute for Studies in Education and the late Roby Kidd.

The effect of all these calls for public policy has been to influence and guide discussion within the educational jurisdictions of individual nations. The most important effect has been to promote adult education and its several conceptions

---

[35] OECD, *Reviews of National Policies for Education—Canada* (Paris, Organization for Economic Co-operation and Development, 1976).

[36] Council for Cultural Co-operation, *A Contribution to the Development of a New Education Policy* (Strasbourg, Council of Europe, 1981).

[37] *Convergence*, Vol. IX, No. 4 (1976) p. 9.

(such as lifelong learning, recurrent education, learning society) to the point where these conceptions are accepted by educational planners and even, in some cases, by policy making bodies. The rate of acceptance is ever increasing, particularly as those precursor circumstances, which are the products of a rapidly expanding and ever changing world, force policy makers to take action on specific issues. The purpose of the next chapter, then, is to examine the policy situation within Canada respecting adult education.

Public Policy Relating to Adult Education

In 1966 the Canadian Association for Adult Education (CAAE) issued a paper outlining its ideas on the development of a Canadian policy for adult education (referred to in the paper as continuing education).[1] In its call for an articulated system of continuing education the CAAE insisted that its development could not be left to chance. Rather it needed to develop on the basis of an overall conception of learning where learning and the learner were placed in a central position in society. "Underlying all is the premise that all citizens should have reasonable access to any part or level of the system at any time in his life and with reasonable convenience to his circumstances." Numerous provincial and national studies on aspects of adult education have been prepared both before and since but the element of chance concerning its development persists to this day. There is more that is implicit than explicit about policy respecting adult education.

Many reasons are advanced for the lack of an explicit Canadian policy on adult education, and always the first to be cited is the constitutional provision in the Constitution Act 1867 (known as the British North America Act prior to 1981) which stipulates that education is a matter of provincial, not federal, jurisdiction (Section 93). Many in the adult education field consider the advancing of this reason as a subterfuge in that Section 93 deals only with provincial jurisdiction regarding youth education, and particularly to the guaranteeing of the right to sectarian education.[2] The suggestion of a subterfuge is supported by the fact that at the provincial level there are only a few governments which have embraced a broad conception of adult education and have developed policies to support its development. The other provinces have chosen instead to allow adult education to develop within general educational or job training policies, preferring not to recognize it by way of specific public policy.

---

[1] CAAE, *A White Paper on the Education of Adults in Canada* (Toronto, CAAE, 1966).

[2] For example, A. Thomas, "Other Voices, Other Rooms: The Emergence of New Educational Constituencies in the 1980s," in Ivany and Manley-Casimir, *Federal-Provincial Relations: Education Canada* (Toronto, Ontario Institute for Studies in Education, 1981) p. 84.

Federal Government Policy Initiatives

Despite the apparent exclusion of the federal government in matters of education by virtue of Section 93 of the Constitution Act, the national government has had, and continues to have, a quite considerable involvement. Prior to the 1950s this involvement was predominately in the area of technical and vocational education encompassing both youth and adults. Beginning in the 1950s, and using the 1951 Report of the Royal Commission on National Development in the Arts, Letters, and Sciences (Massey Commission) as a marker, the federal government also committed itself to the support and development of provincial post-secondary educational systems, i.e. universities, colleges and institutes.[3] More recently, with the passage of the Official Languages Act and with the influx of large numbers of non-English or French speaking immigrants, the federal government has funded language training in both official languages at the elementary and secondary school level. In each of these cases the involvement has been justified by the general commitment of the federal government to national interests such as economic and social development.[4]

Specific federal policy developments in support of technical and vocational education and occupational training programs begin with the appointment in 1910 of the Royal Commission on Industrial Training and Technical Education and with the first legislative enactments, the Agricultural Instruction Act of 1913 and the Technical Education Act of 1919. Ever since, the federal government has maintained its presence in these areas through the funding of different initiatives in conjunction with the provinces.

Whereas the earlier fiscal interventions of the federal government were directed at supporting programs at the secondary school level, beginning in 1937 with the Unemployment and Agricultural Assistance Act it also became involved with supporting the training of unemployed youth and, during the war, the training of skilled workers.[5] This increased involvement was prompted by the immense dislocation in the workforce brought about by the Great Depression. The outbreak of the Second World War provided added impetus to the need to prepare persons for new occupations, in this case to sustain the war effort through the training of both armed forces personnel and civilian production workers. Thus, the federal government was now proactive in not only supporting programs conducted in educational institutions but also training initiatives addressed

---

[3] For an account of this involvement see Secretary of State, *Federal and Provincial Support to Post-secondary Education in Canada: A Report to Parliament, 1987–1988* (Ottawa, Secretary of State, 1988).

[4] For an elaboration on this involvement see E.D. Hodgson, *Federal Intervention in Public Education* (Toronto, Canadian Education Association, 1976).

[5] Dupre et al., *Federalism and Policy Development: The Case of Adult Occupational Training in Ontario* (Toronto, University of Toronto Press, 1982) p. 14.

to the needs of those requiring training beyond their formal schooling, and particularly the unemployed. The significance of this federal involvement was the precedent it set for future interventions. "This pairing of federal support to educational institutions with federal training initiatives to combat unemployment, all via the intermediary of the provinces, was to be the hallmark of [federal] postwar policy."[6]

The federal involvement in occupational training increased by a quantum amount with the passage of the Technical and Vocational Training Assistance Act (TVTA) of 1960. This legislation was part of the government's response to the sluggish economic condition of the country at the time when, for example, in the summer of 1960 the unemployment rate was at a postwar high of eight per cent. Particularly noteworthy for the interests of adult education was that part of the measures in the TVTA were directed at the retraining of workers threatened with job obsolescence. The significance of this is its foreshadowing of a greatly expanded federal government role in manpower planning policy, when national economic interests would be allowed to supersede jurisdictional reservations surrounding the provision of education. This expanded federal role was proclaimed in the heady year of 1967, which marked Canada's centennial of confederation and witnessed the exhilaration of Expo 67 in Montreal.

The Adult Occupational Training Act of 1967 represents a watershed event in federal involvement in matters of education. At the 1966 Federal Provincial Conference Prime Minister Lester Pearson stated, "We propose to change the emphasis of our policy for training in a way that accords with the national economic priorities which are the inescapable concern of the federal government. That is to say, we propose to clarify our purposes and expand our activities in adult training."[7] The explanation put forward justifying this assertive action was that the federal government had "a constitutional and necessary role in the training and development of our adult labour force for economic growth and full employment."[8] By way of circumventing the jurisdictional issue of provincial autonomy in matters of education the federal government accentuated an existing artifice so as to serve its constitutional needs, namely making formal a distinction between training and education. In order to directly influence the availability of particular skills and knowledge necessary for economic development the federal government couched its manpower initiatives by designating them as the training of adults, a specific area not dealt with in the Constitution Act under

---

[6] Dupre et al., *Federalism and Policy Development: The Case of Adult Occupational Training in Ontario*, p. 15.

[7] As quoted in Dupre et al., *Federalism and Policy Development: The Case of Adult Occupational Training in Ontario*, p. 26.

[8] As quoted in Dupre et al., p. 26.

Section 93. At the same time, and so as not to raise the ire of the provinces by appearing to infringe on their educational jurisdiction, the federal government concurrently provided generous funding to the provinces by way of cost sharing arrangements so that each could continue to develop and operate their particular post-secondary educational system free of federal interference.[9] The impact of these measures on adult education was twofold. For one there was now considerable federal funding available to support job training programs, including adult basic education. For another the expansion of provincial post-secondary educational institutions had the unspecified effect of making considerably more adult education opportunities available, as departments of continuing education or similar structures were created in the new colleges, institutes and universities.

The Adult Occupational Training Act (1967) marks the first time in Canada that adult learning needs have been explicitly identified and singled out in public policy. (Note: For the purposes of the Act an adult was defined as a person who had been out of the school system for at least three years and who was attached to the labour force.) The provisions of the Act were such that the federal government would pay both the training costs and living allowances of persons assisted under the Act, and that citizens could deal directly with federal agencies in accessing the various training programs and benefits available. In turn, however, the federal government was still obliged to look to provincial institutions to provide the requisite training.[10]

It is important to note that the learning needs addressed in the Adult Occupational Training Act were those as perceived by the federal government. In terms of public policy the federal adult training initiative represents one of the two major views on the purpose of adult education, namely the "human capital" view as contrasted with the "humanistic" view. These views are not to be seen as in opposition to each other; rather, they represent a placing of emphasis. According to the human capital view the economy requires a skilled and knowledgeable workforce capable of creating wealth. This workforce forms the human capital which, along with investment capital, ensures a vital economy. Just as investment capital moves around to seek out opportunities with greatest profit potential, so must the human capital be available to take advantage of these opportunities. Thus, skilled and knowledgeable workers form part of the economic equation for a healthy economy, which is measured by such indices as the Gross National Product (GNP), employment levels, and international competitiveness.

The humanistic view of adult education takes a different point of view by looking at the whole person and appreciating the individual as capable of achieving his or her full potential as a human being. Rather than the individual being

---

[9] This was by way of the Federal-Provincial Fiscal Arrangements Act (1967) and subsequently in 1977 by the Federal-Provincial Fiscal Arrangements and Federal Post-Secondary Education and Health Contributions Act.

[10] A. Thomas, "Legislation and Adult Education in Canada: A Comparative Study," *International Journal of Lifelong Education*, 8, 2 (1989) pp. 103–125.

seen in terms of an economic unit, as in the case of the human capital view, the humanistic view instead values the individual in terms of his or her total life contribution including at work, in the community, with family and through self actualization. The purpose of adult education, then, is to enable individuals in achieving their full potential.

As noted, the two views are not in opposition to one another. However there can be, and often is, disagreement as to the emphasis placed on one over the other. This is particularly the case when emphasis gets translated into policy, which has definite implications for resource allocation. This resource allocation can then be interpreted as an expression of philosophic orientation on the part of government in its relationship with its citizens. There is, of course, more sophistication to the two views than sketched here; for example, it is easily argued that only through economic independence, made possible by the human capital emphasis, that workers are better able to pursue their humanistic interests. Another example, arising from the Adult Occupational Training Act (1967), is how the Act enabled a considerable amount of adult basic education to be provided, and this opened the doors of possibility and opportunity for trainees. In analyzing policy, however, one looks for the underlying assumptions and the evenness of the policy's application to the general situation. Thus, in the case of the human capital view, it is only those who are part of the workforce, or potentially part of it, who are singled out for attention. There are many adults who are not part of this group and thus not in a position to benefit, such as adults with handicaps, those retired from the workforce, and those who are devoting full time to domestic life, including child rearing.

The federal government emphasis on labour force planning (a term which replaces the gender specific "manpower planning") and on adult training was updated by way of the 1982 National Training Act. The thrust of this Act was to assert that the federal government had the right to determine the providers of federally funded training, outside of being bound to provincial educational institutions as had been the case with the Adult Occupational Training Act. The federal government declared that henceforth it was free to develop contractual relationships also with employers, private training establishments, and other training entrepreneurs.[11] This policy shift was amplified in 1985 with the introduction of the federal government's new job creation program called "Canadian Jobs Strategy."[12] Most recently, in 1989, a further initiative was taken by the federal government with its introduction of a new strategy for equipping the

---

[11] Collins and Long, "Federal and Provincial Adult Education Agencies in the United States and Canada," in Merriam and Cunningham, (Eds.), *Handbook of Adult and Continuing Education* (San Francisco, Jossey-Bass, 1989) p. 390.

[12] F. MacDonald, *The Canadian Jobs Strategy* (Ottawa, Employment and Immigration Canada, 1985).

labour force to adapt to changes and meet new requirements. Referred to as The Labour Force Development Strategy, this initiative is in response to "an evolving work environment brought on by technological and demographic change."[13] By way of example, whereas previous training programs have largely been directed to entrants to the labour force, the proposed strategy pays particular attention to the plight of displaced older workers and their need for retraining.

The above outline has traced the federal government's direct involvement in adult education through occupational training policies. It would be wrong to suggest that this involvement has been at the exclusion of adult education represented by the humanistic view; however policy involvement in this area is not as easily discerned. Through the years there have been numerous federal government initiatives which amount to support of the humanistic view. Examples include the establishment of the Canadian Broadcasting Corporation and the National Film Board, the sponsorship of innumerable citizenship type programs by the Department of the Secretary of State, and the financial support of provincial post-secondary educational systems. While these initiatives are not construed in terms of adult education policies, they nonetheless are responsible for considerable adult learning opportunity being made available.

Adult Education Policy in the Provinces and Territories

The development of provincial educational systems has historically been focused on providing publicly supported education for youth. Initially this was directed at the grade school system and then expanded from there to the post-secondary system, first with its universities and latterly with its colleges, institutes and an increased number of universities. Only since the 1960s, however, has there been comprehensive development of the post-secondary system in most provinces to parallel that of the grade school system.

By way of generalization, the pattern respecting the development of publicly provided adult education has followed that of the formal educational system, with the significant exception being the absence of enabling legislation. Initially, adult education was associated with the night school offerings of the public grade schools, then additionally with university extension departments and vocational training centres and, more recently, with the continuing education units of community colleges and institutes. As noted, these are institutions which are part of the formal educational system. In addition to these institutions it is readily possible to identify other publicly funded institutions which provide adult education such as libraries, community centres and various government departments (e.g. departments of health and of recreation). This review will confine itself, however, to the formal educational system, as it is possible to trace this system's

---

[13] Canadian Labour Market and Productivity Centre, *Report of the CLMPC Task Forces on the Labour Force Development Strategy* (Ottawa, Canadian Labour Market and Productivity Centre, 1989) p. 1.

gradual acceptance of the responsibility for the education of adults as well as youth. As pointed out in Chapter 6, this acceptance by way of statutory provision carries with it considerable financial implications, and explains why Thomas describes it as being for the most part, "benign and enabling."[14] The acknowledgement of the need for adult education, however, is now as undisputed as was the need for youth education a century ago. This acknowledgement is evidenced by the widespread use in official documents of such terms as adult learning, continuing education and lifelong learning.

The point has already been made that learning is pervasive regardless of the age of the individual. With youth, however, the organizing of learning into a formal educational system makes it possible to easily observe and analyze its component parts, such as its enabling legislation, its level of funding, its structuring and its physical presence. With non-formal education, by contrast, there is no containment into a particular system, but rather a multiplicity of independent systems, e.g. school boards, voluntary associations, trade unions, employers, etc., which are involved in addressing the gamut of adult learning needs. Because of this multiplicity, and because of the absence of any coherence among the various systems, it is impossible to observe and analyze non-formal education as an entity in the same terms as formal education.

A particular anomaly of adult education is how it sits astride both systems of formal education and non-formal education. Seen in terms of structure, a significant portion of its activity comes about by virtue of its direct association with the formal educational system, for example an adult education department within a school board or an extension department within an university. Equally, it is possible to see training departments within corporations and adult education sections within voluntary organizations. Seen in terms of program content, many programs can be offered as readily by a community group or another government department as by an institution attached to the formal educational system, for example a course on coping with stress. Because of this dual existence in both formal and non-formal education it has proven difficult to circumscribe adult education for the purpose of public policy development. It is this fact which makes it difficult to pinpoint specific instances of public policy supporting adult education. The diverse nature of adult education has mitigated against the development of a cohesive public policy. Instead, the pattern is much more of a patch work.[15] For this reason it is necessary to first determine what it is we are looking for when we search out public policy in support of adult education.

---

[14] A. Thomas, "Legislation and Adult Education in Canada: A Comparative Study," p. 123.

[15] In taking this point further, Alan Thomas of O.I.S.E., who has been researching the legal foundations for adult education in Canada for a number of years, observes the diverse nature of its statutory provision. He notes that the diversity "reveals something about the nature of adult education which is both necessary and desirable" and that the aspiration to have all concerns for adult learning contained in legislation exclusively designed for adults "seems to be vain and not very constructive." See A. Thomas, "Policy Development for Adult Education: The Law," in Rivera (Ed.), *Planning Adult Learning: Issues, Practices and Directions* (London, Croom Helm, 1987) p. 60.

It is ironic that so much publicly supported adult education is in fact conducted when there is such a paucity of explicit policy. In attempting to explain this situation the first item to search out is the source of the statutory authority which enables the particular adult education activity to be conducted. Even when found the source may only make an oblique reference to adult education; for example, the enabling legislation establishing community colleges in several provinces appends adult education as one of the functions of a college. There is no further mention made, and it is up to the individual college to then sort out the extent of its offering in this area. Thus, legislation is often an insufficient indicator of adult education policy and it is necessary to look for other sources.

Because the wording of enabling legislation does not usually spell out the administrative details necessary to carry out the statutory provision, regulations are developed for this purpose. These regulations are approved by the Executive Council of Government, i.e. the Cabinet, or by Executive Committees of individual ministries. With regard to regulations, Thomas makes the point they are less public in their pronouncement and much more difficult to track. He makes the further point regarding the harmony between legislation and regulations that, "Regulations are not supposed to contradict the letter of the law, and they rarely do, but they often impede or destroy what many supporters of the legislation believed to be the spirit."[16]

Legislation and regulations result in some level of provision being made, and it is this provision which indicates the extent of the actual commitment to adult learning. Indicators of this commitment include:

- the published goals and objectives which promote the commitment
- the level of funding provided to support the commitment
- the type of leadership provided to direct the commitment, i.e. how is adult education placed within the bureaucracy and what are the capabilities of the persons employed
- the comprehensiveness of the provision which makes up the commitment, i.e. what range of programs is provided to whom
- the results of the commitment, i.e. how many people participate and what is the extent of the learning
- the extent to which adult education is incorporated into other areas of policy, i.e. adult education is recognized as an instrument of change
- the degree to which adult education has become established as a necessary and integrated part of the public educational system.

These are but some of the indicators that might be used to determine the presence and certitude of adult education.

Before looking at specific provincial policies it is possible to make some generalizations about the Canadian situation regarding public policy and adult education, even though individual provinces have exercised their autonomy in educational matters in several distinct ways.

---

[16] A. Thomas, "Policy Development for Adult Education: The Law," p. 63.

1. Initially adult education was conducted as part of the work of provincial departments of agriculture, public health and education. In the case of departments of education it developed as an adjunct to the public school system, and this arrangement has remained strong.

2. In the post World War I era universities conducted extension work, initially in agriculture and then in areas of social development and liberal education. University extension departments remain as important providers of adult education, with a proud tradition in this field.

3. The dislocation of the depression years and the Second World War gave impetus to the federal government to fund vocational training programs for adults. Since then there has been considerable direct federal funding made available in support of occupational training.

4. Since the Second World War and particularly since the 1960s there has been considerable expansion of the post-secondary educational system in terms of vocational/technical institutes, community colleges and universities. Adult education is seen to be an included function of these new institutions, and distinct departments carry out "continuing education" work.

6. The amount of adult education, broadly defined, being conducted has grown significantly, and publicly supported educational institutions have become the largest providers.

7. The expansion of provincial education systems in the period since 1960 has resulted in some provinces splitting their ministries of education into dual ministries, approximately along the lines of grade school education and post-secondary (advanced) education. The post-secondary system is often described as providing "continuing education" to distinguish it from "youth education" as provided by the grade school system.

8. With the splitting of a single education ministry into dual ministries adult education is left straddling both, and a not insignificant amount of bureaucratic time is spent attempting to bring coordination to the now divided work.

9. The prevailing emphasis on occupational training in the post-secondary education system has in some cases resulted in "training" or some such synonym being included in the names of post-secondary education ministries.

10. While many provinces have acknowledged the role of adult education, and have appointed commissions which have studied this role, adult education has not been officially recognized as a distinct system, likened with the grade school system and the post-secondary educational system. Instead adult education continues to have a secondary status within most provincial education systems.

11. While correspondence study has always been one means for adults to complete their grade school education, the introduction of distance education technology has allowed some provinces to venture into technologically based distance education, and much programming has been designed to meet needs of adults.

12. Government sponsored adult education is not limited to education ministries. Instead several ministries are involved in sponsoring a variety of programs.

13. The economic recession of the early 1980s and the consequent fiscal restraint by government adversely affected support for adult education, and particularly general interest and community education. Provincial governments cut back on funding and forced the emphasis on a "user pay" approach.

14. Most of the inquiries into provincial education systems have acknowledged the essential place of adult education and have made recommendations for adult education to be a legitimate function of the post-secondary system.

All the provincial and territorial jurisdictions make provision for adult education in one form or another, and some are more deliberate in this regard than others. While there is a discernable pattern of development, there is no uniformity in either philosophy or structure. Each jurisdiction has determined its provision in keeping with its particular social-historical context.[17] What follows is a review of the steps taken within each province towards the development of public policy favouring adult education.[18]

Alberta

Statement of the General Situation

Adult education is offered by most provincial educational institutions in the province through departments of adult education (or similarly named sections of institutions). These institutions have latitude in their governing legislation which enables them to be active in this area. A particular feature of the Alberta situa-

---

[17] There is, however, increasing collaboration among the provinces in educational matters as evidenced by the formation in 1967 of the Council of Ministers of Education. The Council is a national forum which serves to enable the provinces to speak collectively to the federal government on educational matters and which also promotes interprovincial consultation and co-operation. The Council has no constitutional authority, nor are its decisions binding. It does select delegates to international conferences sponsored by the United Nations Educational, Scientific and Cultural Organization (UNESCO) such as the International Conference on Adult Education and by the Organization for Economic Co-operation and Development (OECD).

[18] For an early assessment of this work see P. Sandiford, *Adult Education in Canada: A Survey* (Toronto, University of Toronto, 1935).

tion, however, is the policy involvement by the government in facilitating access by adults to non-vocational and non-credit adult education. This access is both financially supported and coordinated by the government through a system of Further Education Councils. The government's formal recognition of, and involvement in, further education (a synonym for adult education) dates from the early 1970s, and specifically with the publication in 1975 of the policy statement, "Further Education Policy, Guidelines, Procedures."[19] By establishing the councils the government acknowledged the large number and variety of public educational institutions and voluntary organizations engaged in offering adult education courses, and the councils provided a mechanism for coordinating government services in this area at the local level.

The Banff Centre is another unique feature of the Alberta situation, having been established as an adult learning centre separate from its parent, the University of Alberta through the Banff Centre Act (1977).

There are two departments responsible for education, the Department of Education and the Department of Advanced Education.

Historical Developments

The origins of adult education in Alberta stem from the first legislative session of the new province in 1906 when a bill was passed creating the University of Alberta.[20] Soon after opening in 1908, the university became very active in extension work, and particularly in providing service to Alberta's rural population. The provincial Department of Agriculture also carried out a noteworthy program of adult education. A second development of note occurred in 1958 when Lethbridge Junior College opened, thereby becoming one of the first public two-year community colleges in Canada.[21] Included in its functions was the provision of community education. The further development of colleges was stimulated that same year when the Public Junior Colleges Act was passed and when, in the next year, a Royal Commission on Education delivered its findings which helped clarify the role of the new colleges. Additional definition was provided in 1969 with the passing of the Colleges Act, and Alberta's colleges

---

[19] Province of Alberta, *Further Education Policy, Guidelines and Procedures* (Edmonton, Ministry of Advanced Education and Manpower, 1975).

[20] For an historical account see D. Berghofer and A. Vladicka, *Access to Opportunity, 1905–80: The Development of Post-Secondary Education in Alberta* (Edmonton, Alberta Advanced Education and Manpower, 1980).

[21] Dennison and Gallagher, *Canada's Community Colleges: A Critical Analysis* (Vancouver, University of B.C. Press, 1986) p. 19.

were confirmed in providing, among other things, access to "wider educational opportunity to a broader segment of society."[22]

The pivotal thinking with respect to public policy and adult education in Alberta stems from the appointment in 1969 of the Educational Planning Commission, chaired by Dr. Walter Worth. The Commission was given a broad mandate in order that it might make recommendations to guide the Alberta government in developing its system of public education for the next decade.[23] While a change in government occurred in the interval of the Commission's appointment and the tabling of its report, *A Choice of Futures*, and this mitigated against many of its recommendations being adopted, nonetheless the document contains important statements about the place of state supported adult education in Alberta. Much of the thinking in this regard was done by the Lifelong Education Task Force appointed by the Commission.[24]

The first explicit policy on adult education in Alberta was introduced in 1975 when the Department of Advanced Education published the document, *Further Education Policy, Guidelines and Procedures*.[25] This policy was the outcome of a process begun in 1972 which involved input from a wide source of interested public and private organizations and of government branches. The distinguishing feature of the policy is the Local Further Education Council (LFEC), which the original policy described in the following way:

> The ultimate goal of a LFEC is to mobilize all available resources to offer coordinated, comprehensive, meaningful courses of further education to adults in the community. A LFEC is not intended to assume the operation of any of its member agencies. The major function of a LFEC is to coordinate non-credit further education programming on an inter-agency basis. A LFEC is intended to serve people within a region which may be defined by city, county, or school division boundaries.

Today there are approximately eighty-five LFECs functioning throughout the province. Because they are the mechanism by which the Alberta government has chosen to facilitate non-formal adult learning they enjoy not only a structural integration with the provincial educational bureaucracy, which includes fiscal arrangements, but also an integration with the political system. This has had the effect of bringing adult education as a matter of policy much closer to the level of the learner than in any other jurisdiction in Canada.

---

[22] Dennison and Gallagher, *Canada's Community Colleges*, p. 22.

[23] H. Roberts, *Culture and Adult Education: A Study of Alberta and Quebec* (Edmonton, University of Alberta Press, 1982) p. 69.

[24] Commission on Educational Planning, *A Choice of Futures* (Edmonton, Queen's Printer, 1972).

[25] Province of Alberta, *Further Education Policy, Guidelines and Procedures* (Edmonton, Ministry of Advanced Education and Manpower, 1975).

The original 1975 policy has recently been restated and now asserts that "Alberta Advanced Education will facilitate involvement in further education by adult Albertans, and encourage systematic inter-agency communication, co-operation and coordination in the provision of learning opportunities for adults."[26]

There are other examples in Alberta of public policy favouring adult education. These include provision by the Department of Education for adults who are completing their high school education, the establishment in 1972 of Athabasca University to provide distance education, and the formation in 1973 of the Alberta Education Communications Corporation—popularly referred to as ACCESS Alberta—for the production and broadcasting of educational programming. Additionally, the Banff Centre enjoys an international reputation as an unique adult learning centre.

In sum Alberta's provision of adult education, as assured by public policy, is seen to be generous. The effect of this provision appears to be positively reflected in participation figures which indicate that adults in Alberta are the most active in Canada in pursuing their continuing education.[27]

British Columbia

Statement of the General Situation

Adult education is offered by most of B.C.'s public educational institutions, although there is no coherent policy providing for this. Instead the component sectors of the province's public educational system have latitude in their governing legislation which enables them to be active in the area of adult education. In the early 1970s school districts were encouraged to give over their adult education programming to the newly created community colleges, and many of them did so. In 1988 the Ministry of Education extended free education at the public schools to adults over 19 years of age, to the grade 12 level.

There are two ministries responsible for education, the Ministry of Education and the Ministry of Advanced Education, Technology and Job Training.

Historical Developments

An early policy development occurred in 1910 when the province's *Public Schools Act* was amended to permit school boards to conduct night school

---

[26] Department of Advanced Education *Further Education Policy, Guidelines and Procedures* (1988)—made pursuant to Schedule 4 of the Advanced Education Grants Regulation, Alberta Regulation 316/83, as amended.

[27] Statistics Canada, *One in Every Five: A Survey of Adult Education in Canada* (Ottawa, Ministry of Supply and Services Canada, 1985).

courses.[28] In 1915 the University of British Columbia was established, and extension work began shortly thereafter. In 1963 the *Public Schools Act* was again revised in a way favourable to adult education, this time to allow for the formation of community colleges. Over the next fifteen years fifteen colleges and five institutes were created. Also in 1963, the *Universities Act (B.C.)* created Simon Fraser University and the University of Victoria. Both developments were as a result of a report by the then President of the University of British Columbia titled, *Higher Education in British Columbia and a Plan for the Future.*[29] Continuing education was included in the mandate of all these new post-secondary institutions. Additionally the province took advantage of federal funding under the federal government's Technical and Vocational Training Assistance Act (1960) to expand its occupational training programs and facilities.

In 1976 the government appointed committees to investigate three aspects of the province's educational system: the Commission on University Programs in Non-Metropolitan Areas (Winegard Commission); the Commission on Technical, Vocational, and Trades Training (Goard Commission); and the Committee on Continuing and Community Education (Faris Committee).[30] The outcome of this activity was the passage of the *Colleges and Institutes Act* (1977) which, among other things, created the Open Learning Institute with responsibility for developing a provincial distance education program. Educational broadcasting was begun in 1980 with the formation of the Knowledge Network of the West Communications Authority (KNOW-BC). Most recently, in 1988, the province's initiatives in distance education, educational broadcasting and open learning were brought together under the aegis of the Open Learning Agency.

Despite these institutional developments in British Columbia there has been a corresponding demise in the currency of continuing education within the two ministries of education. A Division of Continuing Education, established within the singular Ministry of Education in 1977 and later transferred to the new

---

[28] For a detailed account see G. Selman, *The Invisible Giant: A History of Adult Education in B.C.* (Vancouver, U.B.C. Centre for Continuing Education, 1988). This is the only published adult education history for any of Canada's educational jurisdictions.

[29] J. Macdonald, *Higher Education in British Columbia and a Plan for the Future* (Vancouver, University of British Columbia, 1962).

[30] There had been an earlier Task Force appointed to review the role of the community colleges in the province, in 1973 under the NDP administration. Its report made a number of recommendations supporting continuing education in the colleges, even to the extent that the colleges should become the public agency responsible for the funding, provision, and (or) coordination of adult and continuing education in each college region. The report was not acted on when the NDP was voted out of office in 1975. Task Force on the Community College in British Columbia, *Towards the Learning Community* (Victoria, Department of Education, 1974). See also the *Report of the Committee on Continuing and Community Education in British Columbia* (Victoria, Ministry of Education, 1976).

Ministry of Advanced Education and Job Training, was systematically dismantled by the provincial government in the early 1980s. As Selman observes, " ... the improvements which appeared to have been made during the seventies in government's acceptance of responsibility for leadership and support for adult education have proven to be illusory, or at best, short term."[31]

The one area of adult education which has been maintained by way of policy is that of adult basic education, which includes basic literacy, academic upgrading, pre-vocational training, and English language training. As part of the policy development process initiated through the Division of Continuing Education, a policy statement on adult basic education programs was accepted by government.[32] This document recognizes the responsibility of the Ministry of Education (since transferred to the Ministry of Advanced Education, Technology and Job Training) to "foster learning opportunities for adults in British Columbia who have not had the opportunity to develop some or all of those skills required to function successfully in Canadian society." The policy of the Ministry is to provide "to adult citizens and landed immigrants residing in the province, reasonable access to high quality adult basic education programs." A more recent expansion on this policy is the provision for adults over 19 years of age to receive free education to the grade 12 level in the province's public schools.[33] A difficulty in this area, however, stems from the establishment of a separate Ministry of Advanced Education and Job Training in 1986. This development has had the consequence of introducing jurisdictional confusion as to which Ministry is responsible for what, given that public schools are in one ministry and colleges now are in another, and both offer adult basic education programs.

Manitoba

Statement of the General Situation

There is a well developed system of government support for adult education in Manitoba. Manitoba was the first province to conduct a Royal Commission solely on adult education (1945) and at that time the importance of co-operation and coordination in the provision of adult education was emphasized. Today the Ministry of Education and Training, through the Adult and Continuing Education Branch of the Division of Post-Secondary, Adult and Continuing Education, gives tangible support to the adult education which is conducted through the school districts, community colleges and community-based organizations. Priority for this funding assistance is given to those groups which are seen as educa-

---

[31] G. Selman, *The Invisible Giant: A History of Adult Education in British Columbia*, p. 33.

[32] Province of British Columbia, *A Ministerial Policy on the Provision of Adult Basic Education Programs including English Language Training in the Public Education System of British Columbia (1982)* (Victoria, Department of Education, 1982).

[33] Ministry of Education, *Ministry of Education Information Circulars # 275 and # 353 (1988)* (Victoria, Ministry of Education, 1988).

tionally disadvantaged. In addition the province's three universities offer a variety of continuing education courses.

There is one department responsible for education, the Department of Education and Training.

Historical Developments

The promotion of rural life has historically been important to Manitoba's social and economic fabric, and in the earlier years the absence of publicly funded institutions active in adult education work saw the co-operative movement play a lead role in this area. As an example, from 1939 onwards the Manitoba Federation of Agriculture and Co-operation encouraged and supported study groups through supplying speakers for meetings, organizing film circuits, and maintaining a central lending library.[34] Exigencies of the Second World War caused the Manitoba government to become active in the area of vocational training, and this was stimulated by the federal government's Vocational Training Coordination Act of 1942 which provided for generous joint funding arrangements. This work continued at war's end as part of the resettlement process for returning veterans under the terms of the Veterans Rehabilitation Act (1945), which assisted veterans wishing to pursue vocational or post-secondary education.

Soon after the war the Manitoba government was lobbied to appoint a Royal Commission on Adult Education with the hope that increased coordination and co-operation, including government involvement, would result from such a study. The Commission was chaired by Dr. A.W. Trueman, President of University of Manitoba, and reported in 1947.[35] Its two principal recommendations were: (1) that a Manitoba Adult Education Council be established, and (2) that an Inter-departmental Committee on Adult Education be established to make most effective use of federal assistance, to establish more efficient coordination of provincial government adult education programs, to avoid duplication and waste, and to co-operate with voluntary agencies. There were, however, no policy developments on the part of government, as had been anticipated. However the influence of federal assistance to Manitoba's vocational training remained strong and accounted in large measure for developments in the late 1960s.

The next major development was the adaptation of Manitoba's vocational institutions into three community colleges, in 1969. By this date vocational training had become a significant portion of the adult education provided in the province, due mainly to the funding made available under various federal programs. This change had a general effect of increasing the number of adults participating in a variety of both formal and non-formal programs.

---

[34] B. Fairbairn, *Building A Dream* (Saskatoon, Western Producer Prairie Books, 1989) p. 84.

[35] Royal Commission on Adult Education, *Report* (Winnipeg, King's Printer, 1947).

Within a few years the government determined a study of the province's post-secondary system was required, and in 1972 a Task Force on Post-Secondary Education was appointed.[36] The subsequent report did not specifically address the area of continuing education (which it defined as "education that does not lead to a high school or college diploma or to a university degree") but it noted how lifelong learning had become an "articulate public demand." Particular concern was expressed for the ability of disadvantaged groups to access and participate in continuing education. The report put forward the consideration that, "Continuing education—a co-ordinated system of life-long learning—may provide some solutions to the problems of accessibility and participation."[37] Despite this inclination the report further noted the difficulty of finding a systematic way to fund and support such a system. Regardless, one of the hallmarks of adult education in Manitoba continues to be the attention paid to the disadvantaged referred to in the report. An example is the ACCESS programs, designed to allow Native adults from the northern region to participate in a variety of post-secondary programs leading to professional designations.

Through a reorganization of the Department of Education in 1982 a Post-Secondary, Adult and Continuing Education (PACE) division was created with the following as part of its mission:

- To increase accessibility to post-secondary education for Manitobans who have participated only marginally in post-secondary education;
- To increase the system's ability to respond to the diversity of learners' needs in the province;
- To contribute to human resource development in the province.[38]

In 1989 the responsibility for the education of adults, including employment services and job training initiatives, was consolidated in a new Department of Education and Training. Within the PACE Division there is an Adult and Continuing Education Branch which in turn is composed of a Continuing Education Unit and an Adult Language Training Unit. One of the programs of the Continuing Education Unit is to provide grants to school districts for part-time adult programs and grants to rural school divisions for evening use of facilities for adult education programs.[39]

There have been no specific adult education policy developments emanating from Manitoba. Instead the school boards, community college, and university adult education programs have maintained a traditional pattern of service and delivery.

[36] Province of Manitoba, *Report of the Task Force on Post–Secondary Education in Manitoba* (Winnipeg, Queen's Printer, 1973).

[37] Province of Manitoba, *Report of the Task Force on Post–Secondary Education in Manitoba*, p. 179.

[38] Manitoba Education, *Annual Report 1987–88* (Winnipeg, Manitoba Education, 1988) p. 33.

[39] Manitoba Education, *Annual Report 1987–88*, p. 41.

New Brunswick

Statement of the General Situation

Adult education is provided by all levels of New Brunswick's educational system: school districts, the community college and the six universities. As well, several government departments conduct occupational training. It is the New Brunswick Community College, however, which has a particular mandate to meet all the post-secondary, non-university education and training needs in the province. In the area of academic upgrading for adults (adult basic education, ESL, etc.) the community college reimburses school districts who plan and conduct this work. The community college instead focuses on providing continuing education in its various program areas. As for any formal structure in the government bureaucracy to support adult education, there is none. In addition, general interest courses are not part of the public provision and instead it is the voluntary and non-government sector which conducts this programming.

The government also encourages the use of public schools by community groups in the carrying out of their educational, cultural, recreational or other activities, although it does not provide leadership for this purpose.[40]

There are two departments responsible for education, the Department of Education and the Department of Advanced Education and Training.

Historical Developments

An early public provision was made for adult education in New Brunswick in the case of the adult vocational night program conducted by the Department of Education, which followed on the 1918 Vocational Act and the opening of Carleton County Vocational School a year later. By 1930 there were nine centres operating with an enrollment of 2,556.[41] The Department of Agriculture also conducted courses to promote improved farming techniques.

Similar to Nova Scotia, New Brunswick has a rich history of university level higher education, and this includes extension services. As late as 1969 studies on post-secondary education in New Brunswick were still committed to maintaining the province's system of higher education.[42] By the early 1970s it was evident, however, that the universities were not able to readily respond to training needs as they existed in various parts of the province. To address this situation the government in 1973 passed the New Brunswick Community College Act,

---

[40] New Brunswick Department of Education, *Policy Statement: Community Use of Schools— Schools Act, Section 67* (Fredericton, 1990).

[41] P. Sandiford, *Adult Education in Canada: A Survey*, Chapter 2, p. 1.

[42] Dennison and Gallagher, *Canada's Community Colleges*, p. 58.

thereby establishing a single community college with campuses in each of the province's five regions. The purpose of the new college was to meet the needs of all post-secondary, non-university education on a regional basis.[43] The college was described as being "neither a school nor a training programme but it is a comprehensive educational institution designed to provide a wide range of educational opportunities throughout the province."[44] This philosophy was reaffirmed in a 1978 planning document on the future of the New Brunswick Community College, *Quinquennial Plan, 1978–1983.*

Originally the New Brunswick Community College Act was administered by a new Ministry of Continuing Education which was renamed in 1983 as the Ministry of Community Colleges and is now the Ministry of Advanced Education and Training. When first established, the college absorbed the Vocational Branch of the Department of Education, which included two institutes of technology and five trade schools.

The college is intended to provide a wide range of educational opportunities, including adult education programs offered through the community service sections of each college campus. The primary focus of adult education delivered through the college remains, however, with vocational training programs and programs of continuing education for occupational groups.

It is important to note how in New Brunswick, Canada's only officially bilingual province, the establishing of the New Brunswick Community College is viewed as an educational reform measure designed to ensure a greater equality of access to post-secondary, non-university education for both linguistic groups. In addition, the college is an important aspect of the province's strategy for economic development by virtue of its capacity in the area of job training. This expectation has recently been amplified in a government planning document where one of the guiding principles states, "Our education and training system must be made accessible to all New Brunswickers, so that all of our citizens may participate fully in the province's economic life."[45] From this statement there is no doubt as to the direction which adult education is currently being taken in New Brunswick.

---

[43] Government of New Brunswick, *A Statement of Policy and Intent* (Fredericton, Government of New Brunswick, 1974).

[44] W.B. Thompson, "The New Brunswick Community College," *Canadian Vocational Journal, 10,* 4 (1975) p. 32.

[45] Province of New Brunswick, *Toward 2000—An Economic Development Strategy for New Brunswick* (Fredericton, Province of New Brunswick, 1989) p. 14.

Newfoundland

Statement of the General Situation

Adult education is provided by all of Newfoundland's post-secondary institutions, including Memorial University, the community colleges and the provincial institutes. The province's post-secondary system has only recently been expanded to include community colleges, however, and is still undergoing development. One aspect of this is that the extension services of all institutions are being reviewed in an attempt to rationalize the delivery mechanisms of these several services.[46] An encouraging feature of this rationalization is that, in a province with a generally low rate of educational achievement, participation rates in the post-secondary system are now showing a steady growth, and the government seeks to encourage this trend.

There is one department responsible for education, the Department of Education.

Historical Developments

The provision of education in Newfoundland and Labrador has always been made difficult by such overwhelming factors as rugged geography, scattered settlement and limited budget. Despite this, governments over the years have recognized the importance of adult education as a means of helping the working population especially to cope with the vagaries of the economy and the resulting impact on their livelihoods. Newfoundland has a proud adult education tradition, established well before the province entered Confederation in 1949.

The founding of Memorial University College in 1925 and the initiating of its evening and extension classes shortly thereafter marks the first consistent offering of adult education classes in the then colony of Great Britain. Another development occurred in the early 1930s as a result of funding from the Carnegie Foundation. In a concerted effort to reach the isolated communities and provide academic upgrading classes "Opportunity Schools" were established whereby instructors would travel from one community to another, presenting eight week courses in each location. By 1936 a total of 140 of these schools had been conducted with some 5,000 adults participating.[47] Recognizing the importance of adult education work, the government in 1936 formed an Adult Education Branch within the Department of Education. Under the direction of this Branch a varied program was offered in St. John's (where a permanent centre for adult education was established) and in nine other centres.

---

[46] Government of Newfoundland and Labrador, *Equality, Excellence and Efficiency: A Postsecondary Educational Agenda for the Future* (St. John's, Department of Education, 1990).

[47] F. Rowe, *The Development of Education in Newfoundland* (Toronto, Ryerson, 1964) p. 167. There is an updated version of this work by the same author entitled, *Education and Culture in Newfoundland* (Scarborough, McGraw-Hill Ryerson, 1976).

The entry of Newfoundland into Confederation precipitated further developments. Memorial University was accorded university status, and this provided additional stimulus to its adult education program of evening classes and extension services. To give greater guidance to this work a Director of Extension Services was appointed by the University in 1959. The next significant development saw Newfoundland in the post World War Two era taking advantage of the federal programs supporting technical and vocational education. Initially federal funding went to programs at the secondary school level only but, beginning with the TVTA Act of 1960, funding went to the construction of eleven separate vocational schools. As well, two colleges were established, the College of Trades and Technology and the College of Fisheries, in addition to two training centres at Stephenville in connection with the construction of the Churchill Falls Hydro Project.

The 1960s was a time of change in Newfoundland's educational system, as reflected in the appointment of a Royal Commission on Education and Youth in 1964 (P.J. Warren, Chairman). The Commission reviewed the entire provincial educational system and in its recommendations proposed that six regional colleges be established. These colleges would improve access to post-secondary education throughout the province and would also support continuing education for adults. The recommendations regarding the college regions were not acted upon and instead resources went into constructing additional vocational schools.[48] As for the Department of Education's Adult Education Division, its name was changed in 1959 to the Division of Adult Continuation Classes. The Division retained responsibility for "the organization and supervision of adult education centres (night schools), the institutional programmes, and adult education projects generally."[49] This name change reflected the orientation of the Division's work to academic upgrading. In 1965 the responsibility for adult education was transferred to the Division of Technical and Vocational Education and then, ten years later, reinstated as a separate Division of Adult and Continuing Education. The emphasis of the Division was on adult basic education as well as continuing and community education.

The idea of community colleges was again recommended in the 1980 report of a task force investigating Newfoundland and Labrador's post-secondary system. The community colleges would be assigned responsibility "for all post-secondary non-university education and for adult and continuing education, with the exception of those functions specifically assigned to other institutions ... "[50] Again this recommendation was not acted upon, although other developments at

---

[48] For additional commentary see Dennison and Gallagher, *Canada's Community Colleges*, p. 66.

[49] F.W. Rowe, *Education and Culture in Newfoundland*, p. 176.

[50] Task Force on Education, *Improving School Retention and Post-secondary Participation: Educational Challenge of the 80's* (St. John's, Province of Newfoundland and Labrador, 1980).

the time resulted in a campus of Memorial University being established outside of St. John's and with the institutions at Stephenville being amalgamated into what effectively was a community college. The impetus for change in the provision of post-secondary education continued, however, and in 1984 a new Department of Career Development and Advanced Studies was established which included responsibility for both adult and vocational education as well as manpower planning. The divisions of Adult and Continuing Education and of Technical and Vocational Education moved into the new Department. One of the initial policy initiatives of the Department was the release in June, 1985 of a planning document, *White Paper: Reorganization of Vocational School System*.[51] In this White Paper the Government outlined its intention to reorganize the provincial vocational school system into a provincial college system. This change took place officially in June, 1987 with the passage of "An Act to Establish a Community College System in the Province." Changes brought about as a result of the Act included a new Fisher Institute of Applied Arts and Technology being created and the two existing institutes being renamed as the Cabot Institute of Applied Arts and Technology and the Newfoundland Institute of Fisheries and Marine Technology. As well, the one community college at Stephenville and the fifteen district vocational institutes were regrouped into five multi-campus community colleges serving all the regions of the province.[52] At this time the government moved out of the delivery of adult education services and turned this responsibility over to the community colleges. The services of the Division of Technical and Vocational Education, which also accounted for a considerable amount of adult training, were similarly absorbed by the colleges.

The responsibility for adult education services is now a mandate of the community colleges which, besides their academic programs, offer short-term and part-time programs of education and training in response to needs as expressed within their regions. This is not an exclusive mandate, however, as Memorial University still operates learning centres for both credit and non-credit courses, as well as delivering courses by distance education. The institutes also continue to offer evening courses and short-term programs. It is this multiplicity that causes the government to presently call for a rationalization of delivery systems "to ensure that efficiency is increased and that the various services are complementary to each other."[53] As part of this rationalization, the government has consolidated the ministerial responsibility for education back into a single Department of Education. None of these moves, however, is intended to reduce the

---

[51] Department of Career Development and Advanced Studies, *White Paper: Reorganization of Vocational School System* (St. John's, Department of Career Development and Advanced Studies, 1985).

[52] P. Gallagher, *Community Colleges in Canada: A Profile* (Vancouver, Vancouver Community College Press, 1990) p. 14.

[53] Government of Newfoundland and Labrador, *Equality, Excellence and Efficiency: A Postsecondary Educational Agenda for the Future* (St. John's, Department of Education, 1990) p. 24.

provision of adult education, which is viewed as being a crucial factor in determining the province's future prospects.

Nova Scotia

Statement of the General Situation

Until quite recently the school boards throughout the province were the main providers of adult education, and this work was coordinated through the Continuing Education Division in the Department of Education. Specialized vocational and technical institutions and the several universities in Nova Scotia also offered extension services. This situation has recently been revamped, however, with the creation in 1988 of the Nova Scotia Community College system and its six regional campuses (plus a provincial francophone campus). It is now the mandate of the community college campuses to provide and coordinate adult education and training in their respective regions, and the orientation of their work in this regard is very much occupational training. The school boards, however, continue to be active in offering their long-standing adult education programs.

There are two departments responsible for education, the Department of Education and the Department of Advanced Education and Job Training.

Historical Developments

Nova Scotia can claim a long history of both public and private support for adult education. As early as 1889 the provincial government was operating Coal Miners' Schools and in the next year it was conducting Government Night Schools for Adults.[54] St. Francis Xavier University established an Extension Department in 1928, with Father Moses Coady as its first Director. From this event developed an internationally acclaimed adult education program known as the Antigonish Movement. Additionally, the Nova Scotia Department of Agriculture utilized adult education in its field work program.

The Province's formal commitment to adult education began in 1945 when the Adult Education Division was established within the Ministry of Education and, two years later, a Vocational Education Division. From the outset the purpose of Adult Education Division was to provide "a variety of educational services designed to aid adults in enhancing the quality of life in their communities."[55] This work of continuing education was promoted by field representatives who assisted in the organizing and instructing of many courses, workshops and demonstration projects at the local level. One example of the community development philosophy guiding the Adult Education Division's

---

[54] Province of Nova Scotia, *Report of the Royal Commission on Post-Secondary Education* (Halifax, Province of Nova Scotia, 1985) p. 227.

[55] F.K. Stewart, *Learning Opportunities for Adults: A Study of Adult and Continuing Education in Nova Scotia* (Halifax, Department of Education, 1981) p. 29.

work is the residential Folkschools that were conducted to foster active participation in community affairs.

By 1979 the adult education work had expanded to the point that, in addition to the field representatives, there were part-time and even a few full-time local administrators appointed by the school boards. Another feature of the Division's leadership was the encouraging of school boards to operate community schools so as to provide recreational and general interest courses for all members of the community.

As for the Vocational Education Division, it also carried out an active program throughout the province, in this case primarily of evening classes. This form of vocational instruction had been initiated by the Department of Education beginning in 1907, and was an important aspect of its mandate. In the area of technical education, the Division took on the responsibility for such programs as the School for Marine Engineers, the Land Survey School and the Navigation Schools at Yarmouth and Halifax. Other technical training institutions were subsequently established, the Nova Scotia Institute of Technology and the Nova Scotia Eastern Institute of Technology, as a result of federal assistance made available through the Technical and Vocational Training Assistance Act of 1960. Also as a result of federal training initiatives, a number of Adult Vocational Training Centres (AVTCs) were established to deliver occupational courses to unemployed adults.

The extent of adult education being conducted by the Department of Education by the end of the 1960s was such that the responsibilities of the two divisions were reorganized and brought under a single administration in 1969. The new unit was referred to as the Adult Education Program and consisted of three activity areas: Continuing Education Activity (to serve the general adult education needs of the population), the Applied Arts and Technology Activity, and the Adult Vocational Training Activity. The work of this unit continued to expand in all areas through the 1970s such that one knowledgable observer commented, "Adult education—continuous learning has obviously become a significant, essential, and integral part of the total educational system."[56] The shortcoming that was noted, however, was the absence of any formal statement by the Department of Education outlining its responsibility and support for adult education. This absence was echoed in the report of the Royal Commission on Post-Secondary Education in 1985. The Commissioners noted particularly that the area of continuing education had not been "as fully recognized or accepted as part of the lifelong process of education as it should be."[57] This observation very much reflected what was happening in the continuing education area.

---

[56] F.K. Stewart, *Learning Opportunities for Adults: A Study of Adult and Continuing Education in Nova Scotia*, p. 48.

[57] Province of Nova Scotia, *Report of the Royal Commission on Post-Secondary Education*, p. xi.

The Adult Education Program unit was reorganized within the Department of Education such that continuing education was now a division of the subdepartment of Vocational and Technical Training. Fiscal restrain brought on by the recession of the early 1980s caused the government to amend the financing of continuing education as provided through the school boards. The provincial coordination and support for continuing education all but vanished when the Department of Education's field staff was reduced from six to a single person, and then to the point where no one was given responsibility for this work. Meanwhile other developments in Nova Scotia's post-secondary system were beginning to unfold which were about to have a considerable influence on the structuring of adult education.

In the 1970s, at a time when other provinces were developing their post-secondary education systems with the creation of community colleges, Nova Scotia maintained its existing system of universities and specialized vocational and technical institutions. In its 1974 report, the Royal Commission on Education, Public Services, and Provincial-Municipal Relations (Graham Commission) examined the idea of a community college system but did not recommend it over what already existed in Nova Scotia. The Report of the Royal Commission on Post-Secondary Education, in 1985, did not consider such a system, given the advanced nature of the existing post-secondary institutions. The government began a process in 1986, however, of discussion, debate and public hearings on the idea of a community college system. Subsequently, in February of 1988, a blueprint of the system was revealed in a *White Paper on a Community College System for Nova Scotians.*[58]

In promoting the idea of a community college system, the Nova Scotia government was responding to the dual influences of technological advancement and structural change in the economy. It maintained that Nova Scotians needed to continuously "upgrade and update their education achievements and work skills in order to remain competitive in a changing world economy."[59] Six regional colleges were proposed along with a provincial college for Francophones. Their mandate was to provide training and education on both a full-time and part-time basis to students with or without grade 12 graduation who entered directly from school or at other times in their lives.

The community college proposal was implemented in 1989 and the new colleges began as a consolidation of the facilities and programs of existing institutions. The ministerial responsibility for the colleges lies with the Department of Advanced Education and Job Training. This Department has its genesis in 1985 when a Department of Human Resources and Training was created and then renamed the following year as the Department of Vocational and Technical

---

[58] Province of Nova Scotia, *Foundation for the Future: A White Paper on a Community College System for Nova Scotians* (Halifax, Province of Nova Scotia, 1988).

[59] Province of Nova Scotia, *Foundation for the Future: A White Paper on a Community College System for Nova Scotians*, as quoted in the Foreword.

Training. In 1987 it became the Department of Advanced Education and Job Training.

The community colleges offer a varied program, including academic upgrading, trades training, applied arts, technical and technological training, community-based education, and courses targeted to groups with special needs. While the emphasis throughout is on training and occupational education, the colleges are also mandated to co-operate with local school boards and universities to provide continuing education classes. "Regional college administrators or Community Education and Training Officers will work with directors of continuing education programs offered by school boards and universities to determine the courses most appropriately delivered by each type of educational institution."[60]

It is yet too early to determine the effectiveness of the college system in carrying forward the Province's achievements to date in adult education. In particular the relationship with school boards remains to be worked out satisfactorily. The exigencies of the economy are, however, most apparently skewing the emphasis away from liberal adult education in favour of a job market orientation.

Ontario

Statement of the General Situation

All components of Ontario's public education system provide adult education—the public schools, colleges and universities. In the case of the public schools and the colleges, this activity is carried out with the clear support of the provincial government, although there is an absence of policy specific to adult education. The college system, however, has been developed with adult education intentionally as a major aspect of its mandate. School boards have the authority to admit adults to day school programs, evening classes, summer school, and vocational courses.[61]

There are three departments responsible for education, the Ministry of Education, the Ministry of Colleges and Universities, and the Ministry of Skills Development.

Historical Developments

Similar to two other provinces (Nova Scotia, Saskatchewan) Ontario established an official adult education body at the end of the Second World War. In the case of Ontario, the Department of Education initially formed a Universities Adult Education Board, consisting of representatives from the universities, voluntary organizations and other interests. The board was given the following duties:

---

[60] Province of Nova Scotia, *Foundation for the Future: A White Paper on a Community College System for Nova Scotians*, p. 97.

[61] Ministry of Education, *Continuing Education: A Resource Document* (Toronto, Ministry of Education, 1987).

1. to promote adult education throughout the province
2. to encourage the formation of local councils for adult education
3. to make provision for the training of leaders in adult education
4. to co-operate with all voluntary agencies in the promotion of adult education
5. generally to co-operate with educational authorities and government departments, municipal, provincial or dominion, in promoting the purposes of the Board.[62]

Two years later the Department of Education established a Division of Adult Education and, until the mid 1960s, adult learning opportunities were provided by public schools through night classes and by the universities through extension courses.

As early as 1950 the idea of developing a system of junior colleges was proposed for Ontario.[63] While no action was taken at that time, in 1963 a committee of university presidents issued a report which advanced ideas to remedy a number of perceived deficiencies in Ontario's educational system.[64] The first deficiency was "a striking lack of opportunity for adult education in the province."[65] In the context of the report, adult education referred to learning opportunity for those who were high school graduates and who desired to continue their education, although not at a university level. This report and other developments at the time, including the federal government's post-secondary funding initiatives through the 1960 Technical and Vocational Training and Assistance Act, were influential in Ontario establishing a college system. In May, 1965 amendments were introduced to the Department of Education Act that resulted in the creation of a provincial system of Colleges of Applied Arts and Technology.

The new colleges were given an explicit mandate to provide adult education. When the Minister of Education (and future Premier), William Davis, introduced the college legislation, he outlined the colleges' adult education and vocational and technical emphasis as being to offer the following types of courses, among others:

- general adult education programs, including cultural and leisure time activities
- programs of recreation including physical education

---

[62] As quoted in the *Report of the Royal Commission on Adult Education* (Winnipeg, King's Printer, 1947) p. 153.

[63] Royal Commission on Education in Ontario, *Report* (Toronto, King's Printer, 1950).

[64] Committee of Presidents of Provincially Assisted Universities and Colleges of Ontario, *The Structure of Post-Secondary Education in Ontario*, Supplementary Report No. 1 (Toronto, 1963).

[65] Dennison and Gallagher, *Canada's Community Colleges*, p. 33.

- general or liberal education courses, including remedial courses in basic subjects
- re-training, upgrading and updating courses
- other courses to meet local needs.

The colleges were to be comprehensive institutions, "providing a wide variety of programs of varying lengths including work experience programs, by day and in the evening, for adults as well as for youths, and for probably more part-time than full-time students."[66]

Since the introduction of colleges in Ontario in the mid 1960s there have been several efforts to clarify adult education's particular situation within the total public educational system. These efforts have been made more difficult, however, by the frequent political restructuring of education in the province. In 1975 the Ministry of Education was divided so as to create a separate Ministry of Colleges and Universities. In 1979 the two ministries were combined for administrative purposes under a single Minister and then separated again in 1985, with some of their responsibilities shifting to a Ministry of Skills Development. Despite this restructuring of political accountability, adult education has continued to be the subject of formal attention.

An early affirmation of adult education's role in Ontario occurred in 1972 when the Commission on Post-Secondary Education in Ontario (referred to as the Wright Commission after its Chairman) issued its report titled, *The Learning Society*.[67] In this report "continuing education" was given great credence within a process of "lifetime learning," and this laid the groundwork for further study by government.[68]

In 1981 the joint ministries of Education and of Colleges and Universities issued a discussion paper titled, *Continuing Education: The Third System*.[69] In this document a conceptual distinction was made between the educational process which takes place on a full-time basis, and that which occurs after a learner ceases to be a full-time student. Two systems serve the full-time student, the first one being the elementary/secondary system (elementary and secondary schools, separate schools, private schools) and the second one being the post-secondary system (colleges, universities, and private vocational schools and colleges). The paper posited that continuing education represents a third system in the educa-

---

[66] As contained in *Continuing Education: The Third System. A Discussion Paper* (Toronto, Ministry of Education and Ministry of Colleges and Universities, 1981) p. 103.

[67] Commission on Post-Secondary Education in Ontario, *The Learning Society* (Toronto, Ontario Ministry of Public Services, 1972).

[68] For an assessment of the impact of this report and others of the time see G. Selman, "1972—Year of Affirmation for Adult Education," *Canadian Journal for the Study of Adult Education*, *3*, 1 (1989) pp. 33–44.

[69] Ministry of Education/Ministry of Colleges and Universities, *Continuing Education: The Third System*.

tional process, made up of "educational resources and agencies through which adults obtain learning opportunities throughout their lifetime after their initial schooling is terminated."[70] Included in this system are both the continuing education available through the two established systems of education and the full spectrum of learning activities available outside of the traditional institutions. The paper identified twenty-one issues specific to the third system which pertained to the two ministries, and noted that a fundamental question was the extent to which they should commit themselves to a philosophy of lifelong education. As for policy, the paper suggested that at least a clear policy statement needed to be issued so as to clarify that which was implied in existing regulations and other documents.

In response to this call for clarification the government in 1983 issued a statement, *Continuing Education in the Schools, Colleges and Universities in Ontario*. This statement, while consolidating the government's views on various aspects of adult education, did not provide any clarification by way of specific policy. Instead, the next year a Continuing Education Review Project was initiated by the two ministries to provide recommendations on policy, organization and funding for continuing education as supported by the two ministries. (When the Project submitted its findings in 1986, a new Ministry of Skills Development was included in the report.)[71] Again there was a call for formal recognition of lifelong education and for policy which provides for adult education, e.g. "That adult continuing education which addresses the civic, social and economic needs of adults through their various phases of development be formally recognized as being as important as that of the education of children and youth."[72]

The question of policy for adult education remains subsumed in issues specific to the colleges. In the spring of 1990 the Council of Regents for Colleges of Applied Arts and Technology released a report in which it put forward ideas for renewing the mandate of the college system. Concern for adult learners permeates the report, and a major focus is on enhancing access to learning opportunity of various kinds. The status of part-time learners—who outnumber full-time students in the colleges by almost six to one—is described as being peripheral, as

---

[70] Ministry of Education/Ministry of Colleges and Universities, *Continuing Education: The Third System*, p. 3.

[71] Continuing Education Review Project, *Project Report: For Adults Only* (Toronto, Ministry of Colleges and Universities, 1986).

[72] Continuing Education Review Project, *Project Report: For Adults Only*, p. 15.

evidenced in program and service orientation and funding, and the report seeks to redress this situation.[73]

On the basis of this report there is no question that adult education is accepted by the colleges as an essential and major part of its mandate. To the extent that infrastructure arrangements can be made in the colleges to act on this acceptance will determine the degree to which adult education can be melded into this system.

Prince Edward Island

Statement of the General Situation

Adult education services in Prince Edward Island are, for the most part, provided by Holland College, the province's only community college. Vocational education and academic upgrading are the two major programs offered to adults at the three campuses—in Charlottetown, West Royalty and Summerside—and in others centres throughout the Island. The University of Prince Edward Island also conducts non-credit extension courses for adults, both on and off campus. Additionally there is an active Community Schools Movement which is organized on a co-operative basis and which offers adult education programs during the winter months. Modest financial assistance is provided by the provincial government to assist with the coordination of the community schools.[74]

There are two departments responsible for education, the Department of Education and the Department of Industry.

Historical Developments

It is only recently, and specifically since the creation of Holland College in 1969, that adult education has been given a distinct role in the province. Prior to this time there were only intermittent efforts at meeting adult learning needs. For a few years following World War One vocational courses were conducted in the evening for veterans. Beginning in 1934 and continuing through the depression and war years, the Extension Department of St. Dunstan's University initiated an adult education program for the province's rural population which addressed the

---

[73] Ontario Council of Regents, *Vision 2000: Quality and Opportunity* (Toronto, Ontario Ministry of Colleges and Universities, 1990). The report identifies three categories of programs: (1) college credential programs, i.e. programs for which a college post-secondary credential is granted; (2) non-credential programs, i.e. those career-oriented programs over which the colleges do not control entry and exit standards and those programs which are not primarily vocational in nature; and (3) general education, i.e. the broad study of subjects and issues which are central to education for life in our culture and, generic skills, i.e. practical life skills essential for both personal and career success. (p. 34).

[74] E. MacDonald, *A Community of Schools* (Charlottetown, Institute of Island Studies, 1985).

difficult social and economic problems associated with these troubled times.[75] After World War Two, vocational courses were once again provided to returning soldiers, this time through the Department of Education's Division of Vocational and Continuing Education. With the funding assistance for vocational and technical education made available by the federal government in the early 1960s, Prince Edward Island in 1962 built the Prince County Vocational High School in Summerside and two years later the Provincial Vocational Institute in Charlottetown. Both provided trades training for adults as part of their curricula.

The report of a Royal Commission on Higher Education (J.S. Bonnell, Chairman) in 1965 precipitated significant changes in the province's post-secondary system. Following on this report the government made clear its intentions for post-secondary education in a policy statement delivered by the Premier to the legislative assembly.[76] By way of restructuring the system, the two existing, tradition bound institutions, St. Dunstan's University and Prince of Wales College, were transformed into the University of Prince Edward Island, and a community college, Holland College, was created. Both events occurred in 1969.

The college initially conducted a program of applied arts and technology and then, beginning in 1976 when the responsibility for the two vocational centres was added to the college by the Department of Education, vocational education was also offered. To reflect this addition, the mandate for the college was expanded to include, "The object of the college is to provide a broad range of educational opportunity particularly in the fields of applied arts and technology, vocational training and adult education."[77] This change took place in 1977 when the Holland College Act was amended.

The Prince Edward Island Department of Industry is responsible for channelling both federal and provincial funding to the adult basic education and pre-vocation training programs offered by Holland College. An example of this is the Adult Night Class Program of academic upgrading which is presented in a night school format.[78] It is offered free of charge to those 18 years of age or greater who have been out of school for at least one year.

The changing nature of Prince Edward Island's economy away from dependence on the fishery and into new areas of economic activity has considerably influenced the provision of adult education, which has a decided vocational orientation. At the same time, the strong Maritime's tradition of co-operation

---

[75] M. McKenna, S.C., "Higher Education in Transition, 1945–1980," in Smitheram et al. (Eds.), *The Garden Transformed: Prince Edward Island, 1945–1980* (Charlottetown, Ragweed Press, 1982) p. 206. For an account of the program see J. Croteau, *Cradled in the Waves: The Story of a People's Co-operative Achievement In Economic Betterment in Prince Edward Island* (Toronto, Ryerson Press, 1951).

[76] Hon. Alex Campbell, "Policy Statement on Post-Secondary Education" (Legislative Assembly, Prince Edward Island, April 2, 1968).

[77] As noted in Dennison and Gallagher, *Canada's Community Colleges*, p. 106.

[78] Prince Edward Island, *Evaluation of the Adult Night Class Program* (Charlottetown, Department of Industry, 1988).

ensures a continued role of the community schools as a method for developing individuals and their communities.

Quebec

Statement of the General Situation

Adult education is recognized in Quebec by policy as being part of the formal educational system, and in this case it is referred to as continuing education. The provincial government sees continuing education as being a significant means of furthering the distinctiveness of Quebec society, and as a result financial support for it is provided to several public and private organizations. This situation also recognizes that the two linguistic groups (French and English) have somewhat different patterns to their participation and hence no one provider is dominant.[79] As is the case in most provinces, however, there is no legislated commitment for continuing education and as a result the specific support in terms of finances is subject to budget priorities.

Guiding the Quebec government's involvement in continuing education is the *Policy Statement and Plan for Action* issued in 1984. This policy statement document outlines the government's intentions (referred to as "thrusts") in bringing greater acknowledgment to this sector of education. The document is the government's response to the precursor Report of the Commission d'étude sur la formation des adultes (Jean Commission, 1982). In brief, the document concurs with the main orientations of the Jean Commission, namely, "advocating a broader and easier access to existing educational resources, recognition of pedagogical practices determining the specificity of adult education, recognition of the multiplicity of educational facilities, and a clear sharing of responsibilities between the departments of government ... "[80] It also firmly refutes the federal government's role in occupational training.

There are two ministries responsible for education, the Ministry of Education and the Ministry of Advanced Education and Science.

Historical Developments

The most sensational educational developments in Canada during the modern period have occurred in Quebec. Prior to the start of that province's "Quiet Revolution," as signalled by the election of the Liberals under Jean Lesage in 1960, educational matters were within the domain of the Catholic and Protestant churches. Other aspects of life in Quebec were similarly ready for reform, as part of the reaction against the combination of the dominating influence of the Roman Catholic church and the conservative style of government which had

---

[79] Results from the Statistics Canada 1984 Adult Education Survey as reported in a booklet produced by the CAAE and the Quebec Association for Adult Learning, *Adult Education in Quebec* (Montreal, QALL, 1986).

[80] Province of Quebec, *Continuing Education Program: Policy Statement and Plan of Action* (Quebec, Province of Quebec, 1984).

held in check general economic, social and cultural advancement. In the period leading up to the 1960 election and since, Quebec society has found fresh voices by which to express its aspirations, and a new provincial confidence has emerged. Adult education has been a part of the transformation, and has been the subject of various public policy initiatives.

One of the most fundamental changes brought on by the Lesage government was to secularize the education system. A Royal Commission on Education, chaired by Alphonse-Marie Parent of Laval University, was established in 1961 and issued its five volume report in increments between 1963 and 1966.[81] One of the earliest recommendations called for a Ministry of Education to be established, as it was the Commission's view that, "A master plan is needed, an orientation to serve a common good—a job which properly belongs to the political authorities."[82] The recommendation was adopted and the Ministry of Education was formed in 1964. Out of this move has developed a coherent, democratic and modern educational system.

The interest of adult education was well served by the Parent Commission. One of three working committees set up by the Commission was on adult education, chaired by Claude Ryan. Most of the committee's principal recommendations were adopted by the Commission, and an adult education bureaucracy was integrated in the new Ministry of Education with an appropriate status. This move acknowledged and made legitimate the place of adult education in Quebec's revitalized educational system.

The educational system featured a new institutional form at the post-secondary level, namely the CEGEP, an acronym for College d'Enseignement General et Professional. The CEGEP equates with a post-secondary college and provides programs for either university entry or for occupational training and vocational preparation. The CEGEPs were intended to open educational opportunity as never before and, even more, were "instruments in a sociopolitical plan to restructure an entire society."[83]

There were other educational innovations introduced by the Ministry of Education which had an adult education orientation. The first was TEVEC, an investigation into the use of television for mass education, which was tested in the late 1960s in the Saguenay Lac St. Jean region of the province. Following on this experiment was Multi-Media, a program designed to help those who were undereducated to overcome their disadvantaged circumstances. It employed various distance education techniques and media during its operating life from 1972–1978. A third, and lasting, innovation is the Tele-Université, an affiliate of the University of Quebec established in 1972, which offers its programming using

---

[81] Province of Quebec, *Report of the Royal Commission of Inquiry on Education in the Province of Quebec* (Quebec, Les Presses Des Marais, 1963).

[82] As quoted in H. Roberts, *Culture and Adult Education: A Study of Alberta and Quebec*, p. 109.

[83] Dennison and Gallagher, *Canada's Community Colleges*, p. 45.

distance education means. Tele-Université's program emphasis is not so much academic as it is "education populaire," that is, non-vocational, non-credit courses.

The pace of change in Quebec society continued unabated in the 1970s, and especially in the area of Quebec nationalism. In 1976 the Parti Quebecois was elected on a separatist platform, and as never before attention was focused on Quebec's cultural identity and development. Roberts, in his review of social philosophies in Quebec and their impact on adult education, points out how, through the issuance of a White Paper on cultural development, the government recognized the place of education, indeed lifelong education, in cultural development, which in turn was understood as being vital to Quebec.[84] With all the fervour being generated within the province, culminating in the referendum on sovereignty association in 1980, many questions regarding the place of adult education remained to be answered.

In 1980 the government followed through on an earlier commitment to study various aspects of education, including adult education, and appointed a Commission d'étude sur la formation des adultes with Michele Jean as its president. The Jean Commission was given a broad mandate to investigate both vocational and socio-cultural aspects of adult education and to frame a comprehensive adult education policy for Quebec. A feature of the Commission's work was its extensive effort in seeking input, including the conducting of a survey of the participation behaviour of Quebec adults. From these deliberations and with the data gathered, a working document titled *Adult Education in Quebec: Possible Solutions* was published in which the Commission presented its thinking to that point. Essentially the document noted the general disenchantment concerning the status of adult education in the province and suggested that a greater emphasis needed to be placed on adult education within government and in and among institutions and organizations. In its final report, *Apprendre: Une action volontaire et responsable* issued in 1982, the Commission recommended a more centralized approach for those adult education services provided with public funds.[85]

The Jean Report, with its recommendations for greater government commitment to coordination and leadership in the broad area of adult education as well as for an entitlement to all citizens of fifteen years of full-time subsidized education, was submitted at a time of economic recession. As an example of the recession's severity, unemployment in Quebec jumped to seventeen per cent in 1983. Despite the bleak economic climate the government responded to the report of the Jean Commission in 1984 when it published its intentions in the policy statement, *Continuing Education Program: Policy Statement and Plan of*

---

[84] H. Roberts, *Culture and Adult Education*, p. 57.

[85] Commission d'étude sur la formation des adultes, *Apprendre: une action volontaire et responsable* (Quebec, Ministere des Communications, 1982).

Action.[86] The statement, issued under the signatures of the ministers of Education and of Manpower and Income Security, and of the Minister Responsible for the Status of Women, is quite broad in its scope and outlines the agenda not only for developing adult education within the province's educational provision but also in asserting Quebec's constitutional sovereignty over all educational matters. This dual agenda is evident in one of the Report's introductory paragraphs:

> The requirements of the development of human resources in Quebec, so closely related to those of the social and economic development of the community, call for the establishment of an adult education policy. It will not accomplish its goals, however, until Quebec has recovered from the federal government all the resources allocated by the federal government to adult education and is able to exercise its full power in this field, which is under provincial jurisdiction.[87]

The policy statement expressed in no uncertain terms the Quebec government's displeasure at the federal initiatives in the manpower training area within the province, instead seeing this to be a provincial prerogative.

> Despite the failure of all attempts made up to now to have the federal government recognize Quebec's specific jurisdiction over adult education, this policy paper strongly and firmly reiterates Quebec's demand for all its rightful authority in the adult education sector based on its specific cultural, social and economic interests.[88]

Rather than identifying a specific course of action in adult education, the policy statement more generally defines the goals and means of government action. It identifies seven "challenges" facing Quebec's evolving society which "must be met by adult education either now or in the near future"[89]:

- technological change and economic development
- social progress and equality of opportunity
- the elimination of sexism in educational practices
- cultural development and participation in cultural activities
- development of regional communities
- consultation with the parties involved in education
- the recognition of Quebec's jurisdiction.

The policy statement embraces the view that education is a lifelong endeavour. In declaring its policy intentions supporting adult education (continuing education), the government identified twelve areas for action. These twelve "thrusts" (as they are denoted) can be summarized as follows:

- the mandates of the several government departments involved in providing adult education were confirmed in this respect;

---

[86] Province of Quebec, *Continuing Education Program: Policy Statement and Plan of Action* (Quebec, Ministry of Education, 1984).

[87] *Continuing Education Program: Policy Statement and Plan of Action*, p vi.

[88] *Continuing Education Program: Policy Statement and Plan of Action*, p. vii.

[89] *Continuing Education Program: Policy Statement and Plan of Action*, p. 19.

- the Ministere de l'Education would commit its resources in a number of critical areas to ensuring adults have access to continuing education opportunities. These areas include funding, facilities, trained instructors, and inter-departmental coordination;
- the place of non-profit organizations in community education was reaffirmed;
- the ministere de la Main-d'oeuvre et de la Sécurité du revenu was to (a) establish a manpower policy and, (b) be responsible for all Quebec's manpower training programs.

The Policy Statement further identifies action priorities and measures for more effective government involvement in managing the province's adult education provision. In total it represents a grand design for Quebec's social, cultural and economic well-being, as viewed from the adult education perspective. The document is impressive not only for its embracing nature but also for its unequivocable belief in, and commitment to, adult education as an instrument of government intervention.

Impressive as it is, the Policy Statement suffers under practical limitations as well. To begin, adult education is seen as being politicized by virtue of it being an obvious area to put forward in the ongoing constitutional conflict between the federal and Quebec governments. Further, since the Policy Statement was released in 1984 under the Parti Quebecois, a provincial election was held and a new government under the Liberals formed. Finally, and most obviously, action is closely tied to the availability of funding, and adult education still must compete with government's statutory obligations and other priorities for support. Despite these limitations, adult education in Quebec enjoys an enviable situation of having a policy statement in place.

Saskatchewan

Statement of the General Situation

The early provision of adult education in Saskatchewan was associated with non-government organizations, including the Women's Institutes, agricultural societies and the Saskatchewan Wheat Pool, and with university agricultural extension work. In 1973 comprehensive provision of adult education was made available by way of a unique community college system. In the latter part of the 1980s this system was restructured, however, such that adult education programming is now dispersed among public institutions and community agencies on the basis of its content.

In the new structure regional colleges have been given a mandate to provide the rural and northern areas of the province with adult basic education including literacy, English as a second language, and high school completion, in addition to university and technical institute programs. For the urban settings a new Saskatchewan Institute of Applied Science and Technology (SIAST) has been established and which consists of an administrative amalgam of several technical and vocational institutes and the urban community colleges. As part of its program offering SIAST, like the regional colleges, offers adult basic education courses.

A significant program difference in the new structuring is that community interest, hobby and leisure courses are no longer within the mandate of the regional colleges and instead are offered by local interest groups. The two universities, however, continue to conduct an active adult education program through their extension departments. As well, distance education has become a significant method of delivering much adult learning in the province, as provided for by the Saskatchewan Communication Network.

There is one ministry responsible for education, the Department of Education.

Historical Developments

Within four years of Saskatchewan becoming a province in 1905, the University of Saskatchewan was formed.[90] Early on the extension work of the university was connected with the College of Agriculture, as the provincial government mandated the College to teach agricultural education in the farming communities. (It was not until 1965 that the Extension Department received a mandate to work on a university-wide basis.) The voluntary sector also played a significant role in providing adult learning in the province, consistent with the community based self-help values associated with rural living. By way of public provision some limited amount of community education occurred with government assistance by way of the "lighted schoolhouse" idea, i.e. evening classes for adults.

Beginning in 1944 an Adult Education Division was established within the Department to bring a level of coordination to this work. The impetus for this development was the election of the first socialist government in Canada, the CCF under Tommy Douglas.[91] The Department's aims were announced as being:

(a) to liquidate social, scientific and language illiteracy;

(b) to help clarify the thinking of citizens regarding fundamental issues confronting modern society;

(c) to promote responsible and co-operative citizen action;

(d) to encourage integrated and creative community life.[92]

The bold initiatives that were begun to carry out these aims were short lived, however, for reasons of a political nature.

---

[90] For more historical information see R.F. Harvey, *Middle Range Education in Canada* (Toronto, Gage, 1973).

[91] For an insightful account of this event see M. Welton, "Mobilizing the People for Socialism: The Politics of Adult Education in Saskatchewan, 1944–45," in M. Welton (Ed.), *Knowledge for the People: The Struggle for Adult Learning in English Speaking Canada* (Toronto, O.I.S.E. Press, 1987).

[92] Province of Saskatchewan, Department of Continuing Education, *Report of the Minister's Advisory Committee on Community Colleges* (Regina, Department of Continuing Education, 1972) p. 5.

An overriding concern to preserve the quality of rural life in the province moved the Saskatchewan government in 1956 to appoint a Royal Commission on Agriculture and Rural Life. This commission singled out the role of adult education in its broadest terms as being integral to supporting community life and the particular social values associated with it, especially in the face of the changing economic and social environment. The next year a Centre for Community Studies was established as a project of the province and the University of Saskatchewan, and for the next seven years it produced research and resource materials for use by those working in the field.

In 1962 a Minister's Committee on Continuing Education was formed and given the task of delineating a policy of continuing education for the province. This included determining roles and responsibilities of various agencies and voluntary organizations which were active in the field. The following year the Adult Education Branch became the Community Education Branch and began to provide leadership for adult education in rural communities through the efforts of regional field staff. Three years later, however, following on a change in government in 1964, the Branch was phased out as the emphasis in adult education in the province "shifted away from community programming to the pressing need for expansion of technical training capabilities in the Institutes of Applied Arts and Sciences."[93] The confusion caused by this action, along with other expansionary developments in the education field during the 1960s, suggested the need for a reassessment of post-school education in the province. In 1967 a committee on higher education had issued a report (Spinks Report) calling for a system of "middle range" education in the province. This was followed four years later by the McLeod Report which, as part of its review of the role of the University of Saskatchewan within the community, considered the part that community colleges could play in the province's total educational system. Prior to the government taking action on establishing junior colleges, however, the provincial election of 1971 resulted in the return of the New Democratic Party, and implementation plans were put on hold.

An early action of the new government was to establish a separate Ministry of Continuing Education in an effort to oversee the system of post-secondary learning in Saskatchewan. In turn the Minister appointed a Minister's Advisory Committee on Community Colleges, chaired by Dr. Ron Faris. Subsequently, in 1973, the Community Colleges Act was passed, which introduced a unique community college model with an emphasis on community development and community service.

Faris described the Saskatchewan version of the community college as being "colleges without walls but with foundations."[94] They were without walls in that,

---

[93] Saskatchewan, Department of Continuing Education, *Report of the Minister's Advisory Committee on Community Colleges*, p. 5.

[94] R. Faris, "Colleges without Walls but with Foundations" (unpublished speech, Lambton College, Ontario, 1974), as referenced in Dennison and Gallagher, *Canada's Community Colleges*, p. 56.

rather than constructing college institutions in each region of the province, the community colleges were instead to serve the various communities within their regions by utilizing existing facilities. This reinforced the decentralized approach to providing adult education services. As well, rather than employing faculty, the community colleges instead acted as a broker with other educational institutions for delivery of instruction, or else hired instructors on a temporary, fee-for-service basis. The foundations were firm, however, in that they rested on the sense of community in rural Saskatchewan ("traditions of community participation and co-operation blended with self-help") and on the ready access to learning opportunities throughout life.[95]

In their review of Saskatchewan's community colleges Dennison and Gallagher claim that, "In terms of the original goal of improving quality of life, particularly in rural communities, the colleges had proved to be a remarkable success."[96] However, the province's paramount requirements by the mid 1980s were deemed to be in the area of occupational training. A change of government in 1982 and the general economic recession at that time were two precursors of a general assessment of the community college system. In a preliminary move the new government consolidated all post-secondary education, including the Department of Continuing Education, into a single Ministry of Advanced Education and Manpower.

In 1987 the government implemented a major restructuring of the province's educational system. To begin, the total education system in the province was brought together into a single Ministry of Education. In the post-secondary sector a planning document, *Preparing for the Year 2000: Adult Education in Saskatchewan*, was presented in 1987 which reoriented the community college system to emphasize skills training.[97] A new institution was established, the Saskatchewan Institute of Applied Science and Technology (SIAST), which served the urban settings by bringing under one administrative umbrella several vocational and technical institutes and community colleges. To better serve the rural and northern portions of the province regional colleges were formed out of the rural community colleges and given the mandate to make post-secondary education accessible within the regions. In addition, distance education became a major method of delivering adult learning.

Adult education programming was considerably altered in the new system. While the regional colleges and SIAST continued to provide literacy training, English as a second language, adult basic education, and high school completion,

---

[95] Province of Saskatchewan, *Report of the Minister's Advisory Committee on Community Colleges*, p. 7.

[96] Dennison and Gallagher, *Canada's Community Colleges*, p. 113.

[97] Province of Saskatchewan, *Preparing for the Year 2000: Adult Education in Saskatchewan* (Regina, Saskatchewan Education, 1987).

they were no longer mandated to provide community interest, hobby and leisure courses. Instead these courses were to be conducted by "local interest groups."

The change in emphasis in Saskatchewan's college system away from community education to occupational training effectively ended what Dennison and Gallagher referred to as the "great experiment" in community education.[98] The exigencies of the economy dictated that adult education now carry out its several functions in a much more prescribed manner, with some functions, such as those focused on the interests of the individual and the community, no longer included as part of the colleges' sphere. This change reflected a different set of circumstances in the province from those which had existed some fifteen years earlier.

The Yukon and the Northwest Territories

Statement of the General Situation

Adult education, including academic upgrading for adults, is for the most part provided through the post-secondary systems of both territories. These systems, while small in size (comprised of two institutions, Yukon College in the Yukon and Arctic College in the Northwest Territories) are responsible for providing adult education services over enormous land areas. Both institutions operate learning centres in smaller communities to serve the diverse learning needs of the small populations.

In the Yukon, adult education is coordinated through the Advanced Education Branch of the Department of Education. In turn it is Yukon College which delivers adult education through its Community and Continuing Education Division. This division provides a broad range of full-time and part-time learning opportunities for adults throughout the Yukon using a network of Community Campuses.[99] As well it provides resources and supports for other forms of adult education.

In the Northwest Territories adult education is coordinated through the Advanced Education Branch within the Department of Education. Responsibility for the delivery of adult education services throughout the arctic has recently been transferred from this Branch to Arctic College. At present the college has six campuses and operates adult education centres in an additional twenty-five communities. Each centre is staffed with an adult educator who organizes continuing education programs as determined on the basis of local needs and who coordinates college extension programs being offered in that area.

---

[98] Dennison and Gallagher, *Canada's Community Colleges*, p. 116.

[99] Secretary of State of Canada, *Federal and Provincial Support to Post-Secondary Education in Canada: A Report to Parliament 1988–89* (Ottawa, Ministry of Supplies and Services, 1990) p. 32.

Historical Developments

There is not an established tradition of adult education in either the Yukon or Northwest Territories. Unlike the situation in the provinces where there is a history of institutions of higher education initiating extension services followed by school boards, in the north private organizations such as Frontier College and the Y.W.C.A. have had a presence in providing adult basic education. The Departments of Education in both territories have been concerned with providing grade school education to a mix of both Native and non-Native children, and it was not until post-secondary systems were created that adult education became an acknowledged concern.[100]

It was the establishing of vocational training centres that marked the beginning of post-secondary education in both territories. In the Yukon the Whitehorse Vocational Training School opened in 1963 and in the Northwest Territories the Adult Vocational Training Centre opened in 1968. These developments provided an immediate focus on providing opportunities for adult learning beyond just vocational education and beyond the localities of the main centres (in Whitehorse, Yukon and in Fort Smith, NWT). An expanded number of programs were soon offered, and through extension services these were made available in other communities through learning centres.

Further Developments—Yukon

By the late 1970s the demands for increased educational opportunity within the Yukon for adults precipitated a study on how best to meet these needs.[101] Out of this report came a recommendation to establish a college for the Yukon. This recommendation was accepted by the territorial government and action for its implementation was completed in 1982 with the opening of Yukon College. Originally the College operated from within the Department of Education but, with the passage of the College Act (1988), it now operates on a semi-autonomous basis. The mandate for Yukon College is to deliver post-secondary education to residents of the Yukon, and this very much includes continuing education for adults. As an indication of the importance of adult education to the Yukon, one of the offerings of the College is a diploma program in adult education in conjunction with the University of British Columbia.

With Yukon College now well established the next concern is to have the learning needs of adults recognized and protected in statute. Most recently, a new Education Act has been proclaimed in the Yukon, but it does not refer at all to

---

[100] In the case of the Yukon the territorial Department of Education was established under authority of the Yukon Territory Act (1898) while in the Northwest Territories it was only in 1968 that the Department of Education was formed to take over the school system, run up to that time by the Department of Indian Affairs and Northern Development.

[101] E. Ingram et al., *Toward a Yukon College. Continuing Education Opportunities in the Yukon* (Edmonton, University of Alberta: Department of Educational Administration, 1979).

adult education or to continuing education.[102] While the Yukon is an area where there are many difficult educational issues which need addressing, assured access to adult education remains fundamental to a modern educational system. One issue in particular is that of determining jurisdiction for the delivery of educational services to the Yukon's Indian population. The Council of Yukon Indians, for instance, wishes to be active in this regard, including the provision of adult education.

Further Developments—Northwest Territories

The provision of home-management training in the 1960s marked the formal beginning of adult education in the Northwest Territories.[103] In the 1970s there was a considerable infusion of federal funds through different government departments to support various training initiatives. It was the formation of the Northwest Territories' own Department of Education in 1968, however, which provided the opportunity for an indigenous approach to educational planning for the Territories.

The educational needs to be met were quite considerable, as culture, geography, history and language were all factors in attempting to provide for a small and dispersed population. As well, educational attainment levels were generally lower than in the rest of Canada.[104] Some adult education services were delivered by authorities responsible for schools in various areas of the territory and by other government departments. In the area of vocational training it was the opening of the Adult Vocational Training Centre in 1968 which initiated concerted efforts on behalf of adult learners.

A major study into all aspects of education in the Northwest Territories was established by the Legislative Assembly in 1980. Its subsequent report, released in 1982, stated the conviction that learning is a lifelong activity and made eleven recommendations specific to adult education.[105] One of the most significant outcomes of this report for adult education was that responsibility for all post-school education, i.e. beyond grade 10, was consolidated into a new institution, Arctic College, in 1985. The former Adult Vocational Training Centre, renamed Thebacha College in 1981 because of its expanded program base and enrollment, became one of six campuses of the new college system.

To emphasize the importance of adult learning, the Department of Education in 1984 had established an Advanced Education Program (formerly the Voca-

---

[102] D. Burgess, "The Yukon Education Act: Commentary and Discussion on Recent Legislation," in *McGill Journal of Education, 25,* 2 (1990).

[103] Northwest Territories Special Committee on Education, *Learning: Tradition and Change in the Northwest Territories* (Yellowknife, Northwest Territories Legislative Assembly, 1982).

[104] Secretary of State for Canada, *Federal and Provincial Support to Post-Secondary Education in Canada: A Report to Parliament 1988–89,* p. 34.

[105] Northwest Territories Special Committee on Education, *Learning: Tradition and Change in the Northwest Territories.*

tional and Higher Education Division) to be responsible for delivering post-school programs including adult education in communities. Initially thirty-four community adult educators were employed by this section to conduct this work in conjunction with divisional boards of education. With the passing of the Arctic College Act (1987) they have since become part of Arctic College, which is now mandated to deliver adult post-secondary education throughout the territory. This mandate will undoubtedly prove to be as challenging to carry out as are the educational needs covered by it and the sheer dimensions of the geography involved.

International Experiences in Adult Education

A quality of Canadian adult education is its international awareness. This awareness stems in part from historical circumstance but is also an aspect of the national consciousness shaped by a particular Canadian viewpoint. Historically Canada has derived much from its European settlers, be they the dominant French and English or subsequent immigrants from other countries. Also by dint of history, Canada peacefully shares a continent with the United States of America. In light of this historical circumstance, and particularly since the First World War, Canada has paid special attention to developing its own consciousness. Several factors have exerted strong influence on this effort: its geography, being the world's second largest land mass; its comparatively small population, created almost entirely by immigration; its abundance based on rich natural resources and entrepreneurial zeal; and its commitment to harmonious coexistence, both within Canada and throughout the world. Thus the contemporary Canadian consciousness has been shaped by history and self awareness into a broad world view, and is reflected in the understanding of Canada as a multicultural nation as contrasted with the earlier notion of the United States being a "melting pot" nation.

In Canadian adult education this international awareness is personified in the late Roby Kidd. The Second International Conference on Adult Education, chaired by Kidd, was held in Montreal in 1960. Thirteen years later his vision of establishing an International Council for Adult Education was realized, and Kidd became its first Secretary General. Mention should also be made of the Canadian Association for Adult Education—of which Kidd was Executive Director between 1951 and 1961—and how it has been a focus for international communication and exchange since its inception in 1935.

To foster this international awareness three countries are presented here to examine their public policies regarding adult education: Sweden, the People's Republic of China, and Tanzania. This examination serves several purposes. For one it reveals how adult learning opportunity is able to be patterned according to national circumstances. All three countries are very committed to adult education for essentially the same reasons, but each provides for it in quite different ways. For another it introduces the study of comparative adult education. As there is no singular approach to providing adult education it is instructive to know how and why other countries and educational jurisdictions have done so, to see if there is another way or indeed even a better way. Yet another purpose is to recognize there is truly an international exchange of ideas regarding adult learning, and Canada is very much a part of the community of adult educators who participate in this exchange.

Common to all three countries is the conscious use of adult education in nation building, although the political ideology surrounding the implementation differs considerably in each country (democracy in Sweden, autocracy in Tanzania, and totalitarianism in China). The degree of influence which ideology exerts on other aspects of adult learning, e.g. individual growth and community development, is an indicator of the extent to which adult education is contributing to an overall societal well-being and not just to the intentions of those who formulate policy.

China

China has been selected as a country to review its public policy regarding adult education precisely because of the contradictions this appears to present. Since the formation of the People's Republic of China in 1949, the country has been governed by a totalitarian regime, and such regimes do not engage in policy development processes which involve public input. The Chinese Communist Party has effectively controlled all aspects of the political, economic and social lives of the largest population on earth, estimated in 1989 at 1,103,900,000. From the perspective of education, however, the centralizing of control must be understood in the context of a country where educational opportunity has always been very limited. The formal education system was brought under central control in an attempt to eradicate illiteracy and universalize access to primary and secondary education. At the same time a formal system of adult education was established to serve the remedial learning needs of China's 35 million workers, most of whom have little or no formal education. Responsibility for directing this system lies with the Adult Education Department (prior to 1983 the Bureau of Worker and Peasant Education) within the Ministry of Education, and the adult education system is seen as being of equal importance to the system for youth.

Particularly since the death of Mao Zedong (Mao Tse-tung) in 1976 and the subsequent formal end to the Cultural Revolution, China has attempted to rapidly modernize its economy. The adult education system has been given the additional task of making possible this modernization by way of the training and upgrading of workers in industrial and agricultural enterprises. In short, the formal adult education system in China, i.e. the structured system within the Ministry of Education, was established as an instrument of policy to address specific goals as determined by the state. It is apparent that there exists in China a strong political will favouring adult education.

Western adult educators have noted a basic difference in adult education as understood in the West and in China. Whereas in the West adult education is commonly identified with methods of learning which are distinct from grade school education, in China it refers to the formal schooling of adults. "The Chinese have created the Adult Education Department to help China become a massive learning society for the purpose of modernization. They believe this can best be accomplished by 'formalizing' adult education by systematising, accrediting and standardising education programs for adults."[106] Thus two parallel education systems exist in China, youth and adult, with their aims being complementary to the state's requirements.

There is another distinction to be made between the Western and Chinese view of adult education. In the West the purpose of adult education has been stated variously as being to bring about democratic changes in the social, political and economic structures so as to increase the equality of opportunity within individual societies. This view is described as the social transformationist view of adult education, and is the central concern of many adult educators as they attempt to influence government policy to bring about fundamental change. By contrast, in China the "social transformation" occurred in 1949 with the formation of the People's Republic, and adult education is instead a central feature of the government's plans to bring about change which it has determined as being necessary, in this case the modernization of the economy.

The specific policies regarding adult education begin with the massive campaigns organized soon after the People's Republic was formed. By the end of the First Five Year Plan of 1953–1957 it is estimated that the illiteracy rate was reduced from some 80 per cent of the labour force to 30 per cent. During the Second Five Year Plan of 1958–1962 (the "Great Leap Forward") worker and peasant education was established alongside the regular educational system by way of part-time and spare time education. Then came the regressive interlude of the Great Proletarian Cultural Revolution when ideological zeal caused the educational system to fall into disarray. Intellectuals, students and the educated were uprooted and sent to the countryside for re-education alongside the peasants. This massive dislocation brought on by the Cultural Revolution not only interrupted individual lives but also hampered industrial output. New measures were needed to repair the excesses of the Cultural Revolution, which had run from 1966 to its formal end in 1977.

The country's educational situation was critical, as virtually an entire generation of young people either had their education interrupted or had missed it altogether, and those who were only marginally literate had lapsed into illiteracy. For these reasons, in the period since the Cultural Revolution there have existed the parallel systems of formal education—a regular system for youth and an adult education system for workers and peasants. Both systems are focused so as to enable China to achieve the announced goal of becoming a modern industrialized state by the turn of the century. One example of the rehabilitation of the educational system is the policy of allowing students to study abroad, and many scholars from China are enrolled in Canadian universities. As well, the Canadian

---

[106] Hunter and Keehn (Eds.), *Adult Education in China* (London, Croom Helm, 1985) p. 5.

Association for Adult Education currently has a contract with the Canadian International Development Agency to train Chinese students from a major adult education school, Wuhan Institute, in western methods and techniques of adult education, including distance education.

The foregoing is a greatly simplified overview of public policy in China pertaining to adult education. It is apparent that China has experienced considerable changes and disruptions in even the period since the establishment of the People's Republic in 1949. The progressive developments evident in the post Cultural Revolution period have themselves been called into question by the repression of students demanding pro democracy reforms, in Tiananmen Square in June, 1989. Nonetheless the magnitude of the challenges facing China has indicated how pivotal adult education is to public policy which promotes development. The distressing observation is how policy changes within a totalitarian state can fluctuate erratically, and with no accountability to the people through an elected body. In the case of China one looks to the proceedings of the National Congress of the Communist Party of China for details of policy directions.

Sweden

Adult education, or "folkbildung," is highly organized in Sweden, a nordic country with a population in 1990 estimated at 8,400,000. It enjoys strong cultural roots with that country's social movements and also enjoys assured financial support from the central government. As a result it has intentionally evolved as a significant force in sustaining the Swedish democratic way of life, which is noted for its highly developed programs of economic and social welfare. It is this integration of adult education with Swedish social democracy which is significant from a public policy perspective.

There is a nordic tradition in adult education stemming from the folk high schools—schools for life—initiated by Bishop Grundtvig in Denmark. The first Swedish folks schools were formed in 1868 by the efforts of voluntary associations, and were aimed at improving aspects of rural life in particular. This development coincides with an extremely difficult social and economic period in Swedish history as evidenced by mass emigration, mostly to the United States. At the same time there was progressive liberalization in government such that Sweden avoided political upheaval as experienced in other countries. This stability, coupled with industrialization and a foreign policy of neutrality during both world wars, has led Sweden to become a modern nation in the twentieth century. Instrumental in all this were the efforts of the several popular movements which, beginning with the first folk high school, organized educational opportunities to promote cultural and economic development within Sweden's largely homogeneous population.

The value of these efforts to the cohesion of the nation was formally recognized by the government in 1919 with the proclamation of the Folk School law. Financial support in the form of grants-in-aid were provided for the operation of folk schools without there being the exercise of government control over curriculum. The folk schools provided to older youth, i.e. those out of school, and adults both general and civic education. The purpose of the schools as noted in the 1919 law suggested, "Considerable stress should be laid on fostering individual thinking and moral strength, and the students should be encouraged to know their community and their country, its history and present social conditions, its spiritual and material resources."[107] Since the passing of the 1919 law the grant amounts have been increased on several occasions and currently there are approximately 125 folk high schools in operation.[108]

Another adult education format in Sweden which receives state support by way of public policy is the study circle. This format traces its origins to the Chautauqua Literary and Scientific Circle of the United States in the late nineteenth century, and has since been highly developed and institutionalized in Sweden. The first Swedish study circle was formed in 1902 as an effort of the temperance movement, and Oscar Olsson, a leader of that movement at the time, is regarded as the "father of the study circle."[109] In this case the study circle, with its format of group study and discussion, was employed to make the members of the study circle more effective as temperance supporters and, correspondingly, as citizens. The potency of this format lay in the combining of education with action in that what was learned in the study circle was subsequently applied to political life.

The study circle format of informal adult education was soon adopted by other movements and out of this developed ten national adult education associations, each sponsoring learning activities through study circles. The associations are affiliated with either a political organization or a popular movement and include, for example, the Worker's Educational Association, the Y.M./Y.W.C.A., and the Temperance Movement. These ten adult education associations have, generally speaking, two distinct purposes: the improvement of educational standards and the enhancement of democracy.

The government began supporting the adult education associations in the operating of their study circles in 1936, and this was inspired in large measure by the election four years earlier of Sweden's first labour government, the Social Democratic Party. In 1947 the government formalized the operation of the study circles through the ten adult education associations and also began subsidizing the costs of the study circle leader and the learning materials. A study circle has since been officially defined as "an informal group which meets for the common pursuit of well-planned studies of a subject or problem area which has previously been decided upon."[110]

---

[107] P. Stensland, "Adult Education: A Force In Swedish Democracy," in *American-Scandinavian Review*, June, 1945, p. 121.

[108] Swedish National Board of Education, *Adult Education*.

[109] L. Oliver, *Study Circles: Coming Together For Personal Growth And Social Change* (Washington, Seven Locks Press, 1987) p. 2.

[110] L. Oliver, *Study Circles: Coming Together For Personal Growth And Social Change*, p. 6.

The study circle has become an integral part of Swedish life and each year one in five adults participates in a circle. The central government's subsidy covers approximately forty per cent of the cost while the remainder comes from municipal grants and participant fees. The government has even provided additional grants in an effort to promote "priority circles," i.e. study circles which deal with specific public affairs such as the development of nuclear energy in Sweden. There have been additional legislative measures passed with the intention of making the study circle program more effective and particularly as it can operate in the workplace. The Annual Educational Leave Act of 1975 gives employees the right to time off for continuing education and the Co-Determination Act of 1977 enables employees of a company with twenty-five or more employees the option to appoint two board members, "who are then trained in study circle courses which can take place in the company."[111]

In addition to the informal adult education offered through the folk high schools and the study circles, adults in Sweden are able to take courses based on the formal school curriculum. Organized by the local education authorities in every municipality, these courses can be taken in one of three ways: individually, for completion of compulsory schooling, or for completion of any of the three levels of upper secondary schooling. In addition, adults are able to take vocational courses to improve their employment circumstance.

The Swedish provision of both formal and informal adult education is extensive, and its funding support generous. As a result it is estimated that almost one in three adults is involved in some form of education.[112] Noteworthy from a public policy point of view is how the central government has embraced adult education as an instrument of development which benefits the individual, the community, the workplace and, ultimately, the democratic state.

Tanzania

Tanzania is a young East African nation, having gained its independence from Britain in 1961 when the country was know as Tanganyika. It has a long history of colonial domination, first under the Portuguese, then the Germans and, since 1919, as a League of Nations mandate administered by the British. It was renamed Tanzania in 1964 upon merging with the off shore state of Zanzibar and in 1990 has a population estimated at 25,600,000. Julius Nyerere was elected the first president of the republic in 1962 and he immediately began master minding how the country could, in short order, achieve economic self-reliance and social equality. The subsequent developments are of great interest to adult educators as Nyerere was a fervent believer in the role of adult education in bringing about the necessary changes. Adult education became a national priority as part of the Tanzanian nation building effort.

---

[111] L. Oliver, *Study Circles: Coming Together For Personal Growth And Social Change*, p. 31.

[112] Swedish National Board of Education, *Adult Education*.

The democratic socialist direction for the new nation was outlined in 1967 in a policy statement of the ruling party, TANU (Tanzanian Africa National Union) known as the Arusha Declaration. The central national policies were declared as being socialism and self-reliance. In that same year Nyerere developed his ideas for how the educational system would support the twin policies in a document titled, "Education for Self-Reliance."[113] Nyerere's conception of the educational system was that it would serve both the nation and individual Tanzanians by advancing the goals of self-reliance, liberation and development. Furthermore education was understood by Nyerere as being a lifelong undertaking. In order to implement this conception of education it was first necessary to undo a legacy from the colonial period, namely an educational system based on elitism and which placed emphasis on the preparation of students for university level education, a situation which ultimately benefited only a very few. Instead the educational system needed to be transformed to serve the national policies of socialism and self-reliance by providing education to the greatest number. (In studying the Tanzanian public policies by which adult education was enabled to assume its particular role, it is important to note that these policies were subsumed within the national policies. "The Tanzanian conception of education evolved within, and as a part of, the overall policy of socialism and self-reliance. Hence its various aspects were not elaborated nor introduced into the educational system simultaneously by means of a new and comprehensive educational law, but gradually."[114])

During the Tanzanian government's initial five year plan, 1964–1969, Nyerere recognized the need to first educate the predominately uneducated adult population. He declared, "Our children will not have an impact on our economic development for five, ten or even twenty years. The attitudes of the adult, on the other hand, have an impact now. The people must understand the plans for the development of this country: they must be able to participate in the changes which are necessary."[115] Thus adult education was given a national priority, and the special focus for it was in the countryside where ninety per cent of the population lived.

During the second five year plan, 1969–1974, efforts were made to integrate the nation's formal educational system with non-formal education. In particular the primary schools throughout the country were also to serve as adult education centres in a drive to bring about rural development. One of the measures in the 1969 Education Act was for the government to take over responsibility for the schools. The Ministry of Education was reorganized into the Ministry of Na-

---

[113] J. Nyerere, *Freedom and Socialism: A Selection from Writings and Speeches* (London, Oxford University Press, 1968).

[114] H. Hinzen, "Aspects of Conception and Implementation," in Hinzen and Hundsdorfer (Eds.), *The Tanzanian Experience: Education for Liberation and Development* (Hamburg, UNESCO Institute for Education, 1979) p. 7.

[115] J. Nyerere, Presidential Address to Parliament, May 12, 1965.

tional Education and its structure included four educational divisions: primary, secondary/technical, teacher, and adult education. To assist in aspects of educational development and planning, the ministry worked with "parastatal" institutions, i.e. independent institutions closely linked with the ministry. One such institution is the Institute of Adult Education which carries out several aspects of adult education work in the country including planning, research, training of adult educators, and conducting of various national programs.

Ambitious objectives were established for the educational system: provision of universal primary education by 1977; eradication of illiteracy by 1980; and self-sufficiency in manpower requirements by 1980.[116] As for adult education an important policy direction was developed by Nyerere in a speech delivered in 1970. In it he indicated there were three general objectives for adult education in Tanzania. The first was to inspire in the people a desire for change from a traditional way of life which was no longer viable in a modern world. The second was to teach Tanzanians the ways and means to improve their lives. The third objective was to have everyone understand the national policies of socialism and self reliance.[117] Underlying these objectives was the need to develop basic nationalistic feelings within the population so as to gain commitment to the national policies.

To meet the objectives established for the Tanzanian educational system a number of initiatives were undertaken. One initiative was the conducting of mass educational campaigns on topics vital to the national priorities. Six such campaigns were carried out by the Institute of Adult Education between 1970 and 1981 on the topics of politics, economics, history, health, nutrition and forest conservation. Considerable use was made of radio in these campaigns as not only was radio cost effective in reaching large numbers of the population but also it could reach those who were illiterate and those living in isolated areas. Another initiative was to use the workplace as a setting for continuing education. At the directive of Nyerere, a program of Workers' Education was instituted in 1973 whereby each day not less than one hour of time was allotted for workers to pursue learning pertinent to their situation, no matter what their educational attainment. A further initiative began in 1975 with the establishing of a program of Folk Development Colleges. Modelled after the Swedish Folk High Schools the colleges are designed for adults who have attained a sufficient level of literacy to acquire further skills and knowledge. By 1986 there were 52 Folk Development Colleges with an enrollment of 24,186 students.[118]

---

[116] V. H. Hundsdorfer, "Historical Outline," in Hinzen and Hundsdorfer (Eds.), *The Tanzanian Experience: Education for Liberation and Development* (Hamburg, UNESCO Institute for Education, 1979).

[117] J. Nyerere, "A President's Address to His Nation," in *Convergence, 4*, 1 (1971) pp. 30–34.

[118] Sumra and Bwatwa, "Adult Education, Literacy Training, and Skill Upgrading in Tanzania," in *The Alberta Journal of Educational Research, 34*, 3 (1988) pp. 259–268.

A critical feature of these and other initiatives was to first develop the people in order that they in turn would be able to fix their efforts on the national priorities.

As an indication of just how important adult education is to the development of the nation, the year 1970 was declared Adult Education Year in Tanzania. Adult education was promoted as a national movement with millions of adults joining in the various programs. At the international level, Tanzania hosted in 1976 a conference conducted by the International Council for Adult Education around the theme of adult education and development. The conference was held in the capital city, Dar es Salaam, and the opening address by Julius (Mwalimu) Nyerere was adopted as the Council's own basic statement on objectives and strategies for adult education and development. This statement is referred to as the Declaration of Dar es Salaam.[119]

The efforts to improve Tanzania's literacy rate have proven largely successful. According to scores recorded on the National Literacy Test, in 1967 the illiteracy rate was 69%, but by 1986 this had been reduced to 9.6%.[120] While there continue to be programs directed to further reducing illiteracy—and maintaining a high rate of literacy—consideration is now being given to the purposes of the country's program of postliterate adult education. The original objectives as stated by Nyerere in 1970, however, remain as the basis for any new programs that are developed.

[119] *Convergence*, 9, 4 (1976) p. 9.

[120] Sumra and Bwatwa, "Adult Education, Literacy Training, and Skill Upgrading in Tanzania," p. 264.

8

Adult Education as Discipline and Vocation

The Emergence of a Sense of Vocation

The term adult education is generally credited to Thomas Pole, whose history of the Adult School movement was first published in 1814.[1] But although activities which we would term adult education, or the teaching of adults, went on for centuries before that, and although Pole may well have coined the phrase early in the nineteenth century, the development of the modern adult education movement did not take place until the present century.

C.H. Grattan, in his *In Quest of Knowledge,* and Thomas Kelly in his history of adult education in Great Britain have made it clear that the teaching or education of adults has a long history in Western society.[2] Grattan takes us back to "preliterate man" and stresses the educational meaning of the concepts of enculturation and acculturation, the processes by which people achieve competence in their own culture, or in moving from one culture to another. He reminds us of Socrates, who taught only adults and who "must rank as the greatest adult educator of all time."[3] Kelly begins with the Anglo-Saxons and identifies the Christian missionaries of the period who came "to convert the heathen" as "the first recorded adult educators" of that nation.[4] In somewhat the same spirit, J.R. Kidd

---

[1] C. Verner (Ed.), Pole's History of Adult Schools (Washington, Adult Education Association of the U.S.A., 1967); T. Kelly, *A History of Adult Education in Great Britain* (Liverpool, University of Liverpool, 1970).

[2] C.H. Grattan, *In Quest of Knowledge* (New York, Association Press, 1955); T. Kelly, *A History of Adult Education in Great Britain.*

[3] C.H. Grattan, *In Quest of Knowledge*, p. 35.

[4] T. Kelly, *A History of Adult Education in Great Britain*, p. 1.

has traced the beginnings of adult education in Canada to 1605, the earliest days of settlement, when Champlain and Lescarbot founded "l'Ordre de bon temps," an organization which by utilizing "good talk, good books, good music, good food and good plays," helped our earliest settlers get through "the winter's perils."[5] Choosing a more traditional view, E.A. Corbett, in his brief histories of adult education which he wrote in the late 1940s, began the Canadian story with the mechanics' institute movement of the 1850s[6] and the university extension work of the 1890s.[7]

Before the arrival on the scene of a self-conscious adult education movement in the present century, there were clearly large numbers of persons who performed the functions of adult educators, even if they did not use such a term in describing themselves. At least as far back as the thirteenth century, the guild system functioned to protect its members and promote high standards of performance, the craft master teaching the mastery or "misterie" of his craft to the apprentices.[8] The co-operative movement, the Chartist movement, the adult schools and mechanics' institutes, the agriculture and university extension movements, Chautauqua, the Y.M. and Y.W.C.A. organizations—in these and other settings, the teaching or education of adults was being conducted on a very large scale long before those who were engaged in such work thought of themselves as "adult educators." (Indeed there are still many persons today who are in fact educators of adults—some industrial and vocational trainers, agricultural and other "field men," etc.—who do not feel a sense of common interest with "adult education," as they understand the term.)

The terms "adult education" and "adult educator" in their generic sense are generally seen to have been a product of the period between the two World Wars. The landmark "1919 Report" of the Adult Education Committee of the Ministry of Reconstruction in Great Britain helped to put adult education on the map. A combination of the high profile of those involved, the penetration of the arguments stated and the power of the language in which the report was phrased have contributed to its becoming perhaps the most frequently quoted document on the subject of adult education in the English language.[9]

---

[5]   J.R. Kidd (Ed.) *Learning and Society* (Toronto, Canadian Association for Adult Education, 1963) p. 1.

[6]   E.A. Corbett, *A Short History of Adult Education* (Toronto, Canadian Association for Adult Education, 1947).

[7]   E.A. Corbett, in J.R. Kidd (Ed.), *Adult Education in Canada* (Toronto, Canadian Association for Adult Education, 1950).

[8]   See for instance R.A. Leeson, *Travelling Brothers* (London, Geo. Allen & Unwin, 1979); T. Girtin, *The Triple Crowns* (London, Hutchinson, 1964).

[9]   *The 1919 Report* (Report of the Adult Education Committee of the United Kingdom Ministry of Reconstruction) (Nottingham, University of Nottingham, 1980 (1919)).

It is generally agreed that a sense of vocation in the field of adult education, at least one which spanned many of the different settings in which adult education functioned, emerged in the inter-war period, and most strongly in the United States. Before this there was presumably an awareness within particular settings—the Y.M.C.A., the folk schools, university and agricultural extension, etc.—of a specialized interest in and practice of the education of adults, but little sense of common interest or common cause with those involved in adult education elsewhere. A World Association of Adult Education was formed in 1919, based in Great Britain, and this organization held a somewhat limited "world conference" at Cambridge in 1928 and for a time published a journal, but its influence was not felt widely within participating countries and the organization disappeared during the Second World War.[10]

The emergence of a more cohesive adult education movement which spanned the various settings in which the work was carried out and which was accompanied by the development of professional training for the field, came first in the United States. The key elements and mileposts of this evolution are seen to be the decision on the part of the Carnegie Corporation of New York to fund development in this area; the formation in 1926 of the American Association for Adult Education (with financial support from Carnegie); the creation by Columbia University of the first academic department of adult education (in 1930); and the publication in 1936 of what is generally regarded as the first textbook in the field, Lyman Bryson's *Adult Education*.[11] Webster Cotton has interpreted these and related events as signs that adult education was moving from what he termed an "idealistic" phase, in which the education of adults was seen to be for the purpose of transforming society, to a more practical approach. In this newer approach, according to Cotton, adult education became "essentially an *educational* enterprise concerned with the life of the mind, with ideas and the use of intelligence," not as an instrument of social change.[12] It was willing to leave to the individual learner the decision as to the use to which the newly acquired knowledge would be put rather than to harness adult education to a particular view of the direction of social change. The aim was the democratization of

---

[10] J. Lowe, *The Education of Adults: A World Perspective* (Toronto, Ontario Institute for Studies in Education, 1982).

[11] See L. Bryson, *Adult Education* (New York, American Book Co., 1936); W.E. Cotton, *On Behalf of Adult Education* (Boston, Center for the Study of Liberal Education for Adults, 1968); C.O. Houle in G.Jensen, A.A. Liveright & W. Hallenbeck (Eds.), *Adult Education: Outlines of an Emerging Field of University Study* (Washington, Adult Education Association of the U.S.A., 1964); M.S. Knowles, *A History of the Adult Education Movement in the United States* (Huntington, New York, Robert Krieger, 1977); H.W. Stubblefield, *Towards a History of Adult Education in America* (London, Croom Helm, 1988).

[12] W.E Cotton, *On Behalf of Adult Education*, p. 5.

learning and culture—what Stubblefield and others have termed the "diffusion of knowledge," rather than a social transformation of a particular kind.[13]

The idealistic view of adult education which Cotton described in its American setting (and which did not, of course, disappear completely) was well represented in Canada, although the volume of literature was much smaller north of the border. The Canadian expressions of such views, rather than take the form of substantial series of published volumes of the type identified by Cotton and Stubblefield in the case of the United States,[14] must be sought out in such places as *Adult Learning*, the journal published by the Canadian Association for Adult Education (CAAE) from 1936 to 1939, and in the pages of its successor, *Food For Thought*. What Cotton terms idealistic views of the field may also be found in the works of some of the great pioneer figures in Canadian adult education, Alfred Fitzpatrick's account of the early years of Frontier College, *University in Overalls*, Coady's account of the Antigonish Movement, *Masters of Their Own Destiny*, and Corbett's episodic autobiography, *We Have With Us Tonight*.[15] In the case of the Canadian literature, which tended to appear later than its American counterparts, the idealistic views tend to be linked with the account of particular educational programs rather than be stated as general philosophical positions.

Whereas Cotton and other prominent writers in the United States date the beginnings of a more professional approach to adult education from the events in the 1920s and 1930s which were mentioned above,[16] it has been argued that a strong trend towards a more professional approach did not emerge in Canada until the 1950s.[17] This is not to say that the earliest indications of a more professional approach did not appear until that decade. That goes back at least to the 1930s, when the Canadian Association for Adult Education was formed. The CAAE, in connection with its founding conference, conducted a survey of the

---

[13] H.W. Stubblefield, *Towards a History of Adult Education in America.*

[14] W.E. Cotton, *On Behalf of Adult Education*; H.W. Stubblefield, *Towards a History of Adult Education in America.*

[15] A. Fitzpatrick, *The University in Overalls* (Toronto, Hunter-Rose, 1920); M.M. Coady, *Masters of Their Own Destiny* (New York, Harper & Bros., 1939); E.A. Corbett, *We Have With Us Tonight* (Toronto, Ryerson, 1957).

[16] See reference #11.

[17] G. Selman, "The Fifties: Pivotal Decade in Canadian Adult Education," *Canadian Journal for the Study of Adult Education*, *1*,1 (1987) pp. 5–24.

field throughout Canada. The report of the survey was edited by Peter Sandiford, a psychologist from the University of Toronto, and judging by the terms of the report, there was an obvious assumption that the leadership of adult education in Canada would be an increasingly professionalized group, and that the field would become more tightly co-ordinated at the provincial level.[18] At the first Western regional conference on adult education, held in Saskatoon in 1938, the need for trained leaders in the field was stressed.[19] When, for instance, the Public Library Commission of British Columbia conducted a comprehensive survey of the field in that province in 1941, the recommendations in its report called for a co-ordinated system of adult education, led by "specialists in adult education, not child educationists."[20] During the 1940s, at least three Canadians earned doctoral degrees in adult education in the United States—Roby Kidd, Florence O'Neill and John Friesen.[21] During the latter years of the 1940s, articles of interest to professional practitioners began to appear with increasing frequency in the CAAE journal, *Food For Thought.* These included items about the history of the field, comments on related public policy and at least one about the training of adult educators. Soon after he joined the staff of the CAAE in 1947, Roby Kidd formed a committee which looked into the matter of professional training in Canada for adult educators.

The 1950s: Pivotal Decade

Kidd was to be the key person in promoting the professionalization of the field during the 1950s, the period in which he served as Director of the CAAE. During the decade, he travelled back and forth across Canada in connection with his work, was one of a handful of Canadians who had doctoral qualifications in the field, and in the context of his CAAE duties had access to leaders of educational institutions, ministries of government and heads of other organizations, as well as to adult educators themselves. He lost no opportunity to promote the cause of training and other professional development activities for adult educators.

The work of Kidd and others in promoting a more professional approach to adult education in Canada during the 1950s, which has been described as the "pivotal decade" in this respect,[22] may be summed up under four headings: the emergence of a sense of vocation and professionalism in the field; the develop-

---

[18] P. Sandiford, *Adult Education in Canada: A Survey* (Toronto, University of Toronto, 1935).

[19] J.G. Rayner, "Four Western Provinces Discuss Adult Education," *Adult Learning 2,* 6 (1938) pp. 18–21.

[20] British Columbia Public Library Commission, *A Preliminary Study of Adult Education in British Columbia: 1941* (Victoria, B.C.P.L.C., 1942).

[21] C.O. Houle & J.H. Buskey, "The Doctorate in Adult Education 1935–1965," *Adult Education 16,*3 (1966) pp. 131–168.

[22] G. Selman, "The Fifties: Pivotal Decade."

ment of training opportunities; institutional development; and the growth of a body of literature for the field.

A Sense of Vocation and Professionalism

Those working on a full-time basis in the field of adult education in Canada prior to this period saw themselves mainly within the institutional systems within which they carried out their duties, be it agricultural extension, voluntary bodies such as the Y.M. or Y.W.C.A., library work or university extension. The formation of the CAAE in 1935 and its various meetings and publications provided means by which a relatively few of those working in the field began to see themselves as part of a larger social enterprise, and a few short-lived organizations of adult educators functioned briefly in some parts of the country in the thirties and forties.[23] Some Canadian adult educators were aware of developments in other countries, especially in the United States, which were making the field more visible and increasing its sense of importance. But on the whole, Canadian adult educators still had a relatively narrow view of their field, often one which did not extend much beyond the organizational setting in which they happened to be working. The 1950s brought significant change in this respect in the thinking of many adult educators, and Roby Kidd was clearly an important influence in this regard for many people. He has rightly been described as "both architect and symbol" of the development of adult education in this period.[24]

Kidd seemed to lose no opportunity to emphasize the importance of adult education and of the adult educator's calling. In his personal contacts and in his extensive writings about the field during the period, he repeatedly stressed the significance of adult learning for the lives of individuals and for society as a whole. In his contacts with senior people in both government and educational institutions he emphasized as well the need to recruit able persons to take charge of adult education activities and to provide them with satisfactory status and career opportunities. In his contacts with adult educators themselves, he encouraged them to address and make use of the increasing knowledge that was becoming available about how adults could be assisted in their learning. A study of the major addresses, reports and publications produced by Kidd and his organization during the 1950s reveals what a consistent theme this was.[25] For example, in his Director's Report to the CAAE in 1956, which was devoted in large part to professionalism in the field, Kidd spoke strongly about the need for able personnel and for training:

---

[23] G. Selman, "Specialization or Balkanization: Organizations of Adult Educators," *Canadian Journal of University Continuing Education, 14*, 1 (1988) pp. 24–44.

[24] A.M. Thomas in J.G. Schmidt (Ed.) *J.R. Kidd: A Bibliography of His Writings* (Toronto, Ontario Institute for Studies in Education, 1988) p. vii.

[25] G. Selman, *Roby Kidd and the Canadian Association for Adult Education 1951–1961* (Vancouver, University of British Columbia/Centre for Continuing Education, 1982).

I have only one serious apprehension about the future. More and more the conception of continuous learning is being accepted. But will we have the staff who are numerous and talented enough? Every year several important positions are open which require men and women of considerable capacity and long experience. So we quickly look around for a suitable person as if we did not fully understand that such people aren't just found, they must be "grown," and the growing period starts many years before.[26]

Later in the decade, when he was commissioned by the Toronto Board of Education to prepare a major report and set of recommendations on the future development of their work in adult education, he used that opportunity to publish strong recommendations about according appropriate status for adult education personnel.[27]

In addition to appeals to employers of adult educators, Kidd repeatedly addressed adult educators themselves about these issues. He saw to it that a great deal more attention was paid in the Association's journal to matters of professional concern.[28] He spoke to many groups of adult educators across the country and also restructured the activities of the CAAE itself so as to encourage the development of the field in the regions. In 1950, at Kidd's suggestion, the CAAE decided to hold national conferences only every second year, and to sponsor regional conferences in the Western and Atlantic regions in the intervening years. The chief reason for this suggestion was that the regional meetings would be more accessible to practitioners than were national ones and could serve as a vehicle for strengthening both the development of the field and opportunities for in-service professional education. The Atlantic region was the first to pick up on the idea; the "First Atlantic Region Conference" was held at Amherst, Nova Scotia in June of 1951.[29] Further meetings followed every second year throughout the decade, the programs focusing mainly on the social and economic development of the region. In the West, the meetings did not begin until 1953, the first being held in Banff, but were held regularly thereafter. Although the conferences in the West, like those in the Maritimes, devoted some attention to social development, there was much more focus in the West on the formation of provincial organizations of adult educators, their functions and their relationship with the

---

[26] Quoted in G. Selman, "The Fifties: Pivotal Decade" p. 12.

[27] J.R. Kidd, *18 To 80: Continuing Education in Metropolitan Toronto* (Toronto, Board of Education, 1961).

[28] W. Stewart, *A Comparison of A Historical Model of the American Literature in Support of Adult Education with Literature in the Journals of the Canadian Association for Adult Education* (Vancouver, Unpublished Graduating Essay, University of British Columbia, 1983).

[29] "Maritime Conference," *Food For Thought, 12*, 1 (1951) pp. 32–33.

national organization. It is clear from the reports of these meetings, East and West, that the decision to facilitate the holding of regional meetings under CAAE sponsorship was an important factor in stimulating in-service development activities in both regions.[30]

There had been a few local and regional associations of adult educators in Canada prior to the fifties—in Newfoundland (not then yet part of Canada) as early as 1930,[31] in Winnipeg in the mid-thirties, in Ontario and the Eastern Townships of Quebec in the early forties, and in Alberta beginning in 1943.[32] But by the late forties, no such organizations were functioning. Arising out of suggestions discussed at Banff in 1953, steps were taken in British Columbia to create a provincially based organization. An organizational dinner in September of 1954 led to the first of what were to be a continuing series of semi-annual conferences on adult education which continued on a regular basis until 1961. The B.C. organization was a council of agencies rather than a personal membership body, but the B.C. Adult Education Council sponsored a significant series of in-service professional development activities within the framework of the semi-annual conferences. In 1956, all four Western provinces held provincial conferences of adult educators and in all but B.C. (where an organization already existed), plans were discussed for the possible creation of provincial bodies.[33] As it turned out, things developed more quickly in Saskatchewan than in the other two provinces and under the terms of a revision in the CAAE constitution passed in 1958, the B.C. and Saskatchewan organizations became "affiliated" with the CAAE and had representation on that organization's National Council. In the Atlantic region, that development did not take place until the following decade.

Apart from the CAAE, there were other organizational developments in the field at the national level. The French language national body, l'Institute canadien d'education des adultes, which had developed out of a standing committee of the CAAE, was reorganized in 1952 and became a more vigorous and effective instrument for that language group. Those who worked in the field of university extension, after a period of consultation with an already existing organization of colleagues responsible for summer session activities, joined with them in 1954 in forming the Canadian Association of Directors of Extension and Summer Sessions.[34] Educators interested mainly in the rural and agricultural aspects of adult education had formed an Extension Group under the Canadian

---

[30] G. Selman, *Roby Kidd and the CAAE.*

[31] "Newfoundland and Adult Education," *Bulletin* (World Association for Adult Education) *XLIII* (1930) pp. 19–21.

[32] G. Selman, *Roby Kidd and the CAAE.*

[33] G. Selman, "Western Variations on the Theme," *Food For Thought, 18,* 1 (1957) pp. 5–9.

[34] J.R. Kidd, *Adult Education in the Canadian University* (Toronto, Canadian Association for Adult Education, 1956).

Society of Technical Agriculturalists in 1940, but this organization met only sporadically during the following decade and disappeared by 1953. In 1959, a decision was made to revive such a body, and the Canadian Society of Rural Extensionanadian Society of Rural Extension came into existence the following year.[35]

Training Opportunities

Opportunities in Canada for acquiring training in adult education expanded very greatly during the 1950s. There had been some work of this general kind going on for many years in certain quarters. The literature of the forties contains many accounts of "leadership training" activities in fields such as group work, recreation, and especially late in the decade, human relations training. The Y.M. and Y.W.C.A. and other voluntary organizations, the folk school, co-operative and labour movements were active in this work. Roby Kidd recalled that he had been a student in a credit course in adult education at Sir George Williams College in 1934–35, which may have been the first such course in Canada.[36]

When Kidd returned from his doctoral studies in 1947 and joined the staff of the CAAE, the promotion of training opportunities for adult educators was one of his priorities. He suggested the formation of a CAAE Committee on Personnel in Adult Education, whose initial report was discussed at the annual conference in 1948. It indicated that of the 86 full-time adult educators who responded, only two had any training in the field, even a single course. The committee recommended that the CAAE take a lead in the promotion of both formal and non-formal training programs.[37] The endorsement of this report provided Kidd with a mandate for his continuing efforts to these ends during the fifties.

Non-credit in-service development activities for adult educators were an important new feature of the period and Kidd played a leading role. A few examples will indicate the types of programs which were organized. The first training course for adult educators in the western region, a two-week program on "Extension Methods and Techniques," was held at Banff in 1949, co-sponsored by the CAAE and the University of Alberta. Kidd frequently taught courses for adult educators in the labour movement. In 1951, he secured a foundation grant to support a two-year series of training programs designed for workers in the outports of Newfoundland. The first regional training course for the Atlantic region was organized by the CAAE in 1958.

Reference has already been made to the role of CAAE regional conferences— East and West—to the in-service development of adult education leaders.

A further aspect of working towards adequate training opportunities for adult educators involved efforts directed at employers in the field, most notably educa-

---

[35] G. Selman, "Specialization or Balkanization."

[36] G. Selman, *Roby Kidd and the CAAE.*

[37] J.R. Kidd, *Adult Education in Canada.*

tional institutions, school boards and provincial departments of education. At the CAAE conference in 1950, a working group gave attention to "Provincial Divisions of Adult Education" (meaning units within departments of education). In 1957, 1959 and 1961, conferences on the role of governments and school boards in the field were organized in co-operation with the Canadian Education Association. Beginning in the late fifties, the CAAE had standing committees on governments in adult education and on school boards in the field. In 1950, Kidd published a pamphlet dealing with the role of school boards in the field, and reference has already been made to the study of adult education which he carried out for the Toronto Board in 1961. The committee organizing the Second Canadian Conference on Education, to be held in 1962, commissioned Kidd to write a background study on adult education, one of several on specialized topics published in advance of the meeting. By means of this substantial pamphlet, he made the most of the opportunity to address the educational establishment of Canada with respect to the system's responsibilities in adult education.[38]

Kidd was also active in raising funds from foundations for the purpose of financing training opportunities. The funds he obtained for the training of workers in Newfoundland have already been mentioned. In 1953, a party of leading adult educators from English and French Canada was enabled, with funds secured from Carnegie, to visit outstanding projects in Europe. In 1955, school board adult educators from Nova Scotia and New Brunswick were assisted with a study tour to American and Canadian centres. For several years in the late fifties, some $15,000 a year, which he secured from the Fund For Adult Education in the United States, was used to make study tours or degree study possible for individual Canadian adult educators.

This was also the period during which academic degree programs in adult education were inaugurated in Canada. With his doctoral degree, Kidd was clearly qualified to be appointed to teach university courses. In the late forties and during the fifties he taught credit courses in adult education at several Canadian universities (frequently the first such course the institution had offered). In 1951, he taught the first graduate course to be offered in the field in Canada, at the Ontario College of Education. A course he taught at the University of British Columbia in the summer of 1956 was utilized by that institution as the first step in developing a masters degree program in the field, which when introduced in 1957 became the first degree program in adult education in Canada. (By this time there were at least twelve universities in the United States

---

[38] J.R. Kidd, *Adult Education and the School* (Toronto, Canadian Association for Adult Education, 1950); J.R. Kidd, *18 To 80*; J.R. Kidd, *Continuing Education* (Ottawa, Canadian Conference on Education, 1961).

which were offering advanced degree programs in the field.)[39] The University of Guelph became the second institution to offer such a program when it admitted its first masters candidates in this field in 1960 to a Master of Science degree, with a specialization in agriculture and extension work.[40]

It is apparent from the foregoing that during the fifties considerable advances were made in both providing various kinds of training opportunities and also attempting to convince both adult educators and their employers that such training was desirable.

Institutional Development

The matter of institutional development has already been touched upon in several ways. The efforts made during the decade to convince the public educational authorities were in large measure directed to this end. Kidd made use of the available opportunities, at meetings and in the course of his constant travel back and forth across Canada to promote the field and the need for adequate institutional provision for this work. Leading adult educators in the various provinces were also working to this end. CAAE standing committees on school board and government adult education work have already been mentioned, as have several conferences held during the decade with representatives of those sectors of the field. The consultation carried out by Kidd for the Board of Education in Toronto and the opportunity to write one of the study pamphlets for the Second Canadian Conference on Education in 1962 were high profile opportunities to address the educational establishment in Canada. Another opportunity presented itself in 1953, when the National Conference of Canadian Universities commissioned Kidd to write a study concerning adult education in the university. The outcome was a volume entitled *Adult Education in the Canadian University*, which was published in 1956.[41]

There were grounds for encouragement, particularly with respect to provision for adult education within the structure of the provincial departments of education. Saskatchewan had created an adult education unit in 1944. When the government of Nova Scotia created a Division of Adult Education in the late forties, Kidd gave great prominence to that development, carrying frequent news items in the journal and printing a full account of the work as one of several pamphlets

---

[39] C.O. Houle in M.S. Knowles (Ed.), *Handbook of Adult Education in the United States* (Chicago, Adult Education Association of the U.S.A., 1960).

[40] G. Moss, "A Brief History of the Development of Graduate Studies in Adult Education in Canada," in *Papers Presented to a Conference on Research in Adult Education* (Vancouver, Canadian Association for the Study of Adult Education, 1980).

[41] J.R. Kidd, *Adult Education in the Canadian University*.

he arranged to have published in the early fifties.[42] By 1961, all ten provincial departments had such a unit.[43]

Literature of the Field

The literature on adult education in Canada was another area in which there was significant advance during the fifties. It is generally understood that a field of practice, in order to advance towards professional status, must have a body of knowledge on which to base its growth and development. While adult education in Canada could not be said to have reached the stage of theory building or other advanced forms of research and scholarship at this time, what was attempted was to document the nature and history of the field in Canada and to assist adult educators who were ready to do so to take an increasingly serious interest in the methods and problems of practice.

There was very little literature about the field in Canada published before the fifties. There were the accumulated files of the two CAAE journals, *Adult Learning* (1936–39) and *Food For Thought* (1940–61), Fitzpatrick's plea for and account of the early years of Frontier College (1920), the survey of adult education activities edited by Sandiford (1935) as part of the process of founding the CAAE, and Rev. Moses Coady's account of the philosophy and methods of the Antigonish Movement (1939).[44] Aside from a few other articles, institutional and government reports, and a very few pamphlets, these seem to be the only published works on adult education in Canada prior to 1950.[45] Due to the efforts of Roby Kidd as both author and publisher and those of a growing, but still small circle of practitioners in Canada, this picture changed substantially during the fifties.

Walter Stewart, in his study of the content of the CAAE journals over the years, perceived a distinct shift of emphasis in *Food For Thought* in 1950 compared to five years earlier:

> The clearly intended audience of the 1950 issues is those who are engaged in educating adults and not those who were being educated, as had been true in the 1940s.[46]

---

[42] G. Henson, *Adult Education in Nova Scotia* (Toronto, Canadian Association for Adult Education, 1954).

[43] J.R. Kidd, *Continuing Education*.

[44] A. Fitzpatrick, *The University in Overalls*; P. Sandiford, *Adult Education in Canada: A Survey*; M.M. Coady, *Masters of Their Own Destiny*.

[45] J.R. Kidd, *Adult Education in Canada*.

[46] W. Stewart, *A Comparison of A Historical Model*, p. 36.

He commented further that at this time the journal became "a magazine about adult education rather than an instrument of adult education."[47]

Kidd's own writing about the field during the period was prolific, extremely varied, and may be seen to fall into four categories.[48] The first, that of descriptive studies of the field in Canada, is represented by two of his major works, *Adult Education in Canada* and *Learning and Society*,[49] both collections of articles which reflect the development of the field in Canada up to approximately 1960, and which in the absence of any general histories of the field continue to be especially valuable resources. A second category consisted of publications which resulted from consultations he carried out, the two most substantial of which were *Adult Education and the Canadian University* and *18 to 80*, the study commissioned by the Toronto Board of Education.[50] Kidd was becoming progressively more active at the international level during the fifties. Most of his publication in that connection during the decade was in the form of articles, but one major study resulted from a consultation in the West Indies in 1957–58.[51] The fourth category of his writings had to do with the methodology of the field. Several pamphlets he wrote during the period, about such matters as film utilization, field work, and discussion group techniques, fall into this category, as does his most notable publication of the period, a textbook entitled *How Adults Learn*, the first edition of which appeared in 1959.[52] This text was the first to be published in Canada and was a significant departure from those written by others in at least one major respect, the relative prominence given to learning theory. The book was well received in the field, in North America and beyond, and it has since been translated into at least five other languages and has been used as a text in at least forty countries.[53]

Over and above Kidd's own writing, the field benefitted from his efforts in encouraging and publishing a great deal of material through the CAAE. Soon

[47] W. Stewart, *A Comparison of A Historical Model*, p. 54.

[48] For greater detail, see G. Selman, *Roby Kidd and the CAAE*.

[49] J.R. Kidd, *Adult Education in Canada* and *Learning and Society*.

[50] J.R. Kidd, *Adult Education and the Canadian University* and *18 to 80*.

[51] J.R. Kidd, *Adult Education in the Caribbean* (Mona, Jamaica, University of the West Indies, 1958).

[52] J.R. Kidd, *How Adults Learn* (New York, Association Press, 1959).

[53] N. Cochrane et al., *J.R. Kidd: An International Legacy of Learning* (Vancouver, University of British Columbia/Centre for Continuing Education, 1986).

after his publication of *Adult Education in Canada* in 1950, he secured a grant from the Fund For Adult Education, an American foundation, to make it possible to continue the program of documenting Canadian achievements in the field. The result was a series of eleven substantial pamphlets (up to 120 pages in length) in a series entitled "Learning for Living," which appeared between 1952 and 1954. A few other representative examples of CAAE publications during the decade were: a survey of labour education in Canada, a bibliography of Canadian writings in adult education, and a study of residential education.[54] There were as well several other notable volumes about the field which were published commercially at this time. They included Donald Cameron's history of the Banff School of Fine Arts, E.A. Corbett's reminiscences, *We Have With Us Tonight,* and at the end of the decade, A.F. Laidlaw's history of the Antigonish Movement.[55]

Other organizations at the national level were publishing material at this time: the Canadian Labour Congress, the Canadian Library Association, the Canadian Film Institute and the Canadian Citizenship Council. As well, an increasing amount of material about adult education was being published at the local and provincial level. The bibliography published by the CAAE in 1956, already referred to, contained a number of items related to adult education from *Saskatchewan Community* and *Community Courier* (Ontario) and listed a number of other newsletters and bulletins published at the provincial level.

At the beginning of the 1950s there was very little Canadian literature about adult education, whereas by the end of that decade, practitioners and students had a considerable and growing body of writings from Canadian sources on which to call, covering not only aspects of practice, but also Canadian perspectives, policies and achievements.

Since the Fifties: Towards Professionalism

In a widely-cited article which appeared in 1960 in the *Handbook on Adult Education in the U.S.A.,* C.O. Houle described the workforce of adult education as a "pyramid of leadership."[56] The large base of the pyramid was made up of volunteers, who served as teachers, planners and organizers of adult education. The intermediate sector was made up of the smaller number of persons—usually teachers of adult classes—who worked mainly at other activities but were employed on a part-time basis to teach adults. The top of the pyramid, and the

---

[54] D. Smith, *A Survey Report on Labour Education in Canada* (1951); M. Thomson & D. Ironside (Eds.), *A Bibliography of Canadian Writings in Adult Education* (1956); E. Loosley, *Residential Adult Education: A Canadian View* (1960): all Toronto, Canadian Association for Adult Education.

[55] D. Cameron, *Campus in the Clouds* (Toronto, McClelland & Stewart, 1956); E. A. Corbett, *We Have With Us Tonight;* A.F. Laidlaw, *The Campus and the Community* (Montreal, Harvest House, 1961).

[56] C.O. Houle, in M.S. Knowles, *Handbook of Adult Education.*

smallest group of the three, was made up of full-time, career adult educators, with "basic career expectations in the field."[57]

This has generally been accepted as a satisfactory representation of the leadership of the field at the time—in Canada as well as in the United States. It was recognized that a great deal of non-formal education took place outside of educational institutions, organized and conducted in the main by volunteers. Within educational institutions and in many other settings, teachers were employed on a part-time basis because of their expertise developed elsewhere. The career adult educators were relatively few in number, were frequently the organizers and administrators of educational programs, were often full time in those roles, and usually made up the best paid sector in adult education.

Increasing Numbers of Adult Educators

It is useful to speculate as to the degree to which Houle's pyramid is relevant today, some thirty years later. We know that the extent of adult education has increased many times over in the intervening period. But have the relative proportions of the three sectors of the adult education workforce, as described by Houle, stayed roughly the same? The author has discussed this matter with a number of experienced adult educators in recent years and several points have been made. The first is that likely the number of paid persons—part and full-time—in the field has increased, compared to the volunteers. It is recognized that a great deal of adult education in our society goes on in the voluntary sector—voluntary associations, health associations, hobby and interest clubs, churches, etc.—which is largely invisible to the general public view. But systematic attempts in recent years to survey participation in adult education, although they likely do not do full justice to the private, volunteer sector, nevertheless show it to be only a modest portion of organized adult education overall. The second main observation is that with the increasing acceptance by government in recent decades of the need for adult education, vocational and technical training, etc., vastly increased funding has been provided for various forms of adult education. As is described elsewhere in this book, the percentage of adult Canadians who take part annually in organized adult education has increased at least five fold in the last thirty years. This trend has no doubt brought a disproportionate increase in the numbers of full-time, career adult educators, and also the number of part-time paid teachers of adults. At this point one is once again brought up against the definitional question. Is the full-time faculty member of a community college, who teaches adult students, daytime or evening, as part of a regular teaching load, to be considered an adult educator? Certainly such persons are teachers of adults, but we do not normally see them as "adult educators." Even if we steer clear of such moot points in the field, it seems abundantly clear that the number of paid teachers, organizers, counsellors, curriculum developers, etc. in adult education has grown enormously since Houle devised his pyramid. What

---

[57] C.O. Houle, in M.S. Knowles, *Handbook of Adult Education*, p. 120.

sort of geometric representation one might appropriately make today in describing the "workforce" of adult education would perhaps vary, depending on one's answer to the definitional question raised above, but it is the general view that the number of paid workers in the field has increased greatly in comparison with the volunteers.

In addition to the remarkable expansion of the number of adult educators in recent decades, there have been many signs of a growing awareness on the part of those involved in the field that they share interests and concerns with those involved in other sectors of adult education. At the international level, Lowe, Hely and others have described the evolution of adult education towards becoming an increasingly professionalized field.[58] The CAAE, under the leadership of Alan Thomas, continued throughout the sixties to promote aspects of professionalism. A review of the contents of the Association's journal, renamed *Continuous Learning* in 1962, reveals a conscious policy of supporting such a trend. There were articles about professionalism and about professional aspects of adult education. There were annual listings of professional training opportunities in the field. In 1966, the CAAE held a national conference on the theme, "Adult Education: An Emerging Profession," which was attended by some 225 persons. Thomas strengthened the library of the CAAE as a research centre for the field, published aids to research activity, and launched several newsletters for specialized areas of practice. He saw the promotion of such professional activities as crucial to the welfare of both the field as a whole and his own organization, telling his Board of Directors in 1966, "It is our ability here that will either assure us a commanding place in adult education or condemn us to watch the steady erosion of any imaginative unity in adult education."[59]

The emergence of a large number of organizations of adult educators, both nationally and provincially, and of organizations devoted to research in the field, both of which are described in some detail later, are further evidence of the growing number of persons who were ready to identify themselves with the field.

The Roles of Adult Educators

Accompanying the overall growth and institutionalization of adult education activity has come an increased specialization for those who work in the field. Several areas of specialization will be described.

Guidance to the learning process: The role which comes to mind first is that of teacher. The master craftsmen and their apprentices, the literacy teachers of the early Adult Schools, the lecturers at the mechanic's institutes—from the earliest days of the adult education movement up to the present time, the teacher or expert who imparted knowledge to others has been a prominent feature of the

---

[58] A.S.M. Hely, *New Trends in Adult Education* (Paris, UNESCO, 1962); J. Lowe, *The Education of Adults*.

[59] Minutes of the Board of Directors, Jan. 21–23, 1966, quoted in G. Selman, *Alan Thomas and the Canadian Association for Adult Education 1961–1970* (Vancouver, University of British Columbia/Centre for Continuing Education, 1985) p. 20.

work. The teacher has passed on knowledge, has demonstrated how things are done and has directed the educational process. Students have in many instances decided to take part in the educational activity in the expectation that there would be such an expert present "from whom they could learn." In Houle's "pyramid," referred to in the previous section, the large middle portion of leadership in the field was seen to be made up of persons who were teachers and whose expertise was acquired from their work and study in some other setting or occupation—as accountant, artist, technician, academic, professional, etc.

From the earliest days of the adult education movement, there was also a second tradition in the guidance of learners, which was based not, or not only on knowledge of the subject which was being mastered, but on the nature of the educational activity or the study materials. The Methodist Bible classes, the local meetings of those taking part in the "corresponding societies" of the 1790s, the groups interested in forming co-operative organizations, the local chapters of the Chartist movement—these are a few among many examples where the leadership or guidance of learners came from persons who may not have been much, if any better informed in the content of what was to be learned than the rest of the group, but whose role was one of guiding a process, showing the way, assisting in ways other than imparting content to the learners.

The vast majority of adult education activity, it would seem clear, is of the first type and is led by a person (or by a correspondence course or a computer program) where the "instructional agent" both imparts knowledge and directs the educational process. This is almost universally the case in the formal educational sector, but is the dominant mode in the non-formal sector as well.

The subject matter or content expert who serves as teacher in adult education usually is a person who does not associate himself or herself in career terms with the field of adult education. In formal educational settings, the teacher is often an employee of the sponsoring institution and has career expectations which relate to that institutional system. For instance, the teacher of mathematics in an adult basic education program of a community college, though teaching full or part-time adult students, may have little or no sense of involvement in adult education, but rather see himself or herself as a college faculty member or as a mathematics specialist. In many non-formal settings too, the career expectation of the teacher in most cases lies elsewhere, with the person's full-time employer or with the field of specialty. The second kind of leader referred to above—the process specialist—is perhaps more likely to feel part of the field of adult education.

The teacher of adults may have little or no training in the field of adult education. Persons are usually hired as teachers because of the expertise they have in their subject matter, sometimes reinforced by the fact that they already are employed by an educational institution. Neither the organization which hires the instructor nor the student who enrolls in the class care in the first instance about the teacher's instructional skills, but attach priority to the "credentials" of the potential instructor in the subject to be taught. Many such instructors have by various means become very fine teachers. Many organizations provide in-service training opportunities in instructional methodology. An increasing number of persons who find that their career has taken them into teaching adults subsequently seek formal training in instructional procedures. But the overall picture is that the overwhelming majority of teachers of adults, though involved in adult education, do not have a sense of their career being linked to adult education as a field of study and do not seek training in that field.

Program Planners: With the institutionalization of the field in recent decades has come the development of two groups of specialists in the organization and management of the work, here termed program planners and administrators. The two roles tend to merge into one another, and exceedingly few persons perform exclusively one role or the other. The program planner, or "programmer" is concerned with the planning of the educational event, or course, perhaps apart from the process of instruction, which is usually left to the teacher or content expert. The programmer frequently decides what courses will be offered, what resources will be required to carry them out, and what the general objectives of the program will be. The programmer is frequently involved in managing or administering the program while it is in operation and may make decisions about any evaluation procedures which are carried out, formative or summative.

The role of the programmer varies greatly from one institutional setting to another. In certain situations the educator is responsible for hundreds of courses a year and the main tasks may be to decide what courses will be given, recruit suitable teachers and arrange space in which the meetings will be held. This is particularly typical of formal settings and the non-formal offerings of institutions in large centres of population. In other situations the programmer may have fewer courses to manage and may play a significant role in the planning and carrying out of the program. This type of participation is more common in the case of short courses—programs which go on for one or several days on a full-time basis—than in connection with the one-evening-a-week sort of course. The programmer usually has considerable administrative responsibility as well, managing budgets, supervising the work of others, seeking financial resources, and organizing a multiplicity of office activities.

The programmer is the category of practitioner who is most likely already to have, or to seek training in the field of adult education. It has been a fairly typical pattern in adult education that people have by one means or another "found their way" into adult education, only then have realized its potential, and have been drawn to it as a career. They frequently then become aware of the training which is available in the field and decide to take advantage of it. There is a sense, therefore, that what in other professions is pre-service training, in adult education has frequently been engaged in as in-service training. Presumably as adult education becomes better known as a career choice, more young people will take training in the field prior to entering it (as indeed is the case in many countries in the world), but up to now, at least, students in degree programs in adult education (which are mainly graduate programs) are already engaged in the field, and are usually in their thirties or forties.

Administrator: As has been mentioned, the other specialist in the management and operation of adult education programs may spend most or all of his or her time in the management function, rather than in the planning of programs. This person is frequently the dean, director or head of an adult education organization or unit. In large organizations there may be more than one such position. The administrator has particular responsibility for managing the processes within the unit, acquiring and apportioning resources, developing and administering policy, selecting, developing and supervising personnel, and managing relations of many kinds with forces outside the unit itself—in the institutional hierarchy, with other adult education bodies, and in the community. Public relations and publicity, particularly in their institutional dimensions (as distinct from publicity for particular courses) may also be a special concern of the administrator.

The administrator is frequently a person who has had considerable experience in adult education and has acquired advanced training in the field. It is characteristic of the field, however, and perhaps a manifestation of its relative youth and lack of recognition, that this is often not the case. At the time of writing it is not clear that there is even a trend toward a greater reliance in the case of such roles on those who have received advanced training in adult education. Such a state of affairs is a result of several factors. The adult or continuing education unit is frequently a marginal enterprise within the parent organization and factors other than adult education qualifications sometimes take precedence when appointments are made. There is some disagreement in the field too as to whether the "generic" professional training of adult educators is the most satisfactory type of training or whether training in the broader field of education or in the longer-established disciplines is preferable. Many senior appointments have gone to those with advanced training and experience in adult education, but many have not.

Researchers: An increasing number of persons in recent decades have become engaged in research activity in relation to adult education. University faculty members in departments of adult education, of whom there are over 100 in Canada at the present time, have a professional interest in such activity, as do an increasing number of practitioners, especially specialists in large organizations. Government and other public agencies are increasingly seeking research results as part of the policy formation process, and a growing number of consultants in the field are making a living from research activity. There are currently some 400 members of the Canadian Association for the Study of Adult Education, a significant proportion of these being graduate students in the field.

There have been persistent efforts over recent decades to interest specialists in other fields to take an interest in research problems of interest and importance to the field of adult education. By and large such attempts have fallen on deaf ears. It has increasingly been realized that adult education had to "grow its own" body of competent researchers if satisfactory attention was to be paid to the research needs of the field. That process is going on apace at the present time, as a subsequent section will document.

Other Specialists: In the last two decades particularly, several other important specialties in adult education have emerged. They will presumably continue to grow in numbers and significance in the future. The first of these is the counsellor of adult learners. The counselling or advising function has of course been performed as long as there have been adult learners, but the number of practitioners specializing in this field has been extremely small until recently. Matters of definition arise in this connection. Is a counsellor employed by a university or college, working largely with full-time (adult) students, an adult education counsellor? At any rate, there are increasing numbers of persons who do specialize in advising adult students, and presumably this trend will continue. This is one of a number of areas in which the women's movement has shown the way for the rest of the field. Another specialized area of practice which has been emerging is that of curriculum development. Adult education has traditionally thought more in terms of "program planning" than "curriculum development," but in an increasing number of settings in recent years, particularly in post-secondary educational institutions, curricula designed especially for adult education have been required. A great deal of this work has been contracted out to specialists or consultants. This brings us to the third type of specialist emerging in the field, the consultant. Many organizations—educational institutions, government bodies, business and industry, etc.—have made it a practice in recent years to contract out certain research and curriculum development tasks to outside consultants. There are now many small firms and individuals in all large population centres in Canada which undertake this kind of work. The final type of specialty developing in the field s the media specialist. By this is meant not only the "mass media," in the traditional sense of the term (film, video, print and broadcast), but also those who are expert in the use and application of the computer to the instructional process. The foregoing are several among many emerging specialties in the field of adult education which may be expected to grow in size and importance in future years.

Associations of Adult Educators

One clear indication of the growth of adult education in recent decades has been the emergence of a considerable number of organizations which have been formed by those working in the field.[60] This process has been going on since the 1930s, when the Canadian Association for Adult Education was formed, but has accelerated since the end of the fifties. This development may be seen as a reflection of several factors: the increase in the numbers of people who work in adult education and who have come to associate themselves and their careers with the field; increased specialization within adult education activities; and the political facts of life in Canada—the constitutional role of the provinces in the

---

[60] For details on these developments, see G. Selman, "Specialization or Balkanization."

field of education and the trend within confederation towards decentralization of authority to the provinces.

The development of national and regional adult education associations in Canada does not lend itself to tidy summary, but some general observations can be made. Aside from a few short-lived exceptions at the regional level, the first three decades of development, from 1935 to the early sixties, saw the formation of mainly national organizations. The sixties were a period during which provincially based organizations of a general or "umbrella" coverage of the field came into being. The most recent two decades have brought the development of a variety of more specialized organizations at the provincial level, and in the last ten years, at the national level as well.

The Canadian Association for Adult Education was the first national organization of adult educators formed in Canada. A planning meeting was held in 1934, certain preparatory work carried out in the ensuing year, and the CAAE was officially formed in 1935. It followed its American counterpart by some nine years, a point that is worth noting mainly because some of the same dynamics were at work in the two countries, including some stimulation and financial assistance from the Carnegie Corporation of New York.[61] There had been some short-lived more local associations in the thirties and forties (see above) but the CAAE was alone in the field again by 1950, at least as far as English-speaking Canada was concerned. (In French-Canada, the field was at first represented by a standing committee of the CAAE, but in 1946, a separate organization was formed.) The CAAE and the French language body, the ICEA, remain today as the two "umbrella" organizations in the field, representing the two main language groups, and both have for some twenty years received financial support on a regular basis from the federal government.

More specialized organizations came along in the subsequent decades. The Canadian Association of Directors of Extension and Summer Schools (which became the Canadian Association for University Continuing Education) and the Canadian Society of Rural Extension (which later dropped the word Rural from its name) have already been mentioned. In the sixties, French language university extension departments split away from CADESS and formed a separate body, L'ACDEULF. Following the passage of federal manpower training legislation in 1960, which had the effect of expanding the number of persons engaged in vocational training programs, the federal government supported the formation of a national organization, the Canadian Vocational Association.

The sixties were an active period in the formation of associations at the provincial level. The main reason for this was active promotion by the CAAE. There had been provincial associations in Saskatchewan and B.C. in the fifties. The B.C. group, which had been in existence since 1954, put forward a proposal

---

[61] D.P. Armstrong, *Corbett's House: The Origins of the Canadian Association for Adult Education and its Development During the Directorship of E.A. Corbett 1936–1951* (Unpublished M.A. Thesis, University of Toronto, 1968); R. Faris, *The Passionate Educators* (Toronto, Peter Martin, 1975).

in 1961 that the CAAE revise its constitution to allow for the formation of provincial associations, not as separate organizations, but as integral parts or "divisions" of the national body. This change having been brought about, six provinces formed such divisions during the decade: B.C. (1962), Nova Scotia (1963), Ontario (1966), Manitoba (1966), Saskatchewan (1967) and Newfoundland (1967). By the late sixties, it became apparent that a change in the CAAE's structure was imminent once again and for this reason and others, adult educators in Alberta, when they formed an association in 1967, decided not to become a part of the national body. After the CAAE changed its structure in 1971, the provincial divisions were all reconstituted as autonomous organizations, affiliated with the CAAE and with representation on its Board of Directors. A further development provincially was the formation in 1965 of the broadly based Rural Learning Association of Ontario, representing an amalgamation of the Ontario Farm Radio Forum, the Folk School Council and the Rural Leadership Forum.

Because of the growth and increased specialization within the field, the latter years of the sixties were also the starting point in the development of more specialized associations at the provincial level. The timing differed from province to province, but generally the subsequent two decades saw the formation of organizations which brought together those in such fields as: the administration of adult or continuing education in the public educational institutions (especially the school boards and colleges and institutes); teaching English (or French) as a second language; adult basic education and literacy; training in business and industry; community education and community development; education for handicapped persons; education for women; and educators in health fields.

In some cases, one or more of the provincial bodies took the lead in forming national associations in such fields of specialty. In other cases, it worked the other way around. The last decade has brought the formation of several new national organizations. Although it was not established as an autonomous body until 1979, the Canadian Congress for Learning Opportunities for Women traces its beginnings back to committee status with the CAAE in 1973. In 1967, a number of persons interested in literacy work formed the Movement for Canadian Literacy, successor organization to World Literacy of Canada, which was formed in the early fifties. Formation of a national organization in the field of teaching English as a second language, TESL Canada, took place in 1979. The Canadian Association for the Study of Adult Education held an organizational conference in 1980 and a formal founding conference the next year. Laubach Canada Inc., which is concerned with the teaching of literacy, was formally established in 1981, though literacy work utilizing its methods and materials in Canada dated back to 1970. Community educators from several provinces established the Canadian Association for Community Education in 1984. And perhaps most recent among these national organizations, at least at the time of writing, is the Canadian Association for Distance Education, which functioned for a year under the auspices of the university extension body, CAUCE, and became an autonomous organization in 1985.

The organizations referred to above are of several main types. The first group are general or "umbrella" organizations. They aspire to represent the field as a whole, rather than any segment of it. At the national level this would include the two language-based national bodies, the CAAE and the ICEA, and also perhaps the Canadian Association for the Study of Adult Education, whose interests span research about all aspects of the field. At the provincial level, there is in almost all provinces an umbrella association. Typically this organization is an affiliated body of the CAAE and has representation on its board.

A second category of groups is organized along institutional lines. The university extension body, now called CAUCE, was the first of these at the national level. Membership is made up of those responsible for continuing education services offered by Canadian universities. At the provincial level, those administering school board and college-based programs have a separate organization in some places, as do those based in privately-owned vocational training enterprises. In this category, the common focus of interest is that the members all, or mostly all function in similar kinds of settings.

The third category—and it is the most numerous—is made up of organizations on either the content of the programs being offered or the clientele for whom the services are provided. This includes, for instance, associations for teaching English as an additional language, vocational education, literacy education, learning opportunities for women, and the Canadian Society of Extension, which is concerned with agricultural and rural interests. The number of such specialized organizations has increased markedly in the last twenty years, as the field has expanded and as particular needs have become more clearly identified.

Finally, there are organizations of adult educators which are based on the methodology of delivery. The most obvious example in this group is the body concerned with distance education. Although it fits a little less comfortably into this category, the field of community education, with its reliance on community-based methods, falls in this group as well.

One may confidently predict that in the next decade or two additional specialized organizations will be established, both provincially and nationally.

Although there are many differences among these organizations, there are similarities as well. They are generally, for instance, aimed at advancing the interests of adult education, or in some cases of a particular sector of the field. They are concerned with fostering communication among their membership. They are in most cases concerned with the promotion of effective practice. A number are concerned also with a critical examination of their work, seeking by means of research, inter-institutional co-operation and demonstration projects to enhance their contributions to the welfare of adult learners.

There are important differences as well, of course, some arising from the very nature of the categories set out above. There are also differences in what might be termed philosophical orientations among the organizations. Indeed it is clear that some of them were established in the first instance because of such differences of view. This would be true of the Association for Community Education, for instance, the founders of which left the previously existing groups largely because they saw them as devoted to institutional or "content" interests rather than the interests of the learners and their communities. Some of the organizations are made up only of adult educators, and, especially those which are connected with the large educational institutions, they tend to be comfortable with the emerging professionalism in the field. Others, including many in community education, literacy and basic education, are leery of such professionalism, fearing it will tend to increase the "distance" between educator and learner, and fall heir to some of the rigidities and exclusivity which are frequently associated with the older professions. In keeping with this view, a number of associations include in their membership not only the paid adult education workers but also adult learners and representatives of community organizations. Perhaps most basic of all, some organizations—or the vast majority of their members—believe in the "liberal" philosophical approach to adult education and see it as their role to provide services to individuals. In other organizations a "social transformation" view of adult education is held by many members and their aim, beyond that of providing learning opportunities for individuals, is to contribute to social change—through adult education.

Concern has been expressed about the splintering or "balkanization" of the field of adult education which may result from such a proliferation of organizations.[62] While specialization within the field clearly has potential benefits and will presumably continue to be the trend, are there dangers which need to be guarded against? For instance, with respect to advocacy on behalf of the interests of adult learners, if all the organizations in the field are specialized, who will be in a position to take the larger, more comprehensive view? And will governments or institutions respond if they are receiving uncoordinated, sometimes conflicting recommendations from the field? There is no expectation that the trend towards specialization among adult educators and their associations will not continue. But voices are being raised expressing concern about the possible disadvantages flowing from this development and urging that the associations learn to act together, or at least co-ordinate their actions when that would clearly work to the benefit of the adult learners they are attempting to serve.

Training of Adult Educators

It has been pointed out earlier in this chapter that the first degree programs for the training of adult educators in Canada emerged in the late fifties—at the University of British Columbia and the University of Guelph. The United States had taken the lead in such activity, Houle having traced the beginnings of formal instruction in the field back to 1917, at Columbia University.[63] That university was the first to create an academic department of adult education (1930), and its

---

[62] G. Selman, "Specialization or Balkanization."

[63] C.O. Houle in G. Jensen, A.A. Liveright & W. Halenbeck, *Adult Education: Outlines of an Emerging Field of University Study.*

first doctorates were awarded in 1935. By that time formal courses were also being offered at Ohio State, Cornell, the University of Michigan and the University of California at Los Angeles. Before the decade was over, the University of Wisconsin and Syracuse University were offering degree programs as well. By 1962, soon after Canadian programs began to function, American universities had awarded 323 doctorates in the field.[64] In the case of Great Britain, aside from a short-lived graduate diploma course which was offered by the University of Nottingham beginning in 1921, the University of Manchester was the earliest into the field. A Department of Adult Education was created in 1946, part-time courses launched in that year and full-time graduate certificate and diploma courses inaugurated in 1955 and 1961, respectively.[65] Apart from these ventures, however, formal training was slow to develop in Britain.[66] The Eastern European socialist countries, especially Czechoslovakia, Yugoslavia and Hungary, began to provide training in the field systematically in the late forties and fifties, but major teaching programs did not emerge until the sixties.[67]

Three authorities in the field have summed up the situation by indicating that although there were notable pioneers earlier (especially in the United States), the 1960s brought the major expansion of academic degree training for adult educators. In his international review of the field, which was commissioned by UNESCO following the Third World Conference on Adult Education in Tokyo in 1972, John Lowe stated that "since about 1966" there had been in some countries "a spectacular increase in the number and variety of training courses designed for full-time specialists."[68] In his study of training and training needs in the field, Duncan Campbell concluded that it had been largely after 1960 that opportunities for training had been developed.[69] A special issue in 1985 of the international journal, *Convergence*, was devoted to the "Training of Trainers and Adult Educators." In his introduction, Roger Boshier noted "a worldwide increase in the number of adult education planners after 1960,"[70] and the articles in this and

---

[64] As above.

[65] T. Kelly, *A History of Adult Education in Great Britain*.

[66] K.T. Elsdon, *Training for Adult Education* (Nottingham, University of Nottingham/Department of Adult Education, 1975).

[67] J. Kulich in R. Boshier (Ed.), "Training of Trainers and Adult Educators," Special Issue of *Convergence 18*, 3–4 (1985).

[68] J. Lowe, *The Education of Adults*, p. 144.

[69] D.D. Campbell, *Adult Education as a Field of Study and Practice* (Vancouver, University of British Columbia/Centre for Continuing Education, 1977).

[70] R. Boshier, Special issue of *Convergence*, 1985, p. 17.

the subsequent issue of the journal confirm that the 1960s were clearly a decade of rapid expansion of training activities.[71]

Boshier's comment, just quoted, raises an important point—the distinction between the training needs of teachers of adults, on the one hand, and the organizers of adult education programs on the other. It is fair to say that it is the latter group for whom university-based degree programs have been designed, and Houle's study of the persons who had earned a doctorate in adult education in the U.S. by 1966 made it abundantly clear that these indeed were the people who sought such qualifications.[72] There is a relatively long history of short, non-formal courses designed for those who teach adults, or administer programs on a part-time basis. Homer Kempfer stated in his 1955 text that "a generation ago," pre-service education was required for adult education staff functioning under certain federal legislation and he reported that a significant number of states, including New York, were by the early fifties requiring that staff in publicly funded adult education programs receive at least ten hours of training in the field.[73] The Eastern European countries in some cases required such training by the early fifties as well. In many cases, where brief training courses of this kind were not actually required, many institutions which maintained large adult education programs, including some school boards and university extension departments in Canada, provided such training opportunities for instructors, on an optional basis. In an international review of the field written in 1962, Arnold Hely summed up the present trends (as revealed at the Second World Conference on Adult Education held at Montreal in 1960) as a "process of professionalization" and "the passing of the 'gifted amateur.'"[74]

This may have been a realistic view of the field as seen from an international viewpoint by a person who was dealing with top leaders in the field from various countries, but it hardly summed up the picture in a country such as Canada. As we have seen, there were only two universities offering degree programs in adult education by the beginning of the sixties, and only a very few Canadians who had advanced training in the field. The sixties were a period of rapid development in such work in Canada, as elsewhere. Gwenna Moss has indicated in her review of the Canadian situation in the decade that among the significant developments on the academic front were the following: the University of British Columbia introduced a doctoral degree to its program in 1961 (and a diploma program as well in 1966); the Ontario Institute for Studies in Education launched

---

[71] See *Convergence, 18*, 3–4 (1985).

[72] C.O. Houle, "The Doctorate in Adult Education," *Convergence, 1*, 1 (1968) pp. 13–26.

[73] H. Kempfer, *Adult Education* (New York, McGraw-Hill, 1955).

[74] A.S.M. Hely, *New Trends in Adult Education*, p. 14.

masters and doctoral programs in 1965; the University of Saskatchewan introduced a masters and post-graduate diploma in 1966; the University of Alberta began a masters in community development in 1968; and the following year the University of Montreal introduced masters and doctoral programs.[75] In their summary of the situation in 1970, Draper and Yadao stated that by that time, seven universities were offering a graduate program in adult education, the same number a certificate or diploma in the field, and seven were offering individual courses but no degree program.[76] The most recent survey of opportunities for the study of adult education in Canada, which was conducted in 1987, lists ten universities as offering graduate programs in the field, the six already mentioned, plus the Universities of Calgary, Dalhousie, New Brunswick and St. Francis Xavier, of which three—British Columbia, Montreal and O.I.S.E.—offered doctoral as well as masters degrees. Eight institutions were listed as offering certificates or diplomas, the Universities of Alberta, B.C., Calgary, Manitoba, Montreal, O.I.S.E., St. Francis Xavier and Saskatchewan. In addition to those already mentioned, several others were listed as offering "degree courses;" that is, individual courses which could be used for credit towards general degrees in the field of education—the Universities of Toronto, Queen's, Victoria and Western Ontario. There were therefore some 15 universities in Canada which by 1987 were offering degree credit instruction in adult education, three at the doctoral level.[77] The same survey lists a total of 112 faculty who are involved in teaching these programs, 51 of whom are identified as full time in this work. (Two of the larger institutions did not separate full from part time, so the total of full time is likely considerably higher).[78] An early, admittedly incomplete study in 1978 had listed 47 adult education faculty at Canadian institutions.[79] A directory of academic programs published in 1984 had set the figure at 82 faculty, 51 of whom were full time.[80] The figure of 15 Canadian institutions offering degrees in this field may be compared with approximately 80 in the United States.[81]

There is a great deal of closely related degree credit work offered in Canada as well. For instance, many of those training in the field of English as a second language are engaged in teaching adult students. Those interested in community

---

[75] G. Moss, "A Brief History of the Development of Graduate Studies."

[76] J. Draper & F. Yadao, "Adult Education as a Field of Study in Canada," *Continuous Learning 9,* 2 (1970) pp. 65–82.

[77] R.E.Y. Wickett et al., *Adult Education Studies in Canada* (Saskatoon, University of Saskatchewan, 1987).

[78] As above.

[79] R. Boshier & B. Thiesfeld, *Professors of Adult Education in Canada: A Directory* (Vancouver, University of British Columbia/Adult Education Research Centre, 1978).

[80] P. Keane, *Adult Education Studies in Canada–1984* (Halifax, Dalhousie University, 1984).

[81] A.B. Knox (Ed.), *Enhancing Proficiencies of Continuing Educators* (San Francisco, Jossey-Bass, 1979); S. Merriam in R. Boshier, Special issue of *Convergence,* 1985.

school or community development activities frequently seek training in the fields of social work or recreation. And many professional positions in the field of adult education are filled by persons whose backgrounds are in other fields. Boshier has estimated that only one-fifth of the teachers and one-quarter of the planners of adult education see it as their primary professional concern, and quickly adds that these figures are likely too high.[82]

Apart from the degree-credit type of study, on which this account has focused to this point, a great deal of important training in adult education takes place under other auspices, much of it of a non-formal kind. Large voluntary organizations such as the Y.M. and Y.W.C.A., the Red Cross, the Scout and Guide movements and the churches, conduct substantial and sustained training programs in adult education and related matters. Other educational institutions, especially community colleges, carry out adult education training for groups such as vocational instructors and those being trained to work with volunteers. And a number of large business enterprises conduct "training of trainer" activities for those working in their own training programs. It is impossible to provide anything approaching a complete or comprehensive picture of such work. The foregoing are only a few examples of what is clearly a large and growing aspect of training of adult educators in Canada.

Research and Publication

Earlier in this chapter it was pointed out that the 1950s were an important turning point with respect to research and publication for the field. Very little had been published before 1950, but that changed substantially during the decade.

An extremely important factor in the development of research in the field was the formation of academic departments at the universities. There are currently well over 100 faculty members and perhaps two to three thousand graduate students working in the field in Canada. Most, if not all the students, in connection with their courses and for graduating essays, theses or dissertations, must carry out research activities. Almost all are taking courses in research methodology. The faculty members mainly hold doctoral degrees in the field, have produced research in earning their degrees, and must continue to carry out and publish research in order to progress in their academic careers. The establishment of degree programs in the field has undoubtedly been the most important single factor in the very rapid growth of research and publication in the last 30 years or so. All the studies or inventories of research which have been published since 1960, including those concentrating on non-degree research, have demonstrated that the universities were by far the largest source of research activity.

Several attempts have been made over the years to list or describe research in the field. Several persons have played a prominent role in this activity, but James Draper of the Ontario Institute for Studies in Education has been the leading

---

[82] R. Boshier, Special issue of *Convergence*, 1985, p. 17.

figure. He took up this area of scholarship in the latter part of the 1960s and pursued it, frequently in co-operation with others, until the early eighties.

Reference was made earlier to *A Bibliography of Canadian Writings in Adult Education*, which was published by the CAAE in 1956.[83] Early work on this project had been carried out by Murray Thomson and was subsequently completed by Diana Ironside of the CAAE staff. More than 500 items were contained in this bibliography, gathered under a dozen or so topic headings, and each entry accompanied by a brief annotation. The items were drawn primarily from pamphlet and periodical literature and the selection was based on a fairly expansive view of the field of adult education, some items dealing with the social and cultural background of the field. The journals of the CAAE itself, *Adult Learning* (1936–1939) and *Food For Thought* (1940–61), understandably featured prominently in the sources, but a fair range of others were used as well. Much of the material was descriptive, historical or philosophical, but there were sections on community organization and group work methods. As part of Roby Kidd's general strategy of making Canadian adult educators aware of the richness and content of their field, it no doubt played a useful part at the time—and indeed is a valuable source today for information about the 1935–1956 period.

The next substantial effort to prepare a directory of research was conducted by Coolie Verner and Margaret Stott of the University of British Columbia.[84] Commenting on their publication, Verner identified two problems, ones which have consistently plagued such efforts: that of deciding what limits or boundaries should be used to define the field; and the problem of finding the appropriate items. He also referred to the fact that because adult education had been "rarely recognized as a legitimate category of research," the traditional reference works were of limited assistance.[85] Subsequent researchers tried to cope with the problem of locating the studies by working through personnel in the field and asking them where their reports had been published. The Stott-Verner bibliography contained some 290 items. Compared to the Thomson-Ironside listing of seven years earlier, this one was organized along more professional or technical lines. This may be in part a result of the different orientations of the compilers, but was also no doubt a reflection of the evolution of the field in Canada and of the type of research being carried out. It is uncharacteristic of the compilers of such directories to comment on the quality of the research reported on. Verner, however, had this to say:

---

[83] M. Thomson & D. Ironside, *A Bibliography of Canadian Writings in Adult Education.*

[84] M.M. Stott & C. Verner, *A Trial Bibliography of Research Pertaining to Adult Education* (Vancouver, University of British Columbia/Extension Department, 1963).

[85] C. Verner, "Adult Education Research," *Continuous Learning*, 2, 4 (1963) pp. 155–56.

Existing research is severely limited with respect to its use of creative and imaginative processes of social discovery. Most of the research presented in this Trial Bibliography is descriptive and depends largely upon survey techniques. There is little, if any, experimental or analytic research that helps explain our profession. Such research as is here represented is traditionally oriented as well as dull and pedantic.[86]

Four years later, James Draper began his long association with this area of study. In 1967 he wrote an article which appeared in the CAAE journal, *Continuous Learning*,[87] in which he pointed out the advantages for the field of publishing inventories of research on a regular basis. He made reference to the efforts of the American journal, *Adult Education*, to report annually on research and pointed out that a number of Canadian items were included there. He then set forth a plan for the compilation of Canadian inventories. Draper subsequently pursued this goal and played an important role in such work for at least 15 years. He was the author, or one of the authors, of three inventories of non-degree research in Canada (1967–68, 1969, 1970), two studies of degree-related research (1968–69, 1970) and one (1970) which included both.[88] In addition, he published in 1974 a study of thesis research related to adult education which had been written at the University of Toronto from 1900–1970, and in 1981, an inventory of all Canadian theses about adult education prior to that time.[89] Other substantial efforts to describe research in the field include papers delivered at a conference on research in adult education held in Vancouver in 1980[90] and three

---

[86] As above, p. 157.

[87] J. Draper, "A Proposal for Systematically Collecting and Reporting Research Relating to Adult Education in Canada," *Continuous Learning*, *6*, 5 (1967) pp. 211–14.

[88] J. Draper, J. Niemi & C. Touchette, *Degree Research in Adult Education in Canada 1968-69* (Toronto, Ontario Institute for Studies in Education/Department of Adult Education, 1969); J. Draper & F. Yadao, *Degree Research in Adult Education in Canada 1969* (Toronto, Ontario Institute for Studies in Education, 1970); Y. Demers, J. Draper & A. Gray, *An Inventory of Degree and Non-Degree Research in Adult Education: Canada 1970* (Toronto/Montreal, Ontario Institute for Studies in Adult Education/CAAE/ICEA/ University of Montreal, 1971); S. Landry, J. Draper, & L. Bratty, *Non-Degree Research in Adult Education in Canada—1967-68* (Toronto/Montreal, Ontario Institute for Studies in Education/CAAE/ICEA, 1968); A. Setchell, J. Draper, P. Belanger, *Non-Degree Research in Adult Education in Canada 1968* (Toronto/Montreal, Ontario Institute for Studies in Education/CAAE/ICEA, 1969); L. Gagner, J. Draper & A. Setchell, *Non-Degree Research in Adult Education in Canada 1969* (Toronto/Montreal, Ontario Institute for Studies in Education/CAAE/ICEA).

[89] J. Draper, *University of Toronto Thesis Research Relating to Adult Education: An Interdisciplinary Analysis 1900–1970* (Toronto, Ontario Institute for Studies in Education/Department of Adult Education, 1974); J. Draper, *Adult Education Theses: Canada* (Toronto, Ontario Institute for Studies in Education/Department of Adult Education, 1981).

[90] Canadian Association for the Study of Adult Education, *Papers Presented to a Conference on Research in Adult Education—1980* (Vancouver, CASAE/ACEEA, 1980).

subsequent surveys conducted by John Dobson of St. Francis Xavier University, which appeared in 1982, '84 and '86.[91] In addition to these publications, there are two bibliographies about Canadian experience with community development and "citizen action" which were prepared by Arthur Stinson and appeared in 1975 and 1979.[92]

With James Draper providing much of the leadership, the five major inventories which appeared between 1968 and 1971 were published by three organizations—the two national adult education associations (CAAE and ICEA) and Draper's home Department of Adult Education at O.I.S.E. (In the last of the series, the study of research in 1970, the Faculty of Education of the University of Montreal was a sponsor as well.) The publications on non-degree research were bilingual; the first on degree research included reports on activity at the French language universities but the second did not. The last in the series, the volume for 1970, returned to the bilingual format. Over the four year span covered by these reports (1967–70), there was no evidence of growth in the number of studies. As far as non-degree research was concerned, the second year, 1968, provided the largest number of projects reported—118. Only in the case of non-degree studies was there an attempt to categorize by subject matter. In the first year (1967), "clientele" and "evaluation" were the categories containing the largest numbers of entries. The authors commented in the 1969 study that in French Canada there was a heavy concentration of studies on the "motivation, interests, characteristics and needs" of adult students.[93] There continued to be a preponderance of university-based research projects in non-degree as well as degree studies. In the report on 1970, it was noted that the provincial government of Quebec was the source of considerable research.

Draper's other two publications, studies of theses from the University of Toronto and the national survey published in 1981, were both pioneering efforts. In the first of these, special efforts were made to identify theses which had been written in other parts of the university—the humanities and social science disciplines and the School of Social Work of the University of Toronto, and the other departments of O.I.S.E. A total of 62 theses were reported, covering an extremely wide range of subjects, such as learning theory, sociological backgrounds and a range of institutional settings.[94] The national survey of theses on adult education contained a listing and analysis of these prior to 1978, and a "supplement"

---

[91] J.R.A. Dobson, *A Database Management System for Canadian Adult Education Studies* (Vancouver, CASAE/ACEEA,1982); *A Study of People, Programs, Places and Processes: Canadian Adult Education Literature 1977–1984* (Antigonish, Nova Scotia, St. Francis Xavier University); "Canadian Adult Education Literature," *Caravan, 1*, 2 (1987).

[92] A. Stinson, *Citizen Action: An Annotated Bibliography of Canadian Case Studies* (Ottawa, Community Planning Association of Canada, 1975; A. Stinson, *Canadians Participate* (Ottawa, Carleton University, 1979).

[93] L. Gagner, J. Draper & A. Setchell, *Non-Degree Research 1969* p. 4.

[94] J. Draper, *University of Toronto Thesis Research.*

containing ones reported for 1978 and the following two years. Seven universities supplied information for the study, but in this case all the theses were written within departments of adult education. A total of 326 masters theses and 56 doctorals were reported for the pre–1978 period. A further 106 masters theses and 45 doctorals were reported for the three years 1978 to 1980, which provides an indication of the rapid growth of the academic programs and research activity. In the most recent three year period, St. Francis Xavier was the leader in the number of masters awarded and the University of Toronto/O.I.S.E. the overwhelming leader in the number of doctorates completed.[95]

The most recent attempts to summarize what he termed the "literature" of adult education were carried out by John Dobson in the eighties (1982, 1984, 1986).[96] By this time, the Canadian Association for the Study of Adult Education had been established and it was the publisher of the first two of his reports. Dobson summarized his work in an article which appeared in *Caravan*, a publication of the Conference of Canadian Bishops.[97] He reported that by means of his three biennial surveys he had identified 1,483 publications over the six year period, written by 551 different Canadians (or landed immigrants). He found that 80.6 % of the publications were written by men and that 70.5% of the published items were written by persons "sponsored by" universities. 80% of the publications were written by persons who listed only one adult education publication and 5% by those listing 21 or more items. Of this latter group, all were associated with one of 13 different universities, O.I.S.E. (7), British Columbia (5), Saskatchewan (4), Montreal (3) and Guelph (3) accounting for most of these more prolific authors. Dobson categorized into six groups the content or "research interest" of the 112 authors who had published more than one item in the period. The category of "instructional methods" was by far the leader, accounting for 30.4% of the publications. "Community education" (18.6%) and "foundations" (16.8%) followed in second and third place.

A major factor in the development and publication of research in adult education in Canada has been the activities of the Canadian Association for the Study of Adult Education (CASAE), which was founded in 1981. For approximately two decades, two American organizations, the Commission of Professors of Adult Education and the annual Adult Education Research Conference, had attracted and served the interests of some Canadian professors and other researchers. There were some in Canada who wished a forum in which Canadian-based research and related concerns could be discussed. Roby Kidd and James Draper raised the issue in the early seventies and some informal discussions took place, but it was not until 1976 that more formal meetings occurred. In that year the Adult Education Research Conference, which usually met in the United States, held its annual conference in Toronto. On the day prior to that conference, a

---

[95] J. Draper, *Adult Education Theses: Canada.*

[96] See #91.

[97] J.R.A. Dobson, "Canadian Adult Education Literature."

group of Canadians held discussions about matters of mutual interest. This in turn led to a similar meeting the following year in Windsor, Ontario, attached to the conference of the CAAE. By this time, the group was referring to itself as the "Consortium of Canadian Adult Education Professors." This meeting led to the publication of a directory of Canadian professors.[98]

The next major step was the decision to hold a conference in 1980 on research in adult education in Canada, which met in Vancouver, again just prior to the Adult Education Research Conference. From the outset, the planning for the Vancouver meeting was based on the idea that those present would make a decision concerning whether to establish a Canadian research organization for the field. The decision was to proceed. A Vancouver-based committee was assigned the task of drafting a constitution for the new organization and organizing a founding conference, to be held in Montreal in 1981. At that conference, in addition to the delivery of reports on research, the constitution of the new organization was approved and the life of a new, Canadian research organization for the field began.

The new organization, the Canadian Association for the Study of Adult Education/Association canadienne pour l'étude de l'éducation des adultes (CASAE/ACEEA) was to be bilingual in its operation (the first President was Giselle Painchaud of the University of Montreal) and was deliberately constituted with a minimum of structure and organizational apparatus.

CASAE/ACEEA has been a relatively active organization since its formation in 1981. It has actively fostered research in the field in a variety of ways. Perhaps most important, it has sponsored an annual research conference and published a version of the papers delivered at each such meeting. The papers of the 1988 conference held in Calgary, for instance, was a bound volume of 337 pages, containing summaries of some 60 research presentations.[99] The History Committee of the Association has published occasional "bulletins," containing historical research. In the spring of 1987, the Association launched *The Canadian Journal for the Study of Adult Education*, two issues appearing each year thereafter.[100] It is a bilingual, juried publication and carries research on various dimensions of the field.

There have been several other significant periodicals over the years which have published research and other material about adult education in Canada (the reference here is to material in English, in the main). The journals of the Canadian Association for Adult Education go back to 1936, including *Adult Learning* (1936–1939), *Food For Thought* (1940–1960), *Continuous Learning* (1961–1972) and *Learning* (1976-). Publications of the federal manpower training authorities under several titles, *Manpower Review, B.T.S.D. Review* and *Adult*

---

[98] R. Boshier & B. Thiesfeld, *Professors of Adult Education in Canada.*

[99] CASAE/ACEEA, *CASAE/ACEEA 1988: Proceedings/Actes* (Calgary, CASAE/ACEEA, 1988).

[100] See volume 1, No. 1, May, 1987.

Training, were active in the 1960s and 1970s and carried many articles about the field, as did the journal of the Canadian Vocational Association, which also received federal government support. The longest-running juried journal in the field is that published by the Canadian Association for University Continuing Education. Known at first as *Dialogue*, it began publication as a research journal in May of 1973, changing its name the following year to the *Canadian Journal of University Continuing Education*. Other scholarly journals interested in dimensions of the field have appeared during the eighties, such as the *TESL Canada Journal* and the *Journal* of the Canadian Association for Distance Education. The encouragement for engaging in research in adult education and the opportunities to publish the results have grown substantially in recent years.

So far in this discussion attention has been focused on the opportunities within Canada for Canadians to publish their research. There has as well been a long history of Canadians publishing in other countries and in international publications, such as those of UNESCO, the International Labour Organization, and the International Council for Adult Education. However the avenues most frequently turned to have been those in the United States, especially the periodicals produced by the professional associations there.

What is now called the *Adult Education Quarterly*, the research journal of the American Association for Adult and Continuing Education, has been seen as the most high profile, prestige publication in which to publish and has been the focus of much attention in Canada. To a lesser extent, Canadian researchers have looked to journals in Great Britain (and other European countries), Australia, New Zealand and some other countries for opportunities to publish their work.

Canadians and Canadian-based scholars have at times gained considerable prominence in the American research journal. An analysis published in 1974 of the articles carried by the research journal between 1964 and 1973 indicated that the University of B.C. stood second among all North American universities and the only non-American institution in the top eleven. Among individual authors, Gary Dickinson of U.B.C. stood first and Coolie Verner ninth, all others in the top eleven being Americans.[101] A study of the frequency of citations in *Adult Education* between 1968 and 1977 indicated that a Canadian, Roger Boshier, stood first on the list and that two other Canadians were in the top eight—Coolie Verner (4th) and Gary Dickinson (8th).[102] A study published in 1983 of papers delivered at the Adult Education Reseach Conference, a basically American organization, between 1971 and 1980, determined that if presenters were sorted according to their home institutions, three of the top seven universities were from

---

[101] H.B. Long & S.K. Agyekum, "Adult Education 1964–1973: Reflections of a Changing Discipline," *Adult Education, 14*, 2 (1974) pp. 99–120.

[102] R. Boshier & L. Pickard, "Citation Patterns of Articles Published in *Adult Education* 1968–1977," *Adult Education, 30*, 1 (1979) pp. 34–51.

Canada—U.B.C. (4th), Saskatchewan (6th) and O.I.S.E. (7th).[103] The foregoing is significant evidence not only of the fact that Canadians sought opportunities to publish in American journals and present research at research conferences in that country, but also that some Canadian individuals and institutions were extremely prominent in this activity.

There have been several Canadians in recent decades who have acquired international prominence for their research and scholarly work in the field of adult education. Roby Kidd's textbook, *How Adults Learn*, which appeared in 1959 and which emphasized the application of learning theory to the field has had world-wide use. And his writing about the relationship between education and national development has been influential. His colleague, Alan Thomas, had formative influence in the sixties on the field's thinking about lifelong learning, and in recent years has been doing pioneering work on the impact of legislation, public policy and judicial interpretation in adult education. Allen Tough, also based at O.I.S.E., has had widespread international influence through his studies of self-directed learning.

The names of Coolie Verner, Gary Dickinson and Roger Boshier, all of the University of B.C., have been referred to in the previous paragraphs. Verner, before he moved to Canada in 1961, was one of the group of American professors who were influential in defining the field of adult education in the fifties and sixties. After he came to Canada, he continued important work in several areas, perhaps most notably in his analysis of the concepts used in the field, and also his insistence on the importance of social indicators and other sociological tools in identifying community needs for adult education. Dickinson, while he remained a professor in the field, was a prolific researcher in the Verner sociological tradition and produced a widely used book on teaching techniques for use with adults. Boshier has carried out research in several dimensions of the field, but is best known for his work on the motivation of adult learners.

A third group of prominent researchers and scholars in Canada relates itself particularly to rural and agricultural interests—in Canada and abroad—and is divided between two institutions particularly, the University of Saskatchewan and the University of Guelph. Brock Whale and Harold Baker have long been based at Saskatoon and have had a very substantial impact through their writings and consultations on the development of their region and the field. At Guelph, there have been several outstanding figures, whose impact has been considerable both in Canada and abroad. The two representative figures who will be mentioned are Donald Blackburn, who has recently edited two books on agricultural extension,[104] and John Cairns, who was based at Guelph in the years following

---

[103] H.B. Long, "Characteristics of Adult Education Research Reported at the Adult Education Research Conference 1971–1980," *Adult Education*, *33*, 2 (1983) pp. 79–96.

[104] D. Blackburn (Ed.), *Extension Handbook* (Guelph, University of Guelph, 1984); (Ed.), *Foundations and Changing Practices in Extension* (Guelph, University of Guelph, 1989).

his service with UNESCO and who has had considerable influence internationally in development planning and literacy activity.

It remains to point out that there have been a number of significant contributions to our knowledge of and thinking about the field which have appeared in books which have been published in Canada over the last several decades. Only a few—aside from those already mentioned—will be noted here. Draper's book on community development and Brooke's on adult basic education, which appeared in the early seventies, contained the work of many others and had widespread influence at the time, when both fields were developing rapidly.[105] Allen Tough's *The Adult's Learning Projects* first appeared at the same time and was of widespread interest internationally, as well as in Canada.[106] To Kidd's two earlier volumes which reflected the development of the field in Canada was added a third, covering mainly the 1960s.[107] Several books have appeared which provided information about key figures in the field (Coady, England, Kidd, Grierson) and important projects (Antigonish Movement, National Film Board, Citizens' Forum, the Banff School, Chautauqua, the CAAE). New lines of inquiry and critical points of view were developed by such works as Faris's book about the CAAE and the Forum projects;[108] Lotz on community development in Canada;[109] Roberts' comparative study of the field in Quebec and Alberta;[110] and Welton's volume of historical essays.[111] Other professional concerns were addressed by Campbell's volumes on professional training and university policies;[112] several works on aspects of instruction;[113] Blackburn's two compendia about agricultural extension;[114] and Selman's general history of the field in British Columbia.[115]

---

[105] J. Draper, (Ed.), *Citizen Participation: Canada* (Toronto, New Press, 1971); M. Brooke (Ed.) *Adult Basic Education* (Toronto, New Press, 1972).

[106] A. Tough, *The Adult's Learning Projects* (Toronto, Ontario Institute for Studies in Education, 1971).

[107] J.R. Kidd & G. Selman (Eds.), *Coming of Age* (Toronto, Canadian Association for Adult Education, 1978).

[108] R. Faris, *The Passionate Educators* (Toronto, Peter Martin, 1975).

[109] J. Lotz, *Understanding Canada* (Toronto, NC Press, 1977).

[110] H. Roberts, *Culture and Adult Education* (Edmonton, University of Alberta, 1982).

[111] M.R. Welton (Ed.), *Knowledge For The People* (Toronto, Ontario Institute for Studies in Education, 1987).

[112] D.D. Campbell, *Adult Education as a Field of Study and Practice; The New Majority* (Edmonton, University of Alberta, 1984).

[113] G. Dickinson, *Teaching Adults* (Toronto, New Press, 1973); T. Barer-Stein & J. Draper (Eds.), *The Craft of Teaching Adults* (Toronto, Culture Concepts Inc., 1988); I. Mugridge & D. Kaufman, *Distance Education in Canada* (London, Croom Helm, 1986).

[114] D. Blackburn, *Extension Handbook & Foundations and Changing Practices in Extension.*

[115] G. Selman, *The Invisible Giant* (Vancouver, University of British Columbia/Centre for Continuing Education, 1988).

In the brief span of forty years, the literature of the field in Canada has developed from next to nothing to a promising and rapidly evolving area of scholarly concern. Commercial and institutional publishers were by the 1980s prepared to look seriously at proposals in this field. Several hundred persons had become involved in carrying out research and publishing material concerning the education of adults.

What Kind of Profession?

In this chapter considerable information has been provided which relates to a growing sense of professionalism in the field of adult education. An increasing number of workers in this field have sought formal or non-formal training in adult education and identify themselves and their careers with the field. At least 15 universities and many other organizations are providing specialized training in aspects of adult education. The adult education literature contains increasing reference to professional issues, and to the issue of professionalism. The Commission of Professors of Adult Education in the United States are studying the criteria which might be utilized in an accreditation system for academic departments serving the field.

In forty years we have gone in Canada from an almost total lack of attention to professional aspects of the field to the point where some adult educators are concerned about the possible harmful effects of what is seen by some as "creeping professionalism." There is virtually unanimous support for the idea that those engaged in performing roles in the field—as teacher, program organizer, curriculum developer, counsellor, administrator, etc.—should acquire the knowledge and skills which enable them to carry out these tasks effectively. But there are a number of concerns which relate to the development of a more professional corps of leadership.

One of the points most frequently made in this connection is the concern that leadership in the field might be controlled by those who have a particular type of training. This matter came to official notice at UNESCO's Third World Conference on Adult Education in 1972 in Tokyo, where it was agreed that

> the need for professionals in adult education should not, however, lead to the establishment of a closed profession. It [is] necessary both to preserve mobility between adult educators and the general field of education and to ensure a close rapport between professional adult educators and non-specialists.[116]

Lowe comments: "How ironic it would be if those who have railed against the insularity of the teaching profession should themselves set up a closed shop."[117] This matter is particularly keenly felt by those persons in adult education who see it ideally as a democratic movement and one which should consciously play a part in the critique and transformation of the society within which it functions.

---

[116] Quoted in J. Lowe, *The Education of Adults*, p. 144.

[117] J. Lowe, *The Education of Adults*, p. 141.

There is concern in some quarters that along with increased professionalism in adult education will come an attempt to create a "system" of lifelong education. The fear is that one of what is considered to be the "glories" of adult education, namely that participation is voluntary, will increasingly be eroded. Authors such as John Ohliger and Robert Carlson have warned that an inevitable consequence of professionalism will be a tendency for educators to promote more and more circumstances in which adults will be required to use their professional services—be it mandatory continuing education in various professions, mandatory training programs dictated by the courts, or artificially high formal education requirements for workers.[118]

There are as well those who are fearful that a particular type of professional training or qualification will become the only key to enter the charmed leadership circle. There is a view that present training or degree programs in adult education are based on the notion of producing the "generic" adult educator, one who knows a little bit about various things—adult instruction, program planning, administration, research methodologies, etc.—and not enough about any of them. This point of view holds that we should be training experts in all these areas rather than generic adult educators, and further, that by pursuing the present course we are tending to reinforce the barriers between adult education and the rest of the field of education, rather than building bridges with other educators.

Many adult educators agree with the view that what is desirable for the field is perhaps "a profession with a difference." Those making a career of adult education need by one or various means to acquire as much competence as possible with respect to the roles they are performing. But at the same time the field needs to retain flexibility and imagination with respect to utilizing the special talents and knowledge of any who have something of benefit to offer to other learners.

It is also difficult to see the way in which a field as disparate and decentralized as is adult education could become dominated by a "closed" profession. It is true that for instance a provincial department of education, or a federal manpower training department, if they took a narrow view of who could carry out certain functions within their system or sphere of influence, could have the effect of creating a relatively restricted field of operations, but much of the field would still lie outside their influence. The issue does, however, raise the spectre of a deeply divided field of adult education, with an establishment-regulated and dominated system of adult education on the one hand and a counter or alternative system on the other. This has, for different reasons, produced a "Popular Education" movement in a number of Latin American countries, a coalition of organizations and social forces which is in large measure in opposition to, or at least consciously at arm's length from the constituted authority. It is hoped by most

---

[118] R. Carlson, "Professionalization of Adult Education," *Adult Education, 28*, 1 (1977); J. Ohliger, "Is Lifelong Education a Guarantee of Permanent Inadequacy?" *Convergence, 12*, 2 (1974).

adult educators, we believe, that the field will continue to be many-faceted, with many ideologies and points of view co-existing. Likely no single model of professional training will ever fully meet the needs of the field. Adult education will, we hope, continue to welcome skilled and committed people from many backgrounds, holding many different points of view.

9

The Contemporary Scene and Future Prospects

It is the intention in this chapter to focus on adult education in Canada in the most recent two decades, since approximately 1970. This will involve pulling together some material which has already been presented in previous chapters. There are two main reasons for doing this. The first is to describe the main features of the field in Canada at the present time. The other is to identify current trends in adult education, ones which represent forces or directions which appear to be shaping the future of the field.

Why 1970 as Starting Point?

Neither 1970 nor any other date holds any particular magic to mark the beginning of a new era, but the beginning of the seventies is in some respects a reasonable starting point. The impact of the increasing rate of technological and social change was being brought home at that time by such books as Alvin Toffler's *Future Shock*, which appeared in 1970.[1] Some of the social movements spawned in the turbulent sixties were taking form and settling in for the long run. In the case of the women's movement, for instance, government had by this time been persuaded to take their concerns seriously, and the landmark report on the Royal Commission on the Status of Women was issued in 1970. A dramatic devolution of powers from the federal to the provincial governments had gathered pace during the sixties and by the early seventies scholarly books were appearing under such titles as *Canada in Question*, which expressed concern about the degree of decentralization within Confederation.[2]

In the field of education, the community college systems in the various provinces, which began to develop in the mid and late sixties, were rapidly changing the nature of educational opportunities open to adults. The creation of TV Ontario in 1970 was a harbinger of many related educational innovations to follow.

---

[1] A. Toffler, *Future Shock* (London, Bodley Head, 1970).

[2] D.V. Smiley, *Canada in Question: Federalism in the Seventies* (Toronto, McGraw-Hill Ryerson, 1972).

The field of adult education itself was rapidly moving towards professionalism, with the first two books dealing with specialized areas of practice, *Citizen Participation: Canada* and *Adult Basic Education* appearing early in the decade.[3] Allen Tough's influential study of "self-directed" adult learning, *The Adult's Learning Projects*, appeared in 1971.[4] Community development seemed to be taking a new lease on life in Canada with the emergence of the National Film Board's Challenge for Change project, Frontier College's entry into that field, and the launching in Canada of the "community school" movement, all in or around 1970.

The international community of ideas also seemed to be signalling a new era of development in the field. In 1970, two influential books appeared, Ivan Illich's *Deschooling Society* and Paulo Freire's *Pedagogy of the Oppressed*,[5] both of which were to have substantial impact on adult education in this country, as elsewhere. In Europe, new concepts and practices were emerging which were to have widespread influence: the efforts of the Council of Europe to promote the idea of *education permanente*; the work of the Organization for Economic Co-operation and Development in connection with the policy of recurrent education; and the promotion by UNESCO of the concept of lifelong education, particularly by means of its highly-publicized report, *Learning To Be*, which appeared in 1972.[6] In that same year, UNESCO held in Tokyo its Third World Conference on Adult Education. The proceedings of that inter-governmental conference indicated a widespread acceptance among governments in all parts of the world of the place of adult education in educational planning, and also focused attention particularly on the need to increase the effectiveness of adult education in serving the more educationally disadvantaged.[7] Two important royal commissions on education in Canada, the Worth Commission in Alberta and the Wright Commission in Ontario, reported in 1972 and both were clearly influenced by these European and international developments.[8] There are therefore reasons to see the early seventies as the beginning of significant trends in the field of adult education.

The twenty years under review in this chapter were ones of triumph and tragedy for mankind. Conditions such as the extent of famine in Africa, the

---

[3]   J. Draper (Ed.), *Citizen Participation: Canada* (Toronto, New Press, 1971); M. Brooke, *Adult Basic Education* (Toronto, New Press, 1972).

[4]   A. Tough, *The Adult's Learning Projects* (Toronto, Ontario Institute for Studies in Education, 1971).

[5]   I. Illich, *Deschooling Society* (New York, Harper & Row, 1970); P. Freire, *Pedagogy of the Oppressed* (New York, Herder & Herder, 1970).

[6]   UNESCO, *Learning To Be* (Paris, UNESCO, 1972).

[7]   J. Lowe, *The Education of Adults: A World Perspective* (Toronto, Ontario Institute for Studies in Education, 1975).

[8]   *A Choice of Futures*, Report of the Commission [Alberta] on Educational Planning (Edmonton, Queen's Printer, 1972); *The Learning Society*, Report of the Commission on Post-Secondary Education in Ontario (Toronto, Ontario Ministry of Public Services, 1972).

widespread denial of human rights, the arms race, the increasing numbers of illiterates in the world, the challenge of AIDS, and environmental disasters were all serious in themselves and evoked the spectre of future difficulties. The period also brought the first landing on the moon and, twenty years later, the recovery of pictures of Neptune from a spacecraft which had travelled for twelve years and was about to pass beyond the earth's solar system. It was a time which included the oil crisis of 1973 and its aftermath, the Iranian revolution of 1978 and the upsurge of fundamentalist religion, the more developed world's problems of unemployment, and increasing awareness of the aging of their population. In Canada there have been such events as the imposition of price controls, the election of the Parti Quebecois in Quebec and the subsequent referendum, the upsurge of environmental concerns, new recognition of illiteracy levels in Canada, contention over economic relations with the United States, and the controversies over federal-provincial relations, as symbolized by the Meech Lake Accord.

Such were some of the events which affected the kind of society and psychological climate in which Canadians, and Canadian adult education, functioned in these two tumultuous decades. There was wealth—or at least prosperity—for many who could function effectively in an increasingly high-tech world. There was extended or chronic poverty and unemployment for many who did not find a place in that world. In Canada, as in the international community, the gap between the rich and the poor, the haves and the have nots, widened.

There were also important events which affected what might be termed the "intellectual climate" within which Canadian adult education was functioning. There were, first of all, a number of significant reports and other publications which reinforced the sense of importance of the field. The landmark report of UNESCO's International Commission on the Development of Education, *Learning To Be*,[9] which appeared in 1972, was in many respects the most eloquent of them all. Modern conditions demanded the development of what they termed "a learning society" if man was to remain in control of events, and not the other way around. Change was taking place so rapidly in contemporary society, nothing less than lifelong learning—and much of the emphasis was on learning rather than education—would enable men and women to cope. Another influential document of the period was *No Limits to Learning*, a report written in 1979 by J. W. Botkin and others for the prestigious international "think tank," the Club of Rome. They argued that if humanity was to save itself from environmental and other follies which were being perpetrated, it would have to call on its "untapped resources of vision and creativity" in order to "bail humankind out of its predica-

---

[9] UNESCO, *Learning To Be*.

ment." [9] The Organization for Economic Co-operation and Development, a body representing the most highly developed and wealthiest nations in the world, embraced the concept of "recurrent education" in the early 1970s. [11] It was argued that such an approach—an integration or alternation of work and education throughout adult life—would have both social and economic benefits. These three approaches, all of which accorded new prominence to adult education and adult learning, were perhaps the most important among many of the period, which during these two decades brought adult education into prominence among economic and social planners as never before.

At the same time that adult education was gaining this new prominence, it—and the field of education as a whole—was the subject of vigorous criticism, from various quarters. The sixties had been a turbulent time for the field of education, much of the leadership in this process coming from the students or learners themselves. By late in the decade, the crisis of confidence with respect to the educational strategies being employed, what Philip Coombs termed "the linear expansion of existing or inherited educational systems," [12] was being taken seriously by educational and development planners. Two eloquent critics of current educational practice, Ivan Illich and Paulo Freire, published powerful statements of their points of view in 1970. Illich's *Deschooling Society* identified what he saw to be the "institutionalizing" effect that educational systems were having on students—creating dependence on the teaching profession—and he also condemned the attempt, through such institutions, to impose a middle class set of values on all students. He was no less critical of a lifelong education policy, if it was to produce the same effects. [13] Paulo Freire's critique had much in common with that of Illich, and was firmly rooted in adult education practice. His *Pedagogy of the Oppressed* advanced the view, as Illich did, that existing educational systems were based on a largely unconscious assumption that its role was to develop people to "fit" into the society, more or less as it was presently constituted; it was an education for "domestication," whereas what was needed was an education for freedom. In his view, educators were deluding themselves if they thought they were being—or even could be—neutral in their influence with respect to the future of society; they must, in Freire's view, be forces for change, or forces which reinforced the status quo. [14]

These and other critiques of education have had considerable impact on the field of education, including adult education, since they appeared. They have

---

[10] J. Botkin, M. Elmandjra & M. Malitza, *No Limits To Learning* (Oxford, Pergamon, 1979) p. xiii.

[11] Organization for Economic Co-operation and Development, *Recurrent Education: Trends and Issues* (Paris, OECD, 1975).

[12] P. Coombs, *The World Crisis in Education: View from the Eighties* (New York, Oxford, 1985) p. 7.

[13] I. Illich, *Deschooling Society*.

[14] P. Freire, *Pedagogy of the Oppressed*.

made all educators who were willing to listen more sensitive to the implications of their policies and practices. They have also provided great encouragement to those sectors of the field of adult education which sought to use education as an instrument, or at least a handmaiden of social change. More specifically, many of those in the field of literacy or basic education, about which Freire spoke in considerable detail (having developed his ideas while working in such situations himself) have drawn inspiration and methodological assistance from his writings. The result has been a more polarized field than was the case in earlier decades. Much of the field has taken part, or at least fallen in with the move towards professionalism, a "needs meeting" and market orientation model, which have been the dominant trends of the period. On the other hand, the adult educators who have been concerned with linking their efforts with attempts to bring about social change have been strengthened in their views by the radical critiques such as those referred to above. In addition, the national organization representing the field, the Canadian Association for Adult Education, has directed its energies in recent years to allying itself with several social movements—the women's movement, literacy, peace and disarmament organizations, etc.—a further source of encouragement to adult educators who were involved in education for social change.

The Development of the Field of Adult Education

Participation

The last two decades have seen spectacular growth in participation in adult education on the part of Canadians. This has been a period during which some parts of the educational system have experienced slowed rates of growth, but adult education has seemingly not been affected in that way. The simplest way to document this growth is to compare two reports issued by Statistics Canada, one in 1963 and one in 1984.[15] The first of these indicated that "one in 25" adult Canadians had taken part in adult education during the year studied (1959–60) and the second announced in its title, *One in Every Five*, how drastically the picture had changed. These were of course percentages of a growing total population. The numbers of adult learners reported in the 1963 study was stated to be 426,340, and 30 years later, the number was 3,170,900. The number of adult learners had increased by some seven and-a-half times in that period, a much more rapid rate of growth than that of the adult population as a whole. As was pointed out in Chapter 4, the numbers of persons actively engaged in learning was clearly a much higher number.

---

[15] Dominion Bureau of Statistics, *Participants in Further Education in Canada* (Ottawa, D.B.S., 1963); Statistics Canada & Secretary of State, *One in Every Five* (Ottawa, Statistics Canada & Dept. of Secretary of State, 1984).

Providers and Methodologies

Phenomena which have accompanied the rapid growth in the field—and may in part explain it—have been the proliferation of agencies which provide adult education and the development of new, or altered methodologies for the delivery of programs. The three most notable new developments in the case of the providing agencies have been the community college, distance education institutions and delivery systems, and the considerable expansion of the private sector.

The single most important development in the field during this period has undoubtedly been the creation, beginning in the sixties, of community college systems in most of the provinces. As documented by Dennison and Gallagher[16] in their recent study, although the functions of the colleges have differed from one jurisdiction to another, they have all seen as one of their main tasks the provision of opportunities for part-time study for adults in their communities. The importance of their activities in this field was revealed in the participation study, *One in Every Five*, just referred to, in which the colleges (including the Quebec CEGEPs) were shown to be the largest provider of adult education of all the educational institutions.[17]

Distance education—the provision of instruction to learners who are at a distance from the instructor or instructing institution—has grown dramatically in these recent decades, and it has taken a variety of forms. The creation of the Open University in Britain, which began taking students in 1971, has been instrumental in encouraging the growth of similar institutions elsewhere, including Canada. The Open University took the long-established practice of "correspondence study" and embellished it in a variety of ways—supplementary broadcasts, local tutoring and counselling centres, audio and other augmentation of the traditional print materials in the course packages, and brief residential periods of instruction. The three most prominent institutions in Canada of a somewhat similar nature are the Tele-université in Quebec (part of the University of Quebec), Athabaska University in Alberta, and the Open Learning Agency in British Columbia, all created in the 1970s.[18] In addition to these new, special purpose institutions, many already existing ones took a fresh interest in the possibilities of this "new generation" of distance education techniques and have greatly expanded their offerings by this means. A leading example of this has been the University of Waterloo, which by the mid-eighties had approximately 300 courses available, in their case with heavy reliance on audiocassettes con-

---

[16] J. Dennison & P. Gallagher, *Canada's Community Colleges* (Vancouver, University of British Columbia, 1986).

[17] Statistics Canada & Secretary of State, *One in Every Five*.

[18] J. Wilson, B. Bell & W. Powell, *The Provincial Educational Communications Organizations in Canada* (Toronto, Ontario Educational Communications Authority, 1984).

taining versions of on-campus lectures.[19] Teleconferencing and other communications techniques through which an instructor can be in touch with individual students or groups of students at remote locations are also being widely used. Computer managed or computer assisted instruction is being used in many settings, by individuals for their own purposes and also within the programs of educational institutions and other agencies. A third major sector of distance education is that of provincial educational communications organizations, particularly TV Ontario, Radio-Quebec, ACCESS Alberta, and the Knowledge Network (part of the Open Learning Agency) in B.C., all established in the 1970s.[20] Generally, these organizations broadcast both general educational programs (just for general viewing, not as courses of instruction) and also credit and non-credit courses for which people may register. Any "credit" which students gain by means of these courses is normally awarded by other institutions (colleges, universities, etc.) in the provincial system rather than by the broadcasting agency itself. The four organizations differ somewhat in their activities, but are also involved in closed circuit broadcasting, videotape services and computer-related applications.

The expansion of the private sector of the field takes several different forms. First of all, particularly during the eighties, the federal Manpower authorities have as a matter of policy sought to purchase an increasing proportion of the training for their trainees from the private sector and correspondingly less from the public educational institutions. This policy has been particularly emphasized under the terms of the National Training Act of 1982 and the Canadian Job Strategy program of 1985. This has led to the offering of training at the job site, by arrangement with private sector employers, and also to the creation of many private sector educational agencies, established in order to be able to take advantage of the federal government's policies in this area. Quite apart from the impact of federal Manpower policies, there has been a rapid growth in the number of proprietary educational and training institutions in the private sector, and the expansion of many previously established firms. Continuing or adult education having become a more widely accepted phenomenon in our society, expanded opportunities have presented themselves for the sale of services in this area— everything from learning about deep sea or scuba diving, to learning how to operate a computer. A further dimension of this trend has been a considerable increase in the extent of private consulting in the area of adult education and training. But by far the most significant dimension of the private sector was the training conducted by business and industry for its own employees (and in some cases, for the employees of other corporations as well). The national study published in 1985 revealed that education provided by "employers" was the largest

---

[19] E. Burge et al., *Communications and Information Technologies and Distance Education in Canada* (Toronto, Ontario Educational Communications Authority, 1984).

[20] J. Wilson, B. Bell & W. Powell, *The Provincial Educational Communications Organizations.*

single category of "course provider," accounting for 18 per cent of the total. And employers provided 42 per cent of "job related" courses.[21]

Two further, somewhat conjectural points might be made with respect to who provides adult education. The statistics available relate in the main to formal and non-formal education; the reports refer to numbers of "enrollments" and "courses." Education takes place in other ways as well. Social movements such as the environmental movements, for instance, have seen that "media events" and other forms of influence over people's attitudes, ones which are not educational programs in the traditional sense of the term, nevertheless can be effective in informing (and perhaps persuading) people with respect to the issues being dealt with. There seems at this time no dependable way of quantifying such activity, much less attempting to evaluate its educational effectiveness, but it does appear to be the case that such approaches to alerting people to issues and providing information about them has greatly gained in usage in these most recent decades.

The second point perhaps does not logically fall under the heading of "providers," but it is closely related to it. We refer to the increased awareness in recent years of what is referred to as "self-directed learning." This phenomenon is of particular interest to Canadian students of adult education because the leading figure in research into this area is a Canadian, Allen Tough.[22] The point of view taken in this work is that most of the education engaged in by adults does not take the form of enrolling in a course or a program, but is directed by the learner himself/herself. Research has revealed that virtually everyone undertakes such self-directed learning projects in the course of a year. Tough was the main figure in launching investigation into this form of learning effort, but it has had wide influence and has been picked up by many other investigators.[23] This research is controversial: some question the soundness of the research; others, for ideological reasons, prefer not to take self-directed learning seriously as part of what Philip Coombs has termed the educational "network,"[24] perhaps because it is slippery to define and not easily directly controlled by policy. A new kind of "provider" of adult education—the learner himself/herself—has come into our ken.

Program Areas

It is a safe assumption that all program or content areas of adult education have grown significantly in these past two decades. In what follows the emphasis will be given to a number of areas which have, for various reasons, grown especially rapidly.

[21] Statistics Canada & Secretary of State, *One in Every Five.*

[22] A. Tough, *The Adult's Learning Projects.*

[23] See for instance A. Tough, "Major Learning Efforts: Recent Research and Future Directions," *Adult Education 28*, 4 (1978) pp. 250-63.

[24] P. Coombs, *The World Crisis in Education.*

In Canada, as in many other countries, vocational and technical training have received priority treatment in recent years. The conservative governments which have been in power in many Western countries for much of this period have had a particular interest in promoting the industrial sector and in providing the skilled labour force necessary for such economic development. The great interest shown in vocational training and in such concepts as "recurrent education," which links further education and worker proficiency, have been manifestations of such priorities.[25] The emphasis on vocational education has become so pronounced in this period that some international experts in the field of education have expressed concern about the extent of its dominance in public policy over other areas of adult learning.[26]

Both senior levels of government in Canada have been giving strong emphasis to vocational training. The stage was set at the federal level by two developments, the vast expansion of funding for this field initiated by the Technical and Vocational Training Assistance Act of 1960, and the decision by the federal authorities in the mid-sixties to assume authority in the field of vocational and technical education. The federal government drew a line between education, which was clearly a provincial responsibility, and training, which it now claimed to be within its powers, arising out of its constitutional responsibility for the economic development of the country. The Occupational Training Act of 1967, the National Training Act of 1982 and the Canadian Jobs Strategy of 1985 have been based on this interpretation and have radically altered the basis of public policy towards this aspect of adult education in Canada. At the same time the various provinces pursued their own policies in this area, and at the time of writing, the vocational and training picture across the country is in many respects uncoordinated and lagging behind the need. Federal initiatives to explore a comprehensive "paid educational leave" policy for Canada, have produced two major reports on the subject[27] but were not successful in securing the active support of the three major interested parties, management, labour and government.

An area of adult education which has grown spectacularly since 1970 is that of continuing professional education. It is almost in the nature of professions that practitioners must keep up to date with new knowledge and conditions affecting their fields of practice, in order to be able to perform at the expected level. Professional people have traditionally continued their education through reading, professional conferences, study groups and the like. In the sixties and early seventies, professional groups, responding to a realization that they were facing a severe problem in keeping up with an accelerated rate of change, and as well to a

[25] J. Bengtsson in T. Schuller & J. Megarry (Eds.), *Recurrent Education and Lifelong Learning* (London, Nichols Publishing, 1979).

[26] See for instance J. Lowe, *The Education of Adults*.

[27] R.J. Adams, *Education and Working Canadians*, Report of the Commission of Inquiry on Educational Leave and Productivity (Ottawa, Labour Canada, 1979); National Advisory Panel on Skill Development Leave, *Learning For Life*, Report of the Panel to the Minister of Employment and Immigration, 1984).

new level of scrutiny from the "consumer," stepped up their educational efforts. Typically, the professional body and the pre-service training institution (universities, institutes of technology, etc.) co-operatively established continuing education programs through which needed information and education could be provided for practitioners. In some cases professions have established regulations which make the continuation or renewal of licenses to practice conditional upon the practitioners being able to show evidence of efforts to update their knowledge and skills. Continuing professional education has in many instances been at the growing and innovative frontier of methodologies in adult education. While it is not possible to quantify the growth or extent of continuing professional education in Canada, it is clear to anyone at all knowledgeable about the field as a whole that this has been one of the areas of most rapid growth in the last two decades.

One of the areas of the field which has been developing most quickly is that of full and part-time study towards academic credentials. For present purposes, this will be examined in two sections, post-secondary education and adult basic education. Growth in the post-secondary field has been the most spectacular. The creation of the systems of community colleges and institutes in the various provinces has undoubtedly been the most important single factor. These institutions, which began their spectacular growth in the sixties, have by their very existence encouraged many to continue their education, have brought many new programs and fields of training into being, and have made post-secondary education much more accessible, both geographically and financially. Furthermore, the colleges generally have from the outset seen the adult and part-time student as one of the main clientele they intend to serve, so they have designed services of many kinds for this group.[28] As has already been mentioned, as of the Statistics Canada study published in 1984, the community colleges served more adult students than any other sector of the educational system.[29]

The universities of the country greatly expanded their services to adult part-time students in this period. Although it is not possible to state all the reasons with assurance, it would appear that demographic trends which resulted in decreased demand for university services in the traditional 18 to 24 year age groups encouraged the universities of the country to become more interested in older, part-time students. New, special purpose units within certain universities, such as Atkinson College at York University and Woodsworth College at the University of Toronto, have been established to serve the part-time student. New distance education institutions such as Athabaska University (Alberta), Tele-Université (Quebec) and the Open Learning Agency (B.C.), and other distance education programs have made many post-secondary educational opportunities more accessible. The statistics available indicate that in the period between 1970 and the

---

[28] J. Dennison & P. Gallagher, *Canada's Community Colleges.*

[29] Statistics Canada & Secretary of State, *One in Every Five.*

late 1980s, part-time credit course enrollments at Canadian universities increased enormously, reaching 279,850 by 1985–86, the most recent detailed figures available.[30] This represented approximately 38 per cent of all credit enrollments. Of the part-time enrollees, approximately three quarters of these persons were 25 years or older.[31] In his study of the matter, Campbell indicates that in 1974–75, the number of part-time students in Canadian universities (credit and non-credit) exceeded the number of full-time students for the first time.[32]

Another area of rapid development during the seventies and eighties was the field of adult basic education (ABE), which is here meant to include everything from literacy education through to high school completion for adults, and beyond the literacy level, at least, is normally closely related to formal educational credentials. education Two developments during the 1960s laid the foundations for this rapid expansion. The census of 1961 revealed as never before the extent of under-education in the Canadian population.[33] Secondly, with the rapid expansion of vocational and technical education made possible by the Technical and Vocational Training Assistance Act of 1960, it soon became clear that many of the persons who were most in need of such training did not have a sufficient level of basic education to enable them to cope with the training which was being made available. As a result, the federal Manpower authorities were drawn into financing a great deal of basic education for adults.[34] These efforts, and those of the provincial authorities (where the record was very uneven) led to a dramatic expansion of adult basic education programs across the country. In 1982, the federal authorities cut back their support for ABE activities and the initiative began to shift increasingly to provincially and privately sponsored programs. In addition to the various Manpower-related programs, the provinces have in most cases developed alternative curricula and programs through which adults can gain formal qualifications at the high school level—through the General Educational Development (GED) examination system and by other means.

The field of literacy education has been a prominent concern in the Third World for several decades. Canadian activity in this area began to take shape in the 1960s and came into prominence in the mid–1970s.[35] Although federal authorities cut back on their commitment to the full range of ABE activities in the 1970s, they have in recent years provided leadership in the field of literacy education. In this case, literacy was seen to be an essential element of citizenship in contemporary society, and the federal initiatives have come through the Secre-

---

[30] *University Affairs*, May, 1986.

[31] As above.

[32] D.D. Campbell, *The New Majority* (Edmonton, University of Alberta, 1984).

[33] M. Brooke, *Adult Basic Education*.

[34] M. Taylor & J. Draper (Eds.), *Adult Literacy Perspectives* (Toronto, Culture Concepts Inc., 1989).

[35] As above.

tary of State's Department rather than through Employment and Immigration. Federal funds were provided on a larger scale than previously for this work, beginning in 1988, in support of work by the non-governmental and voluntary sector, and through joint initiatives with the provinces. At the time of writing, literacy education is a rapidly expanding part of adult education in Canada.

Reference must be made as well to the emergence in the past two decades of adult education programs and services intended for, and in many cases under the sponsorship of the Native people of Canada. In keeping with the proclamation by the Native Indian Brotherhood (since 1982, the Assembly of First Nations) in 1972 of the intention of the Native people to develop educational services under their own control, and with the support in many respects of the federal government, there has been a dramatic expansion of adult education activities, much of it under the direction of Native organizations.[36] This educational activity has been of various kinds, perhaps most notably in three areas: education related to the aspirations of the Native people in such areas as human rights, cultural and political development, and land claims; general educational development, largely in the area of adult basic education; and increased access to post-secondary education and professional training. This activity has been developed both on the reserves and in the cities of the South, where many special purpose organizations and institutions have been established. Widespread concern was expressed recently when the federal government announced a reduction of funds available for post-secondary education of Native people.

The women's movement, in its contemporary form, was a product of social forces during the 1960s and by 1970, when the Royal Commission on the Status of Women reported, was very much a going concern. From the very beginning there was a strong educational dimension to the movement, at first aimed largely at "consciousness raising" among women, but increasingly as time went on concerned as well with assisting women to gain the confidence and qualifications needed as they altered their goals and moved into new roles in Canadian society. Some of the longer-established women's organizations, such as the Y.W.C.A., took a leading role in the new women's movement, but the most prominent women's groups of the recent decades have been newly-established ones. The Voice of Women organization was prominent in the early years, especially in the area of political and social action. Other bodies, most notably the National Action Committee on the Status of Women, an umbrella organization which speaks for 230 women's organizations, have become more prominent in the 1980s. In the field of education, many important developments have taken place. A new organization which emerged in the seventies, the Canadian Congress on Learning Opportunities for Women, has taken a vigorous lead in promoting educational opportunities for women, through the creation of new programs and promoting satisfactory access for women to existing ones. Many

---

[36] See for instance, *Affiliation and Accreditation: Research Study Report for the First Nations Federation of Adult Educators* (Vancouver, The Merritt Group, 1988).

educational institutions in Canada have created new programs of interest to women, such as "women's studies," and have provided support services for women students, particularly by means of peer support groups and counselling services of various kinds. Particular attention has been paid by the women's movement to the vocational training programs provided by the two senior levels of government, to the end that access (and benefits) be fairly available to women, including those programs related to occupations which have not traditionally been women's fields of work.

An important phenomenon of these decades has been the educational activities undertaken by the various social movements already referred to. The peace movement, groups representing the interests of Native people, those concerned with aspects of the environment, the women's movement, and those concerned with the welfare of the growing number of older persons—to name only some—have engaged in a great range of informational and educational endeavours, which have reached and influenced many Canadians. Much of the activity of these movements has not taken the form of traditional types of adult education—courses, classes, etc.—but none would question their educational impact, in the broad sense of the term. The women's movement has utilized perhaps the broadest range of educational activities of any of these groups and as well has pioneered many approaches to the field of educational counselling.

The Canadian Association for Adult Education, the national organization for the field in English-speaking Canada, which has cultivated links with the voluntary sector throughout its history, resolved during the celebration of its fiftieth anniversary in 1985 to strengthen its co-operative working relationships with six social movements—adult literacy, the peace movement, cultural sovereignty, environmental citizenship, local economical development, and the women's movement. In each case, the commitment of the CAAE is to co-operative endeavours in connection with the educational, as distinct from the social or political action of these groups. For the CAAE, this represents a re-focusing on a theme which has run through its history. During the 1950s and the following decade, the CAAE was prominent as well in the profession-building aspects of the field, but since that time, and especially since the mid-eighties, the organization has returned to a more dominant commitment to the social movement roots of the field.

Many other aspects of the rapidly growing field of adult education could be mentioned here, but those discussed above represent a number which have developed most remarkably during these decades. There is a concern on the part of many adult educators that a combination of conservative government policies and trends towards professionalism in the field of practice are producing an adult education enterprise which is increasingly concerned with vocational and academic aspects and correspondingly less interested in the social and citizenship dimensions of adult learning in this country.

Canadian Adult Education and the International Community

No account of the concerns and character of Canadian adult education in recent decades would be complete without reference to the active part played by Canadians and Canadian institutions in the world community. There is to our knowledge no account of this activity. Many Canadian organizations—churches, voluntary organizations, co-operatives, labour unions, professional associations, etc.—have sent personnel or in some way have contributed to international aid efforts. Some of these organizations have taken advantage of funds available from the Canadian International Development Agency (CIDA) on a matching basis for such work. There have been several organizations—CIDA, the World University Service of Canada, the Canadian University Service Overseas, etc.— which have specialized in such activities and have sent and maintained large numbers of Canadians abroad, many of them involved in organizing adult education work or teaching adults. CIDA has also financed projects which have been carried out by others, for instance the Association of Universities and Colleges of Canada, the Association of Canadian Community Colleges, the Canadian Association for Adult Education, and many individual institutions. Individual Canadians have been recruited by international organizations such as UNESCO, the World Health Organization, the International Labour Organization, and others, to work at headquarters or in Third World countries carrying out educational work. Some Canadians have occupied key positions in international bodies—Eugene Bussiere and John Cairns at UNESCO, Kalman Kaplansky and John Whitehouse at the International Labour Organization, etc.—and organized work in many countries.

In addition, successful and innovative adult education projects in Canada which were seen by other countries as having something to offer to their development processes were invited to share their experience. The Antigonish Movement in Nova Scotia and other Canadian co-operative organizations were active in this work in recent decades, as they had been earlier.[37] The Challenge for Change projects of the National Film Board, which made use of film and videotape as part of the community development process, was of great interest in other countries, and persons connected with it were asked to go abroad and share their expertise.[38]

A particularly important Canadian contribution during this period was the creation of the International Council for Adult Education (ICAE), largely as a result of leadership provided by a Canadian, Dr. Roby Kidd. International co-operation in the field of adult education at the intergovernmental level had been encouraged and facilitated since the Second World War by the relevant United Nations specialized agency, UNESCO. Roby Kidd played a leading role in

---

[37] E. Stabler, *Founders* (Edmonton, University of Alberta, 1987); P. Milner (Ed.), *Human Development Through Social Change* (Antigonish, Nova Scotia, Formac Publishing, 1979).

[38] D.B. Jones, *Movies and Memoranda* (Ottawa, Canadian Film Institute, 1981); The John Grierson Project, *John Grierson and the NFB* (Montreal, ECW Press, 1984).

UNESCO activities in the latter part of the fifties, and it was partly in recognition of this fact that UNESCO accepted Canada's invitation to hold its Second World Conference on Adult Education in Montreal, in 1960. Kidd was elected President of that conference and by means of resourceful leadership brought the conference to a successful conclusion, in spite of it being a time of heightened Cold War tensions. As a result he emerged from the conference as one of the best known adult education leaders in the world.

It was recognized in the field that an organization such as UNESCO could accomplish only so much. The resources it could devote to any one of its enormous range of interests were limited, and such an intergovernmental organization was of necessity somewhat unwieldy and slow to act. There had been a non-governmental international body in the field between the wars, the World Association for Adult Education, but it was disbanded during World War II. There was some discussion at the Montreal Conference in 1960 of establishing a new organization, but the time and conditions were judged not to be appropriate. Kidd was committed to the idea of creating such a body and as the time for the Third UNESCO World Conference approached, which was to be held in Tokyo in 1972, he began to encourage leaders in the field in various parts of the world to think in those terms. At Tokyo, he "lobbied" on behalf of the idea and arranged for a meeting of interested delegates (outside the formal agenda) to discuss the idea. From this meeting he received strong support and in the ensuing months he sought out persons and organizations willing to support such a new body. In the following year, 1973, the ICAE was formally established with its headquarters in Toronto. Kidd thereafter served for six years as Secretary-General of the organization, with early funding coming from CIDA, the Kellogg Foundation, the governments of West Germany, Iran and the United Kingdom, and international organizations such as OECD, UNESCO and the Commonwealth Secretariat. It is generally agreed that Kidd's leadership was the crucial factor in the creation of the Council which, since its formation, has done much important work in the international community with respect to adult education and development concerns.[39] Kidd remained a leading figure in the ICAE until his death in 1982, and the headquarters of the organization continues to be located in Toronto.

Disparate Forces in the Field

Many aspects of the foregoing discussion document the rapid growth of adult education in recent years and indicate something of the extent to which the education of adults has been accepted increasingly as an important social and

---

[39] J. Lowe, *The Education of Adults*; N. Cochrane et al, *J.R. Kidd: An International Legacy of Learning* (Vancouver, University of British Columbia/Centre for Continuing Education, 1986).

personal concern. We have been moving towards the ideal stated in the well-known *1919 Report* on adult education in Great Britain, that education should become "both universal and lifelong,"[40] though the limitations as to who is being served and who is not is a matter of widespread concern. There are a number of identifiable groups in our society which are not being served by adult education as well as are those with higher incomes and with higher levels of formal education. These groups are identified in a 1982 publication issued by the two Canadian national adult education organizations, *From the Adult's Point of View*. They were listed as: women, Native people, older adults, the handicapped, immigrants, adults with low educational attainment, and francophones outside Quebec.[41]

Although there is clearly a great deal to be done yet—in Canada as elsewhere—in terms of what has been described as the democratization of adult education, the field has made substantial strides in the last two decades, in terms of the general acceptance and understanding of the idea; its acceptance as a basis for public policy in areas such as manpower training, public health, citizenship and economic development; the development of institutional structures, curricula and methodology; and the training of professional manpower for the field.

Reference has already been made to the expansion of government's role in vocational and technical training. In addition, there have been a series of commissions appointed by government in recent years which have in their reports placed emphasis on the importance of adult education. There have of course been reports commissioned specifically on adult education and related policies, and this in itself has been a sign of increased recognition of the field. But what has been more remarkable is the fact that public bodies which were asked to examine other subjects have also chosen to give prominent place to the role of adult education. The Worth Commission in Alberta and the Wright Commission in Ontario, both of which reported in 1972 and gave a prominent place to recommendations concerning adult and lifelong education, have already been mentioned, as have the two government-commissioned studies of paid educational leave. Perhaps typical in some respects of the increased recognition accorded to adult education was the report of the Parliamentary Task Force on Employment Opportunities for the 1980s. Though the mandate of this body was focused on employment and economic development, ten out of the sixteen recommendations featured in its summary of outstanding recommendations dealt with education and training. Finally, it should be pointed out that in several of the provinces in Canada in the past two decades, ministries of government have been established which have been devoted in large part to the education of adults. The designations have included phrases such as "further education" and "job training."

---

[40] *The 1919 Report*, Report of the Adult Education Committee of the Ministry of Reconstruction of the United Kingdom (Nottingham, University of Nottingham/Department of Adult Education, 1980 (1919)) p. 4.

[41] CAAE/ICEA, *From the Adult's Point of View* (Toronto/Montreal, CAAE/ICEA, 1982).

Another indication of the increasing acceptance of the importance of adult education has been the establishment of institutional structures which have been put in place largely to meet the educational needs of adults. A number of these have already been dealt with in this chapter—provincial broadcasting organizations, distance education agencies, and perhaps most pervasive in their influence, the community college and institute systems in the various provinces.

No figures exist to document this matter, but the "work force" of adult education in this country has clearly expanded enormously in this period. Reference was made in Chapter 9 to Cyril Houle's analysis of those who provide leadership in the adult education enterprise.[42] He saw them falling in three categories: full-time career adult educators; part-time teachers of adults (whose chief livelihood and/or expertise lies elsewhere, such as the business accountant who teaches a night class in his specialty); and the volunteers, who organize, give leadership to, and teach so much of adult education activity. A field which has gone in Canada in 25 years from involving 1 in 25 Canadians (1960) to 1 in 5 Canadians (1983) has clearly grown in all those dimensions, but perhaps most noticeably in the career or full-time category. With a great expansion in the number of institutions actively engaged in offering programs, the number of administrators and program organizers alone has clearly increased many fold. The number of full-time teachers of adults, in the new college systems and in the private sector particularly, has also expanded enormously. (It should be noted that the vast majority of these full-time teachers do not think of themselves as "adult educators" and would not feel drawn to membership in adult educators' organizations, but identify themselves with the institution which employs them and/or with the content of the field in which they teach.) And a number of more specialized fields within adult education have developed during this period: for instance, curriculum developers, media and computer specialists, counsellors of adults, and consultants in the field. It is not known how many hundreds of thousands of persons are now involved in the field of adult education in one of these capacities, but the number is certainly of that order.

A further indication of the growth of the field is the increase in the number of persons who seek professional education in adult education. Those who engage in such study are mainly those who are in full-time positions in the field, and predominantly those who are in, or wish to be in, administrative, programming or other specialized roles. University degree programs in the field of adult education, as described in an earlier chapter, have grown from offerings at two institutions in 1960 to fifteen at the present time (with other universities as well offering individual courses, as distinct from degree programs). Within these programs there are several thousand persons engaged in degree studies in adult education, and most if not all these programs are not able to accept all the qualified persons who apply to enter.

---

[42] C.O. Houle in M.S. Knowles (Ed.), *Handbook of Adult Education in the United States* (Chicago, Adult Education Association of the U.S.A., 1960).

There is extensive training of adult educators in other settings as well. Business and industry typically provide such training for the instructors within their programs. Most of the large educational institutions, public and private, provide opportunities for the persons they employ to teach adults to learn more about teaching. Many of the voluntary organizations, such as the Y.M. and Y.W.C.A., the Red Cross, the St. John's Ambulance Association, the Guide and Scout organizations, and many churches, provide training in the field for their leaders and instructors.

There has as well been a rapid increase in the volume of research and publication in Canada on aspects of adult education. The growth of graduate degree programs has perhaps been the most important factor in the expansion of research activity. The volume of publication about adult education has grown very quickly since the beginning of the seventies. In 1970, there were no academic journals devoted to publishing in this field, though the Canadian Association for Adult Education was publishing its more "popular" journal, *Continuous Learning*. Since that time, four academic, juried journals have been created, all of which are publishing at the time of writing. As well, commercial publishers and university presses across Canada have taken an increasing interest and have published a number of volumes over the years. In addition, many Canadian researchers publish in journals and books which are produced outside Canada. The most recent survey of material being published by Canadian scholars in adult education revealed that in the six years from 1982 to 1987, there had been 1,483 publications in the field, written by 551 different Canadians.[43] This represents a very substantial change from the situation which existed in 1970.

Further to the matter of research and publication, during recent years there have been some studies published which have moved our view of the field to a different level of analysis. Much examination of the historical development of adult education in this country has been of a traditional type, based on institutional and biographical studies, and generally approached with little evidence of a strong theoretical framework or an informing world view on the part of the authors. In the past two decades this has begun to change. One of the earliest book length studies to appear which involved the application of theory from the social sciences was Faris's *The Passionate Educators*,[44] a study of the CAAE and other voluntary associations and the role of interlocking "elites" in the development of the CAAE and broadcasting policy. Another significant study, of a very different type, was Lotz's book *Understanding Canada*, a somewhat journalistic and strongly revisionist view of Canadian experience with community development. Gregory Baum's *Catholics and Canadian Socialism* was not essentially a book about adult education, but it brought to the field from another quarter an arresting view of the Antigonish Movement. Another important work is the study by Hayden Roberts entitled *Culture and Adult Education*, which

---

[43] J.R.A. Dobson, "Canadian Adult Education Literature," *Caravan 1*, 2 (1987).

[44] R. Faris, *The Passionate Educators* (Toronto, Peter Martin, 1975).

presents a comparative study of adult education as it has developed in two provinces, Quebec and Alberta, and utilizing theoretical models from political science and sociology. A final example is a paper entitled "Learning in Society" written in 1983 by Alan Thomas, which utilizes insights from sociology, political science, cultural and communications theory in a study of the relationship between public policy, learning and education in our society.[45] These several works, selected as examples of various perspectives and not intended to be a complete list, are representative of analyses of the field which are based on more theoretical approaches, and in some cases a more strongly revisionist world view than has been true of much of the literature of the field. They are no doubt as well an indication of some future directions of scholarship in adult education.

Contending Forces and the Future

There have in the last twenty years been two sets of forces which have had impact on the field of adult education, one having the effect of strengthening adult educators' sense of the importance, identity and cohesion of the field, and the other set working in the opposite direction. On the one hand, educators who are engaged in working with adults, and who take an interest and feel a stake in the field as a whole, have many reasons to believe that much progress has been made. In 25 years, participation in adult education programs by Canadians, as we have seen, has risen from 4 per cent to 19 per cent. Government support for adult education, particularly in the vocational and academic areas, has increased enormously. A whole new institutional system has emerged in Canada—the community college—which has from its very inception attached central importance to meeting a wide variety of adult learning needs. Royal commissions and other major studies, many of a type which in past decades tended to ignore or make only passing reference to adult education, have given major emphasis to the importance of the field. Government and other planners at the national and international levels are according an important place in development planning to the education of adults. Some figures such as Freire, Illich and Coombs, reports of the Club of Rome and other international bodies, to name just a few, who have attracted the attention of the whole educational and social planning sectors throughout the world, have attached importance to adult education as part of their proposals. An increasing number of priorities which are espoused by governments—clearly in the belief that they will find favour with the voting public—such as vocational training, literacy training, environmental, public health and multicultural education, etc., are ones which consist of, or rely heavily upon forms of adult education. There are many grounds for adult educators to feel that the field has gained enormously in recognition and participation.

At the same time, there are a variety of forces which are preventing, or at least working against, a sense of cohesion and common concern among those in the

---

[45] A.M. Thomas in M. Hogue and C. Quinn (Eds.), *Learning in Society: Toward a New Paradigm* (Ottawa, Canadian Commission for UNESCO, 1985).

field. Four of these will be mentioned. The first is the nature of our constitutional arrangements in Canada. The fact that public education in this country is not one system, but at least thirteen (ten provinces, two territories and the federal government) means that most educators have a "compartmentalized" view of the field. When to these jurisdictional boundaries we add the effects of regionalism, with its widely pervasive impact on the thinking of Canadians, it is clear there are strong forces working against a sense of community of interest in the field.

A second, and perhaps even more important factor preventing a cohesive view is the effect of specialization of role and the wide dispersal of adult education in society. Adult education never has been and shows no sign of ever becoming an integrated or cohesive field. The enormous variety of organizations and institutions which sponsor adult education—chess clubs, churches, colleges, unions, secretarial schools, the women's movement, government departments, etc.—is in itself an obstacle to cohesion. As well, there is an increasing specialization of function within the field. To the long familiar specializations of administrator, teacher and programmer have now been added many others—curriculum developer, counsellor, computer and media specialist, consultant, to name only some. What do the course designer in a distance education institution, a specialist in multicultural programs in a local Y.W.C.A. and a teacher of breadmaking in a local school board night class feel they have in common professionally?

A third barrier to a sense of cohesion in adult education is the effects of institutionalization. As some of the providing institutions in the field have become large systems in themselves, such as university-based continuing education, large training units within industry, or training groups within government, such areas easily come to be seen as worlds of their own. More and more teachers of adults are employed on a full-time basis, but such persons typically come to this work on the basis of their competence in their subject matter fields and feel no sense of common cause with, nor do they even identify themselves with, adult education as a field of activity.

A fourth barrier to a sense of cohesion might be termed philosophical differences. For instance, adult educators in social movements or in community development projects may feel they have little in common with those in the public institutional systems, or in business and industry. The former see adult education as a way of bringing about change in society, and they tend to see the other segments of the field as devoted to adjusting people to the system, rather than helping people to examine and change the system. This "sense of distance," or at times even antagonism within the field works against achieving any sense of common cause.

In fact, the question must be raised—and will, if anything, be even more relevant in the future—as to whether it is sensible to think in terms of "adult education" any longer as a single field. There is ample confusion at the present time about the boundaries or limits of the field. Reference was made in the first chapter to the 40-year-old woman who returns to her education. If she attends college or university full time, or even part time, in the daytime, she will not show up in the adult education statistics. But if she took the same program by means of part-time evening study, she likely would. Under any of these circumstances, she would fit within the definition of adult education which has been produced by UNESCO, but she does not, if a daytime student, fall within most Canadian definitions. There are deep cleavages in adult education at the present time, as is attested to by the fact that in most provinces there are now 10 or 12 separate organizations of adult educators, and at that, many adult educators don't feel they are represented by any of these groups. Some of the reasons for these cleavages have already been described.

As we look towards the future, it is possible to discern several main clusters or groupings of adult education services. They are not discreet, or mutually exclusive sectors, and some providing agencies may be operating in more than one area.

1. *Academic, credential and vocational.* This category includes much of the work done by the formal educational systems (public and private), business and industry, professional associations, and vocational and technical education in the public and private sectors. Much of this activity is publicly mandated and subsidized, much is provided by employers, but an appreciable amount is simply purchased by individuals in the market place. In the "neo-conservative" 1980s, it has been this sector of the field which has been the predominant focus of government support.

2. *Personal interest and development.* This includes much of what has been termed "general interest" or "community education," and relates to hobbies and the expanding of personal skills, understanding or horizons. It includes the arts, humanities, hobby-related and cultural matters generally, as well as other areas of personal development and inter-personal skills. Some such activities are provided by the public educational system, but where that is the case, there is a growing tendency for such work to be required to be financially self-supporting, if not profit-making. A great, perhaps growing portion of this kind of adult education is being provided by the private sector, including membership organizations and local community and neighbourhood agencies of various kinds.

3. *Social action and social change.* This includes various kinds of educational activity which are dedicated to, or "harnessed" to active efforts to critique and change society in some way. (Note that it is meant to include education in relation to these matters, not propaganda, though the line is sometimes difficult to draw.) While the public educational system is mandated to be active in type 1, above, and on a fee-for-service basis provides some of type 2, it has of late done little in this third area, and the trend is perhaps in the direction of complete withdrawal. The sponsors of activity in this third area tend to be groups and organizations whose purpose is to seek social change—social movements (environment, women's movement, peace and disarmament, etc.), groups which are

broadly humanitarian in purpose (human rights, some churches, etc.) or groups which are working on behalf of parts of the population who are suffering under a sense of grievance (Native people, older persons, the poor, handicapped persons, etc.). In some other societies, this third category is described as "popular education." In the Scandinavian countries, the popular education movement is encouraged and supported out of public funds. In many Latin American countries, this popular education sector has an openly adversarial relationship with the constituted authorities.

What future for adult education? At the present time, it seems reasonable to predict continued growth, such as has been experienced in recent decades. It seems likely that the forces of change in society which have prompted such growth will continue, and if anything accelerate. The "patternless mosaic" of adult education providers, programs and services which exists at the present time would seem likely to continue, though provision of services in the public sector (and those elsewhere which receive support from public funds) may be more tightly co-ordinated and controlled in the future. In those sectors too, we can expect a continuation of the trend toward the professionalization of the field. Public funding for adult education may well continue to be focused more and more exclusively on vocational and academic kinds of adult education. We can expect two main results to flow from that trend. The first is that "general interest" kinds of adult education—matters related to personal and recreational interests—will increasingly be "forced out" of the public sector (which will have to charge higher fees than people will be willing to pay) and will be taken up by voluntary and other non-public agencies. The second result of the public sector concentrating increasingly on vocational and academic education is that the gulf between the public sector of the field and those elements of it which see adult education as the key to promoting social change will widen. To what extent the various movements and organizations working for social change will work together or coalesce in their adult education efforts remains to be seen. But it does seem likely (to the regret of many adult educators) that increasing public sector concentration on vocational and academic aspects of adult education, to the exclusion of its historic role in citizenship and social education, will have the effect of creating a wider and wider gulf between the public sector on the one hand, and on the other hand, those interested in adult education as a component of social critique and social change.

10

Accessing the Literature

In this chapter the authors wish to share some information and insights concerning the literature of the field with those who are seeking to go beyond this volume and to work with the kinds of sources on which it is based. We first offer some general observations on the literature as a whole, and then comment more specifically on six sub-divisions which correspond with the main themes covered in this volume: history and biography, functions and philosophy, public policy, participation, program development, and the contemporary scene. It should be emphasized that the authors are referring in what follows to the literature of the field in Canada which relates primarily to the topics covered in this volume, not to other aspects of adult education.

The General Picture

We in Canada have much to learn from research and thought about adult education which originates in other lands. This is clearly the case in such areas as learning theory, functions and philosophy, the program planning process, and research methodology, for instance. But in some of the "foundations" areas, which are the focus of this book, there are important and obvious reasons why we have to rely particularly on Canadian sources if we are to understand the historical and social roots of the field as it has developed in this country. The belief that this is so was the chief factor which moved the authors to write the present volume.

By any standard, the literature of adult education in Canada must be judged to be in its infancy. Although the volume of publication—books, monographs, conference proceedings and journal articles—has increased greatly in the last two decades, compared with other disciplines and fields of practice, the amount of publication is as yet small. That this is so may in part be the result of the fact that many Canadian scholars have in the past, and to some extent still do, feel that publication in foreign journals and presses is more prestigious than in Canadian publications, and that subject matter that is not specifically Canadian is more likely to be of interest to foreign editors. This situation is changing, a fact which is reflected in both the quality and extent of publication in Canada in recent years. It is also apparent in the proceedings of the annual research conference on adult education which has been held since 1981.

It should be pointed out that it is possible to take too narrow a view of what is important to the field in Canada. We have learned, and hopefully will continue to learn, from the experience of others. However, the present authors have attempted in some respects to restore what seems to us a more balanced view, starting from our Canadian experience and calling upon literature and insights from beyond our borders where it seemed relevant and helpful.

One encouraging development in recent years has been an increase in the number of Canadian publishers who have been willing to publish Canadian materials about the field. For many decades, the Canadian Association for Adult Education was our chief publisher—books, proceedings, monographs, pamphlets and journal publications. In the last two decades, several of the universities—either the official "presses" or the continuing education units—have entered the field. As well, several of the professional associations have begun to publish journals, juried and otherwise, and the outlet for Canadian materials is much greater than ever before.

Gaining access to Canadian material has also been greatly facilitated as a result of efforts by individuals in compiling inventories and directories. This, combined with advances in the technology of storing, retrieving and sending information, holds great promise for the future. In the case of inventories and directories, the section in Chapter 8 on Research and Publication provides information about a number of directories of published material which have been produced over the years. In addition there are other directories and indexes of government documents, research reports and scholarly articles, such as the *Government of Canada Publications Catalog*, the *Microlog: Canadian Research Index* and the *Canadian Education Index*, which contain subject headings pertaining to adult education as well as cross referenced entries under both author and title. (Indeed the several headings under which adult education materials can be indexed, including community development, continuing education, distance education, further education, lifelong education and university extension, suggest the researcher should consult the index of each directory.) As for the technology of storing, retrieving and sending information, developments in these areas have enabled libraries in particular to access publications without necessarily having to acquire them for their own collection, or at least not in their original format. For example, government reports are made available to libraries in microfiche, and duplicates can easily be made at a nominal charge. Another significant technological development is the creation of computer data bases capable of storing vast amounts of bibliographic information which can be accessed in an instant and then "outputted" in a variety of ways according to the needs of the researcher. Many libraries have now used data base technology to catalogue their collection. As for a data base specific to adult education publications, there is none in Canada. However the Educational Resources Information Centre (ERIC) in the United States maintains a clearing house on adult, career and vocational education which is accessible by computer search. Again, care with respect to the selection of "descriptors" is essential. It is all too easy to find yourself with "more than you had in mind." The services of a modern library are now so advanced that it is advisable to consult with a librarian when beginning one's research.

History and Biography

We have perhaps done more in Canada in this area than in any other, but that is not saying a great deal. The usual library-based catalogue and reference systems are the most effective means of locating such publications. The periodic listings of Canadian publication in the field which were described in Chapter 8 are also particularly useful in this subject area. Historical writing has appeared in all the usual forms—books, monographs, research conference proceedings, pamphlets and periodical articles. In addition, special attention should be given in this case to university graduating essays, theses and dissertations.

There is no general history of adult education in Canada. The closest we come are the three volumes of readings about the field in this country edited by J.R. Kidd (and in the third case edited by Kidd and G. Selman). Those volumes only bring us up to the early seventies, however. The single attempt at a general history of the field in any of the provinces is Selman's *The Invisible Giant* (about British Columbia). There are a number of biographies and institutional histories which contain historical information and insights. The Antigonish Movement is by far the most thoroughly documented of our institutional programs. In addition, books about particular aspects of the field, such as Draper (Ed.) on community development, Brooke (Ed.) and Taylor and Draper (Eds.) on ABE and literacy, contain valuable historical material. As indicated in Chapter 9, a "new generation" of historical work, some of it revisionist in point of view, has begun to appear in the last two decades particularly. Attention is drawn there to some of the work of Faris, Lotz, Baum, Roberts and Thomas, and Welton's *Knowledge for the People* is among those which could be added to the list. A great deal of useful work of this kind is contained in university theses as well.

Institutional histories are perhaps the most numerous form of historical writing we have. The Antigonish Movement, as mentioned above, has been the subject of more studies than any other program (Coady, Laidlaw, Milner (Eds.), Delaney, Stabler, etc.). Other programs on which there are major studies include Farm and Citizens' Forum, agricultural extension, the Banff School, aspects of the work of the National Film Board, Frontier College, the co-operative movement, several university extension departments, and aspects of manpower training and related public policy. There are also several histories of organizations of adult educators, the Canadian Association for Adult Education having received the most attention. Histories of organizations such as the Y.M.C.A., the Y.W.C.A., the Women's Institutes and the Home and School/Parent-Teacher Associations contain valuable information as well.

We have a number of biographies and autobiographies which are valuable resources, but this is an underdeveloped aspect of the literature. The reminiscences of Corbett and Coady are important, and are supplemented by other works about both of these pioneers. Studies of aspects of the work of Thomson,

Fitzpatrick, Hoodless, Tompkins, Grierson, Cameron, Robbins, England, Kidd, Thomas and others are valuable sources. University theses are currently adding rapidly to the fund of biographical studies.

With each passing decade, it is increasingly realized how valuable a resource we have in the journals and fugitive literature which has been published by the field over the years. These publications are of interest not only for the information they contain, but also from the point of view of what they reveal about the field at the time. The clearest example of this is provided by the four journals which have been published by the Canadian Association for Adult Education since 1936 (*Adult Learning, Food For Thought, Continuous Learning,* and *Learning*). Also of great interest are various newsletters, bulletins and occasional publications which have been published by other organizations over the years.

There is increasing awareness of the importance of locating and preserving the archives of the field—institutional and organizational records, personal papers, occasional publications, etc. Some organizations have taken appropriate steps to ensure the care of their records, by means of deposit in archives or libraries, but in many cases the need for this has not been recognized. Adult educators have tended to live for the present, and in many cases have failed to perceive that with the passage of time, materials in their possession are acquiring significant historical importance. However, scholars will find, upon inquiry, that the records of a number of organizations in the field are available in public collections—national, provincial or institutional.

Functions and Philosophy

There is no sustained scholarship in these fields (as they relate to adult education) which has been produced in Canada. One will look in vain for books or monographs by Canadians which address these subjects directly. The closest one comes are the relevant sections of Kidd's two volumes of readings, *Adult Education in Canada* and *Learning and Society*, and the volume published for the fiftieth anniversary of the Canadian Association for Adult Education, Cassidy and Faris (Eds.), *Choosing Our Future*. A diligent search through the Canadian literature of the field, however, will reveal that a great deal has been said about the functions, goals and philosophy of the work, almost always as part of telling another story—often describing the work of a particular agency or program.

The only professional philosopher who has given attention to adult education in Canada was George Grant, who worked briefly for the Canadian Association for Adult Education in his younger years. A few articles by him are to be found in *Food For Thought* in the early fifties. The section of the present volume by Dr. Mark Selman on matters philosophical is hopefully the beginning of a new process.

A number of leading adult educators spoke and wrote with some passion about the purposes of adult education. Alfred Fitzpatrick wrote eloquently about the potential of adult education to provide more equal access to opportunity for the working men on the frontier. Corbett and others saw adult education as the key to a more effective democracy and the building of Canadian society and culture. Watson Thomson, John Grierson and their spiritual successors saw adult education as a factor in promoting radical social change. The Antigonish leaders, including Tompkins and Coady, embraced the field's potential for social betterment and for improving the quality of individual life and thought. Kidd and Thomas promoted a humanistic, liberal-professional view of the field, the latter being more consistent in advancing a strong personal set of beliefs which placed learning, as distinct from education, at the forefront of social and individual development. These and other leading figures, although not writing as philosophers, advanced with eloquence views which came from the progressive, humanistic, liberal and radical points of view.

For the source of their ideas, many adult educators have relied on writings originating in other countries. Prior to 1970, these sources were largely in the United States, Britain, and Scandinavia. In the last two decades, voices such as those of Freire and Illich from Third World settings have been blended with radical thought from elsewhere to support revisionist and radical views of the field and its goals. The humanistic views which undergird much of the literature about lifelong learning have in the present period been challenged consistently by more radical, policy-oriented views.

Material about the functions of adult education has been largely implicit in the philosophical literature. Textbooks for the field have usually contained a section which addresses this topic. A focal point for much of the current debate about the purposes of adult education which is to be found in the literature, predominantly a debate between liberal and more radical points of view, lies in the area of the purposes or functions of the enterprise, as seen from both an individual and a social perspective. There is, as a result, a great deal of discussion of the functions of adult education and of priorities among the various functions in the contemporary literature.

The Current Scene

In some respects this topic cannot be seen as a separate one but represents a pulling together of threads from contemporary aspects of all the other categories. The reader is referred to various works cited in Chapter 9. But it bears pointing out that during the last two decades particularly, something approaching a world community of ideas has been established in adult education, as in many other spheres of activity. Canada, which is a member of the rich and more industrially developed groupings of nations, such as the Organization for Economic Co-operation and Development, a member of the "European" region within the UNESCO structure, a member of the Commonwealth, and now of the Organization of American States, is thoroughly involved in many aspects of our "global village." Canadian adult educators who are interested in doing so are able to share in the research and thought about adult education from all parts of the world, through such avenues as the International Council for Adult Education, UNESCO and other specialized agencies of the United Nations system, the growing number of journals which are intentionally international in their scope, and the academic and commercial publishing business, which now serves worldwide markets.

Speaking in terms of domestic publication, and with regard to areas covered in this volume, bibliographic resources have expanded incrementally in recent years, but much is yet to be done, in terms of both opportunities to publish and communication of information about what is already available. The number of Canadian journals in the field has increased significantly in the eighties. University-based publishers—and some others—are giving greater attention to the field. The Canadian Association for the Study of Adult Education, through its *Proceedings* of the annual research conference, its journal and other services, is strengthening information networks in the field in Canada. Many Canadians connect themselves to parallel organizations and information networks, in the United States and Britain, particularly.

There is a trend towards more specialized information and bibliographic networks. Those working in particular subject matter areas—learning, adult basic education, critical theory, women's issues, agricultural or university extension, distance education, and history—are meeting on a more regular basis and exchanging information within the group.

But finding out about and accessing the literature of the field is still a constant struggle. In many respects, adult education is not one field but many, and information does not travel easily across the boundaries (whether geographical or subject matter), not to speak of the gulf between the two language communities in this country.

The field is beginning to take advantage of the various bibliographical and communications services which the computer has made possible, but has been slow to do so. There has been a tendency for adult education to isolate itself from other branches of education, perhaps as a sort of self-defence mechanism, a response to its marginality in so many settings. As it has become less marginal in many respects—largely a product of developments in the last two decades— there are encouraging signs of its willingness to join the rest of the educational world and to take greater advantage of the information and bibliographical services now available, and coming on stream.

Participation

The notion of participation in adult education has two basic aspects, as found in the literature on this subject. The first is ascertaining the extent to which adults do participate and the second is providing explanations for it. The interest in participation in the literature is quite recent and in Canada one of the earliest presentations of comparative data was by Kidd in his study of continuing education in Toronto *(18 to 80)*. He used statistics gathered from several sources including the Dominion Bureau of Statistics (as Statistics Canada was then known), in a chapter headed "The Participants in Adult Education." In 1957 the Bureau established an Adult Education section. When it conducted the first national survey on adult education participation in 1960, one of the initial issues which its findings confirmed was the high incidence of adult illiteracy, and this at a time when attention was being directed particularly at the urgent need for job training and retraining. The situation spurred on government sponsored programs of remedial education, and adult basic education became the subject of numerous publications.

The beginning of scholarly interest in participation can be traced to the study conducted by the American, Cyril Houle, and published in 1961 (*The Inquiring Mind*). His conclusions concerning the reasons why adults participate in adult education prompted other theorists to carry out further investigation into both participation and non-participation.

There have been only a few surveys conducted in Canada on the extent of participation and on related questions such as the reasons for participation and the characteristics of participants and non-participants. The most recent such survey was the one conducted by Statistics Canada in 1984, but at the time of writing it is unclear when or whether further studies of this kind will be carried out. However, some useful data may be derived from other Statistics Canada sources, such as its decennial census and its monthly labour market survey. The figures published by the provinces are limited to annual enrollment data for provincially sponsored programs. In many cases information specific to adult education is difficult to extract from the data, and comparisons among the provinces are difficult because data is organized and presented in varying ways. The only comprehensive surveys of participation at the provincial level have been carried out in Ontario (*Demand for Part Time Learning in Ontario*, 1976) and in Quebec (as input to the 1982 Quebec Study Commission on Adult Education).

The work of the Canadian Association for Adult Education during the 1980s to "popularize" statistical information warrants special mention. Believing that the contemporary advocates for the cause of adult education needed to base their arguments on solid information rather than on emotional appeals alone, the CAAE made a determined effort to produce the data in a readily usable form. Its initial effort in this regard was carried out in collaboration with its French language counterpart organization, the ICEA, and published in booklet form, *From the Adult's Point of View*. The CAAE has also worked closely with provincial adult education associations in the presentation of Statistics Canada data as it applies to individual provinces.

There are a small number of researchers and theorists who have made notable contributions to the literature of participation. In the latter part of the 1960s Coolie Verner and Gary Dickinson of the University of British Columbia conducted socio-economic research on rural regions of B.C., focusing on participation in adult education. There have been several masters and doctoral theses on aspects of participation. Another researcher from the University of British Columbia, Roger Boshier, has concentrated on motivational aspects of participation, and has been widely published in academic journals. One of the best known figures in the whole field is Allen Tough of the Ontario Institute for Studies in

Education. Tough's research on "adult learning projects" conducted by means of "self-directed learning" has challenged the whole basis on which participation is conceptualized. More recently Kjell Rubenson of the University of British Columbia has developed a "Model of Recruitment and Barriers" in an attempt to explain the motivational forces at work which determine the decision to participate or not in organized education. Rubenson presented his model in 1983 as one of the background papers to the federal Skill Development Leave Task Force. The two volume report of the task force, *Learning a Living in Canada*, put forward recommendations for policy development which, if implemented, would have the effect of removing some barriers to participation.

The concept of participation is fundamental to adult education, and for this reason it is referred to in virtually all areas of the literature. For instance it is an aspect of marketing, of motivation, of program planning, and of policy development. Working with the notion requires a facility for conceptualization (as is well summarized by Cross in *Adults as Learners*) and skill in statistical interpretation, as noted in Chapter 4.

Program Design

The literature on program design can be divided in general terms between program descriptions and methodological outlines. The former can consist of anything from a brief summary (perhaps for use by a decision-making body) to a book length study. Methodological studies tend to present the ideas of particular authors on the process. There are works on all phases of the program planning process, from needs assessment, through implementation, to evaluation. The intent of these publications is to influence the practice of adult education and, in the case of scholarly works, to add to the theoretical underpinnings of adult education as a discipline.

Many program descriptions used by institutions for internal purposes remain in files and have a very limited circulation. As for more formal publications, the section on "History and Biography" earlier in this chapter makes reference to these. It is worth noting that many works can be found under headings which relate to adult education program areas such as adult basic education, community development, citizenship and vocational training. In addition, there are a number of films which effectively convey something of the nature and inspiration behind the programs which are studied. The Antigonish Movement and Chautauqua have been the subject of excellent films. There is as well a videotape on Roby Kidd's contributions to the field which contains useful insights (University of Guelph).

Of the methodological studies, the most accessible of these are the texts which describe features of both program design and adult learning (Brookfield, Brundage and MacKeracher, Cross, Dickinson, Houle, Kidd, Knowles). Articles in scholarly journals which deal with program design tend to focus on one or two aspects of the process only. There are a number of more practice-oriented journals which frequently deal with matters of program design and do so in terms of the needs of those working in such areas as business, government and educational institutions.

The professional development needs of practitioners have been the subject of a large number of commercial publications. Some of these are written by respected adult educators (Knowles, *The Modern Practice of Adult Education*) while some others tend to oversimplify and to reduce the process to a series of checklists and forms. The large commercial market for such works has been such that there are many publications in this field, of widely varying quality or soundness.

Public Policy

There is a considerable amount of material which addresses the matter of public policy related to adult education. This material is of three main kinds: (1) input into policy making in the form of advocacy briefs, position papers and the like; (2) the resulting policy, be it in the form of legislation, policy statements, texts of speeches, etc.; and (3) assessments of policy, in the form of commentaries, analyses and histories. Unfortunately the deliberations of policy makers tend not to be available—or even recorded.

Submissions which are made to public inquiries such as royal commissions or government task forces are typically difficult to access. The organizations which provide input will frequently publish their submissions. If this is done in journals, it becomes readily accessible; otherwise it falls into the category of "fugitive" literature and is frequently difficult to find. Recognizing this, the Pacific Association for Continuing Education, for example, published recent submissions to government by several adult education associations in British Columbia in its PACE Papers series (*Advocacy for Adult Education in British Columbia*). An example of a quite different kind was the publication in 1966 by the Canadian Association for Adult Education of *A White Paper on the Education of Adults in Canada*, which was simply issued to interested persons and authorities, rather than as a response to a public inquiry.

Government has become increasingly interested in receiving input into its policy making processes and frequently takes the initiative in establishing fact-finding and opinion-seeking bodies. These bodies often commission research studies on specific issues. Their final reports are commonly published in attractive formats, to encourage public interest. Frequently, interim reports or discussion papers are also issued, designed to encourage input from the community. This was the case, for example, with the working document released by the 1982 Quebec Study Commission on Adult Education, *Adult Education in Quebec: Possible Solutions*.

Another relatively recent feature of educational policy making in Canada has been intergovernmental consultations, frequently carried out through the various organs of the Council of Ministers of Education. As a result of the work of this agency, documents are being produced which have implications for policy development. The federal government also produces valuable material relating to public policy, a recent example being the report by the Secretary of State, *Federal and Provincial Support to Post-Secondary Education in Canada: A Report to Parliament 1986–87*.

It is helpful to the researcher that most government reports and documents are accorded special attention by large libraries. To assist with access to these materials, catalogues and directories are published on a regular basis which are indexed and cross-referenced, using consistent headings for the most part. In the case of the *Microlog: Canadian Research Index*, a monthly catalogue is produced. Another feature of government reports is that those of any consequence are produced in microfilm or microfiche formats.

Material about public policies themselves is not at all easily accessed. One of the reasons for this is that public policy, as noted in Chapter 6, is communicated in a number of ways, including legislation, written policy statements, and through bureaucratic actions, which may not be in writing. The search for relevant policy is also complicated by the fact that adult education policy is not to be found only in Ministries of Education (in some provinces there is more than one of these). Ministries of labour, or social welfare, the solicitor general and others are likely to have developed policies related to adult education which are relevant to their mandates. Alan Thomas has reported on this situation in connection with his ongoing research on adult education and the law. For these reasons it is difficult to conduct research on public policy in this field, all the more so considering how policies can change or be ignored without any public debate or notice.

The most developed aspect of adult education literature regarding public policy is found in the various commentaries, analyses and histories which have been written. Some of these are subject oriented, such as the study on vocational training by Dupre et al., *Federalism and Policy Development: The Case of Adult Occupational Training in Ontario* and the study by Audrey Thomas, *Adult Illiteracy in Canada*. Others are broader in their orientation, such as the essays in the volume edited by Cassidy and Faris, *Choosing Our Future: Adult Education and Public Policy in Canada*.

In the area of understanding the public policy process and the relationship between a government and its society, Alan Thomas of O.I.S.E. has conducted ongoing research on this subject. His findings have been published in a number of journals, in Canada and abroad. Indeed, works on comparative aspects of adult education are useful sources in the public policy field. Roby Kidd (formerly of O.I.S.E.) and Jindra Kulich (formerly of U.B.C.) and others have been active in publishing material on international comparative adult education. Within Canada, Hayden Roberts' work, *Culture and Adult Education: A Study of Alberta and Quebec*, demonstrates the value of comparisons between provincial jurisdictions.

As for historical pieces on public policy, there has been very little written. Faris uses the case of radio broadcasting in his book, *The Passionate Educators*, to record the struggle to preserve the airways in public rather than private control during the formative years of broadcasting policy. Selman has compared two periods in B.C. history when government was particularly active in giving leadership to adult education activities, and has written a history of advocacy on behalf of adult education in the province. Dennison and Gallagher trace the development of provincial community college systems in their work, *Canada's Community Colleges*. There are also theses and dissertations which address specific aspects of public policy matters, mainly through case studies.

There are a few publishers which have periodically produced works dealing with policy issues. These are the Canadian Association for Adult Education, the Ontario Institute for Studies in Education, the Canadian Commission for UNESCO, and the University of B.C.'s Centre for Continuing Education. The federal and provincial governments and educational institutions produce documents such as background reports, study findings and policy statements. In many cases, policy about adult education is not the main focus of these reports. An example of this is the recent review of the mandate of Ontario's colleges, *Vision 2000: Quality and Opportunity*. The fact that the student of these matters is forced consistently to "dig" for material related to adult education in documents whose main focus lies elsewhere is, of course, a continuing reminder of the marginality of the field.

Index